If You Call Yourself a Jew

If You Call Yourself a Jew

Reappraising Paul's Letter to the Romans

Rafael Rodríguez

CASCADE *Books* • Eugene, Oregon

IF YOU CALL YOURSELF A JEW
Reappraising Paul's Letter to the Romans

Copyright © 2014 Rafael Rodríguez. All rights reserved. Except for brief quotations in critical publications or reviews, no part of this book may be reproduced in any manner without prior written permission from the publisher. Write: Permissions, Wipf and Stock Publishers, 199 W. 8th Ave., Suite 3, Eugene, OR 97401.

Cascade Books
An Imprint of Wipf and Stock Publishers
199 W. 8th Ave., Suite 3
Eugene, OR 97401

www.wipfandstock.com

ISBN 13: 978-1-62564-680-4

Cataloguing-in-Publication data:

Rodríguez, Rafael, 1977–.

If you call yourself a Jew : reappraising Paul's letter to the Romans / Rafael Rodríguez.

xx + 318 pp. ; 23 cm. — Includes bibliographical references and indexes.

ISBN 13: 978-1-62564-680-4

1. Bible. Romans—Criticism, interpretation, etc. 2. Bible. Romans—Commentaries. 3. Israel (Christian theology)—Biblical teaching. I. Title.

BS2665.53 R637 2014

Manufactured in the U.S.A.

New Revised Standard Version Bible, copyright 1989, Division of Christian Education of the National Council of the Churches of Christ in the United States of America. Used by permission. All rights reserved.

Scripture and/or notes quoted by permission. Quotations designated (NET) are from the NET Bible® copyright ©1996-2006 by Biblical Studies Press, L.L.C. All rights reserved.

Dedicated to:

Andrea, Janelle, and Josephina

Contents

Preface   ix

Abbreviations   xii

1. Introduction: Paul the Apostle, to the Beloved Gentiles in Rome   1
2. The Gospel, the Power of God: Paul Begins to Write   13
3. The Wrath and Impartial Judgment of God: Gentiles in Pauline Perspective   25
4. Introducing the Gentile Proselyte: A Gentile Who Calls Himself a Jew   47
5. The Righteousness of God apart from Torah: Or, Not a Law-Free Gospel   73
6. Christ, the New Adam: Undoing the Curse of Death   95
7. Baptized, Buried, Raised: Freed from Sin, Enslaved to Righteousness   108
8. *Nomos*, Flesh, Spirit: The War Waging Within   125
9. Creation Renewed by the Spirit: Security in the Presence of God   147
10. Israel and Christ: Paul's *Pathos* for the People of God   169
11. Israel and Christ, Pt. II: Torah's *Telos*   190
12. [Re-]Grafted Olive Branches: The Persistence of Hope   213
13. Living Sacrifices: One Body, Many Members   232
14. The Offering of the Weak: Paul and the Particular Assemblies in Rome   257

15   In Sum . . . : The End of Paul's Rhetoric and of His
     Letter   283

Bibliography   297
Index of Names   305
Index of Ancient Documents   309

Preface

I half-jokingly describe *If You Call Yourself a Jew* as a book I accidentally wrote. With so many books written on Paul and/or Romans every year (with rumors of one recent behemoth tipping the scales at over 1,600 pages!), and with my own area of expertise centered on Jesus and the Synoptic Gospels, I never anticipated having anything original to contribute to the vibrant and sometimes bewildering discussion of Paul and Romans in the academic literature.

When I was asked to prepare a graduate-level course on Romans in 2010, I decided not to use notes on Romans that I had prepared a few years earlier, but instead to start from scratch. As I worked through the text afresh, I was surprised to discover early on that I had changed my mind on a number of significant issues, including Paul's intended audience (I now agree with Stowers, Das, *et al.* that Paul wrote for gentile readers) and the identity of Paul's interlocutor in the first half of Romans 2 (whom I now view as a gentile figure). When I came to Rom 2:17 ("But if you call yourself a Jew, if you take comfort in Torah, if you set your boast on God . . ."), the possibility occurred to me that perhaps Paul continues to envisage a gentile interlocutor *even here*. At the time the stakes seemed rather low. After all, how much difference could it make whether Paul imagined himself in dialogue with an actual Jew or a gentile who calls himself a Jew? I decided to read Paul's diatribe as a dialogue with a gentile proselyte to Judaism—a "Judaizer"—simply to see what effect it would have on my reading of Romans as whole.

I soon made two discoveries. First, I was not the first person to propose that the person whom Paul portrays as "calling himself a Jew" was not an *ethnic* Jew. Runar Thorsteinsson's monograph, *Paul's Interlocutor in Romans 2* (Almqvist & Wiksell, 2003), not only *considered* this possibility but *argued* for it on the basis of the function and features of diatribe in Greco-Roman epistolographers. Thorsteinsson's work is often neglected or summarily dismissed. However, a small but growing number of commentators have taken account of it and have been building upon it to reappraise our understanding of Pauline theology and his missionary activity among gentile communities of Jesus-followers in the early Roman empire. Second,

Preface

the shift from an actual Jew to a gentile who calls himself a Jew makes all the difference for a number of perennial problems in Romans, including Paul's dark assessment of Torah's effects in Romans 3, his first-person discourse in Romans 7, and his *apologia* of Israel in Romans 9–11.

This book, then, provides a reading of Paul's entire letter on the basis of the hypothesis that Paul constructs a dialogue with a gentile proselyte to Judaism as his interlocutor. Space constraints prevent us from providing a comprehensive, verse-by-verse commentary, but we will read through every section of the letter. In the course of the pages that follow, we will see Paul's exposition of the revelation of the righteousness of God—God's faithfulness to his covenant promises to Abraham and his descendants. Those promises climaxed in the announcement that, through Abraham and his family, "all the tribes of the earth will be blessed" (Gen 12:3). However, Paul insists that the righteousness of God is revealed, "for the Jew first as well as for the Greek," not through Torah but through the faith[-fulness] of Jesus. Torah and the prophets provide corroborating witness for God's righteousness, but the gentile who bends his neck to Torah's yoke misses the actual mechanism for finding peace with God. Romans never claims that Torah was never intended to reveal God's righteousness or that Torah was somehow fundamentally flawed. In Torah, God set before Abraham's descendants the choice of life and blessings, on one hand, and death and curses, on the other. On any reading of Israel's history and the socio-political situation of the late Second-Temple era, Israel chose the latter. Nevertheless, Paul found in the story of Jesus, the son of David and of God, the image of complete faith in/faithfulness to God, and in the account of Jesus' resurrection to newness of life he found the image of God's complete faithfulness to his promise of life and blessings, "for the Jew first as well as for the Greek." Whereas Torah resulted in curse and death, it also anticipated the unconditional faithfulness of God for both Jew and gentile. For Paul, the gospel of Jesus Christ is the account of the outworking of God's faithfulness: the end of Torah's curses and the fulfillment of its blessings.

But now we are getting ahead of ourselves. Chapter 1 offers a rough outline of the biblical narrative of Israel's history that forms Paul's symbolic universe and provides the formative matrix for Paul's theologizing. It also briefly introduces two key components of our reading of Romans: (i) the ethnic make-up of Paul's intended audience, and (ii) Paul's reason for writing Romans. Chapters 2–15 provide our reading of Romans 1–16 as Paul's dialogue with a gentile proselyte to Judaism and his exposition of the revelation of God's righteousness. As we will see, the hypothesis of a gentile Judaizer results not only in a coherent reading of Romans but also a reading that avoids and/or solves a number of perennial problems in the history of interpretation of Romans.

A number of people have supported and encouraged me throughout the process of writing *If You Call Yourself a Jew*. The administration of Johnson University (especially John Ketchen and Chris Davis) provided the occasion and the support for developing this book. The library staff of Johnson University (especially John Hale and Heidi Berryhill) provided every resource I asked for. My student worker, Hannah McCord, proofread an earlier draft of the manuscript and helped compile the original translation of Romans in chapters 2–15. Robin Parry expressed interest (though not without skepticism) in my reading of Romans at the British New Testament Conference (King's College London, 2012); I thank him and Christian Amondson, of Cascade Books, for accepting this book for publication and guiding me through the production process. I would also like to thank the following individuals, who in various ways impacted the development of this project: Bill Baker, Mike Bird, James Ernest, Les Hardin, Chris Keith, Matt Novenson, Peter Oakes, Richard Pervo, Minna Shkul, Matt Thiessen, Runar Thorsteinsson, Chris Tilling, Brian Tucker, Gary Weedman, Mark Weedman, Sarah Whittle.

Part of chapter 11 ("Israel and Christ, Pt. II: Torah's *Telos*") appeared in slightly different form in my volume, *Oral Tradition and the New Testament: A Guide for the Perplexed* (London: Bloomsbury T & T Clark, 2014). I am grateful to Bloomsbury for permission to include that material here.

Abbreviations

Technical Abbreviations

§(§)	section(s)
BCE	before the Common Era
ca.	circa
CE	Common Era
cf.	*confer* (compare)
chap(s).	chapter(s)
cp.	compare
ed(s).	editor(s), edited by
e.g.	*exempli gratia* (for example)
esp.	especially
etc.	*et cetera* (and the rest)
f(f).	and the following one(s)
ftn	footnote
Grk	Greek
Heb.	Hebrew
ibid.	*ibidem* (in the same place)
i.e.	*id est* (that is)
inter alios	among other persons
MT	Masoretic Text
Mt.	Mount
lit.	literally

Abbreviations

LXX	Septuagint
mng.	meaning
n.	note
NA28	Nestle-Aland, 28th edition
NT	New Testament
OG	Old Greek (version of the lxx)
OT	Old Testament
p(p).	page(s)
pace	with all due respect
par(r).	parallel(s)
passim	here and there
plur.	plural
pt.	part
sic	*sic erat scriptum* (thus it is written)
s.v.	*sub verbo* (under the word)
v(v).	verse(s)
viz.	*videlicet* (namely)
w.	with
Θ	Theodotion (version of the LXX)

Translations and Secondary Sources

AB	Anchor Bible
ABRL	Anchor Bible Reference Library
AOTC	Abingdon Old Testament Commentaries
BBE	Bible in Basic English
BBR	*Bulletin for Biblical Research*
BDAG	Bauer, W., F. W. Danker, W. F. Arndt, and F. W. Gingrich. *Greek-English Lexicon of the New*

Abbreviations

	Testament and other Early Christian Literature. Third edition. Chicago: 1999
BDF	Blass, F., A. Debrunner, and R. W. Funk. *A Greek Grammar of the New Testament and Other Early Christian Literature.* Chicago: 1961
BECNT	Baker Exegetical Commentary on the New Testament
Bib	*Biblica*
BNTC	Black's New Testament Commentary
BR	*Biblical Research*
BSac	*Bibliotheca sacra*
CBQ	*Catholic Biblical Quarterly*
ConBNT	Coniectanea Biblica New Testament
COQG	Christian Origins and the Question of God
CTR	*Criswell Theological Review*
CurTM	*Currents in Theology and Mission*
DJG	*Dictionary of Jesus and the Gospels.* Edited by J. B. Green and S. McKnight. 1st ed. Downers Grove, IL:1992
DLNTD	*Dictionary of the Later New Testament and Its Developments.* Edited by R. P. Martin and P. H. Davids. Downers Grove, IL: 1997
DNTB	*Dictionary of New Testament Backgrounds.* Edited by C. A. Evans and S. E. Porter. Downers Grove, IL: 2000
DPL	*Dictionary of Paul and His Letters.* Edited by G. F. Hawthorne, R. P. Martin, and D. G. Reid. Downers Grove, IL: 1993
EC	*Early Christianity*
ESCO	European Studies on Christian Origins
ESV	English Revised Version
ExAud	*Ex Auditu*

Abbreviations

ExpTim	*Expository Times*
FRLANT	Forschungen zur Religion und Literatur des Alten und Neuen Testaments
HTR	*Harvard Theological Review*
ICC	International Critical Commentary
JBL	*Journal of Biblical Literature*
JETS	*Journal of the Evangelical Theological Society*
JSNT	*Journal for the Study of the New Testament*
JSNTSup	Journal for the Study of the New Testament: Supplement Series
JTSA	*Journal of Theology for Southern Africa*
KJV	King James Version
L&N	Louw, J. P. and E. A. Nida. *Greek-English Lexicon of the New Testament: Based on Semantic Domains.* 2nd ed. New York: 1989
LCL	Loeb Classical Library
LNTS	Library of New Testament Studies
LPS	Library of Pauline Studies
LSJ	Liddell, H. G., R. Scott, and H. S. Jones. *A Greek-English Lexicon.* 9th ed. with revised supplement. Oxford: 1996
NASB	New American Standard Bible
NET	New English Translation, NET Bible®
NETS	New English Translation of the Septuagint
NICNT	New International Commentary on the New Testament
NIDNTT	*New International Dictionary of New Testament Theology.* Edited by C. Brown. 4 vols. Grand Rapids, 1975–85
NIGTC	New International Greek Testament Commentary
NIV	New International Version

Abbreviations

NKJV	New King James Version
NLT	New Living Translation
NovT	*Novum Testamentum*
NRSV	New Revised Standard Version
NTS	*New Testament Studies*
PCNT	Paideia Commentaries on the New Testament
PNTC	Pillar New Testament Commentaries
PRSt	*Perspectives in Religious Studies*
RBS	Resources for Biblical Study
ResQ	*Restoration Quarterly*
RevExp	*Review and Expositor*
SBLDS	Society of Biblical Literature Dissertation Series
SCJ	*Stone-Campbell Journal*
SJT	*Scottish Journal of Theology*
StBL	Studies in Biblical Literature
TDNT	*Theological Dictionary of the New Testament.* Edited by G. Kittel and G. Friedrich. Translated by G. W. Bromiley. 10 vols. Grand Rapids: 1964–76
TynBul	*Tyndale Bulletin*
WBC	Word Biblical Commentary
WUNT	Wissenschaftliche Untersuchungen zum Neuen Testament

Primary Sources

Hebrew Bible/Old Testament

Gen	Genesis
Exod	Exodus
Lev	Leviticus
Num	Numbers

Abbreviations

Deut	Deuteronomy
Josh	Joshua
1–4 Kgdms	1–4 Kingdoms (mt = 1–2 Samuel; 1–2 Kings)
1–2 Chr	1–2 Chronicles
Job	Job
Ps(s)	Psalm(s)
Prov	Proverbs
Eccl	Ecclesiastes
Isa	Isaiah
Jer	Jeremiah
Lam	Lamentations
Ezek	Ezekiel
Hos	Hosea
Jonah	Jonah
Hab	Habakkuk
Mal	Malachi

Apocrypha/Deuterocanon

Bel	Bel and the Dragon
1–2 Esd	1–2 Esdras
1–2 Macc	1–2 Maccabees
Sir	Sirach/Ecclesiasticus
Wis	Wisdom of Solomon

New Testament

Matt	Matthew
Mark	Mark
Luke	Luke

xvii

Abbreviations

Acts	Acts
Rom	Romans
1–2 Cor	1–2 Corinthians
Gal	Galatians
Eph	Ephesians
Phil	Philippians
Col	Colossians
1–2 Thess	1–2 Thessalonians
Titus	Titus
Heb	Hebrews
Jas	James
1–2 Pet	1–2 Peter
1–3 John	1–3 John
Rev	Revelation

Pseudepigrapha

Apoc. Abr.	*Apocalypse of Abraham*
Apoc. Mos.	*Apocalypse of Moses*
1 En.	*1 Enoch*
Jub.	*Jubilees*
L.A.B.	*Liber antiquitatum biblicarum* (Pseudo-Philo)
L.A.E.	*Life of Adam and Eve*
4 Macc.	*4 Maccabees*

Josephus

Ag. Ap.	*Against Apion*
Ant.	*Jewish Antiquities*
J.W.	*Jewish War*

Philo

Creation	*On the Creation of the World*
Decalogue	*On the Decalogue*
Mos.	*On the Life of Moses*
Sacr. Abel	*On the Sacrifices of Cain and Abel*
Spec. Laws 1–4	*Special Laws 1–4*

Apostolic Fathers

Ign. *Phld.*	Ignatius, *To the Philadelphians*
Mart. Pol.	*Martyrdom of Polycarp*

Targumim

Tg. Neof.	*Targum Neofiti*

Greco-Roman Authors

Aen.	Virgil, *Aeneid*
Clem.	Seneca, *De clementia*
Cyr.	Xenophon, *Cyropaedia*
Eth. nic.	Aristotle, *Nichomachean Ethics*
Geog.	Strabo, *Geography*
Hist.	Herodotus, *Histories*
Lucil.	Seneca, *Ad Lucilium*
Quaest. rom.	Plutarch, *Quaestiones romanae et graecae*

Introduction

Paul the Apostle, to the Beloved Gentiles in Rome

Paul is a man of enormous influence, a religious genius whose capacity for creative thought and original writing has made him a mountain on the landscape of Christian history. . . . The New Testament contains just one letter ascribed to James, two attributed to Peter, and three short ones attributed to John; but even taken all together their influence is far outweighed by just one of Paul's letters, written to the Christians in Rome.[1]

David Horrell's description of the apostle Paul—"a mountain on the landscape of Christian history"—strikes me as exactly the kind of thing we must say about the man from Tarsus. One can hardly imagine what would remain of the rich and multilayered heritage of Christian theology and ethics if we sought to strip it of all traces of Pauline influence. Certainly the stream of Christian tradition begins with Jesus of Nazareth. But that stream's disposition and description at present are, in large measure, the product of Paul's influence. And, of course, readers throughout history have often landed on Paul's epistle to the Christians in Rome as his seminal and most influential letter. This introductory discussion briefly sets out some basic presuppositions about Paul and his letter that will guide our reading of Romans.

---

1. Horrell, *Introduction*, 1.

The Story of Pauline Theology

In this book, we will locate Paul's thinking within the world circumscribed by Israelite biblical tradition. The stories of Abraham and the patriarchs, Moses and the wilderness, Israel and the covenant did not provide prooftexts or examples or prefigurations of Paul's gospel; they did not provide a resource that Paul "used" to help communicate his message.[2] Rather, these stories provide "the symbolic universe within which Paul lives, within which he is rooted in his thought and life before as well as after his call."[3] In what follows, I will outline the basically *storied* basis of Pauline thought and theology. In other words, this section will briefly describe the underlying narrative—the *story*—that informs Paul's thinking.[4]

That story begins "with God's act of creation, closely followed by the fall of Adam."[5] Very quickly humanity fails at its vocation as "the image of God" amidst creation, resulting in a rupture between God, as Creator, and humanity, as creation. The first move toward healing that rupture occurs in the story of Abra[ha]m: God calls Abraham out of his land and promises him:

> [2] I will make you a great nation [LXX: *ethnos mega*], and I will bless you and magnify your name. And you will be blessed. [3] I will bless those who bless you, and those who curse you I will curse. And in you all the tribes of the earth [LXX: *pasai hai phylai tēs gēs*] will be blessed. (Gen 12:2–3 LXX[6])

Abraham received these promises—and others as well—by *faith* (see Gen 15:6) and responded in *trust* that God could and would provide what he had promised. Eventually, God would bring Abraham's descendants out of slavery in Egypt and establish them as his people, making a covenant with them. We call that covenant "the Torah [*nomos*] of Moses." God promised life and blessing to those who kept the terms of the covenant (see Deuteronomy 30). To understand Paul, however, we must remember the original promise to Abraham in Genesis 12: God promised to bless Abraham and

2. See Ehrensperger, "Scriptural Reasoning."

3. Ibid.

4. See Grieb, *Story*; Gombis, *Paul*, chap. 3.

5. Horrell, *Introduction*, 58.

6. All translations of the Septuagint are my own. I generally cite the LXX because, as far as we can tell, it looks like Paul read the Bible in its Greek translation. At the very least, Paul typically cites the Hebrew Bible in its Greek form; but see the table in Silva, "Old Testament in Paul," 630–31.

his descendants, and through them to bless "all the tribes of the earth." Paul understood Torah in light of this promise.

At the height of its geo-political influence, YHWH promised Israel's king, a shepherd named David, that he, YHWH, would establish an eternal Davidic dynasty. Centuries earlier, when the Lord commissioned Moses on Mount Sinai to return to Egypt and bring the people out of slavery, the Lord called Israel his "son": "But you shall say to Pharaoh, 'This is what the Lord says: "Israel is my first-born son"'" (Exod 4:22 LXX). In David's day, YHWH promises the expansionist king,

> 12 And it shall be when all your days are fulfilled and you go to sleep with your fathers, that I shall raise up your seed after you—who shall come from your loins—and I shall prepare his kingdom. 13 He will build for me a house for my name, and I shall establish his throne forever. 14 *I shall be like a father to him, and he shall be like a son to me.* If his unrighteousness comes, then I will reprove him with the rod of men and with the ropes of the sons of men. 15 But I will never remove my mercy from him, the way I removed it from those whom I removed from my presence. 16 And his house and his kingdom shall be made trustworthy before me forever, and his throne shall be established forever. (2 Kgdms 7:12–16 LXX; my emphasis)[7]

Eventually, however, the people of Israel would incur the punishments and curses established by their covenant with YHWH (*viz.* exile and death). We typically understand this failure in terms of the nation's "sin"; that is, the people of Israel worshipped the gods of other nations, they oppressed the poor (widows, orphans, and aliens), and so on. But in addition to their sin, Israel failed to be the blessing that God originally promised to Abraham. If nothing else, the nations around Israel were confirmed in their idolatry because of the apparent strength of their gods *vis-à-vis* Israel and YHWH (see Isa 52:5; Ezek 36:22–23). Israel's faithfulness to the covenant would have put YHWH's glory and faithfulness on display for all the nations to see. But her sin obscured the glory of the Lord and blocked the Abrahamic promises.

Despite the people's spectacular failure and rebellion against YHWH, the Lord reiterated his own faithfulness to his promises to Abraham and his covenant with Israel. Two examples will suffice. First, YHWH promises the people of Israel and of Judah through the prophet Jeremiah:

---

7. Similarly, see Ps 2:7 LXX.

> **31** "Behold! The days are coming," says the Lord, "when I will make a new covenant [*diathēkēn kainēn*] with the house of Israel and the house of Judah, **32** not according to the covenant which I made with their fathers on that day when my hand grasped them to lead them out of the land of Egypt. For they did not abide in my covenant, and I turned away from them," says the Lord. **33** "For this covenant, which I will make with the house of Israel after those days," says the Lord, "I will undoubtedly give my *nomoi* upon their mind, and upon their hearts I will write them. I will be their God, and they will be my people." (Jer 38:31–33 LXX)[8]

Jeremiah 38 affirms both (i) that the people did not abide in the covenant God had made with the people, and (ii) that the Lord will nevertheless establish a new covenant with his people—with the house of Israel and with the house of Judah. Paul takes up these ideas in very telling ways in 2 Corinthians, where he speaks of himself and his companions as "ministers of a new covenant, not of letter but of s/Spirit" [*diakonous kainēs diathēkēs, ou grammatos alla pneumatos* (2 Cor 3:6)]. He then goes on to speak of the comparative glory of the old and new covenants and the persisting veil over Israel "at the reading of the old covenant" [*epi tē anagnōsei tēs diathēkēs* (3:14)]. Jeremiah insists that God does not abandon his promises even when his people have abandoned him. Paul makes the same point using similar language.

As a second example, when the Lord re-establishes his covenant with his people, it will bring the fulfillment of God's original promise to Abraham, that all the tribes of the earth will be blessed. Isaiah is particularly emphatic in this regard. For instance,

> **5** And now, thus says the Lord who fashioned me from the womb to be his very own slave [*doulon heautō*], in order to gather Jacob and Israel to himself—I will be gathered and glorified before the Lord, and my God will be my strength— **6** and he said to

---

8. I left *nomoi* ("laws") untranslated because, in context, the prophet has more in mind than is conveyed by the English word "laws." The Greek translates the Hebrew word *tōrā*, which encompasses a number of meanings, including "law," "teaching," "instruction," and so on. When I do translate *nomos*, I will prefer "Torah" over "Law" or, worse, "law." Mark Nanos helpfully explains the wider significance of *tōrā*: "'Torah' is a Hebrew word that denotes 'teaching' rather than simply 'law,' including laws/commandments but also many other teachings, stories, warnings, consolation, etc. For Paul, 'Torah' is not the opposite of 'love' or 'freedom' but embodies 'teaching' about important values, including 'commandments' that clarify how those whom God has 'freed' from Egypt, from sin, and so on, are to treat ('love') others" (Nanos, "To the Churches," 12 n.2).

me, "It is a great thing for you to be called my child, so that you may make the tribes of Jacob stand and return the dispersion of Israel. Behold, I have set you as a covenantal race [*eis diathēkēn genous*], as a light for the nations [*eis phōs ethnōn*] so that you might be for salvation as far as the end of the earth [*eis sōtērian heōs eschatou tēs gēs*]." (Isa 49:5–6 LXX)

Paul does not cite Isa 49:5–6 in any of his extant writings.[9] However, as Luke portrays Paul responding to the Jews in Pisidian Antioch, he cites Isa 49:6. Scholars have expressed the need for caution in appealing to Luke's portrayal of Paul in order to reconstruct Paul's own theological persona.[10] Even so, this idea fits so squarely with Paul's self-presentation at key points (esp. Gal 2:8; Rom 11:13; see also Paul's references to "light" [*phōs*] in Romans and elsewhere) that Luke has certainly captured something of the historical Paul.

If it is appropriate for us to appeal to Isa 49:5–6 in our attempt to recover the foundational, scriptural narrative that undergirded Paul's theologizing, I find it striking that this passage closely aligns the restoration of the scattered tribes of Israel with the redemption of the nations (or gentiles).[11] In some strands of Jewish thought (e.g., in many of the Dead Sea Scrolls), the restoration of Israel would take place when YHWH vindicated his people and defeated their enemies. And certainly we can find similar sentiments in the Hebrew Bible. But here in Isaiah 49 and throughout Isaiah as a whole, when Israel is brought back into her covenant with God, the nations will join with Israel and offer their worship to the Creator God. In this vision of the world, the nations are blessed rather than crushed when YHWH restores his people Israel.

This narrative—the [hi]story of God's relationship with Abraham and his descendants—finds its climax in the life, death, and resurrection of a craftsman from Nazareth, Yeshuʽa bar Yosef. While Paul originally opposed Jesus and his followers, his encounter with the risen Jesus convinced him that God had indeed chosen Jesus to bring his promises to fulfillment. More than that, God had shown Paul mercy and grace, making Paul his slave [*doulos*][12] and sending him across the eastern Mediterranean basin

---

9. He does, however, cite Isaiah 49 in two places (see 2 Cor 6:2 [Isa 49:8]; Rom 14:11 [Isa 49:18]). And, of course, Paul frequently cites or alludes to Isaiah as a whole.

10. Recently, see Eisenbaum, *Paul*, 11–16.

11. But see Das, *Paul*, 120–28, esp. pp. 120–23, who cites Donaldson, "Curse of the Law."

12. See Rom 1:1, passim; recall Isa 49:5 LXX.

proclaiming the gospel. His message centered on Israel's Messiah (Jesus), the restoration of God's people (Israel), and the invitation to the nations to acknowledge YHWH as their true God. As Paul prepared to deliver a collection he had coordinated and taken up from the churches in Asia Minor and southeastern Europe for the church in Jerusalem, he apparently considered his task in the east finished. And so he turned his eyes west and envisioned a mission to Spain, the edge of the then-known world. At some point, as he made plans to return to Jerusalem and then to head west toward Rome, he wrote what would become one of the most influential letters in history: his epistle to the Christians in Rome.

Two Other Questions

Romans suffers a perplexing irony. On the one hand, some of this letter's introductory issues are rather non-controversial. For example, our letter's *who* (i.e., *who* wrote Romans?) enjoys almost total consensus. If Paul did not write Romans, he did not write any of the letters that bear his name.[13] Similarly, we are relatively certain about the *when* and *where* of Romans' authorship as well as the letter's *what* (i.e., its literary integrity).[14] On the other hand, other introductory issues are subject to considerable debate, so much so that scholars frequently refer to these issues as "the Romans debate."[15] As a result, we are simultaneously more certain and more uncertain about Romans than about the other letters in the Pauline corpus. The

---

13. Longenecker, after chronicling eighteenth- and nineteenth-century attempts to disprove Romans as a Pauline letter, rightly says, "Scholars today, however, are united in recognizing Romans as having been written by Paul. And all earlier denials of his authorship are commonly viewed today as aberrations in the history of NT study, and rightly so" (Longenecker, *Introducing*, 5).

14. The textual history of Paul's letter to the Romans is among the most complicated of all the NT texts. Put simply, we have evidence of fourteen-, fifteen-, and sixteen-chapter versions of the letter, and both the grace-formulae at 16:20, 24 and the doxology at 16:25–27 appear in various places or not at all in different manuscripts (see the discussion of Romans 16, below). Nevertheless, in comparison with 2 Corinthians or Philippians, the integrity of the bulk of Romans is relatively established.

15. Das describes Romans scholarship as a "furious debate [that] has raged in Pauline scholarship for the last forty years over the occasion behind the Letter to the Romans. Paul's letters generally address specific issues facing local congregations. The apostle confronted Jewish Christian teachers at Galatia. He comforted the Thessalonians when members of their congregation died shortly after his departure. He combated division at Corinth. . . . When scholars turned their attention to Romans, the situation presupposed in this letter proved more elusive" (Das, *Solving*, 1). See also Donfried, *Romans Debate*.

Paul the Apostle, to the Beloved Gentiles in Rome

remainder of this chapter briefly considers two final questions: *for* (or *to*) *whom* did Paul write Romans? and *why* did he write this letter?

The Recipients of Romans

The *who*, *where*, and *when* of Romans are relatively straightforward: Paul of Tarsus, at Corinth, in 57 CE, respectively. Things get significantly more complicated when we turn to Romans' *to whom*. Granted that Paul addressed his letter "to all those in Rome who are beloved of God [and] called saints" (1:6), the question remains: Did Paul envision his readers as primarily Jewish, gentile, or as some combination of the two?

Commentators typically understand Romans' original audience, insofar as Paul imagined it,[16] as a mixed congregation of both Jewish and gentile believers in Jesus (or, alternatively, as a number of congregations, some Jewish and some gentile). For example: "The most important background information for reading Paul's letter is that these Roman house churches were probably composed of both Jewish Christians and Gentile Christians."[17] Similarly, Richard Longenecker concludes,

> Undoubtedly the life of Jews in Rome after Claudius's edict was severely restricted, particularly with the loss of their right to free assembly in their synagogue groupings. *But we need not insist that a Jewish component was no longer part of the Christian presence at Rome.* Likewise, it may be posited that Jewish believers in Jesus continued to live in the city and had some influence within the developing Roman church, whatever is postulated regarding their numbers compared to those of Gentile believers within the Roman Christian community.[18]

Longenecker certainly speaks with the majority of commentators. However, in the last few decades a relatively small but important minority of scholars has argued that Paul wrote Romans for an exclusively gentile audience. One of the stronger voices here belongs to Stanley Stowers, who

---

16. This is an important distinction. There is a real difference between the actual audience who first read Romans (or who first *heard* Romans being read), on the one hand, and the audience that Paul had in mind as he dictated the letter. Whether or not there were Jewish Christians in Rome, our question asks whether Paul *imagined* Jewish Christians as recipients of his letter.

17. Grieb, *Story*, 5.

18. Longenecker, *Introducing*, 80 (my emphasis); for a discussion of the history of Judaism in Rome, see Das, *Paul*, 50–61.

7

is almost polemical in his critique of the view that Paul wrote for a mixed audience.

> The assumption of a Jewish Christian element in the audience forms another pillar in the traditional reading of Romans and of Paul's letters in general. The obsession with finding Jewish readers is so great that interpreters ignore or disallow the letters' explicitly encoded audience. Although the text explicitly addresses itself only to gentiles and nowhere explicitly encodes a Jewish audience, interpreters persistently speak of the predominantly gentile audience and the gentile majority. The logic of this nearly willful dismissal of Paul's encoded audience goes something like this: Because we know that there were Jewish believers in Rome and because Paul's subject matter at times seems fit for Jews, there must have been a Jewish Christian element in the audience in Paul's mind as he wrote.[19]

In other words, contemporary readers insist on reading Paul's letters—especially Romans—as though they were written to groups of Christians comprising both gentile and Jewish believers, *even though Paul himself addresses his letters to exclusively gentile believers in Jesus.*[20]

Andrew Das argues that Paul explicitly identifies his readers as gentiles when he speaks of having received grace and apostleship "for the obedience of faith among all the gentiles [*en pasin tois ethnesin*] for his name's sake, among whom you also are [*en hois este kai hymeis*], [you who are] called by Jesus Christ" (Rom 1:5–6).[21] This, in fact, explains why Paul took it upon himself to write to the Roman Christians in the first place: even though he had not founded the Roman church and indeed had never even visited them, Paul was appointed "the apostle to the gentiles." Therefore,

---

19. Stowers, *Rereading*, 29–30.

20. Francis Watson complains, "It is often *wrongly assumed* that Paul addresses Romans exclusively to Gentiles—*on the basis of a misinterpretation of 11:13*, where 'I am speaking to you Gentiles' refers only to the immediate context and not to the letter as a whole" (Watson, "Law in Romans," 105). How ironic, then, that Watson's essay comes bound in the very same volume as Das's essay, "The Gentile-Encoded Audience of Romans," which argues—*not assumes!*—on the basis of a "consistent and conspicuous" identification of Paul's audience in four—*not one!*—passages: Rom 1:5–6; 1:13; 11:13; 15:15–16 (Das, "Gentile-Encoded Audience," 33). Moreover, Das's argument in this essay was not new; see Das, *Solving*, which was published *five years* before Watson's dismissive characterization!

21. Even if there were Jewish believers in Jesus in Rome, and even if Paul assumed that some of them would have eventually heard or read his letter, Das's thesis is simply that nothing in Romans suggests that Paul had these Jewish believers in mind as he wrote. See also Thorsteinsson, *Interlocutor*, 87 n.2; 99–100.

the gentile Christians in Rome fell "within the sphere of Paul's apostolic authority because they too are gentiles."[22]

Das finds corroborating evidence for his conclusion in Rom 1:13-15, where Paul says he wants to bear fruit "among you, also, just as among the rest of the gentiles [*en tois loipois ethnesin*], Greeks as well as barbarians, wise as well as foolish." In the letter's closing, Paul clearly indicates that the sphere in which he exercised his apostolic authority was "among the gentiles" [*eis ta ethnē* (15:16)], and that he endeavored to bring "the offering of the gentiles" [*hē prosphora tōn ethnōn* (15:16)] as an acceptable and sanctified gift to Israel's God. Paul also refers to the "obedience of the gentiles" [*hypakoēn ethnōn* (15:18)], which again suggests that Paul conceived his apostolic task in gentile—and even *exclusively* gentile—terms.[23] Thorsteinsson, in a provocative statement, is even more sure of a gentile audience for Romans than for any other Pauline letter: "[I]n no other extant letter by Paul is the audience so distinctly identified as in Romans."[24]

This is not the place to answer the objections to a thoroughly gentile audience for Romans. However, we should recognize the speculative (rather than textual) tenor of most discussions of Romans' supposedly mixed audience. As one example, which is neither uncharacteristic nor unusual:

> Originally, the Roman Christian churches had been populated by Jewish Christians, but after the expulsion of the Jews, including Jewish Christians, the Christian churches *must have continued* under Gentile Christian leadership. In the meantime, these churches *had become disconnected* from the Jewish synagogues, and *other factors had probably shifted*. Some of the communities *may have switched* to Sunday worship *or discontinued* the dietary regulations prescribed by Torah.... At Claudius's death, Jews—including Jewish Christians—*probably returned* to Rome in great numbers, and suddenly the Roman house churches *must have experienced* a merger of two rather different groups

---

22. Das, *Solving*, 55. See Das's earlier discussion in *Paul*, 63-69.

23. See Das's larger discussion (*Solving*, 54-70). Thorsteinsson also provides an extensive discussion of Paul's audience, arguing that Paul's readers "are included among the people to whom Paul was appointed apostle, namely, non-Jews. In other words, the rather general identification of the letter's recipients in the adscription has already been demarcated by Paul's introductory account of his mission to 'all the gentiles' (vv. 5-6). Hence, the letter is addressed to all those gentiles in Rome who stand in a loving relationship to God" (see Thorsteinsson, *Interlocutor*, 87-122; p. 87 quoted).

24. Thorsteinsson, *Interlocutor*, 88.

who had been divided for five years and were now learning to live together.[25]

Even if we grant every facet of this reconstruction of the Roman church, the fact remains that Paul only ever explicitly identifies the audience he imagines himself addressing as gentiles.[26] Moreover, most of the details of this reconstruction have very little concrete evidence supporting them; the italicized phrases highlight those parts of Grieb's reconstruction that (i) are central to the traditional understanding of the context of Paul's audience and (ii) rely completely on historians' assumptions about what "must have," "may have," and "probably" happened. But *why* should we assume that gentiles who took an interest in Jesus, *as Israel's Messiah* (!), "had become disconnected from the Jewish synagogues" or formed a "rather different group" than Jews who also identified Jesus as the Messiah? No answer is immediately forthcoming. As we work through the text of the letter, then, we will defend the thesis of Paul's gentile-Christian audience.[27]

The Purpose of Romans

If Paul wrote for gentile Christ-believers in Rome (Romans' *to whom*), *why* did Paul write this letter? Here are three of the more compelling reasons scholars propose for Romans.

1. Das makes a compelling case that Paul writes Romans to exercise his authority as the apostle to the gentiles.[28] Paul did not found the

---

25. Grieb, *Story*, 7; my emphases.

26. See Rom 1:5–6, 13; 11:13; 15:15–16. The one possible exception is Rom 2:17 ("But if you call yourself a Jew . . ."), though, as we will see below, even here Paul is imagining himself addressing *a gentile* who "call[s him]self a Jew." Paul's "for the Jew first as well as for the Greek" formulae (Rom 1:16; 2:9, 10; see also 3:9, 29; 9:24; 10:12) do not explicitly identify his intended audience.

27. I retain the use of the traditional term, *Christian*, throughout this book despite the fact that Paul nowhere uses the term. Joshua Garroway (*Gentile-Jews*, 4–7) argues that this word is anachronistic, and of course it is. But his own proposal, that we refer to them as "Gentile-Jews," is no more consonant with Pauline usage than the traditional designation. However, I agree with the substance of his argument (that "Gentile-Christians of the first century should in fact be considered Jews"; p. 1), and so I stipulate that my use of the term *Christian* assumes a fundamentally ("according to the flesh") Abrahamic understanding of the term, which understanding usually applies only (or primarily) to the label, *Jew*.

28. Das, *Solving*, 56–57; passim.

church(es) in Rome; neither had he ever visited them, though he says he intended to. Paul understands himself, however, as one commissioned to take the message of the gospel to the gentiles (see Gal 1:1, 16), and even the Jerusalem church had recognized this commission (Gal 2:1–10, esp. v. 9). Paul's letter, therefore, spreads the umbrella of Paul's apostolic authority over the community/-ies of gentile believers in Rome.

2. Similarly, Paul mentions his intention to launch a preaching mission west, through Rome and on to Spain. By the time he wrote Romans, Paul has been engaged in preaching the gospel throughout the eastern Mediterranean for nearly two and a half decades. Now he plans to travel to Rome, and he hopes they will send him out west (Rom 15:22–24). But before he can do that, he has to take the offering he has collected from the gentile congregations in southeastern Europe and Asia Minor and deliver it to the Jewish congregation(s) in Judea and Jerusalem.

3. The lengthy discussion of Israel in Romans 9–11 suggests that Romans' original audience exhibited some animosity toward Israel and/or Jewish brothers and sisters (= believers). In Romans 14–15, Paul addresses a schism within or among the Roman churches and provides a lengthy admonition for the "strong" and the "weak" brethren to accept one another. Since most commentators interpret Romans in light of a mixed audience that comprises both Jews and gentiles, we usually imagine a division between the Jewish and gentile believers in Rome. If, however, Paul is addressing an exclusively gentile audience, then we will have to re-think this interpretation of Romans 14–15.

We could mention other purposes, but these three seem to be the primary and the most significant proposals frequently made by Pauline scholars.[29]

Thus, Paul writes to the gentile believers in Rome in order (i) to extend his apostolic authority over the established communities of gentile believers and place his gospel at the center of their theological perspective; (ii) to lay the foundation for a mission to Spain, on the western edge of the Empire; and (iii) to manage (≠ solve!) tensions between various expressions of the nascent Christian faith and restore unity between them without requiring conformity to a single pattern of faith or piety.

---

29. See Longenecker's chapter, titled simply, "Purpose" (*Introducing*, 92–166). The three purposes I have singled out pertain to Longenecker's first, second, and fourth options (Longenecker mentions five possible purposes for Romans).

1

The Gospel, the Power of God

Paul Begins to Write

> *The study of classical rhetoric reveals the crucial role of the exordium for the understanding of a subsequent argument. The exordium not only introduces the speaker in a manner calculated to appeal to the audience and lend credence to the speaker's cause, but it also frequently introduces the topics to be addressed in a speech. When one compares this opening with Greco-Roman letters, its length and complexity are unmistakable. . . . Even in comparison with the other Pauline letters, the opening of Romans is considerably expanded.*[1]

Pauline scholarship has increasingly appreciated the ways that Paul directs his audiences' reading of his letters in the opening sections. As such, Jewett's observation (cited in the epigraph, above) that Romans' opening section is long and complex ought to give us pause before we jump right into the theologically rich text awaiting us in later chapters. Paying especially close attention now might just enable us to better understand the more complicated moments in this letter later on.

---

1. Jewett, *Romans*, 96.

Paul, to All Those in Rome (Rom 1:1–7)

> **1** Paul, a slave of Christ Jesus, called [to be] an apostle, one set apart for the gospel of God **2** (which was promised beforehand through his prophets in the Holy Scriptures) **3** about his son—who was from the seed of David according to the flesh **4** and was declared son of God with power according to the Spirit of holiness by the resurrection from the dead—Jesus Christ our Lord, **5** through whom we received grace and apostolic vocation for the obedience of faith among all the gentiles for his name's sake, **6** among whom you also are, you [who are] called by Jesus Christ, **7** to all who are in Rome, beloved of God, called [to be] holy. Grace to you and peace from God our Father and from the Lord Jesus Christ.

The three-fold self-description—"a slave of Christ Jesus, called [to be] an apostle, set apart for the gospel of God" (1:1)—presents Paul as an authoritative figure whose teaching deserves to be heard and accepted. Paul does very little to defend his apostolic status or to convince anyone who might doubt him. Instead, simply on the basis of his self-presentation in the opening verses, we might infer that Paul expects his readers to accept his apostolic status fairly readily. In addition, the numerous personal notes in Romans 16 suggest that Paul knows a number of Christians in Rome and has numerous personal relationships already established there. Even though Paul had never visited Rome and was not involved in founding any of its churches, he seems to think he already has a favorable audience among his readers.

Paul identifies himself in three distinct terms: *slave*, *apostle*, and *set apart*. I will address the second term first. There is nothing particularly emphatic or defensive about Paul's self-identification as an apostle in Rom 1:1. The title *apostolos* appears at the beginning of all thirteen of the letters that bear Paul's name, with only two exceptions:

1. In his letter to the Philippians, Paul uses *apostolos* only at 2.25, where he refers to Epaphroditus as the Philippians' "apostle and priest for my need."
2. Paul never uses the word in his letter to Philemon.

Contrast the opening of Galatians, in which Paul defends his apostolic status as being "neither from men nor by men but by Jesus Christ and God the Father, who raised him from the dead" (Gal 1:1). As we turn to Romans, if Paul's claim "to have been set apart for the gospel of God" [*aphōrismenos eis euangelion theou*] is meant to defend his authority and status, it is a very mild and laconic defense. As I will explain below, I think Paul mentions his "set-apart-ness" for other reasons.

The same could be said for his self-identification as "a slave of Christ Jesus" [*doulos Christou Iēsou*]. Though Paul identifies himself as a slave less often than as an apostle, he uses the designation often enough. Paul refers to both himself and Timothy as slaves in Phil 1:1, and Titus 1:1 also identifies Paul as "a slave of God." In the highly polemical letter to the Galatians, in which Paul emphasizes his authority rather than his servant-status, he refers to himself as "a slave of Christ" [*Christou doulos*], though the designation occurs outside the letter's address (Gal 1:10). If we were to attach any particular significance to Paul's self-designation as "slave" in Rom 1:1, we would probably want to read this verse in light of his comments on slavery in Romans 6.

Finally, as I already mentioned, Paul describes himself as "set apart for the gospel of God" (cp. Gal 1:15). Nothing about this phrase strikes me as a defense of his authority, as if Paul felt the need to counter any potential opponents among the Roman believers who might have denied his apostolic commission. Rather, this phrase subtly introduces a theme that we will encounter later in the letter, especially in Romans 15, in which Paul describes his role in God's plan using priestly and/or cultic language. "The basic meaning of *aphorizō* is to set apart, to separate, which occurs in the OT most prominently in the context of separating the clean from the unclean."[2] Paul's language here is striking because the typical usage of *aphorizō* refers to setting apart *from*—whether Israel's being set apart from the pagan nations (see Lev 20:26), Peter's setting himself apart from gentile believers "because he was afraid of those from the circumcision" (Gal 2:12), or whatever. Paul, however, speaks of being set apart *for* something: the gospel of God. This unusual usage might just signal something deeper about the transformation in his thinking about purity/impurity (or, similarly, holiness/profanity) in light of the gospel. That is, Paul's concern for purity may have been just as strong after his encounter with the risen Jesus as it had been before. But now, rather than trying to keep himself separate *from* potential sources of impurity, Paul's "set-apart-ness" propelled him *into* gentile situations to advance the gospel of God.

This last designation—as one "set apart for the gospel of God"—places Paul's apostolic calling within the framework of Israel's prophetic tradition. The prophet Isaiah described Israel as "set apart from Abraham," the chosen offspring from among Abraham's descendants (Isa 29:22). Later, the prophet

---

2. Ibid., 102.

encourages the children of Israel and exhorts "those who bear the vessels of the Lord" to "separate themselves" from impurity. Ezekiel refers to the first-fruits of the harvest, which are "set apart" for the Lord and given to the priests (see Ezekiel 45; 48). Paul, like the earliest produce of the season or, significantly, like Abraham's offspring, has been set apart for God's purposes, and as such he stands in the venerable tradition of Israel's prophets.

Paul explicitly links "the gospel of God" [*euangelion theou*] with Israel's written, biblical traditions. Romans 1:2 provides a parenthetical description of the gospel mentioned in v. 1: "the gospel of God (which was promised beforehand through his prophets in the Holy Scriptures) about his son."[3] The closest connection elsewhere in Romans between "gospel" [*euangelion*] and Israel's Scriptures comes at 10:16, where Paul laments, "Not everyone has obeyed the gospel," and then explains this perplexing situation by appealing to Isa 53:1. However, despite the fact that Paul does not use *euangelion* in Romans 3, the connection between the gospel and the Hebrew Bible is arguably most powerfully expressed in Rom 3:21. At this pivotal moment in Paul's rhetoric, the righteousness of God is "attested to by Torah and the Prophets."[4] Just ten verses later, at the end of Romans 3, Paul insists that his gospel *establishes* rather than *nullifies* Torah (3:31).

Pauline scholars largely agree that Paul quotes an early credal formula in vv. 3-4, though they disagree on (i) the precise contours of that formula, and (ii) whether and how Paul has redacted it. One of the key issues is whether Paul's description of Jesus' Davidic descent ("according to the flesh") marginalizes that descent or merely qualifies it with respect to Jesus' status as son of God. I take a weak view of the contrast between "flesh" and "spirit." That is, I do *not* read "according to the flesh" as Paul's way of minimizing or down-playing Jesus' descent from Israel's illustrious king. Rather, the descriptive phrase "according to the flesh" places Jesus' physical ancestry on a lower plane than his "spiritual" descent. Unlike his physical, Davidic descent, which was "according to the flesh," Jesus'

---

3. Matera presents these verses in a similar fashion: Rom 1:2-4 presents "the gospel Paul preaches," and these verses describe that gospel in two ways: (i) it was "promised through the prophets in the Scriptures (1:2)"; and (ii) it is "about God's Son (1:3-4)" (*Romans*, 27; see also p. 29).

4. Remember also that though this text speaks of "the righteousness of God" instead of the gospel, at a programmatic moment in this letter Paul had already equated the *euangelion* that he proclaimed with the power of God for salvation and the revelation of the righteousness of God (see Rom 1:16-17).

spiritual descent as the son of God was "declared . . . with power" [*horisthentos . . . en dynamei*].

The two descriptors of Jesus in 1:3–4 emphasize Jesus' royal status, an idea that Paul does not usually stress.[5] The description of Jesus' descent "from the seed of David" conveys obvious royal connotations. The reference to Jesus' physical relation ("according to the flesh" [*kata sarka*]) maps David's reputation as Israel's illustrious king, "a man after God's own heart," onto Jesus. But later Christian controversies about the nature of Christ make it difficult for us to see clearly that the language of being "the son of God" also referred to chosen and/or royal identity. In other words, "son of God" language did not relate directly to Trinitarian ideas of God's or Jesus' nature. For example, in Psalm 2, the king of Israel expresses consternation that the surrounding nations conspire "against the Lord and his anointed one" (Ps 2:2 LXX). "His anointed one" refers to Israel's king, as we see four verses later: "I am appointed king [*basileus*] by him on Zion, his holy mountain" (2:6 LXX). In the very next verse the Lord declares to Israel's king, "You are my son [*huios mou*]; today I have begotten you" (2:7 LXX). The context makes clear that the anointed, the son of God, is Israel's king.

This same idea is found in the Lord's promise to David in 2 Sam 7. After David tells the prophet Nathan of his plans to build a permanent temple in Jerusalem, the Lord prevents him and declares instead a significant promise:

> 12 And it shall be that when your days are fulfilled and you sleep with your fathers, then I will raise up your seed [*to sperma sou*]—who will come from your loins—and I shall prepare his kingdom. 13 He shall build for me a house for my name, and I will establish his throne forever. 14 I will be for him as a father [*eis patera*], and he will be for me as a son [*eis huion*]. And if his unrighteousness comes, then I will correct him with the rod of men and with the wounds of the sons of humans. 15 But my mercy I will not remove from him, the way I removed it from those whom I removed from my presence. 16 Both his household and his kingdom shall be made sure forever in my presence, and his throne will be established forever. (2 Kgdms 7:12–16 LXX)

However, the idea of a special relationship with YHWH—being a "son of God"—was not limited to Israel's king. As we saw in the previous chapter, the entire people of Israel could also be described as "God's son." The

---

5. Jesus as Israel's king, and Jesus' message of the kingdom of God/the heavens, are central ideas in the Synoptic Gospels. Though they are not central in Paul's letters, these ideas nevertheless appear at key moments in his writings.

Lord instructed Moses to tell Pharaoh, "Israel is my firstborn son [*huios prōtotokos mou Israēl*]" (Exod 4:22 LXX). And, in a text that Matthew cites in his account of Jesus' birth, the prophet Hosea says, "I have loved Israel like a child, and out of Egypt I have called my son [*libĕnî*]" (Hos 11:1).[6] Whether the status "son of God" applies to Israel as a whole or to Israel's king, the idea is the same. The Davidic king stands between the people of Israel and God and mediates between them. Israel stands between the peoples of the world and God and mediates between them. We should read this language in the NT (including in Rom 1:4) along these lines, rather than in overtly Trinitarian terms.

Paul continues to pile up phrases that describe "his [= God's] son" (v. 2). In addition to being (i) the son of David according to the flesh and (ii) the son of God according to the Spirit of holiness, Jesus is also the vehicle of the grace and apostolic calling that God has given Paul (Rom 1:5). Although Paul will not formally identify his audience until vv. 6–7, already in v. 5 we catch a glimpse of the implied reader. Paul's apostolic office—his responsibilities and his tasks—centers on procuring the "obedience of faith" [*hypakoēn pisteōs*] from "all the gentiles." These phrases provide an important glimpse into Paul's reason for writing Romans. The strong gentile community/-ies of faith in Rome fell under Paul's divine commission as "apostle to the gentiles" (see Rom 11:13), even though he had not proclaimed the gospel in Rome nor founded any of the churches there.

In the context of Jesus' royal identity, understood within the framework of Israel's biblical—and especially prophetic—traditions, Paul portrays himself as an ambassador dispatched on behalf of Jesus, Israel's king, to procure the allegiance ("the obedience of faith") from all the nations of the earth. Paul explicitly identifies his Roman readers among these gentiles/nations and names them as among those who are subject to Jesus ("you [who are] called by Jesus Christ"; v. 6). Verse 7 brings the letter's address to an end: "To all who are in Rome, beloved of God, called [to be] holy. Grace to you and peace from God our Father and from the Lord Jesus Christ." This greeting ("grace and peace . . .") is considerably expanded from typical Greco-Roman epistolary greetings, "Greetings" [*chairein*].[7]

---

6. I have translated the Hebrew text here because the LXX text of Hos 11:1 differs significantly from the MT: "Therefore Israel is a child, and I loved him, and I recalled his children [*ta tekna autou*] out of Egypt." See Matt 2:15.

7. This more typical greeting is found three times in NT letters; once at Jas 1:1, once in the Jerusalem church's letter to gentile believers in Asia Minor (Acts 15:23), and once in Lysias's letter to the Roman governor Felix (Acts 23:26). However, see Lutz Doering's study (*Jewish Letters*, esp. pp. 406–15) for a compelling explanation of Paul's

However, all of Paul's letters begin by wishing grace and peace [*charis kai eirēnē*] to his readers, and the practice seems to have caught on among other Christian writers.⁸

Romans 1:1–7 contains a number of important terms that Paul will discuss through the course of his letter, including "slave" [*doulos*], "son" [*huios*], "power" [*dynamis*], "faith" [*pistis*], and others. The fact that the letter's opening contains such important vocabulary suggests that Paul is setting the stage now for his discussion later on. Moreover, the opening of this letter (through 1:17) forms a piece with the letter's closing in Romans 15. This tight structure strongly encourages us to see the argument that spans the length of Romans 1–15 as a unified argument. Unlike 1 Corinthians, where Paul addresses a number of disparate issues facing the churches in Achaia, or comparatively short letters such as Galatians, Philippians, or 1 Thessalonians, Romans is a lengthy, focused, direct communication that does not get distracted from its main point: the gospel message of the righteousness of God revealed in Jesus, the son of David and of God, which results in peace with God, for the Jew first as well as for the Greek.

A Prayer of Thanksgiving (Rom 1:8–15)

> **8** First of all, I give thanks to my God through Jesus Christ for all of you because your faith is proclaimed throughout the whole world. **9** For God—to whom I give priestly service with my spirit by the gospel of his son—is my witness, how unceasingly I remember you **10** always in my prayers as I ask if, somehow now at last I will be granted success by the will of God to come to you. **11** For I long to see you so that I may impart some spiritual gift to you in order to strengthen you, **12** that is, to be encouraged together with you through the faith we have together, both yours and mine. **13** But I do not want you to be ignorant, brethren: I often intended to come to you (though I was prevented [from doing so] up until now) so that I might have some fruit even among you, just as [I have] also among the rest of the gentiles. **14** I am under obligation to Greeks as well as the barbarians, to the wise as well as the foolish; **15** likewise I have been eager to proclaim the gospel also to you who are in Rome.

---

purportedly distinctive greeting within the contexts of ancient Jewish letters.

8. See 1 Pet 1:2; 2 Pet 1:2; and Rev 1:4. Second John 3 mentions both *charis* and *eirēnē*, but it is sufficiently different from these other, "Pauline" greetings that it likely was not influenced by Paul's letters.

If You Call Yourself a Jew

The second section of Romans' opening gives a prayer of thanksgiving for the Christians in Rome. Prayers of thanksgiving are a commonplace in Greco-Roman epistolary practice, and every one of Paul's letters except Galatians contains a thanksgiving prayer. If Das is right that Paul intends his letter for a gentile (rather than a mixed) audience, we should appreciate what we have in Rom 1:8–15: Paul, a diaspora Jew, writing the message of the "good news" that God has appointed a king of Israel and sending this message to gentiles *in the imperial capital, Rome!* These gentile residents of the imperial capital had "put their hope in the Davidic Messiah risen from the dead, with the intent that *he is and will be their ruler, too.*"[9] Instead of announcing the king's victory over the enemies of God's people, or warning of the king's impending judgment, this Jew says flatly, "I give thanks to my God through Jesus Christ for all of you" (1:8). Paul names the reason for his gratitude to God: the spread of reports of the Romans' "faithfulness," or "trustworthiness" [*pistis*], throughout the Empire. This really is amazing (or it would be if we were not already so familiar with Paul's letters): a non-Jewish population of a pagan imperial power is known across the Empire as being faithful, trustworthy subjects of Israel's God and king!

Paul invokes God as his witness of this amazing development in v. 9. Once again Paul surprises us here, because he describes himself as a priestly servant of God. Of course, only Levitical Jews could serve God as priest. But Paul, a Benjamite Jew, understands his apostleship (see 1:5) in priestly terms.[10] He describes God as the one "to whom I give priestly service [*hō latreuō*] with my spirit by the gospel of his son" (Rom 1:9). Paul will use the same language again in Romans 15. The LXX provides some valuable insight into the use and meaning of *latreuō* and related terminology:

- a *leitourgos* ("servant or minister") was either a servant (like Gehazi to Elisha, or one of the king's attendants) or one of the personnel of the temple. Of the thirteen uses of *leitourgos* in the LXX, six certainly refer to temple personnel, two probably do, and the remaining five refer to a prophet's or king's servant (or a political official);

- the related adjective *leitourgikos* ("serving or priestly"), used six times, only ever describes cultic activities or implements;

---

9. Stegemann, "Coexistence and Transformation," 19; emphasis added.

10. Martha Himmelfarb discusses a number of Jewish texts from the Second Temple era that "reflect not a revolt against priestly hegemony, but rather a desire to appropriate the status of priests for non-priests" ("Kingdom of Priests," 89). This—"appropriat[ing] the status of priests for non-priests"—is precisely what Paul does for himself in Romans.

- of the nine uses of *latreia* ("worship"), eight refer to the cultic service associated with either the tabernacle or the Jerusalem temple.

Paul will use this sphere of Judaic worship (i.e., its cultic ministry) to frame his proclamation of the gospel among the nations/gentiles at the close of the letter. But for now, he simply refers to this self-understanding as he assures his Roman readers of his unceasing prayers for them.

Before we move on, perhaps we should mention that city and public officials throughout the Empire often did (and were expected to) offer prayers for the Emperor. Even in Jerusalem, the priests in the temple would offer sacrifice on Caesar's behalf. One of the precipitating events of the Jewish War in 66 CE was the cessation of sacrifices to God on Caesar's behalf.[11] Paul, who presents himself as a priest in service of Israel's God, does not offer prayers on behalf of the Emperor. Instead, he prays for the gentile subjects of Israel's God who live in the capital city.

Paul expresses his desire to come and visit the believers in Rome in vv. 10–12. Commentators rightly focus on Paul's stated desire to "impart some spiritual gift" to the Roman believers and on his hope for mutual encouragement of his and his readers' faith. This desire clearly provides (at least part of) the impetus for Paul's letter. But the reciprocality of Paul's desire for *mutual* encouragement ought not lead us to miss the authoritative posture Paul takes *vis-à-vis* his audience. Paul does not seem in any way apologetic for thinking he has an obligation toward and authority over the Romans. As the apostle to the gentiles writing to gentile believers in the imperial city, Paul is especially concerned to bring the Romans under the ambit of his apostolic calling. We will see this played out further in Romans 15.

The disclosure formula in Rom 1:13 provides an important indication of Paul's purpose for writing to Roman gentile believers in Jesus: he has been prevented from visiting them, and this letter solves that problem (at least temporarily). Of course, Romans is much more than a short note saying, "I have been meaning to visit; I promise I will as soon as I can." But given Paul's authoritative (= apostolic) stance *vis-à-vis* his readers, we can probably say that Paul has wanted for some time to bring the gentile churches in Rome under the aegis of his ministry. He has been prevented from coming to them in person, so now he sends a letter. This reading makes sense of the end of v. 13: Paul perceives some difference between the Romans and "the rest of the gentiles," namely that he cannot claim any "fruit" among the Roman believers. The whole of the gentile world falls

---

11. See Josephus, *J.W.* 2:409–10.

under Paul's apostolic vocation—Greeks as well as barbarians; the wise and the foolish (Rom 1:14). The fact that Paul had not spread his apostolic blanket over Rome was, at least to him, a conspicuous problem.

A Thematic Statement (Rom 1:16–17)

> **16** For I am not ashamed of the gospel, for it is the power of God for the salvation of everyone who believes, for the Jew first as well as for the Greek. **17** For in it the righteousness of God is being revealed by faith for faith, just as it is written, "But the righteous one will live by faith" (Hab 2:4).

This first section of Romans ends with a thematic statement that most commentators describe as the thesis of the whole letter.[12] The rhetorical movement across vv. 14–15 and through vv. 16–17 exhibits a four-fold progression (I have added explanatory questions in square brackets to emphasize the passage's logical development):

a. **14** I am under obligation to Greeks as well as the barbarians, to the wise as well as the foolish; **15** likewise I have been eager to proclaim the gospel also to you who are in Rome. [*Why, Paul, are you eager to proclaim the good news of Israel's God to believers in the imperial capital, Rome?*]

b. **16** Because [*gar*] I am not ashamed of the gospel. [*Why, Paul, aren't you ashamed of the good news of Israel's crucified king, especially as you proclaim it in the heart of Caesar's empire?*]

c. Because [*gar*] it is the power of God for the salvation of everyone who believes, for the Jew first as well as for the Greek. [*Why, Paul, is this the message that results in the salvation of everyone who believes it, Jew as well as gentile?*]

d. **17** Because [*gar*] in it the righteousness of God is being revealed by faithfulness to faithfulness, just as it is written, "But the righteous one will live by faith."[13]

---

12. For example, Jewett (*Romans*, 135) calls these two verses the *propositio*, or the "thesis, basic contention" of Romans and refers to this passage as "the argumentative burden of the entire letter." Karl Barth (*Romans*, 35–42) also discusses Rom 1:16–17 under the heading, "The theme of the epistle."

13. Paul's citation of Hab 2:4 is ambiguous. I have provided the translation, "the righteous one will live by faith," but the Greek can also be translated, "the one who is righteous by faithfulness shall live." Katherine Grieb provides an interesting suggestion: "There are a number of possible meanings and Paul probably intended more than one of them: it could mean that Jesus, God's righteous one, will live again (be raised from

The Gospel, the Power of God

I agree that this passage is the thematic statement of the whole letter. Each section of Romans in some way relates to what Paul says here. Paul's obligation to the entire gentile world on behalf of Israel's God compels him to proclaim the good news of Israel's king, Jesus. The result of this good news is the life of faith, the life that characterizes the one who lives under God's rule (i.e., "the righteous one" [*ho dikaios*]).

Before we move on to the remainder of Romans 1, we need to say something about "the righteousness of God" [*dikaiosynē theou*].[14] N. T. Wright suggests that when Paul refers to the righteousness of God, he is talking about God's faithfulness to his covenant with Israel and, through Israel, to all creation.[15] Robert Jewett agrees: "[T]he biblical concept of righteousness was primarily relational, associated with covenantal loyalty."[16] Katherine Grieb identifies "three interrelated meanings" for "the righteousness of God" in Jewish literature before Paul: "(1) God's covenant faithfulness to Israel; (2) God's justice, especially for the poor and powerless; and (3) God's eschatological (end-time) saving power to make things turn out right."[17] I regularly relate the concept of God's faithfulness back to the original Abrahamic covenant:

> 1 And the Lord said to Abram, "Depart from your land and from your family and from the house of your father, for the land which I will show you. 2 I will make you a great nation, and I will bless you and magnify your name. And you will be blessed. 3 I will bless those who bless you, and those who curse you I will curse. And in you all the tribes of the earth will be blessed. (Gen 12:1–3 LXX)

The next significant moment in God's covenant with Abraham was the Mosaic covenant at Sinai. At the end of that covenant, just before Israel

---

the dead) because of his fidelity or that he will be raised because of his trust in God. It could mean that those who put their trust in God and Jesus will live by their faith in the God who has put them back in right relationship. It may refer to the resurrection of those who, like Jesus, put their trust in God. It may mean all of these things at once" ("Righteousness of God," 71).

14. This phrase occurs six times in Romans (1:17; 3:5, 21, 22; 10:3 [twice]); in addition, Paul refers to "his righteousness" [*dikaiosynē autou*], referring to God, twice (3:25, 26).

15. See Wright, "Romans," 397–405; Wright, *New Testament*, 271–72.

16. Jewett, *Romans*, 141.

17. Grieb identifies the first—"God's covenant faithfulness to Israel"—as "[t]he most important and primary meaning of God's righteousness" (Grieb, *Story*, 21–25 [p. 21 quoted]; see also Grieb, "Righteousness of God," 65–78).

entered the land of promise, YHWH explained to the people exactly what was at stake: life and death.

> **19** I call both heaven and earth to swear to you today: I have set before you both life and death, blessing and curse. Choose life, so that you might live, you and your seed. **20** Love the Lord your God. Listen to his voice and hold to it, because this will be your life and the length of your days, for you to dwell in the land, which the Lord promised your ancestors—Abraham, Isaac, and Jacob—to give to them. (Deut 30:19-20 LXX)

The problem, of course, was that God's chosen people, Israel, did not choose life. As we move through Romans, Paul will have to explain how God will keep his promise to Abraham (see Gen 12:1-3) in light of Israel's failure to choose life and blessing (see Deuteronomy 30). This faithfulness to his promise to Abraham—*the righteousness of God*—is revealed in the gospel of God's son (remember: Israel's king), Jesus.

3

The Wrath and Impartial Judgment of God

Gentiles in Pauline Perspective

The wrath of God is the judgement under which we stand in so far as we do not love the Judge; it is the "No" which meets us when we do not affirm it.... The whole world is the footprint of God; yes, but, in so far as we choose scandal rather than faith, the footprint in the vast riddle of the world is the footprint of His wrath. The wrath of God is to unbelief the discovery of His righteousness, for God is not mocked. The wrath of God is the righteousness of God—apart from and without Christ.[1]

Karl Barth's massively influential commentary on Romans provides a breathtaking theological exposition of the text of Paul's longest epistle. The First World War had placed an undeniable question mark against the very foundation of Western theology in the traditions of the Enlightenment. In the aftermath of the War, Barth's commentary blazed a new trail and read Romans with eyes firmly focused on Paul's gospel of Jesus Christ, the Son of God. Nevertheless, Barth's theological reading of Romans suffers from certain exegetical shortcomings, not least of which is his too-eager universalization of Paul's words. Barth uses first-person plural pronouns, referring to "the judgement under which *we* stand in so far as *we* do not love the Judge." Romans 1 convicts Barth and confirms him in his conviction—correct as far as it goes—"that we are sinners, and

1. Barth, *Romans*, 42, 43.

that we must die."² As Barth navigates Paul's sudden turn from the revelation of the righteousness of God in the gospel (Rom 1:17) to the revelation of the wrath of God "against all ungodliness and unrighteousness of men" (v. 18), he writes: "These are the characteristic features of *our* relation to God, as it takes shape on this side [sic; of] resurrection. *Our relation to God is ungodly*."³ When Barth reads Rom 1:18–32, he finds Paul addressing him directly! However, in a letter replete with first- and second-person pronouns, we should note that Paul only uses third-person pronouns in this section. Paul is not writing about "us" or even "you"; he is writing about "them."⁴

But First, the Wrath of God (Rom 1:18–32)

18 For the wrath of God is being revealed from heaven against all the ungodliness and unrighteousness of people who by their unrighteousness suppress the truth, **19** because the knowledge of God is evident among them (for God made it evident to them). **20** For ever since the creation of the world his invisible qualities are perceived through created things; they are clearly discerned—whether his eternal power or also his deity—so that they might be without excuse, **21** because although they knew God they did not glorify him as God or give thanks, but they were rendered foolish in their thoughts and their senseless heart was darkened. **22** Although they claimed to be wise they were made foolish, **23** and they exchanged the glory of the incorruptible God for the likeness of an image of a corruptible mortal or bird or four-footed creature or reptile.

24 God, therefore, by means of the lusts of their hearts, handed them over to uncleanness, in order to dishonor their bodies among themselves. **25** They exchanged the truth of God for a lie, and they worshipped and gave priestly service to the creation rather than the Creator, who is blessed forever. Amen. **26** For this reason, God handed them over to dishonorable passions, since their females exchanged the natural function for that which is contrary to nature, **27** just as the males, also, abandoned the natural relation with a female. They were inflamed by their longing for one another, males committing this shameless deed with [other] males, so they also received the consequence that was required for their mutual deception.

28 And just as they did not approve to have God in knowledge, God handed them over to a worthless mind, to do things that are not proper, **29** since they are filled with all unrighteousness, wickedness, greediness,

---

2. Ibid., 43.

3. Ibid., 44; my emphases.

4. For an excellent discussion of this very issue, see Garroway, *Gentile-Jews*, 86–89.

> and malice; they are full of envy, murder, strife, treachery, malevolence. They are gossipers, **30** slanderers, haters of God, insolent, arrogant, boasters, contrivers of evil deeds, disobedient to their parents, **31** senseless, faithless, heartless, merciless. **33** Although they knew the righteous requirement of God—that those who practice such things are worthy of death—they not only practice such things but also approve of those who do them.

"But the righteous one will live by faith." Habakkuk 2:4, along with the rest of Rom 1:14–17, is somehow related to the stark description of the ungodliness and unrighteousness that immediately follows in 1:18–32. Again we have the Greek conjunction *gar* ("for, because"), which "introduces the reason for a statement, which usually precedes."[5] Given the connection between vv. 14–17 and 18–32, the change in tone should surprise us. The gospel is the power of God for salvation, because in it the righteousness of God is revealed, along with the life of faith. And what comes next in Paul's mind? "For the wrath of God is being revealed from heaven against all the ungodliness and unrighteousness of people who by their unrighteousness suppress the truth" (1:18).[6] Ekkehard Stegemann helpfully explains the movement from Rom 1:14–17 to vv. 18–32:

> The key theme of Romans is not only the gospel and God's power of salvation mediated by the revelation or appearance of God's *dikaiosynē* ["righteousness"], which makes faithful believers righteous. The revelation of God's wrath as soon coming into force is also part of it. There is, so to speak, a *dysangelion* ["anti-gospel"], too.[7]

The question, however, remains: why does Paul follow up on the exuberant confidence of Rom 1:14–17 with the stark depravity of vv. 18–32?

Romans 1:18–32 introduces the problem for which the gospel provides the solution. That is, the righteousness of God is being revealed with

---

5. LSJ, s.v. (cited above); see also Jewett, *Romans*, 151.

6. The present-tense verb, *apokalyptetai* ("is being revealed") may convey future-oriented connotations (i.e., "will so certainly be revealed in the future that we speak of it as a certainty in the present"); however, as Jewett rightly notes, "[s]ince 'wrath' is an expression of Paul's gospel, described in 1:16 with the identical present passive verb, *apokalyptetai*, the present progressive translation 'is being revealed' is appropriate for both" ("Anthropological Implications," 26).

7. Stegemann, "Coexistence and Transformation," 9.

power,[8] in contrast with the revelation of his wrath against gentile idolatry. In other words, Paul contrasts the life of faith (v. 17) with the life of unrighteousness that suppresses the truth [of God]. Among the gentiles to whom Paul proclaims the gospel, sin, wickedness, unrighteousness, and ungodliness result from their failure to distinguish God, as Creator, from creation, the works of his hands.[9] This is not a new state of affairs; it has characterized gentile society for as long as they have exchanged the worship of the Creator God for worship of hand-made idols.[10] In light of the gentiles' misdirected worship, the world is less than the "good" God repeatedly declared over creation in Genesis 1. The gospel of God (Rom 1:1) reveals God's plan to rectify precisely this situation.

The beginning of Paul's discussion of the wrath of God (1:18–23) employs standard Jewish rhetoric against gentile idolatry, which strongly suggests that Paul's critique aims at gentiles and not Jews. Certainly the opening shot of Paul's harangue has universalistic possibilities. When he declares, "For the wrath of God is being revealed from heaven against all the ungodliness and unrighteousness of humans" (1:18), the reference to "humans" (*anthrōpōn*) easily gives the impression that Paul has all humanity in view. And how does Paul describe or qualify the *anthrōpōn*—the "humans"—he has in mind? They "suppress the truth . . . by their unrighteousness" (v. 18). It takes little imagination to apply this general description at the feet of the human race *in toto*, to read Paul the way we read the psalmist: "there is none righteous, not even one" (Ps 14:1; see Rom 3:10). We have already seen Karl Barth offer this exact reading of Romans.[11]

A careful reading of the text, however, reveals that Paul does not apply his comments either to himself or to his gentile readers. The knowledge of God is evident "among *them*," for God has revealed it "to *them*" (v. 19). Therefore, "*they* are without excuse" (v. 20), for "*they* neither glorified God nor gave thanks" (v. 21). "*They* were rendered foolish" (v. 22), and "*they*

---

8. Remember the reference to *dynamis theou* ("the power of God") in Rom 1:16.

9. We are emphasizing the point here, in contrast to other prominent commentators on Romans, that Rom 1:18–32 characterizes the "ungodliness and unrighteousness" of gentile idolatry and not "the human plight" (*pace* James D. G. Dunn, "Adam and Christ," 127).

10. *Pace* Robert Jewett, who interprets *gar* at the start of Rom 1:18 as an indication that "divine wrath is "in some sense at least, *a new or newly revealed phenomenon* and this implies that it is in some way related to the gospel" ("Anthropological Implications," 25; emphasis added; quoting Finamore, "Wrath," 140).

11. More recently, Victor Paul Furnish discusses Rom 1:18—3:20 under the heading, "Humanity's Plight" ("Living to God," 188). James Dunn uses the same phrase ("Adam and Christ," 127).

The Wrath and Impartial Judgment of God

exchanged the glory of the incorruptible God for the likeness of the image of the corruptible: a human, or birds, or quadrupeds, or reptiles" (v. 23). And so on. Though we could read certain verses as general and universal condemnations of human depravity, especially vv. 18-22, this reading falters completely beginning at v. 23. Paul has something very specific in mind: not "the ongoing human effort to suppress the truth about their evil inclinations" but rather the worship of graven images patterned after mortal creatures.[12]

We need to resist the temptation to see Paul's critique as a general condemnation of gentile religiosity as a whole, as if all gentiles enthusiastically worshiped hand-made gods and only the Jews rejected idols as the works of human craftsmen.[13] The criticism of idol-worship, though nearly universal among the Jews, "is also found among Graeco-Roman intellectuals, who ridiculed idol-worship as vulgar superstition (e.g., Heraclitus, Cicero, Plutarch, and Lucian)."[14] We will see soon enough that Paul fits comfortably within the Jewish tradition of idol-critique. But first we should appreciate that Paul aims his critique not against gentiles *tout court* but against a specific and particular phenomenon among the gentiles. Paul tilts against the basest of the most debased aspects of gentile culture, aspects that other gentiles also critiqued, as we will see in Romans 2. More traditional readings construe Rom 1:18—3:20 as "the story of a world gone wrong," with 1:18-32 conveying "special emphasis ... on Gentile sinfulness, probably in order to stress the universal condition of human bondage to Sin and Death."[15] But why should "Gentile sinfulness" equate—let alone "stress"!—"the universal condition of human bondage"? Instead, we would *expect* that a Jew (such as Paul was) would emphasize gentile sinfulness in order to throw Israel's election and status as the

---

12. *Pace* Jewett, "Anthropological Implications," 27. Dunn reads Rom 1:18-32 as an allusion to "the failure of Adam and Eve to obey the explicit command of God." He has mischaracterized the target of Paul's condemnation. Paul is not critiquing some general, vague notion of "fail[ure] to give God the glory and thanks due to him"; rather, he chastises the gentiles' idolatrous worship of created, corruptible images in lieu of the Creator God (*pace* Dunn, "Adam and Christ," 127-29; pp. 128 and 127 quoted).

13. *Pace* Schreiner, who speaks too universally of "Gentiles who have received a revelation of God through the created order [and] suppress and distort the revelation given to them" ("Justification," 138). Paul never suggests he is describing all gentiles in Romans 1. He does use *pas* ("all") twice in Rom 1:18-32, both times in reference to the vices that merit God's wrath ("all the ungodliness and unrighteousness of humans" [v. 18]; "all unrighteousness, wickedness, greed, and malice" [v. 29]).

14. See Goodwin, *Paul*, 81 n.53, and the literature cited there.

15. Grieb, *Story*, 25-26.

people of God into sharper relief! Moreover, if gentiles also recognized Israel's Torah as a means to overcome weakness and their passions (see our discussion of Romans 6–7, below), then nothing about Paul's anti-idol harangue in Romans 1 suggests "the universal condition of human bondage."

Paul argues that gentiles, who did not have the benefit of the Law, still perceived in God's creation the truth of the Creator.[16] Jewish tradition already critiqued both pagan idolatry and Jews who succumbed to the influence of pagan idolatry. For example, the deuterocanonical Wisdom of Solomon condemns both idols and those who make them: "But the idol made with hands [*to cheiropoiēton*], it is even more accursed—both it and the one who made it—first because he made it, and second because, although it was corruptible [*phtharton*; see Rom 1:23], it was called a god" (Wis 14:8). Similarly, Isaiah receives a vision in which the Lord, seated upon a cloud, comes to Egypt. "The Egyptian idols made with hands [*cheiropoiēta Aigyptou*] will be shaken from his face, and their hearts shall wither within them" (Isa 19:1 LXX). Both the Egyptians and their handmade idols quake before the presence of YHWH.

We could mention other striking examples of Jewish polemic against idol-worship. The clearest of them, however, comes from one of the deuterocanonical additions to Daniel, Bel and the Dragon, which ridicules gentile idolatry. Devotees of the idol Bel claimed the god consumed a daily diet of twelve measures of flour, forty sheep, and six measures of wine. Moreover, the Persian king, Cyrus, worshipped Bel daily. Daniel, the most esteemed of the king's friends, worshipped his own God. This puts Daniel in considerable danger, but his persistent faithfulness to Israel's God and his refusal to honor pagan gods ends up saving him and putting the Babylonian priests of Bel to shame.

In the narrative of Bel and the Dragon, both Daniel and the Babylonian priests are known quantities: Daniel will remain steadfastly faithful to Israel's God, and the priests of Bel will persist in idol-worship. The unknown variable, however, is Cyrus, a pagan who is genuinely open

---

16. Contemporary readers, mostly Christian and, therefore, mostly gentiles, may not appreciate the benefit and advantage Paul sees in having Torah. As Christians we affirm that Torah is the word (or Word) of God, but we nevertheless see it in third place, like God's revelatory step-child (compared to Jesus, God's one and only, beloved son). Paul never denigrates Torah in this way, though we will encounter a couple of texts later in Romans in which Christian exegetical tradition has attributed such a view to Paul. For Paul, however, Torah was and remained the word (or Word) of God.

(according to the narrative) to worshipping the true God of Israel.[17] Bel and the Dragon narrates the following exchange: "The king asked him, 'Why don't you worship Bel?' And [Daniel] replied, 'Because I do not worship idols made by hands [*eidōla cheiropoiēta*]; instead [I worship] the living God who created heaven and earth and who holds dominion over all flesh'" (Bel 1:5 [Θ]).[18]

Paul stands squarely in this Jewish tradition of critiquing gentile idol-worship. God through his creation was revealing himself—"his eternal power or also his deity" (Rom 1:20)—to all flesh. Gentiles, however, became enamored with the works of his hands and neglected the one whose hands made all things. Whereas God created humanity in his image and directed his image to worship him, humans—not all of them, but many of them—created gods in their image and served the works of their hands. Paul is relentless in his critique. Even though the gentiles "knew God, they did not glorify him as God or give thanks" (1:21); as a result, they were made senseless, futile, moronic. Their futility is on display in multiple venues, from their worship of corruptible images of humans, birds, quadrupeds, and reptiles, on the one hand, to their unnatural and aberrant sexual practices. The chapter ends with a scathing and extensive vice list (1:29–31) that leaves no question as to the revealed wrath of Israel's God. The gentiles knew God's standard of judgment: "those who practice such things are worthy of death" (Rom 1:32). Their wickedness, however, extended not only to doing such things but also approving of others who did them. They not only failed to imitate (= obey) the good God who created all things, but they also judged God unworthy of imitation (= obedience). For all these reasons, then, "the wrath of God is being revealed from heaven" (Rom 1:18).

Paul will shortly turn to address a gentile persona more characteristic of his implied readers. But for now, in Rom 1:18–32, we should take seriously the character of Paul's rhetoric as a discussion *with* one party (gentile Christians in Rome; see Rom 1:7, 13–15) *about* another party (debauched, idol-worshiping gentiles). If anything, rather than the stark condemnation of humanity as a whole, such as Barth reads into the letter, we should

---

17. The Persian [= gentile] Cyrus already holds an honored place in biblical tradition; the Lord even calls him "Cyrus, my anointed one" [*tō christō mou*; Isa 45:1 LXX]!

18. The Old Greek version of Bel and the Dragon differs significantly here from Theodotion: "The king said to Daniel, 'Why don't you worship Bel?' And Daniel replied to the king, 'I worship nothing except the Lord God who created heaven and earth and who holds dominion over all flesh'" (Bel 1:5 [OG]). In both, however, the distinction between Creator and creature is central to the text's critique of idol-worship.

probably imagine Paul's audience nodding in agreement along with him, scandalized at the depths to which "some people" will go and confident that Paul's harangue is neither intended for nor applies to them.

You, Like Them, are without Excuse (Rom 2:1–16)

1 Therefore, you are without excuse, all of you who judge, for you condemn yourself by that for which you judge another because you who judge do the very same things. **2** But we know that the judgment of God is according to truth against all those who do such things. **3** But do you think in this way—you who judge those who do such things but also do them—that you will escape the judgment of God? **4** Or do you despise the riches of his kindness, his forbearance, and his patience, being ignorant that the kindness of God leads you to repentance? **5** But, in accordance with your obstinacy and unrepentant heart, you are storing up for yourself wrath on the day of wrath and the revelation of the righteous judgment of God, **6** who repays each person according to their deeds: **7** To those who persistently seek the glory and honor and immortality of a good deed, eternal life. **8** To those who disobey the truth out of selfish ambition and instead obey unrighteousness, wrath and indignation. **9** Affliction and distress [shall fall] upon every human soul who practices evil, the Jew first as well as the Greek; **10** but glory and honor and peace for everyone who practices good, for the Jew first as well as for the Greek.

11 For there is no favoritism with God. **12** For all who have sinned in a lawless manner, shall perish in a manner befitting lawlessness. All who have sinned while living within Torah, shall have their case judged by Torah. **13** For the hearers of Torah are not right with God; instead, those who keep Torah will be justified. **14** For whenever gentiles, who by nature do not have Torah, do the things of Torah, they—although they do not have Torah—are Torah for themselves. **15** They demonstrate the work of Torah written on their hearts, their conscience testifying on their behalf—even as their thoughts are divided, alternatively accusing and then defending them— **16** on the day when God judges humanity's secrets, according to my gospel, through Christ Jesus.

One of the biggest obstacles facing Western readers of Romans 2 might be that the word "pagan" means, among other things, "immoral." We often think of polytheists as godless hedonists who were only interested in life's pleasures: food, drink, sex. Or we think of them as violent barbarians, like Klingons, who would just as quickly knife you in the back as give you the time of day. Paul's description of gentile godlessness in Rom 1:18–32 easily fits into this understanding.

When we get to Romans 2, we often experience difficulty imagining that Paul still has gentile pagans in view.[19] In Romans 1, Paul focuses on gentiles who forsake the Creator to worship images of created things, and, as a result, plunge into godless immorality. In Romans 2, Paul turns his attention to a class of individual who, like him, condemns the very people he described in 1:18–32.[20] We took special note of Paul's third-person rhetoric in Rom 1:18–32, but his rhetoric changes suddenly and dramatically in Rom 2:1. Now, Paul emphatically and directly addresses his audience, whether his actual audience—the readers of Romans—or an imagined audience, as we will suggest. If Paul's description of immoral masses in Romans 1 strikes us as so obviously referring to pagan gentiles, the hypocritical self-righteous moralist of Romans 2 has an equally obvious identity: the Jew, and especially the Pharisee.

James Dunn argues that Rom 2:1–16 presents a spiral that "consists of the increasing specificity of the Jewish identity of the viewpoint rebutted."[21] Dunn reads the entire section in terms of general Jewish ideas (e.g., election): "The underlying thrust of 2:1–11 now becomes explicit: the target is Jewish presumption of priority of privilege."[22] Elsewhere, he refers to "a typically Jewish attitude" and "the overconfidence in their election on the part of many of his fellow Jews."[23] Dunn even draws direct links with Pharisees in particular:

> [S]uch self-confidence had been typical of Paul himself in his days as a Pharisee before Christ, apparently oblivious of his own need of a fundamental repentance. In fact we would probably not be far from the mark if we were to conclude that Paul's

---

19. See Schreiner ("Justification," 140–41 n.29) for a lengthy and helpful list of commentators who espouse the view that "Paul addresses Gentiles in Rom 1:18–32 and Jews in 2:1–16." Schreiner attributes this view, in 1993, to "most commentaries"; his own argument appears on p. 141. However, Thorsteinsson (*Interlocutor*, 177–96) conclusively demonstrates that Paul's rhetoric in Rom 2:1ff. is so closely linked to 1:18–32 that a change in subject (or addressee) in Rom 2:1 is unlikely.

20. The second-person singular addresses begin in Rom 2:1: "Therefore, *you are* without excuse, all of you who judge . . ."

21. Dunn, *Romans*, 1:76–77.

22. Ibid., 1:88.

23. Ibid., 1:90, 91; respectively. Similarly, Cranfield comments on v. 1: "That the truth thus stated applies to the heathen moralist, to the civil magistrate, to the ministers of the Church, is indeed true; but Paul himself, it is scarcely to be doubted, was thinking *especially of the typical Jew*" (Cranfield, *Romans*, 1:142; my emphasis).

interlocutor is Paul himself—*Paul the unconverted Pharisee*, expressing attitudes Paul remembered so well as having been his own![24]

Dunn is hardly unique in this interpretation. Thomas Schreiner offers a similar point, though he offers little by way of argumentation.[25] Twice Cranfield affirms that Paul is "apostrophizing the typical Jew" in Rom 2:17–24,[26] and between these two referents he generalizes to Paul's rhetoric earlier in Romans 2: "An attitude of moral superiority toward the Gentiles was so characteristic of the Jews ... that, in the absence of any indication to the contrary, it is natural to assume that Paul is apostrophizing the typical Jew in 2:1ff."[27] My own reading of Paul and of Romans hopes to demonstrate this interpretation's fatal flaws.

Contrary to Cranfield's implication that there is no "indication to the contrary," there are reasons to think Paul still has a gentile in view when he turns from the base immorality of Romans 1 to the judgmental interlocutor of Romans 2.[28] The intrusion of a new chapter here may mask the flow from the end of Romans 1 into the beginning of Romans 2.[29] If we do not

---

24. Dunn, *Romans*, 1:91; my emphasis.

25. Note the weight Schreiner puts on the terms "most likely" and "would": "Rom 2:1–5 *most likely* refers to the Jews because it is the Jews who *would* consider themselves morally superior due to possession of the law. They, as God's elect people, *would* reckon that God's kindness to them *would* make punishment unlikely (2:4)" (Schreiner, "Justification," 141; my emphases). Apparently, Schreiner supposes that gentiles did not consider themselves "morally superior." However, Roman expressions of their "moral superiority" *vis-à-vis* other nations were ubiquitous, were communicated by means of a broad range of communicative media, and invited the interactive participation of subjects of the Empire: "Imperial theology promoted the claims that *the gods, especially Jupiter, had chosen Rome and its emperor to rule the world and manifest the gods' will and blessings among the nations*. These messages were asserted through civic celebrations of victories and rulers, as well as by image-bearing coins, statues, buildings, imperial personnel, festivals, poets, writers, and so forth. The imperial cult, frequently promoted by local elites, provided a way of understanding the world and Roman presence as reflecting the will and pleasure of the gods. It offered residents of a city like Ephesus a mostly voluntary means of marking their participation in that world by expressing loyalty and gratitude through sacrifices to images in temples, and at games, street parties, artisan guild meals, and so on" (Carter, *John and Empire*, 57; my emphasis).

26. Cranfield, *Romans*, 1:137, 139.

27. Ibid., 1:138.

28. My discussion of the rhetorical flow from Romans 1 into Romans 2 is heavily dependent on Thorsteinsson's discussion of "Paul's gentile interlocutor in Romans 2:1–5" (*Interlocutor*, 177–96). In order to avoid the multiplication of footnotes, I have provided references only to verbatim quotations from *Paul's Interlocutor*.

29. For this reason, I have intentionally ignored the chapter division and focused on

The Wrath and Impartial Judgment of God

let the new chapter prejudice us into assuming that Paul shifts subject, the continuity between these two chapters becomes immediately evident:

> **1:28** And just as they did not see fit to acknowledge God, God handed them over to an unfit mind, to do things that are not fitting, **29** because they are filled with all unrighteousness, wickedness, greed, and malice, full of envy, murder, strife, treachery, malevolence. They are gossipers, **30** slanderers, haters of God, insolent, arrogant, boasters, contrivers of evil deeds, disobedient to their parents, **31** senseless, faithless, heartless, merciless. **32** Even though they knew the just requirement of God—that those who practice such things are worthy of death—they not only do such things but also approve of those who practice them! **2:1** *Therefore* [*dio*], you are without excuse, all of you who judge, for you condemn yourself by that for which you judge another because you who judge do the very same things. (Rom 1:28—2:1; my emphasis)

The most telling indicator that Paul continues to address a gentile must be the very first word of v. 1: *dio*. Thorsteinsson offers the following as three of the more popular understandings of *dio*:

1. a "colorless transition particle" that does not connect what follows (Rom 2:1-16) with what precedes;
2. a link between what follows with the immediately preceding sentence (1:32); or
3. a link between what follows with the entire preceding pericope (1:18–32).

Thorsteinsson rightly rejects the first interpretation: "A survey of Paul's usage of *dio* shows that there are no instances of it being used as a 'colorless transition particle.' Though the referential scope may vary, *dio* always marks a conclusion drawn from the preceding."[30] He likewise rejects the second proposal in light of the contrast between Rom 1:32 and 2:1. Paul describes the target of his polemic in 1:31 as those who "approve of those who practice [such things]"; in 2:1, he portrays his interlocutor as "you who judge" (= condemn) those he described at the end of Romans 1.

That leaves the third option, that *dio* links Rom 2:1-16 with 1:18–32 as a whole and "provides the cause for the interlocutor in 2:1

Rom 1:18—2:16 in this chapter.

30. Thorsteinsson, *Interlocutor*, 178.

being 'without excuse' when he judges others."[31] Most contemporary commentators advocate this understanding of the conjunction, *dio*, but this agreement has not led to any consensus regarding Paul's intention in 2:1–16 and the identity of the interlocutor he imagines. Thorsteinsson attributes the source of the problem to a non-linear, "retrogressive" reading of Romans 2:

> It seems to me that the different conclusions reached in this respect depend largely upon the way in which scholars approach the text as text, i.e., whether they prefer to read it (more) linearly and progressively (in this case, from 1:18 onwards) or (more) reversely or retrogressively (from 2:17 backwards). . . . Would Paul, then, have intended his audience to read the letter repeatedly in order to perceive fully the reverse reference assumed by Cranfield and others? Hardly.[32]

In light of these arguments—(i) the typical interpretation of *dio* and (ii) the preference for a linear reading of the text—the identity of Paul's interlocutor in Rom 2:1–16 can only be a gentile who participates in the revelation of God's wrath, just like the gentiles described in 1:18–32. The only hindrance to this clear and necessary reading of the text is, unfortunately, the text's history of interpretation.[33]

Romans 2:1ff. is the first instance of Paul's use of diatribe.[34] Stanley Stowers's doctoral thesis offered the seminal study of diatribe, which had not advanced noticeably since the doctoral work of Rudolf Bultmann.[35] Stowers demonstrates that the "dialogical style" of the diatribe "[grew] out of the situation of the philosophical school"[36] and is a pedagogical tool with which a teacher instructs a student rather than a polemical tool with which a disputant debates an opponent.[37]

---

31. Ibid., 179.

32. Ibid., 180, 181.

33. Thorsteinsson also identifies "certain presuppositions about Jews in antiquity" as a culprit in the misreading of Paul's interlocutor at 2:1ff. (see ibid., 183–88).

34. For a contemporary use of diatribe in imitation of Paul's style, which helpfully illustrates not simply its style but also its tenor and purpose, see Keesmaat, "Reading," 47–64.

35. See Bultmann, *Stil der Paulinischen Predigt*.

36. Stowers, *Diatribe*, 76.

37. Similarly, see Campbell, "Separation," 461. *Pace* Garroway (*Gentile-Jews*, 75), who refers to Romans' "obviously polemical character" and argues that Paul "is responding to actual accusations made against him."

> *The diatribe is* not the technical instruction in logic, physics, etc., but *discourses and discussions in the school where the teacher employed the "Socratic" method of censure and protreptic.* The goal of this part of the instruction was not simply to impart knowledge, but to transform the students, to point out error and to cure it. Our review of the sources suggests that the dialogical element of the diatribe was an important part of this pedagogical approach. The two major categories of dialogical features are address to the interlocutor and objections from the interlocutor.[38]

At this point in Romans, Paul's interaction with the interlocutor conforms to Stowers's first category of dialogical features ("address to the interlocutor"). In Romans 3–11, Paul will both address the interlocutor and field objections and/or questions from him.[39] As we work through Paul's use of diatribe throughout Romans,[40] we will need to remember the function of diatribe in Hellenistic rhetoric: instruction, not disputation.

Paul leaves behind his stark description of gentile depravity, which climaxed in 1:31, and conjures up an imagined dialogue partner, a gentile moralist who, like Paul, disapproves of those who lose control of their emotions or desires and succumb to the power of their passions (*ta pathē*;

---

38. Stowers, *Diatribe*, 76–77; original italics. Stowers emphasizes the pedagogical aspect of diatribe: "Our study has suggested very strongly that the dialogical element in the diatribe is basically an attempt to adapt this method to a dogmatic type of philosophy in the school situation. Thus, *censure is not an aspect of real inquiry, but an attempt to expose specific errors in thought and behavior so that the student can be led to another doctrine of life*. . . . [Our sources] use *diatribē* as a term for the school as we would speak of 'going to school.' They also use the term to designate various forms of education activity in the school (lecture, discussions)" (ibid., 77; my emphasis). Similarly, Changwon Song refers to "the so-called 'Pauline schoolroom'" (Song, *Reading*, 82).

39. I use masculine pronouns to refer to Paul's interlocutor in light of the likelihood that Paul imagines a male student dialogue partner. As we will see later in Romans 2, circumcision looms large in the discussion, and this would not have been such an issue had Paul imagined himself addressing a female interlocutor. However, as we will see in Romans 16, Paul is in no way unaware of high-status, influential, even educated women, and I am open to the possibility that Phoebe herself was the original reader—or *lector*—of Paul's letter to the Roman Christians.

40. Changwon Song rightly notes that the diatribe begins in Romans 2 and continues through Romans 14 (*Reading*, 22). As a result, "the 'body' of Romans as a whole, not partially, may well be considered a pure diatribe that was performed in the so-called 'Pauline schoolroom'" (see ibid., 55–82; p. 82 quoted). Song goes on to prefer, solely on this basis, "a short version of Romans . . . as a reasonable option in choosing which text to use when reading Romans." However, as we will see in our discussion of Romans 15, the rhetorical format of the diatribe continues into Romans 15, and Paul continues to speak in the manner of a letter-writer even after he finishes speaking in the manner of a rhetorical instructor (see Rom 15:15—16:27).

see Rom 1:26).⁴¹ "Therefore, you are without excuse, all of you who judge, for you condemn yourself by that for which you judge another because you who judge do the very same things" (Rom 2:1). Matera helpfully discusses the close links between Rom 1:18–32 and 2:1–16, despite the change in tone and rhetorical style:

> In this first address to his imaginary interlocutor (2:1–2) . . . Paul draws a close relation between those whom he has indicted in 1:18–32 and the arrogant interlocutor who judges them. That interlocutor may think that he is morally superior but, in the light of the gospel that Paul preaches, Paul knows that such a person is the same as those whom he judges.⁴²

Witherington rightly notes that Paul is not necessarily "accusing the 'you' addressed here of committing all the same sort of moral sins listed in 1:18–32, or of idolatry. Paul is accusing such a person of judgmentalism and some hypocrisy, and thus of carrying forward a pagan life into Christian existence to some degree."⁴³ However, nothing in Rom 2:1–16 suggests that Paul has shifted from idolatrous gentiles in Romans 1 to gentiles who have entered "Christian existence."⁴⁴ In fact, the arrogance Paul critiques in 2:1–16 becomes problematic not simply for being arrogance but also for its failure to set God apart from all of creation and worship him alone.⁴⁵

In his *Epistles to Lucilius*, Seneca offers the kind of gentile moralism against which Paul writes.⁴⁶ Paul's point in v. 1 is not that those who

---

41. Historians often refer to "ethical monotheism," the idea that pagans could pursue a righteous and moral lifestyle and worship a single (or supreme) deity without necessarily subscribing the *Jewish* monotheism (e.g., Bird, *Crossing*, passim). Pagans could and often did exhibit considerable interest in virtue, piety, justice, and so on. See the discussion of the Greco-Roman value of self-mastery, especially in my discussion of Romans 6 and 7, below.

42. Matera, *Romans*, 61.

43. Witherington and Hyatt, *Romans*, 79.

44. As Witherington himself notes (see Witherington and Hyatt, *Romans*, 81)!

45. Similarly Thorsteinsson: "Hence, unless simply swept over, the inferential conjuction *dio* indicates that the judging individual addressed in 2:1 is 'without excuse' (*anapologētos*) precisely because he is one of the people described previously in 1:18–32, viz. gentiles, the very people who are 'without excuse' (*anapologētous*, 1:20) *because they failed to acknowledge and worship God properly*" (*Interlocutor*, 182; my emphasis).

46. For example, in his letter, *On Practising What You Preach* (written ca. 63–65 CE), Seneca admonishes Lucilius: "[P]hilosophy teaches us to act, not to speak; it exacts of every man that he should live according to this own standards, that his life should not be out of harmony with his words, and that, further, his inner life should be of one hue and not out of harmony with all his activities. This, I say, is the highest duty and

judge immoral people are themselves immoral (though popular Christianity often reads Rom 2:1 in precisely this way[47]). Paul's point is that the moralizing gentile who condemns the immoral, unphilosophical pagan also "knew God [but] did not glorify him as God or give thanks" (1:21), also "claimed to be wise [but was] made foolish" (1:22), also "exchanged the glory of the incorruptible God for the likeness of an image" (1:23). In other words, even gentiles who do not indulge in debased sexual immorality (see 1:26–27) but who nevertheless refuse to honor the one Creator God give their worship to things that are not really gods. Garroway rightly describes the judgmental gentile's problem in terms of failure to acknowledge God, so that "by consequence [he] became foolish, senseless, idolatrous, debased, and wicked."[48] They have all "exchanged the truth of God for a lie, and they worshipped and gave priestly service to the creation rather than the Creator, who is blessed forever. Amen" (1:25). The problem, for Paul, is that gentiles worship created gods rather than the Creator God. The debased and debauched immorality of some gentiles is simply the by-product of their misdirected worship.

In vv. 2–6, Paul distinguishes himself, a Jewish writer, from his imagined gentile interlocutor: "Now *we* know that the judgment of God is according to truth against all those who do such things." (Whether Paul distinguishes himself, as a Jew, from his rhetorical audience [the interlocutor] or his actual audience [gentile Christians in Rome] is unclear, though I prefer the former.) God judges everyone who refuses to acknowledge him as Creator, regardless of their moral status. The moral gentile who imagines he will fare any better than morally debauched gentiles who worship idols deceives himself. Ironically, by imagining that he does not need God's offer of mercy and forgiveness, the elitist moral gentile misses the gospel's offer of repentance, which the God of Israel, the Creator God,

---

the highest proof of wisdom,—that deed and word should be in accord, that a man should be equal to himself under all conditions, and always the same" (Seneca, *Lucil.*, 20:2 [Gummere, LCL]). Other commentators similarly appeal to Seneca in order to understand either the kind of letter Paul imagined himself writing or the kind of person he or his audience might have imagined as they read that letter (see Witherington and Hyatt, *Romans*, 79; Stowers, *Rereading*, 124; *inter alios*).

47. For example, in an essay linked to Romans 2 on bible.org, Bob Deffinbaugh claims, "Those who enthusiastically condemned the Gentile 'heathen' as sinners, on the basis of Paul's argument in 1:18–32, were self-condemned. They practiced the very same things which they condemned in others (2:1, 2, 3). . . . Did the Jews really sin in the same way as the Gentiles? Were the Jews guilty of immorality, sexual impurity and perversion, idolatry, robbery, and even murder? The answer is a clear and undeniable, 'Yes!'" (Deffinbaugh, "Coming Wrath of God").

48. Garroway, *Gentile-Jews*, 90.

extends to everyone (even the depraved humanity described in 1:18–32!). Despite their common judgment against idol-worship and its immoral consequences, the elitism of gentile moral philosophy runs counter to the God of Paul's gospel.[49] This elitism leads moral gentiles to "despise the riches of his kindness, his forbearance, and his patience" (2:4).[50] Instead of espousing the virtues of self-mastery and self-control,[51] Paul tells the moral gentile to allow the kindness of the jilted Creator God to lead him into repentance. If he does not, he is storing up for himself the wrath of God, the very wrath the gentile moralist seeks to avert by means of moral effort.

Paul's citation of Ps 61:12 (LXX) and Prov 24:12 comes out of the blue and appears, at first blush, to reinforce rather than rebut the gentile moralist's point of view, that God "will repay each person according to their deeds." At the very least, we have to admit that Paul takes an interest in one's works and anticipates that the judgment of God will take account of these works. Later in the letter we will even see Paul construe one's behavior in terms of slavery, whether to sin or to righteousness (Romans 6), and he will admonish his readers to "walk according to the Spirit" (Romans 8) and even provide some glimpse of what that walk should look like (Romans 12–15). However, at this point in the letter, in light of Paul's

---

49. I assume the answer to Paul's question in 2:3 is "yes" (i.e. the gentile moralist does actually expect to escape God's/the gods' judgment), primarily because this moralist, who agrees with Paul's indictment against the undisciplined immorality of the masses, has not born the signs of God's wrath described in 1:18–32. Robert Jewett aptly describes Paul's rhetorical texture here: "Paul's formulation indicates that 'the objector doubtless did suppose this, and not without reason, for the visible handing over to reprobate mind and behavior (i. 24, 26, 38), which was the token of God's wrath upon Gentile sinners, did not apply to him.' Thus the rhetorical question is meant to be answered by the imaginary conversation partner in the affirmative" (Jewett, *Romans*, 200, citing Barrett, *Romans*, 44). A little further on Jewett rightly says, "each group is obligated to accept others as equally beloved by God" (Jewett, *Romans*, 203); this gets to the heart of Paul's critique of the gentile moralist and his elitist condemnation of others.

50. "To despise God was for the Greco-Roman and Jewish worlds an unspeakable offense" (Jewett, *Romans*, 201).

51. For example, notice the self-reliant tenor of Seneca's instructions to Lucilius in his letter, *On Siren Songs*: "Work is the sustenance of noble minds. There is, then, no reason why, in accordance with that old vow of your parents, you should pick and choose what fortune you wish should fall to your lot, or what you should pray for; besides, it is base for a man who has already travelled the whole round of highest honours to be still importuning the gods. What need is there of vows? *Make yourself happy through your own efforts*; you can do this, if once you comprehend that whatever is blended with virtue is good, and that whatever is joined to vice is bad" (Seneca, *Lucil.* 31:5 [Gummere, LCL]; my emphasis).

The Wrath and Impartial Judgment of God

harangue against idol-worship in Rom 1:18–32 and against gentile moralism in 2:1ff., "the deeds" [*ta erga*] he has in mind in 2:6 must be the worship of the one true God. In context, both Psalm 61 LXX and Proverbs 24 refer to God vindicating the one who persists and perseveres in faithfulness to God and refuses to go with others into unrighteousness. In light of the context of these passages, God does not judge people primarily on the basis of whether they have been self-controlled, compassionate, pious, and so on. He judges people on the basis of whether they have set him apart, as God, from those things that are not-God. The psalm and the proverb both demonstrate the same assumption, which Paul shares: for those who have set the Creator God apart from his creation, the other virtues will follow as a result.

Paul switches from using second-person singular addresses (= you) to third-person plural addresses in vv. 7–10. All of Rom 2:6–16, however, "continually points back to v. 5, in which Paul exposed the interlocutor's wretched position on the day of judgment," and so Paul's focus remains on his imagined interlocutor throughout.[52] As such, Rom 2:7–10 extends the second-person singular critique of 2:1–6 to everyone who fails to worship God. Moreover, Paul picks up the word *ergon* ("deed") from his quotation in v. 6, but he uses the singular, *deed*, rather than the more typical plural, *erga* ("deeds").[53] Paul's use of the singular term, *ergou agathou* ("good deed") in v. 7 is unusual. Paul also uses the singular terms *kakon* ("evil deed") and *agathon* ("good deed") in vv. 9 and 10, respectively, in exactly the same ways. The question is: what "deed"—whether an "evil deed" or a "good deed"—does Paul have in mind?

I will argue shortly that the difference between *erga* ("deeds") and *ergon* ("deed") is negligible; these have the same referent. However, some commentators who have come to the same conclusion nevertheless misconstrue Paul's point by conforming the singular term to the plural (rather than the plural to the singular). Moo, for example, suggests, "Paul goes out of his way to stress that the work that God so rewards is a persistent lifestyle of godliness."[54] We saw in Romans 1 that Paul's critique centered

---

52. Thorsteinsson, *Interlocutor*, 159.

53. In Romans alone, Paul uses *ergon* fifteen times. Of these, ten are plural; he uses the singular at Rom 2:7, 15; 13:3; 14:20; and 15:18.

54. Moo, *Romans*, 137; see also Dunn, *Romans*, 1:85–86. Schreiner (*Romans*, 113) inexplicably paraphrases the singular *ergou agathou* as plural ("Verses 7–10 clarify that the repayment for good works [sic!] is either eternal life or eschatological wrath"). Elsewhere he translates v. 7 more ambiguously: "V. 7 describes such people as 'seeking glory and honor and immortality by patient endurance in good work'" (Schreiner, "Justification," 142). He then immediately slips right back into paraphrasing v. 7 with

on the fundamental error of worshiping graven images rather than the Creator God of Israel. "They exchanged the truth of God for a lie, and they worshipped and gave priestly service to the creation rather than the Creator, who is blessed forever. Amen" (Rom 1:25). This is "the evil deed" that leads to the judgment of God against those who worship other gods. In contrast to this evil deed, "the good deed" in 2:7–10 must refer to recognizing and acknowledging the Creator God of Israel as the true God. God grants eternal life to those who steadfastly seek after him and refuse to turn away from him to worship anyone (or anything) else. To those who turn aside from God, who are "disobedient to the truth and even persuaded by unrighteousness" (2:8), God will repay their evil deed with "wrath and anger" [*orgē kai thymos*].[55]

Therefore, we can agree with Jewett that "the use of the plural 'works' in v. 6 and the singular 'good' in v. 10 appear to reflect roughly interchangeable meaning."[56] Paul demonstrates a consistency across Rom 1:18—2:10 that "the deed(s)" God expects from gentiles (and for the lack of which God reveals his wrath against them) is to worship him as Creator. The offer of eternal life, on the one hand, or wrath and anger on the other applies to everyone, "the Jew first as well as the Greek" (vv. 9–10). These verses do not *redefine* Jewish election so much as they *clarify* the point that one's response to the Creator God—rather than one's national identity—determines one's eschatological fate.[57] Both Jews and gentiles would come under God's judgment. YHWH reserves eternal life for those who worship him as God (first for the Jew as well as for the Greek), and he guarantees

---

a plural reading *ergou agathou*: "And it should be noted that Paul does not focus only on the negative, but he also brings in the positive: *those who do **good works*** will receive an eschatological reward, namely, eternal life" (ibid., 143; original italics; my emphasis in bold).

55. Paul's references to God's wrath [*orgē*] in 2:5 (2x) and 2:8 harkens back to his declaration of the revelation of God's wrath in 1:18. Moreover, this entire section (2:1–16) is closely linked with Paul's rhetoric in Romans 1 by the double reference to "the Jew first as well as the Greek" (2:9, 10; cp. 1:16).

56. Jewett, *Romans*, 204.

57. This is an important point. Christian readings of Paul often denigrate Jewish ideas of election as if Jews thought that just being "a Jew" resulted in a certain relationship with God. Jews knew full well that some descendants of Abraham refused to acknowledge God as God (e.g., any of Judah's and/or Israel's miserable kings). But given God's special relationship with Abraham and his descendants, being "a Jew" certainly provided additional opportunity to know the true God, opportunity that gentiles did not normally or naturally have.

wrath and indignation for those who worship anything/one else (first the Jew as well as the Greek).

Paul continues to use third-person plural rhetoric through the remainder of 2:11–16. Paul explains why worship of the true God and not ethnic or national identity played such a definitive role for one's eschatological fate. In one sentence: "For there is no favoritism with God" (2:11). Paul argues against an implicit claim that God favors one particular people or nation over others. We all know that Jews thought of themselves as God's chosen people.[58] We need to be careful, however, to avoid seeing Jewish ethnocentrism here, as if Jews were the only people who imagined themselves as especially favored by God (or the gods).[59] Romans, Greeks, and just about every other people group (including Americans!) fancy themselves the peculiar objects of God's (or the gods') affections.

The Romans certainly saw their political, economic, and military supremacy throughout the Mediterranean region as a sign that the gods had appointed Rome for greatness. Early in Rome's founding *mythos*, Virgil's epic poem *Aeneid*, Jupiter announces his intentions for the Roman people to Aeneas' mother: "For these [the Romans] I set neither bounds nor periods. Dominion without end (*imperium sine fine*) I give to them" (Virgil, *Aen.* 1:278–79).[60] Texts like these lead Warren Carter to extract three principal themes from Roman imperial ideology of the first century CE:

---

58. The idea of Jewish election is ubiquitous. But for one particularly striking expression, see the expansive retelling of Genesis 1 in the pseudepigraphal book, *Jubilees*. According to this Second-Temple-era text, God set Israel apart from the very beginning of creation: "And he gave us a great sign, the sabbath day, so that we might work six days and observe a sabbath from all work on the seventh day. And he told us—all of the angels of the presence and all of the angels of sanctification, these two great kinds—that we might keep the sabbath with him in heaven and on earth. And he said to us, 'Behold *I shall separate for myself a people from among all the nations*. And they will also keep the sabbath. And I will sanctify them for myself, and I will bless them. Just as I have sanctified and shall sanctify the sabbath day for myself thus shall I bless them. *And they will be my people and I will be their God. And I have chosen the seed of Jacob from among all that I have seen. And I have recorded him as my firstborn son, and have sanctified him for myself forever and ever.* And I will make known to them the sabbath day so that they might observe therein a sabbath from all work'" (*Jub.* 2:17–20; my emphases).

59. James Dunn (*Romans*) bases his entire reconstruction of Paul's perspective on Torah, Israel, and Judaism on the idea that Paul critiques Jewish ethnocentrism. That idea is partly correct, but Dunn does not take sufficient account (i) of the fact that other nations—even *every* other nation!—viewed themselves as unique, elect, chosen, and (ii) of the likelihood that Paul's Jewish contemporaries did not assume that national identity *apart from Torah-observance* sufficed to merit God's favor. See Das, *Paul*.

60. Collins, "Eschatologies of Late Antiquity," 331.

- The gods have chosen Rome.
- Rome and its emperor are agents of the gods' rule, will, and presence among human beings.
- Rome manifests the gods' blessings—security, peace, justice, faithfulness, fertility—among those that submit to Rome's rule.[61]

Against ideas of Roman election such as these, Paul writes that there is no favoritism with God, and so elite (and elitist) Romans will have no basis for confidence on the day of God's judgment.

Paul continues to explain that both egregious sinners and those who transgress the Law, even as they attempt to observe it, find themselves subject to God's judgment (Rom 2:12).[62] I have struggled with Paul's apparent argument in 2:13–15 that the gentiles, who do not have the Torah, do "the things of Torah" [*ta tou nomou*] and so demonstrate that Torah has been inscribed on their hearts. Torah, of course, includes commandments such as circumcision, Sabbath observance, dietary restrictions, and other distinctive markers of Jewish identity, and these are precisely the things that gentiles do *not* do.[63] So what does Paul imagine himself talking about when he refers to gentiles doing "the things of Torah," even though they do not (apparently) do all of the things of Torah?[64]

---

61. Carter, *Roman Empire*, 83. Carter goes on to explain, "[These claims] expressed their understanding that Rome's dominating place in the world was the will of the gods. These ideas justified efforts to force people into submission to Rome."

62. Remember that elite Greco-Roman moralists were as susceptible to the charge of self-righteousness and hypocrisy as were Jewish moral rigorists (see the discussion above). When we account for Roman (rather than Jewish) ideas of election, Stanley Stowers' translation of Rom 2:11–12 makes good sense: "God shows no partiality. For all who have sinned in a lawless manner, shall perish in a manner befitting lawlessness. All who have sinned while living within the law, shall have their case judged by the law" (*Rereading*, 139). In Rom 2:14–15 Paul refers to gentiles "who do not have the *nomon*" but who nevertheless "do the things of the *nomou*," who "are a *nomos* unto themselves" and who "demonstrate the work of the *nomou* inscribed on their hearts." In these verses *nomos* clearly refers to the Torah of Moses. Therefore, I find it likely that already in vv. 12–13 *nomos* likely refers to the Mosaic covenant.

63. There were, of course, gentiles who practiced circumcision, and every culture differentiates what can be eaten from what cannot. My claim, "these are precisely the things that gentiles do *not* do," capitalizes on the *distinctive* role these practices played in the differentiation, construction, and maintenance of a peculiarly Jewish identity.

64. We can draw a helpful analogy with the illegal immigration debate in contemporary American politics. Politicians have struggled with the concept of law-abiding illegal immigrants. After all, such people regularly break the law simply by means of living this side of the American borders; in addition, there are myriad employment, tax, and other civil laws that such people cannot help but violate. Nevertheless, there

The Wrath and Impartial Judgment of God

We have already seen the answer: the "good deed" or "righteous act" *par excellence* is the recognition and acknowledgement of YHWH as Creator God.[65] Simon Gathercole rightly argues that the sense of *ta tou nomou poiōsin* ("they do the things of Torah") in Rom 2:14 "is neither 'vague' nor 'partial', nor utterly perfect."[66] However, his own explanation, that "the reference is to the fundamental knowledge of God and orientation to his will that is lacking in the Jewish contemporaries of these Gentiles" is hardly more explanative or precise than the "vague" and "partial" explanations he rejects.[67] The question remains, *how* can Paul envisage uncircumcised gentiles who work on Sabbath and do not observe *kashrut* as "doing the things of Torah," or, in Gathercole's words, demonstrating "the fundamental knowledge of God and orientation to his will"?

Gathercole's reading imports a contrast between gentiles and Jews, the former who do the things of Torah and the latter who do not. However, Paul's rhetoric operates with a contrast between gentiles and other gentiles: on the one hand, certain gentiles do the things of Torah, while other gentiles exhibit the depravity and debauchery Paul described in Rom 1:18–32.[68] When Paul refers to "the work of Torah" [*to ergon tou no-*

---

is clearly a difference between illegal immigrants who try to take care of their family without doing any harm to others and those who steal, murder, or commit other violent offenses. The language of "law-abiding illegal immigrants" is meant to account for just this sort of difference. I think Paul's language of gentiles who do "the things of Torah" functions similarly.

65. Curiously, despite his masterful rereading of three perennially difficult sections of Romans, Garroway (*Gentile-Jews*, 95) preserves a more traditional explanation that lacks any basis in the text of Romans itself: "In 2:17–29, Paul reconfigures Jewish identity so that its sine qua non is no longer the literal circumcision of the penis, or performance of the literal decrees of the Law, but a spirit-mediated circumcision and the consequent performance of the righteous decrees of the Law, *which are presumably its moral, rather than ceremonial, requirements*" (my emphasis; see also p. 107). My own explanation (*viz.* that Paul reduces Torah [*nomos*] to the recognition and worship of God, as Creator, distinct from all of creation) derives from Paul's rhetoric in Romans 1 and his development of that rhetoric in Romans 2.

66. Gathercole, "Law unto Themselves," 35.

67. Similarly, Das (with whose reading of Romans I am largely sympathetic) claims, "Romans 2 critiques Jewish confidence on the basis of mere possession of the Law. Paul seeks to disturb that comfort by reminding the hypothetical Jew that he or she must also obey that Law" (*Paul*, 9; original emphasis). But can we really suppose that Paul thought any of his Jewish contemporaries would have forgotten the expectation that they not only possess but also obey Torah?

68. Surprisingly, Gathercole himself notes this contrast ("Law unto Themselves," 43). However, his reading of an ethnically Jewish interlocutor in Rom 2:17ff. and the striking parallels between vv. 14–15 and 25–29 wrongly lead him to import a gentile/Jew

mou] in v. 15 that some gentiles, apparently, have inscribed on their heart, the work he has in mind is the worship of the Creator God.⁶⁹ Despite not circumcising their sons, abstaining from work on the Sabbath, and so on, Paul portrays gentiles who nevertheless distinguish the Creator God from the created world and only worship the former as those who demonstrate "the work of Torah written on their hearts."

Before we move on to consider Paul's dialogue with an interlocutor who "calls himself a Jew" (2.17ff.), let me summarize our discussion of 2:1–16 in two points:

- First, Paul turns from the base depravity he described in 1:18–32 and critiques a gentile moralist in 2:1–16 who would have been nodding his head approvingly at Paul's harangue against the passionate, unnatural, undisciplined lifestyle of the masses. Despite appearing to be on his side, Paul turns on this gentile moralist ("all of you who judge") because he, too, has forsaken the worship of the Creator God.

- Second, in 2:1–16 Paul reduces Torah to worshipping the Creator God rather than the hand-made gods of the gentiles. Each person—the Jew first as well as the Greek—will stand before the Creator God and be judged on how they responded to "the knowledge of God [that] is evident" to all peoples (see 1:19). This is how Paul can speak of gentiles—people who did not circumcise their sons on the eighth day, observe the Sabbath, or keep the distinctive Jewish dietary regiment—as those "who by nature do not have Torah" and yet who "do the things of Torah" (2:14).⁷⁰

---

contrast rather than to recognize the gentile/gentile contrast operative in Romans 1–2.

69. A few paragraphs later, Gathercole will refer to "[t]hose who do not belong to the nation that received the Torah" but who "nevertheless obey *its ultimate requirements*" (ibid., 37; my emphasis). In light of Paul's anti-idolatry polemic in Romans 1, I would interpret Torah's "ultimate requirements" as the necessity to distinguish the Creator God from the created cosmos.

70. Gathercole rightly argues that *physei* ("by nature") modifies the participle *ta echonta* ("who have") rather than the subjunctive *poiōsin* ("they do"; see Gathercole, "Law unto Themselves," 35–37).

4

Introducing the Gentile Proselyte

A Gentile Who Calls Himself a Jew

> *Rom 1:18—2:16 presented the competent ancient reader with a Jewish teacher's "missionary" sermon spun out of the rhetorical technique of speech-in-character. . . . At the point we expect Paul to get to the heart of the matter, he turns away from the Greek. The apostle has just mentioned his good news and Christ Jesus (2:16) when he spots one of his competitors in the crowd, a Jew who has committed himself to teach gentiles about the Mosaic law. Paul knows that many gentiles in the audience have been attracted to such teachers and decides that he can best continue his missionary appeal by provoking a debate with the other Jewish teacher in front of his gentile audience (2:17—4:21).*[1]

We have already encountered the debate among commentators regarding whom, precisely, Paul has in mind when he switches from the third-person plural rhetoric of Rom 1:18-32 to the second-person singular rhetoric of Rom 2:1-5. Traditionally, scholarship has tended to read the switch as Paul's move from writing about gentile depravity in Romans 1 to confronting Jewish arrogance and pride in Romans 2.[2] Recently, however, another interpretation has become increasingly

---

1. Stowers, *Rereading*, 142.
2. For example, see Moo, *Romans*, 125-57; Schreiner, *Romans*, 105-26.

popular, in which Rom 2:1–16 continues to address a faulty *gentile* ethic. Nevertheless, a significant change occurs at 2:17, where Paul describes his interlocutor as one who "calls himself a Jew." However, even here we will argue that Paul envisions a gentile interlocutor. In fact, this will prove to be a watershed moment in our reading of Romans as a whole.

You Call Yourself a Jew?! (Rom 2:17–29)

17 But if you call yourself a Jew, if you take comfort in Torah, if you set your boast on God, **18** if you know the will [of God] and approve of superior things (since you are instructed by Torah), **19** and you have persuaded yourself that you are a guide for the blind, a light for those in darkness, **20** an instructor of the ignorant, a teacher of children (since you have the shape of knowledge and truth in Torah) . . . . **21** Therefore, you who teach another, do you not also teach yourself? You who preach, "Do not steal," do you steal? **22** You who say, "Do not commit adultery," are you adulterous? You who abhor idols, do you rob temples? **23** You who boast in Torah, by your transgression against Torah you dishonor God, **24** for "because of you the name of God is reviled among the gentiles" (Isa 52:5) as it is written.

25 For circumcision is beneficial if you keep Torah. But if you are a transgressor of Torah, your circumcision has become uncircumcision. **26** Therefore, if the uncircumcision keeps Torah's just commandments, won't his uncircumcision be considered as circumcision? **27** Then the one who is naturally uncircumcised and who fulfills Torah will judge you, the transgressor of Torah through the letter and the circumcision. **28** For it is not the outward Jew, nor the outward circumcision in the flesh, **29** but the hidden Jew, and the circumcision of the heart (in spirit and not the letter), whose praise is not from humans but from God.

Paul resumes the second-person singular address to an imagined interlocutor in Rom 2:17. The difficulties regarding Paul's rhetorical audience in Romans 2 take a significant turn in vv. 17–20, where Paul offers an elaborate and extensive description of his interlocutor: "But if you call yourself a Jew [*Ioudaios eponomazē*], if you take comfort in Torah, if you set your boast on God, . . ." (Rom 2:17). In classical literature, *eponomazō* meant to "apply a word as a name, denominate, give a second name or surname, nickname."[3] With respect to Rom 2:17, Bietenhard rightly explains, "Here Jew is a title of honour, the heir to the legacy described in

---

3. Bietenhard, "ὄνομα" (part), 2:648. He carries this nuance forward into his discussion of *eponomazō* in the NT (see ibid., 2:655).

vv. 17–20."[4] However, in the very next sentence Bietenhard makes clear that he thinks the interlocutor in 2:17 does not simply *claim* to be a Jew but actually *is* one.[5] Stanley Stowers agrees; in the text that I cite in this chapter's epigram, Stowers imagines Paul, speaking as a Jewish missionary to interested gentiles, espying a fellow Jewish missionary in the audience and deciding to engage him in front of the letter's gentile hearers.[6] While the specific understanding of Paul's rhetorical strategy varies among commentators, nearly all agree that in 2:17 Paul imagines and addresses an actually Jewish interlocutor.[7]

Given the weight of this consensus among commentators, I hesitate to offer my dissent.[8] Nevertheless, I suggest that Paul still imagines a gentile in vv. 17ff., only now this gentile has taken on the yoke of Torah and, in contrast to the pagan moralist of 2:1–6, worships the Creator God of Israel. Runar Thorsteinsson argues at length that the interlocutor in Romans 2 (i) represents Paul's imagined (or intended) audience: gentile Christians in Rome, and (ii) maintains a consistent identity throughout the entire letter. This is a critical component of Thorsteinsson's argument. If Paul portrays a gentile interlocutor in Rom 2:1–5, and if "in any given letter an interlocutor remains the same unless otherwise indicated,"[9] then the bur-

---

4. Ibid., 2:655.

5. "The Jews stand under the divine judgment like the Gentiles" (ibid.).

6. Stowers, *Rereading*, 142. Earlier, Stowers gave Rom 2:17–24 the label, "Apostrophe to the proud but inconsistent Jewish teacher" (*Diatribe*, 80).

7. Dunn, *Romans*, 1:109; Elliott, *Rhetoric*, 127–32; Moo, *Romans*, 157–58; Schreiner, *Romans*, 127–30; Witherington and Hyatt, *Romans*, 85; Wright, "Romans," 445–46. Jewett (*Romans*, 221–22) is ambiguous, but seems to agree. Matera (*Romans*, 59, 60) eschews speculating about the identity of Paul's interlocutor, who is, after all, a fictive persona, a figment of Paul's rhetorical imagination.

8. Since first developing this argument, I have slowly become aware of other readers who likewise read Rom 2:17 in terms of a gentile who wants to call himself a Jew. Runar Thorsteinsson (*Interlocutor*) provides the most detailed and explicit argument in favor of this reading. Recently, Joshua Garroway (*Gentile-Jews*, 84–109) has argued for a similar reading of Rom 2:17ff. In unpublished formats, both Matthew Thiessen ("Romans 2:17") and Matthew Novenson ("Did Paul") have also developed this reading. I thank Drs. Thiessen and Novenson for sharing their papers with me. The earliest example of this reading that I have found comes from David Frankfurter ("Jews or Not?"): "We might well ask, who 'calls oneself' a Jew anyway? Certainly not someone who is *recognized* [original emphasis] as Jewish by birth or by community. Rather, this suggestion of self-chosen Jewishness would denote *a Gentile who has taken to practicing certain elements of Jewish observance and thereby has come to claim that self-definition—as a constituent part of Jesus devotion*" (ibid., 419; my emphasis; additional thanks to Matthew Thiessen for the reference to Frankfurter's essay).

9. Thorsteinsson, *Interlocutor*, 144.

den of argument shifts toward those who envision a *Jewish* interlocutor beginning in 2:17.[10] Thorsteinsson proceeds to argue at length that Paul's interlocutor in Romans 2 "is thought of not as a (native) Jew but as an individual of gentile origin who wants to call himself a Jew."[11] Throughout the remainder of our discussion of Romans, I will refer to this figure as "a gentile proselyte to Judaism" (or simply as "a proselyte").[12] Moreover, in light of the evidence we saw that Paul's gentile interlocutor in the first half of Romans 2 was a moralizing pagan gentile *and not a gentile who worshipped Israel's God*, we will disagree with Thorsteinsson in that we see a *different* interlocutor introduced at Rom 2:17 than in 2:1–5, but we will agree with him that the interlocutor in 2:17ff. is not an ethnic Jew.

If this is the right approach to v. 17, this gentile has taken on the name [*eponomazē*] "Jew" and gone on to assume the signs of the Mosaic covenant, including circumcision (see 2:25–29). Paul, however, seems to regard the interlocutor with suspicion, as though his claim were based on inappropriate grounds.[13] In just a few verses Paul will make the surprising assertion, "The one who is naturally uncircumcised and who fulfills Torah will judge you, the transgressor of Torah through the letter and the circumcision" (Rom 2:27). We will have to explain how Paul can imagine someone who has submitted himself to Torah's commandment of circumcision a "transgressor of Torah through the letter and the circumcision," especially since he also imagines an *uncircumcised* gentile who fulfills Torah and will judge the circumcised gentile as a transgressor! But that will have to wait until we get to Rom 2:27. Here in 2:19–21, Paul indicates that this gentile proselyte has taken it upon himself to proselytize other

---

10. See ibid., 196. Garroway follows Thorsteinsson closely: "Despite the nearly unanimous view that Paul tangles here with a boastful Jew, nothing in the conversation indicates that Paul's dialogue partner is anyone other than the Gentile whom he just chastised for hypocritically judging his fellow Gentiles" (*Gentile-Jews*, 92).

11. Thorsteinsson, *Interlocutor*, 196–97.

12. If Paul's interlocutor, insofar as Paul portrays him rhetorically, is a gentile who has converted to Judaism (i.e., a proselyte to Judaism), we run into the problem of how to refer to this figure. As a convert, he is now a Jew and no longer a gentile (cp. Josephus, *Ant.* 20:38–39, where the gentile king Izates sought to "be definitively a Jew"; *einai bebaiōs Ioudaios*). However, for our analytical purposes we need to retain a distinction between this proselyte to Judaism and a native-born Jew. For this reason, we will continue to describe Paul's interlocutor as a gentile, one who "calls himself a Jew." The terms "[gentile] proselyte" and "[gentile] Judaizer" similarly highlight that this figure has become—rather than was born—a Jew.

13. Thiessen, "Romans 2:17."

gentiles.[14] If this reading is right, the imagined interlocutor in 2:17–24 might be a Jew *religiously* but is a gentile *ethnically*.

The logical progression from 1:18–32 through 2:1–16 and on into 2:17–29 suggests that Paul tilts at a gentile proselyte who has assumed the name [*eponomazō*] "Jew."[15] The difference might not seem significant, but some interpretive problems arising from the rest of this paragraph (2:17–24) and even through Romans 11 find resolution if we take this exegetical option. I want to underline this point: *The choice between an actually Jewish interlocutor in Rom 2:17–29 and an ethnically-gentile-religiously-Jewish interlocutor will prove to be the fork in the road for our reading of Romans as a whole.* The choice we make here will fundamentally alter the way we read difficult passages throughout the rest of Romans, including Paul's dark tenor in Romans 3, his first-person monologue in Romans 7, and his explanation of Israel's salvation in Romans 9–11. As we stand at 2:17 and consider the different paths before us, the consequences seem slight. Some exegetes configure Paul's letter to the Romans as his response to an "anti-Jewish error among [the Gentile-Christian majority]."[16] Our reading configures Paul's discussion here in terms of an *enthusiasm* for Torah among Paul's gentile audience rather than any anti-Jewish sentiment. Reading Romans in terms of "anti-Jewish error" gets Paul's rhetoric exactly wrong. Few things will affect our interpretation of Paul's letter more than the decision we face here.

Before we continue reading Rom 2:17–24, let us take a moment to ask whether a gentile who commits himself to Torah-observance might "call himself a Jew" in the first place and whether this might be an issue

---

14. Michael Bird, despite concluding that pre-Christian Judaism was not engaged in an active mission of proselytization (defined as a concerted effort to circumcise pagan gentiles), acknowledges that "many pagans adopted Jewish customs, remained sympathetic to Jewish beliefs, and some even went as far as to renounce their ancestral customs and become proselytes to Judaism" (*Crossing*, 4). In light of Bird's reticence to attribute an intentionally missional/missionary motive to pre-Christian Jewish texts, we should take special note of his admission that "Jews in Rome were perhaps unusually active in recruiting converts" (ibid., 149). In other words, even if we accept with Bird that pre-Christian Judaism was not a particularly proselytizing enterprise, "proselytes to Judaism were [nevertheless] made in significant numbers.... Judaism was presented to Gentiles in such a way that there were conversions to Judaism in Greek cities and in sufficient enough numbers to earn the ire of the cultural elites" (ibid., 13, 83).

15. *Pace* BDAG (s.v.), which considers the compound verbal form equivalent with the simple *onomazō* ("*epi*- without special mng."). In Rom 1:18—2:29, Paul moves along a spectrum from morally depraved gentiles (1:18–32) through a morally elitist pagan gentile (2:1–16) to a gentile who has not only assumed a more rigorous moral standard but has explicitly adopted a Torah-observant lifestyle (2:17–29).

16. Elliott, "Political Christology," 40.

that might require Paul's attention.[17] Epictetus provides an interesting and relevant passage. As a Stoic philosopher, Epictetus is especially unhappy that people claim the title "philosopher" without living out a philosophic way of life. "He is sharply critical of those who lightly call themselves philosophers but continue to 'eat in the same fashion, drink in the same fashion, give way to anger and irritation' (*Discourses* 3.15.10)—that is, to continue in a self-indulgent style of life totally at odds with the philosophical teaching they espouse."[18] In the context of critiquing those who call themselves one thing but live as another, Epictetus writes:

> Why then do you call yourself a Stoic? Why do you deceive the many? Why do you act the part of a Jew, when you are a Greek? Do you not see how (why) each is called a Jew, or a Syrian or an Egyptian? And when we see a man inclining to two sides, we are accustomed to say, This man is not a Jew, but he acts as one. But when he has assumed the affects of one who has been imbued with Jewish doctrine and has adopted that sect, then he is in fact and he is named a Jew. Thus we too being falsely imbued, are in name Jews, but in fact we are something else. Our affects are inconsistent with our words; we are far from practising what we say, and that of which we are proud, as if we knew it.[19]

Admittedly, Epictetus does not use the key term *eponomazō* here. When Epictetus speaks of "calling yourself" a Stoic, or people "being called" a Jew or a Syrian or an Egyptian, he uses the more common verb, *legō*. When he refers to the genuine proselyte to Judaism, he uses *kaleō*: "then he is in fact and he is named [*kaleitai*] a Jew." Epictetus does not prove that Paul has a gentile convert to Judaism in mind in Rom 2:17. This passage does, however, raise the possibility that earning and exhibiting the epithet "Jew" was an issue for gentile converts to Judaism.[20] According to Donaldson,

---

17. In his discussion of Galatians, Das points out that Paul "identifies the Galatians in 4:21 as those 'who desire to be subject to the law.' Likewise Paul's comments in 3:1–5 indicate that the Galatians are considering adopting a more comprehensive approach to the Mosaic Law. . . . The Jews celebrated Sabbaths, new moons, seasons of Pentecost and Passover, and sabbatical years. Paul's audience would thus be adopting a Jewish liturgical calendar that ironically corresponded to the pagan calendars of their past" (*Paul*, 19). That is, *gentiles* in Galatia were contemplating the very thing we see Paul portraying a gentile as having done: adopting a thoroughly Jewish lifestyle and submitting to the full yoke of Torah-observance.

18. Donaldson, *Judaism*, 389.

19. Epictetus, *Discourses* 2.9.19–21; Donaldson (ibid., 388–91) discusses this passage in some detail.

20. Nanos rightly warns against the easy assumption that gentiles always or even

"the most significant aspect of the passage is that once they have taken this decisive second step and have fully adopted the Jewish frame of mind and way of life, the convert is seen, by Gentile outsiders at least, as fully a Jew, in fact as well as in name."[21] This conclusion fits well with Ross Kraemer's argument that the term "Jew" in Greco-Roman inscriptions often referred to "non-Jews who affiliated with Judaism," whether they assumed the epithet for themselves, "perhaps as a self-designation, or gave the term as a proper name to their children."[22] Or, as William Campbell explains, "In the ancient world when Gentiles converted to Judaism, in a culture where what we call religion was seen as an innate and not a detachable aspect of identity, this phenomenon was regarded as tantamount to changing one's ethnicity."[23]

Paul continues to describe his imagined interlocutor—the gentile proselyte—as one who "take[s] comfort [lit. rest] in Torah" and "set[s his] boast on God," who "know[s] the will [of God] and approve[s] of superior things" and who is "instructed by Torah" (Rom 2:17-18). As Paul adds depth to his description, he clearly portrays a person who shoulders a burden, not just to keep Torah, but also to spread Torah's influence, almost certainly among sympathetic gentiles (see Rom 2:19-20).[24] In his letter to the Philadelphian Christians, the early second-century bishop Ignatius similarly alludes to gentiles who proclaim Judaism.[25] Verses 21-22 have traditionally been read as Paul's critique of the Jewish teacher who instructs

---

usually despised or looked down on Jews: "When Paul wrote Romans, however, Jews were in general still respected and held in high regard as good citizens who exemplified high ideals, even if upholding some seemingly strange ideas and practices" (Nanos, "To the Churches," 17).

21. Donaldson, *Judaism*, 391.

22. Kraemer, "Meaning," 52. Kraemer's last sentence is especially interesting in light of our analysis of Rom 2:17: "And it may well be that the term was necessary especially in situations where the Jewishness of the individual might not be apparent, not only in cases of burial near pagan graves (as Frey suggested) but *in cases where the individual did not begin life as a Jew*" (ibid., 52-53; my emphasis; Kraemer refers to Frey, "Inscriptions").

23. Campbell, "Rationale," 27.

24. The references to *typhlōn* ("the blind") and *phōs tōn en skotei* ("a light for those in darkness") echo Isa 42:6-7, in which YHWH appoints his servant to be "a light for the gentiles" [*eis phōs ethnōn*] and "to open the eyes of the blind" [*anoixai ophthalmous typhlōn*], and which mentions "those who sit in darkness" [*kathēmenous en skotei*].

25. "But if anyone should interpret Judaism to you, do not listen to him. For it is better to hear of Christianism from a man who has circumcision than Judaism from an uncircumcised man [*akrobystou*]" (Ign. *Phld.* 6:1). For a discussion of this passage, see Schoedel, *Ignatius*, 202-3.

others to do one thing but who does another.[26] Victor Paul Furnish uses language consistent with the majority of Romans commentators when he reads Rom 2:17–29 in terms of "the hypocrisy and self-righteousness of those (Jews) who exult in their possession of [God's Law]."[27]

Once again, I offer a dissenting interpretation. The grammatical fact, which commentators often fail to note,[28] is that Paul's first rhetorical question in 2:21 expects an affirmative answer. He asks: "Therefore, you who teach another, do you not also teach yourself?" The answer, which Paul does not contradict, is, "Yes, I do teach myself."[29] This sets a pattern for the remaining rhetorical questions, all of which point toward the same conclusion:

> Question: Therefore, you who teach another, do you not also teach yourself?
> Answer (implied): Yes, I do also teach myself.
>
> Q: You who preach, "Do not steal," do you steal?
> A: No, I do not steal.
>
> Q: You who say, "Do not commit adultery," are you adulterous?
> A: No, I am not adulterous.
>
> Q: You who abhor idols, do you rob temples?
> A: No, I do not rob temples.[30]

---

26. For example, "Paul first describes these Gentiles in 2:14–15, and then follows this up with his shaming of the Jewish nation in 2:17–24. Here, by contrast, 'the Jew' is in full possession of the Law, and trained in it (2:17–20), *but is disobedient* (2:21–24)" (Gathercole, "Law unto Themselves," 48; my emphasis). The shocking and scandalous nature of the disobedience Paul portrays in 2:23–24 actually depends upon the absurdity of the possibility of disobedience in vv. 21–22, as I shall argue presently.

27. Furnish, "Living to God," 188.

28. For example, "Paul turns immediately to questions that challenge the consistency of the individual who holds so high a view of his or her possession of the Torah. . . . Here [*viz.* Rom 2:21–22] resemblance to the philosophical diatribe is most obvious, for as Stowers has shown, 'one of the most common themes, especially in Epictetus, in texts which address the fictitious opponent, is the attack on inconsistency and hypocrisy.' Exposing the discrepancy between someone's noble profession and actual conduct is a regular part of the *topos*" (Elliott, *Rhetoric*, 128, citing Stowers, *Diatribe*, 101). Paul does go on to make this attack in Rom 2:23–29, but here in vv. 21–22 Paul is not at all accusing his interlocutor of hypocrisy.

29. Grk: *ho oun didaskōn heteron seauton ou didaskeis*. If Paul had expected the answer, "No, I don't teach myself," he would have used *mē* instead of *ou* (see BDF §427).

30. The second and third rhetorical questions contain the negative particle *mē* (see the previous note), but this is not the reason for offering a negative answer to these questions. The particle is not part of the question proper but of the content of the

Introducing the Gentile Proselyte

Paul grants his interlocutor the benefit of the doubt: His moral *behavior* is consistent with his moral *instruction*. The moral pagan of Rom 2:1–16 nodded in agreement with Paul's harangue against "all ungodliness and unrighteousness" in 1:18–32, only to have Paul turn on him for doing the very same things (2:1). In contrast, the gentile proselyte of 2:17–20 does *not* do the very things he teaches against, and up through vv. 21–22 he has no reason to suspect that Paul is about to spring a rhetorical trap from beneath his own feet.[31]

This interpretation avoids a perennial exegetical problem that has perplexed commentators: why does Paul expect his audience to receive as true-to-life a fictive Jewish interlocutor who robs temples?[32] Jewett, following Edgar Krentz, reads the question as a metonym for reviling or blaspheming the gods of other peoples and so, somehow, to have "no respect for the concept, the name, the honor of God."[33] Dunn supposes some Jews may have rationalized taking items from pagan temples, "since they lacked an owner anyway!"[34] Matera reads the question in terms of the Decalogue: "the fourth question insinuates that the Jewish interlocutor has violated the first commandment (Exod 20:2–3) by his involvement with pagan temples."[35] Schreiner argues that Paul chastises the Jews for (rightly) detesting idols but (wrongly and hypocritically) profiting from idol worship: "[The Jews] claim to detest idolatry and spurn any association with idols, yet they are willing to be defiled by profiting from the very idols they detest (cf. Deut 7:25)."[36] And so on.

---

interlocutor's preaching and speaking ("Do *not* steal" and "Do *not* commit adultery," respectively).

31. I have adopted the imagery of Paul's "trap" for the interlocutor from Matthew Thiessen ("Romans 2:17"): "Rom 2:21–22 set the trap for the interlocutor: of course, they would condemn the person who does the very thing he preaches against. Rom 2:23 leads to the principle Paul and his interlocutor will agree on—the one who breaks the very law he boasts in, dishonors God. All of this sets up the elaborate trap Paul intends to spring upon his gentile interlocutor, who boasts in circumcision and preaches circumcision, but, as we shall see, does not actually keep the law of circumcision."

32. BDAG (s.v.) gives two definitions for *hierosyleō*: 1. to take objects from a temple by force or stealth, and 2. to commit irreverent acts.

33. Jewett, *Romans*, 229, citing Krentz, "Disrepute," 433–35.

34. Dunn, *Romans*, 1:115. Moo argues similarly, but he acknowledges that, on this reading, "Paul would be accusing his Jewish target of an offense that was, at best, rare" (*Romans*, 164).

35. Matera, *Romans*, 73.

36. Schreiner, *Romans*, 133.

I find none of these interpretations compelling, and my reading avoids all of the problems associated with them. The series of four rhetorical questions in Rom 2:21–22 do not accuse Paul's interlocutor of hypocrisy. Instead, they concede that the gentile proselyte has forsaken the depravity described in 1:18–32, turned from the pagan moralism described in 2:1–16, and taken on the yoke of Torah-observance (as described since 2:17). This raises the question: what could Paul possibly have against such a person? Paul's imagined gentile proselyte has condemned the base immorality of passionate paganism in 1:18–32, just as Paul had. He condemned the elitist moralism of the philosophic pagan in 2:1–16, just as Paul had. This interlocutor, a proselyte to Judaism, practices a positive moral ethic *and* worships the Creator God of Israel. What could Paul have against this man?

The question finds an easy answer: Paul regularly and vociferously rails against the idea that *gentiles* should subject themselves to Torah, YHWH's covenant with *Israel*.[37] This is the driving theme throughout Galatians.[38] The proselyte who has taken on the name "Jew" and set his boast in Torah, *instead of worshipping the Creator God of Israel by means of the promise that precedes Torah*, and who teaches others to do the same (Rom 2:19–20), dishonors God. "You who boast in Torah, by your transgression against Torah you dishonor God" (Rom 2:23). What "transgression" could Paul have in mind? Here commentators often read Paul through the lens of Jas 2:10–11: failure to keep one point of Torah resulted in transgression of the whole of Torah.[39] But, as Thiessen points out, this is not what

---

37. In her discussion of Romans 14–15, Kathy Ehrensperger rightly concludes that Paul "confirms that the general Jewish perception concerning these laws in relation to Gentiles applies also to Gentiles who are now in Christ. The Jewish distinctions relevant for Jews do not apply to Gentiles in Christ. This cannot be otherwise. If they were to adhere to Jewish food laws now that they are in Christ this would actually mean they would be required to take on Jewish identity. *This is precisely, however, what Paul in other contexts and discussing other issues opposes.* Gentiles in Christ should under no circumstances aspire to become Jews. Not because there is anything wrong with Judaism or the Torah, nor because the Torah is actually obsolete and it is only a matter of time until its validity for Jews is overcome, but because in the eschatological time inaugurated by the coming of Christ, Jews and Gentiles together will with 'one voice glorify the God and Father of our Lord Jesus Christ'" (Ehrensperger, "Called to Be Saints," 107; my emphasis).

38. For example, see Gal 3:1–5. See also Das, *Paul*, 17–48.

39. "For whoever keeps the whole Torah but stumbles at one point, that person is guilty of all points. For he who said, 'Do not commit adultery' (Exod 20:13) also said, 'Do not commit murder' (Exod 20:15). If you do not commit adultery but you do commit murder, you are a transgressor of Torah" (Jas 2:10–11).

Paul says.[40] Paul's gentile proselyte interlocutor transgresses the very same commandment he preaches. Does Paul, then, have a specific commandment in view?

The rest of Romans 2 focuses on circumcision. "For circumcision is beneficial if you keep Torah [*ean nomon prassēs*]. But if you are a transgressor of Torah [*parabatēs nomou*], your circumcision has become uncircumcision" (Rom 2:25). Paul could not possibly be saying that transgression of this or that commandment of Torah (e.g., stealing) nullified circumcision. Torah itself provided the mechanisms for repentance, atonement, and (in the case of stealing) restitution. For example, "When someone steals an ox or a sheep, and slaughters it or sells it, the thief shall pay five oxen for an ox, and four sheep for a sheep. The thief shall make restitution, but if unable to do so, shall be sold for the theft" (Exod 22:1 NRSV). There is no suggestion here or anywhere else that a single violation of Torah renders circumcision as uncircumcision (= nullifies the covenantal significance of one's circumcision).[41] Thiessen argues that vv. 25–27 make clear that Paul portrays the interlocutor as a transgressor of the specific

---

40. "But what James says differs from Paul. James argues that if one obeys one aspect of the law (by not committing adultery), but does not obey another aspect (by committing murder), one has not kept the whole law. If Paul were making this claim, he would need to argue similarly: those who preach against *adultery*, do you *steal*? Those who preach against *stealing*, do you commit *adultery*? But Paul's point is entirely different. The one preaching against *stealing* commits *theft*. The one preaching against *adultery* commits *adultery*. Romans 2:20-21 is meant to illustrate *the absurdity of the person who preaches one thing, but does the exact opposite* [my emphasis]. Paul is not accusing anyone of breaking the entire law because they fail to keep it at one point" (Thiessen, "Romans 2:17").

41. The one possible exception is Jer 9:25, when the prophet declares, "The days are surely coming, says the Lord, when I will attend to all those who are circumcised only in the foreskin [LXX = *episkepsomai epi pantas peritetmēmenous akrobystias autōn*; 'I will attend to all those who have had their foreskins circumcised']: Egypt, Judah, Edom, the Ammonites, Moab, and all those with shaven temples who live in the desert. For all these nations are uncircumcised, and all the house of Israel is uncircumcised in heart [LXX = *panta ta ethnē aperitmēta sarki, kai pas oikos Israēl apertmētoi kardias autōn*; 'all these nations are uncircumcised in their flesh, and the whole house of Israel are uncircumcised with respect to their hearts']" (NRSV). This text does describe "all the house of Israel," the males of which had certainly been physically circumcised, as "uncircumcised in heart," but this is not the result of transgressing this or that statute of Torah. Rather, the people "commit iniquity and are too weary to repent" and "refuse to know me, says the Lord" (Jer 9:5, 6 NRSV). Moreover, "they have forsaken my law that I set before them, and have not obeyed my voice, or walked in accordance with it, but have stubbornly followed their own hearts and have gone after the Baals, as their ancestors taught them" (9:13–14 NRSV). In other words, the people have not merely transgressed this or that statute of Torah but have abandoned Torah altogether!

rite of circumcision.⁴² Thiessen explains the "nonsensical claim" that the circumcised proselyte transgresses the law of circumcision by reading Gen 17:12 and Lev 12:3 closely:

And a child eight days old [*paidion oktō hēmerōn*] shall be circumcised by you, every male unto your generations, the one born of your household as well as the one purchased from every foreign-born son who is not from your descent. (Gen 17:12 LXX)	And on the eighth day [*tē hēmera tē ogdoē*] she shall circumcise the flesh of his foreskin. (Lev 12:3 LXX)

The distinctive feature of Jewish, covenantal circumcision is not simply the removal of the foreskin. Popular conceptions notwithstanding, circumcision was not an exclusively Jewish phenomenon.⁴³ What made Jewish circumcision distinctive was its practice on the eighth day after birth.⁴⁴ "[B]y distinguishing between Ishmael's circumcision and Isaac's, [Genesis 17] stresses the distance between the infant circumcision practiced by Israel and the pubescent or adult circumcision of all the other nations in the ancient Near East that practiced the rite."⁴⁵

If this is Paul's understanding of Jewish, covenantal circumcision, he would not be distinct among Second-Temple Jews.⁴⁶ The Hebrew Bible set

---

42. "But if theft, adultery, and temple robbery are *merely* illustrations of a broader principle, what precise aspect of the law is his interlocutor guilty of preaching but not keeping? The answer, as Romans 2:25–27 makes clear, is the rite of circumcision. . . . Paul's statement that circumcision is of value only if one keeps the law should be taken to refer, not to the entirety of the Jewish law, but specifically to the law of circumcision. In other words, circumcision is of value if one follows the entirety of the law of circumcision" (Thiessen, "Romans 2:17").

43. "Although it was also practiced by other groups, circumcision was widely regarded in antiquity as a specific and defining mark of Jewishness. . . . It was well known in antiquity that the Jews were not the only group that circumcised, though it is not clear how widespread the practice was. Ancient authors include Arabs, Egyptians and some pagan priests (see, e.g., Herodotus *Hist.* 2.104; Strabo *Geog.* 17.2.5; Josephus *Ant.* 8:260–63; Josephus *Ag. Ap.* 1:168–71; Philo, *Spec.* [*Laws*] 1:2; Barn. 9)" (de Lacey, "Circumcision," 226).

44. See the extensive discussion in Thiessen, *Contesting Conversion*.

45. Ibid., 41.

46. "Covenantal circumcision is not merely any form of circumcision, but precisely circumcision on the eighth day. In fact, LXX Genesis 17:14, supported by *Jubilees* and the Samaritan Pentateuch, states that the person not circumcised on the eighth day after birth is cut off from the covenant people" (Thiessen, "Romans 2:17").

forth the "law of circumcision" as a particular practice *for Abraham and the male members of his household* (sons as well as slaves). Luke-Acts, in its references to the circumcision of Jewish male babies, also takes care to emphasize their circumcision *on the eighth day* (Luke 1:59; 2:21; Acts 7:8).[47] Paul presents gentile adults who submitted to circumcision as transgressors "through the letter and the circumcision" (Rom 2:27) because (i) they were not members of Abraham's household, and (ii) they were not circumcised on the eighth day.[48] Paul draws the shocking conclusion that the gentile proselyte, *in the very act of being circumcised*, transgresses Torah's commandment of circumcision. He "boast[s] in Torah,"[49] but his transgression of Torah dishonors God![50] The irony lies thick over Paul's exchange with the gentile proselyte:

> Sympathetic Gentiles would have had no problem observing virtually any aspect of Moses' Law, but circumcision was another matter. It required the ultimate commitment. The procedure was painful and only partially reversible and would be socially compromising in the midst of a Gentile world. A willingness to undergo circumcision would signal a clear intent to live by the other, less painful and stigmatizing aspects of the Law as well.[51]

Paul, however, flips this line of thought on its head: rather than a sign of the gentile proselyte's "ultimate commitment" to observe Torah's commandments and prohibitions, circumcision has become the paradigmatic locus of the proselyte's *transgression* of Torah! This conclusion might seem

---

47. See the discussion of these passages in Thiessen, *Contesting Conversion*, chap. 5.

48. "Any adult gentile male undergoing circumcision fails to keep the law, first because he does not do so on the eighth day after he was born, but more importantly, because he is not Abraham's son or slave. In other words, a gentile undergoing circumcision in order to become a Jew *fails to keep the law of circumcision in the very act of being circumcised.*" (Thiessen, "Romans 2:17," my emphasis.)

49. See my comments on Rom 3:27 for a positive interpretation of "boasting" (in Rom 3:27, *kauchēsis*; here in 2:23, *kauchasai*).

50. Similarly, see Garroway ("Circumcision," 318–19): "Paul's point in Rom 2:25–29, then, is not that circumcision of the heart matters while circumcision of the penis does not. In fact, circumcision of the penis remains crucial. *What has changed is what counts for genital circumcision.* As Paul explains it, the figurative circumcision of the heart determined by compliance with the righteous decrees of the Law at the same time renders adherents as though they were physically circumcised. Circumcision is indeed an internal and figurative matter, just as Paul proclaims in Rom 2:29, but this internal, figurative transformation affects the state of the genital foreskin as much as the foreskin of the heart" (my emphasis).

51. Das, *Paul*, 20–21.

surprising, but it is more plausible than the traditional understanding. For example, Elliott supposes that Paul employs diatribal rhetoric in Romans 2 in order to illustrate a legal principle: "not *possession* of the Law (or circumcision, or the heritage of the covenant) but *obedience* characterizes the true Jew who is 'justified' (2:13) and rewarded from heaven (2:29)."[52] However, Elliott never explains what "circumcision" *is* if not "obedience," adherence to Torah's command rather than mere boasting in the possession of Torah. The circumcision of a Jewish male on the eighth day *is* obedience; of course it is. A gentile's circumcision as an adult, however, amounts to transgression.

Moreover, the proselyte's assumption of Torah's yoke is itself transgression that dishonors God (2:23).[53] By taking on Torah-observance, the proselyte makes it *more* difficult, not less, for gentiles to see "the righteousness of God [that] is being revealed apart from Torah ... through the faith[fulness] of Jesus Christ" (3:21–22). Paul quotes Isaiah against the very same gentile who renounced both godless hedonism (cf. Rom 1:18–32) and pagan moralism (cf. Rom 2:1–16): "'Because of you, the name of God is reviled among the gentiles,' just as it is written" (Rom 2:24, citing Isa 52:5). God sent his son (see Rom 1:4) to unveil his righteousness, first to the Jew as well as to the Greek. But the gentile proselyte neglects the gospel of God's son and subjects himself instead to Torah. Anything that obscures God's appeal to the gentiles through the gospel of Christ equates to reviling God's name, *especially* gentiles who bend their necks to Torah's yoke.

"For circumcision is beneficial if you keep Torah" (2:25a). Israel, of course, failed to observe Torah and was exiled from the land. The proselyte's circumcision is all the more useless *because his very assumption of Torah's rights and responsibilities transgresses Torah*, which was never intended for gentiles in the first place. As a transgressor of Torah [*parabatēs nomou*], the interlocutor's circumcision is counted as uncircumcision (2:25b). On the other hand, Paul has already referred to gentiles in his experience who, without being circumcised and taking on other distinctive practices prescribed by Torah, nevertheless observe Torah (see Rom 2:14–15). We saw earlier that Paul reduced "the things of Torah" down to one: worship of the Creator God. Romans 2 results in a fairly striking irony: uncircumcised gentiles who worship God as Creator "do the things of Torah," while gentiles who submit

---

52. Elliott, *Rhetoric*, 129; original italics.

53. Sinaiticus punctuates Rom 2:23 as a question. While this possibility is interesting and "may reflect the way this text was read and heard in the fourth century" (Elliott, *Rhetoric*, 129 n.1), it ruptures the flow of the text from the four rhetorical questions in vv. 21–22 and the quotation from Isa 52:5 in v. 24.

to Torah's yoke find themselves "transgressors of Torah."⁵⁴ How can this be? Paul provides an explanation in Rom 2:28–29.⁵⁵ By taking on the name "Jew" and submitting to Torah's yoke (= circumcision), the gentile proselyte has missed the mechanisms by which gentiles find adoption into God's family (see Rom 8:14–17) or grafting into Israel's tree (see Rom 11:16–22).

∽

To sum up, I read Rom 1:18—2:29 as Paul's comments for (or to) three types of gentiles: (i) the depraved immoral pagan (1:18–32); (ii) the elitist moralizing pagan (2:1–16); and (iii) the gentile proselyte to Judaism (2:17–29). Each exhibits their own problem *vis-à-vis* Israel's God. In contrast to these stock gentile *personae*, Paul will instruct his Roman readers to be gentiles who worship the Creator God of Israel without assuming Israel's obligations under Torah. To this point, Paul has not said anything negative about Jews. He certainly has not condemned their alleged over-confidence in Torah or their arrogance *vis-à-vis* the gentiles. The problems he has addressed in Romans 1–2 have all focused on *gentiles* and their status in relation to Israel's God. Paul will continue this discussion in Romans 3, and we will continue to read Paul as though he were addressing the fictive interlocutor—a gentile proselyte to Judaism—that he introduced in 2:17.

If Not Torah, Then What? (Rom 3:1–8)

> 1 "What, then, is the benefit of [being called] a Jew, and what is the advantage of circumcision?" 2 Much in every way! First, that they were entrusted with the oracles of God . . . . 3 "What then? If some were unfaithful, their unfaithfulness does not nullify God's faithfulness, does it?" 4 Certainly not! Let God be true and every human being a liar, just as it is written,

---

54. Garroway would offer a helpful correction: The gentiles who are physically uncircumcised are nevertheless circumcised. "What Paul describes is a real, but imperceptible, circumcision, by which Gentiles become reckoned as though they are circumcised and thus become qualified to participate in God's covenantal community" ("Circumcision," 307).

55. I have adopted Thiessen's translation (see Thiessen, "Romans 2:17"). The NRSV differs significantly: "For a person is not a Jew who is one outwardly, nor is true circumcision something external and physical. Rather, a person is a Jew who is one inwardly, and real circumcision is a matter of the heart—it is spiritual and not literal. Such a person receives praise not from others but from God."

If You Call Yourself a Jew

> "... so that you would be vindicated by your words,
> and you will overcome when you are brought to trial"
> (Ps 50:6 LXX).
>
> **5** "So if our unrighteousness demonstrates the righteousness of God, what shall we say? God is not unjust for inflicting his wrath [on us], is he?" (I am speaking in a human fashion.) **6** Certainly not! How, then, would God judge the world? **7** "But if the truth of God abounds to his glory by my falsehood, why am I still being condemned as a sinner?" **8** And should we (as we are being slandered, just as some people claim that we say such things) do evil things so that good things might result? Their condemnation is well deserved!

The beginning of a new chapter should not mask the continuity of Rom 3:1–20 with 2:17–29.[56] "[T]he phenomenon in 3:1–9 has its beginning in 2:17."[57] When Paul turns to an imagined interlocutor and addresses him, "But if you call yourself a Jew, if you take comfort in Torah, if you set your boast on God ..." (2:17), he portrays himself speaking to a proselyte to Judaism.[58] Paul's interlocutor might be a Jew *religiously*, but he is a gentile *ethnically*. Paul continues to address this person in Romans 3, fielding questions and explaining why his confidence in Israel's Torah and its ability to facilitate his worship of Israel's God was misplaced.[59] The

---

56. "This section (3:1–20) continues the form of the diatribe, which Paul has employed in 2:1–5 and 2:17–24 [sic!]" (Matera, *Romans*, 78; see also Stowers, *Rereading*, 165). Stowers reconstructs the dialogue in 3:1–9 differently than I do (but see Jewett, *Romans*, 247 n.86), and the difference matters tremendously for our understanding of Romans 3.

57. Stowers, *Rereading*, 165.

58. The rhetorical portrayal of "full-scale dialogue" usually involves the speaker characterizing his dialogue partner—the interlocutor—"as a certain type either corresponding to a specific vice or sometimes belonging to a school of thought. Thus, the interlocutor might be the cowardly philosopher, the boaster, or a pleasure-seeking Epicurean" (ibid., 163). In my reading, Paul portrays his imaginary conversation partner as a gentile who "calls himself a Jew" (2:17) and has become a full proselyte to Judaism, including submission to circumcision (2:25–29).

59. "In 3:1, this teacher [i.e., the interlocutor] initiates a dialogue by objecting to Paul's insistence on God's impartial judgment. Paul treats him not as an enemy but as a student in need of instruction. The discussion arises (3:1) when the interlocutor reacts to Paul's claim that God will fully accept gentiles—as if they were members of God's chosen people—if they do what the law requires of them (*ta dikaiōmata*, 2:26)" (ibid., 159). Remember that Stowers identifies "this teacher" as an actual Jew. In my reading, the interlocutor's objection to "Paul's insistence on God's impartial judgment" is personal: the interlocutor has taken on the full yoke of the Torah, only to be told

interlocutor's ethnic status becomes a key point in this discussion, and the general failure to recognize Paul's portrayal of a proselyte interlocutor in Rom 2:17ff. has made it difficult for readers to make proper sense of Rom 3:1–20. Before letter's end, Paul will make some very positive statements about Torah (e.g., Rom 7:14), including the approbative label *ta logia tou theou* ("the oracles of God") in 3:2, which is surely synonymous with Torah [*ho nomos*]. Why, then, does Paul go to such great lengths to dissuade his interlocutor from pursuing righteousness and life by means of Torah?

Paul has already explained that doing the "things of Torah" requires only that gentiles differentiate God, as Creator, from everything else and worship him alone (see Rom 2:7–16). The gentile who has taken on the yoke of Torah and who has even submitted to circumcision "in the flesh" has missed this. So the interlocutor interrupts Paul with a question, and the ensuing discussion takes on a dialogic tenor. The proselyte, surprised at Paul's claim that his circumcision transgresses Torah and dishonors Israel's God (2:23–24), asks, "What, then, is the benefit of [being called] a Jew, and what is the advantage of circumcision?" (Rom 3:1). Paul, who has not abandoned circumcision (or Torah!) for Jews, counters that there is an advantage for being—and being called—a Jew. For one thing, the covenant relationship with YHWH, which we call Torah but which Paul refers to here as "the oracles of God" [*ta logia tou theou*], was given to Israel (= the Jews). In his discussion of Paul's use of the passive verb, *episteuthēsan*; ("they were entrusted"; 3:2), Jewett rightly explains,

> [I]n Romans he "means that since the promises were given to Abraham, Israel has been and is now the trustee of the divine word that God wills the salvation of all peoples on the basis of faith." For Paul this is the issue of "chief importance" because of its decisive bearing on his missionary project, because the "oracles of God" given in faith to the Jews contained "good news to the gentiles," as Stowers explains.[60]

The provision of Torah to Israel was a blessing and was meant to provide further blessing. Torah certainly contained good news *for* the gentiles, but it was never given *to* the gentiles. As such, they were never intended to

---

that his circumcision transgresses the law of circumcision. To add insult to injury, Paul explains that God will accept gentiles who have received the sign of circumcision "in spirit" rather than those who have received the sign of circumcision "in the flesh" (see 2:28–29).

60. Jewett, *Romans*, 243 (citing Williams, "Righteousness," 267–68; Stowers, *Rereading*, 167).

keep its covenantal terms. In fact, with regard to the specific issue of circumcision, the gentiles *cannot* keep Torah's terms since they can no longer be circumcised on the eighth day.

Before we read Rom 3:1–8, however, we have to determine when Paul speaks in his authorial voice and when he speaks as the proselyte interlocutor. This is no easy task, in part because Paul does not clearly identify when he is speaking in his own voice and in part because twice Paul interrupts the dialogue with an aside to the audience (see Rom 3:5, 8). Compare the following two reconstructions. The dialogue on the left is my reconstruction based on Frank Matera's comments; the dialogue on the right reproduces Stanley Stower's analysis (I have used bold typeface and quotation marks to mark the voice of Paul's interlocutor):[61]

Interlocutor: **1 "What, then, is the benefit of [being called] a Jew, and what is the advantage of circumcision?"**	Interlocutor: **1 "Then what advantage does the Jew have? Or what good is circumcision?"**
Paul: 2 Much in every way! First, that they were entrusted with the oracles of God . . .	Paul: 2 Much in every way! Above all, the Jews were entrusted with the words spoken by God himself. 3 For how else could it be? If some Jews were unfaithful, their unfaithfulness doesn't nullify God's faithfulness, does it?
I: **3 "What then? If some were unfaithful, their unfaithfulness does not nullify God's faithfulness, does it?"**	
P: 4 Certainly not! Let God be true and every human being a liar, just as it is written, ". . . so that you would be vindicated by your words, and you will overcome when you are brought to trial" (Ps 50:6 LXX).	I: **4 "God forbid! Let God be true and every man a liar, as it is written, 'so that you may be justified in what you say and win when you are challenged'** (Ps 50:6 LXX)."

---

61. See Matera, *Romans*, 80–83 (my translation); Stowers, *Rereading*, 165 (Stowers's translation). Matera agrees that Stowers's reconstruction of the dialogue is unlikely (see Matera, *Romans*, 79–80). Song (*Romans as a Diatribe*, 36, 94–95) presents the same reconstruction of Paul's dialogue as Matera, except for Rom 3:8, which both Matera and Stowers (and I) read in Paul's authorial voice.

Introducing the Gentile Proselyte

I: **5** "So if our unrighteousness demonstrates the righteousness of God, what shall we say? God is not unjust for inflicting his wrath [on us], is he?" P: (I am speaking in a human fashion.) P: **6** Certainly not! How, then, would God judge the world? I: **7** "But if the truth of God abounds to his glory by my falsehood, why am I still being condemned as a sinner?" P: **8** And should we (as we are being slandered, just as some people claim that we say such things) do evil things so that good things might result?⁶¹ Their condemnation is well deserved!	P: **5** But if our unrighteousness demonstrates the righteousness of God, what shall we say? Is God unrighteous when he expresses his anger? (I am speaking in a human way.) I: **6** "God forbid! For then how will God judge the world?" P: **7** But if the truthfulness of God is magnified by my falsity and increases his glory, why should I still be judged a sinner? **8** And shall we then say (as certain people also slanderously charge us with saying), "Let us do evil that good may come"? (Those who slander us in this way are justly condemned.)

I prefer Matera's reconstruction. The interlocutor consistently identifies an (erroneous) implication from Paul's argument, and Paul responds to correct the proselyte's misunderstanding.

On the heels of Paul's shocking claim that the circumcised proselyte (who calls himself a Jew) will be judged by the uncircumcised gentile who worships God as Creator (thereby fulfilling Torah's righteous requirements), the interlocutor interrupts Paul and asks if any advantage accrues to the status of being a Jew. Paul begins to answer that there is, when the interlocutor again interrupts Paul, exclaiming as much as asking: "If some were unfaithful, their unfaithfulness does not nullify God's faithfulness, does it?" (Rom 3:3). The answer, of course, is no. God is faithful even if no one else is, and Paul cites Ps 50:6 [LXX] to the effect that God is vindicated by his words whenever accusations are leveled against him (see Rom 3:4). The interlocutor picks up on the effect of Israel's unfaithfulness to the covenant (*viz.* that it makes God's faithfulness all the more incredible), and he asks how God can pour out his wrath on the very people who demonstrate

---

62. Paul's question, which he tacks onto the interlocutor's question in v. 7, anticipates a negative response. Despite the uncertainty involved with distinguishing Paul's authorial voice from his rhetorical voice as the interlocutor, Song rightly insists, "commentators should read the sections [of question-and-answer dialogue] as a dialogue format, not merely as a straight preaching" (*Reading*, 23).

how faithful he truly is.⁶³ Paul dismisses the suggestion as nonsense; God's people ought to demonstrate God's faithfulness by imitating it, not by testing its limits. Torah was meant to guide Israel in this imitation and, subsequently, to result in the blessing of Abraham upon all the families (= nations) of the earth. Things did not work out this way, and now even Israel requires redemption from Torah's curses. If Torah has not procured Israel's redemption, how much more foolish is it for gentiles to bend their necks to Torah's yoke? Instead, God has provided this redemption in the gospel, first for the Jew as well as for the Greek.

Paul's proselyte interlocutor, however, has neglected this redemption by taking on Torah-observance. In response to "the knowledge of God" (Rom 1:19), the interlocutor has turned to the revelation of God's will as expressed in Torah in order to join the people of God. Paul, however, forestalls that route and claims that other gentiles will actually condemn him as a transgressor of Torah. The interlocutor picks up on an unexpressed assumption in Paul's argument—*viz.* that Torah has not resulted in blessings for Israel—and pushes back. His questions assume that neither Israel's nor his own transgressions of Torah nullify the promises God made with his people, and he attempts to wrangle from Paul a concession that, in fact, his circumcision brings him in the sphere of God's people.

Let me explain. We noted Paul's argument that the proselyte's circumcision amounted to nothing less than a transgression of the commandment of circumcision on the eighth day. But if God demands this level of precise observance of Torah's commandments in order to uphold his promises, then no one could expect to receive his promises. "What, then, is the benefit of [being called] a Jew, and what is the advantage of circumcision?" (3:1). As soon as Paul affirms that Jews do indeed receive a benefit, the interlocutor interrupts Paul and asks whether God's faithfulness is jeopardized by human unfaithfulness. If not, we could expect the interlocutor to object that his circumcision, despite not following the letter of the commandment, nevertheless finds acceptance in light of God's faithfulness. Paul's response in v. 4 affirms God's abiding faithfulness. The interlocutor asks in v. 7: "But if the truth of God abounds to his glory by my falsehood, why am I still being condemned as a sinner?" This is not a crass question, asking if God is really just to inflict his wrath on the kind

---

63. I left out a phrase from the end of Rom 3:5 in my portrayal of Paul's dialogue. Despite my judgment that most of v. 5 represents the interlocutor's response to Paul's citation of Ps 51:4, I think Paul breaks out of speech-in-character in an aside to his Roman readers: "I am speaking in a human fashion." In my reading, Paul distances himself from the claim that God might be unjust for pouring out his wrath on his unfaithful people.

Introducing the Gentile Proselyte

of unrighteousness and depravity Paul described in 1:18–32. Rather, the question is, if God's patient acceptance of my transgression—circumcised, but not on the eighth day—magnifies God's glory, why would circumcision after the eighth day not be reckoned as faithful obedience of God's command? Paul dismisses the question as nonsense in v. 8, but that is not to say he dismisses it out-of-hand. In the next pericope (Rom 3:9–20) Paul will provide a full-throated exposition of just how bleak the interlocutor's transgression, as part of the Jews' transgression, really is.

Reading Torah against Israel (Rom 3:9–20)

> **9** "What then? Are we at any advantage?" Certainly not! For we have already charged that everyone, Jews as well as Greeks, are under sin, **10** just as it is written:
>
> "There is none righteous, not even one;
>   **11** there is none who have understanding;
>   there is none who seek God.
> **12** Everyone turned aside; together they have gone astray.
>   There is none who practices kindness,
>   [there is not] even one" (Pss 13:1–3; 52:2–4 LXX).
> **13** "Their throat is an open grave;
>   with their tongues they practice deceit" (Ps 5:10 LXX).
> "The venom of asps is under their lips" (Ps 139:4 LXX).
>   **14** "Their mouth is full of cursing and bitterness" (Ps 9:28 LXX);
> **15** "their feet are quick to shed blood.
>   **16** Destruction and distress on their paths,
>   **17** and they do not know the path of peace" (Isa 59:7–8 LXX).
>   **18** "There is no fear of God before their eyes" (Ps 35:2 LXX).
>
> **19** But we know that what Torah says, it says to those in Torah, so that every mouth would be closed and the whole world would be accountable to God. **20** Therefore, no flesh will be justified before him by works of Torah, for through Torah comes the knowledge of sin.

I am inclined to understand Rom 3:9 as Paul's continued dialogue with his proselyte interlocutor.[64] So far in Romans 3, most of the questions have

---

64. *Pace* Dunn (*Romans*, 1:129–30), who says that 3:1–8 is "transitional": "Paul at first perseveres with the diatribe style; but the debate becomes increasingly with himself." He then describes the question in 3:9 as "the final spasm of the diatribe which dominated most of 2:1—3:9, but which had already begun to get out of hand [!] in the preceding section" (ibid., 1:145). I disagree; not only is all of 3:1–8 dialogic in nature,

come from the interlocutor (though see 3:6, 8), and the interlocutor asks if "we" (those who call themselves "Jews") experience any advantage.[65] Paul answers emphatically, "Certainly not!" [*ou pantōs*]. Despite the advantage of Israel's election, her being entrusted with Torah/the oracles of God, of being the covenant people, and so on, in actual fact no advantage has attached to being a Jew. Why not? Because Jews, like Greeks, find themselves under sin. "God has made sin into the great equalizer of nations."[66] We still have to distinguish how Jews and Greeks (= gentiles) found themselves in this situation.[67] Gentiles, of course, have been estranged from the Creator God since primordial history, when the descendants of Adam spiraled further and further into sin. Israel, on the other hand, received the special revelation of God. God set life and death, blessing and cursing, before Israel, with the promise that Israel (= Jacob) and his descendants would live (Deut 30:19 LXX). This should have resulted in an advantage for the Jew. *Should have*, but it did not.

Paul then offers a catena of scriptural references to support his argument that both Jews and gentiles are under sin, with no advantage accruing to Israel. The majority of Paul's citations come from the Psalter, though Paul also cites Isa 59:7–8 (see also Prov 1:16). These passages all exhibit a dark point of view, whether with respect to humanity as a whole or with respect to a narrower population.

1. In Rom 3:10-12, Paul cites Pss 13:1-3; 52:2-4 LXX.[68] The psalmist sings about gentiles: among the nations surrounding and attacking Israel,

---

but the diatribe continues through v. 9 and beyond.

65. Stowers translates *Ti oun? proechometha?* in v. 9, "What then? Are we at a disadvantage?" (*Rereading*, 166; see 173–74). I have given a more traditional translation and offered a very different explanation of Paul's rhetoric. If, however, we prefer the passive translation "Are we at a disadvantage?" my explanation of the passage would stand with only minor changes.

66. Ibid., 183.

67. Stowers makes a similar (but not identical) point: "For Paul, the Bible contains two stories about the peoples of the earth. The one story concerns an often-wayward but also repentant people who worship God, and the other concerns the usually wicked and idolatrous gentile peoples. The law does not show how the gentile peoples can become an elect people like Israel, it only chronicles their sin" (ibid., 190).

68. The two passages from the Psalms are nearly identical; Paul's language is closer to Ps 13:1–3 than to 52:2–4, but Paul differs even from some places where the psalms agree. The phrase, "There is none righteous, not even one" [*ouk estin dikaios oude heis* (Rom 3:10)] does not occur in either Psalm 13 or 52 LXX; Paul seems to combine Eccl 7:20 with his citations of the psalm(s). This latter phrase also occurs in Hannah's song (1 Kgdms 2:2 LXX); however, Hannah's song, in which she praises God for her

Introducing the Gentile Proselyte

none seek the Lord. None practice kindness. All have turned aside. But though the nations "devour my people as they eat bread" [*hoi katesthiontes ton laon mou brōsei artou* (Ps 13:4 LXX)], the Lord God will turn back his people's shame and Israel will be glad. Surprisingly, Paul turns this passage even against Israel.[69] Paul, unlike the psalmist, lumps Jews and Greeks together: "there is none righteous, not even one" (Rom 3:10). Rodrigo Morales rightly points out that the psalm passages include "a plea for God to deliver Israel and to 'restore the fortunes of his people' (Ps 14:7)" and "include pleas for God to act to bring about his kingdom."[70] All the more striking, then, that Paul deploys Pss 13 and 52 LXX to *indict* rather than *intercede for* Israel!

2. In Rom 3:13, Paul cites Pss 5:10 and 139:4 LXX, both of which continue the same pattern from vv. 10-12. Once again, the psalmist bemoans the wickedness of his enemies and declares his trust in the Lord for deliverance. Paul, however, turns the psalmist's words against Israel herself: both Jew and Greek have made their throat an open grave and harbored the venom of asps within their lips.

3. In Rom 3:14, Paul cites Ps 9:28 LXX, and we see the same pattern all over again. The psalmist decries the proud and wicked man who oppresses the poor and boasts that God will not act. This man's "mouth is full of curse and bitterness and deceit; beneath his tongue are trouble and toil." However, the psalmist trusts the Lord to act, to avenge the poor who trust in him, and spits out a swear against his enemies: "You gentiles will be destroyed from his land" [*apoleisthe, ethnē, ek tēs gēs autou* (9:37 LXX)]. Paul, however, paints both Jew and gentile in these starkly dark hues.

4. In Rom 3:15-17, Paul puts down the Psalter and cites Isa 59:7-8, and with the change in text we also find a change in our pattern. Unlike the Psalm citations, Isaiah 59 bemoans *Israel's* sins. "*We* have acted with impiety; *we* have lied; *we* have stepped out from behind our God; *we* have spoken unjustly; *we* have been disobedient; *we* have conceived and attended to unrighteous words in *our* hearts" (Isa 59:13 LXX; my

---

son, Samuel, does not match the dark tenor of Romans 3. Not surprisingly, Eccl 7:20 certainly does.

69. "The point becomes clearer when it is recalled that all the Psalm citations presuppose an antithesis between the righteous (the faithful member of the covenant) and the unrighteous" (Dunn, *Romans*, 1:145).

70. Morales, "Promised," 114-15 (p. 114 quoted).

69

emphases).⁷¹ This passage, in fact, gives Paul the warrant he needed to read the psalms as indictments against Israel herself. God's people have not produced the blessing of Abraham;⁷² instead, they have wrought "destruction and distress" [*syntrimma kai talaipōria* (Rom 3:16)] and have failed to know "the path of peace" [*hodon eirēnēs* (Rom 3:17)].

5. *The catena concludes with a final citation from the Psalter (Ps 35:2 LXX)*, which returns to the pattern we saw in the earlier psalm citations. The psalmist decries the wicked and appeals to the Lord to act on behalf of his people, who have set their trust in him. Paul, however, indicts Jews as well as gentiles with the words, "There is no fear of God before their eyes" [*ouk estin phobos theou apenanti tōn ophthalmōn autōn* (Rom 3:18)]. This is why no advantage accrues to bearing the name "Jew," despite the lengths to which the gentile proselyte has gone to merit that label. Israel's failure to nurture and develop a healthy fear of the Lord is not, for Paul, a *theological* problem. He does not say that Israel failed because they were hypocrites, or because Torah was ineffectual, or anything like that. Israel's failure, for Paul, is a *historical* problem: Israel's exile, the Diaspora, and Rome's hegemonic rule all make blindingly obvious that the consequences of sin—curse, exile, death—have come upon Israel just as certainly as they have plagued the gentiles.⁷³ However, Paul's citation of precisely these passages from the Writings and the Prophets strike a contrary harmonic that cuts across the long dark notes of the catena and "emphasize[s] not only human sin, but also, more subtly, God's righteousness and fidelity."⁷⁴

---

71. Paul's use of Scripture depends on a literary device called "metalepsis," in which the unstated elements of the texts Paul quotes and alludes to play an important role in determining how Paul deploys those texts in his own rhetoric; see Morales, "Promised," (he discusses metalepsis on p. 110).

72. The Abrahamic promise of blessing for the gentiles is a vital context for understanding Paul's theologizing about Torah, sin, and what God has accomplished in the gospel (Stowers, *Rereading*, 179).

73. "But for Paul and, he assumes, for his imaginary opponent, the fact of Israel's ongoing exile is evidence enough of Israel's sins, especially of breaking the law that Israel claims as its special privilege" (Grieb, *Story*, 32). John Barclay describes the social context of Pseudo-Philo's *Liber Antiquitatum Biblicarum* in terms of "a demoralised nation," and the recounting (and revision) of the historical narrative is intended to assure its readers that "Israel remains the central thread in God's purposes for the world" (Barclay, "Have Mercy," 97). In other words, Paul—like other Jews—could recognize and address Israel's failures without concluding, as has often been concluded throughout Christian history, that Jews are somehow innately defective and/or ultimately rejected.

74. Morales, "Promised," 115.

Introducing the Gentile Proselyte

Paul draws a stark conclusion for his interlocutor in 3:19-20. Torah speaks to those "in Torah" (i.e., the Jews), and its verdict is that Jews—no less than gentiles!—are under sin. The proselyte has acted foolishly, then, for placing his trust in Torah, which has not kept the Jews holy and was never meant for gentiles anyway. "Here, even more clearly than in 2:12, the character and function of the law as marking the boundary between Jew and Gentile comes to expression. The Jews are defined as 'those within the law,' within the area circumscribed by the law, whose religion, nationality, and lifestyle bears the distinctive marks of the Torah."[75] When we realize that Paul is addressing a gentile interlocutor, who has placed a premium on "the distinctive marks of the Torah" and even bent his neck to the full yoke of Torah, the conclusion that "no flesh will be justified before him by works of Torah" (3:20) becomes all the more dire. The interlocutor has already questioned whether God would really hold it against him that he was circumcised, but not on the eighth day. Paul now reveals the full scope of his answer: everyone, Jew as well as Greek, is accountable [*hypodikos* (3:19)] to God's righteous judgment.

Paul's closes this section with a word directed squarely at his proselyte interlocutor: "Therefore, no flesh will be justified before him by works of Torah, for through Torah comes the knowledge of sin" (3:20). Stowers rightly sees that v. 20 focuses on gentiles, and that *dikaiōthēsetai* ("will be justified") is "a transfer term," one which "has reference only to those who are outside of a positive relation with God."[76] Whatever Paul thinks of the proselyte's *motivation* for submitting to Torah—remember 2:21-22, in which Paul grants that the interlocutor has risen above the depravity described in 1:18-32—he insists that the interlocutor's turn to Torah fundamentally dishonors God.[77] God's own people have amply demonstrated

---

75. Dunn, *Romans*, 1:152.

76. Stowers, *Rereading*, 190. Stowers continues: "As such, it could refer only to gentiles or perhaps to extremely wicked and unrepentant Jews." Stowers rightly insists that Paul knew that Torah made provisions for making Israel acceptable before God without requiring perfect and total obedience to every commandment; he overlooks, however, that the Diaspora and Roman hegemony over Judea clearly suggest that, despite the mechanisms for repentance and reconciliation within Torah, the Jews were nevertheless estranged from God.

77. Stowers prefers a general explanation of the gentiles' inability to perform works of Torah: "Works of the law typically cannot be done consistently by gentiles because God has consigned them to sin as a punishment for their rejection of him. At most, the law gives them only a knowledge of their bondage to sin and their culpability. The

the principle that Torah brings knowledge of sin. The gentile proselyte, then, has turned to the wrong authority in order to properly distinguish the Creator God from created idols. But Paul is about to correct the proselyte's errant turn.

---

law cannot serve to make the ungodly and unrighteous righteous because God did not intend for the law to function that way" (ibid., 192; see also Garroway, *Gentile-Jews*, 94–95). Matthew Thiessen has shown that, according to Rom 2:23–29, the gentile proselyte's submission to circumcision was itself a transgression of Torah, (i) first because it did not adhere to the detailed instructions for circumcision, and (ii) because Torah was given to Abraham and his descendants, not to the gentiles (see Thiessen, "Romans 2:17").

5

The Righteousness of God apart from Torah

Or, Not a Law-Free Gospel

> *Paul not only continues to direct his remarks in 3:21–26 to the fictitious interlocutor, but again resumes their dialogue in 3:27—4:2. Moreover, the groundwork for what Paul announces to the teacher in 3:21–26 has already been laid in 3:1–9. On this reading 3:1–8 no longer seems to be a digression with its own parenthetic digression. Rather, 1:18—3:9 and . . . 3:10—4:25, fit tightly and flow smoothly in a complex and powerful rhetoric constructed with speech-in-character. Instead of forming an appendix or an afterthought on Jewish unbelief, on this reading chapters 9–11 become a climactic resumption of issues already raised in 2:17—3:9 that touch the very heart of Paul's message and ministry.*[1]

Romans 3:21–31 has become one of the most significant texts among Christian theologians and exegetes. Certainly the content of the passage helps explain its centrality. Here Paul announces and unpacks the righteousness of God that is revealed apart from Torah (though which is nevertheless bound with/to Torah). Here Paul explains some of what he sees when he focuses his gaze on the atoning death of Jesus and its effects for those who are "in Christ" [*en Christō*].[2] More than that, this

---

1. Stowers, *Rereading*, 175.

2. This quintessentially Pauline formula occurs for the first time in Romans at 3:24,

passage presents an unusually tight cluster of grammatical and syntactical difficulties that have very significant consequences for its bearing on key doctrinal areas (including Christology, soteriology, and hamartiology). To add yet another complicating factor, exegetes have often neglected this passage's relationship to its immediate context, especially to the discussion of Abraham in Romans 4. As a result, we will spend considerable time on this text, and we will explicitly attempt to understand how this section leads to Paul's reflections on Abraham and Genesis 15.

The Righteousness of God apart from Torah (Rom 3:21–26)

> **21** But now the righteousness of God is being revealed apart from Torah, although it is attested to by Torah and the Prophets. **22** The righteousness of God [is being revealed] through the faith[fulness] of Jesus Christ to everyone who believes. For there is no distinction, **23** for all have sinned and fall short of the glory of God, **24** though they are being justified freely by his grace through the redemption that is in Christ Jesus, **25** whom God put forward as the *hilastērion* through his faithfulness, achieved by means of his blood, to be a display of his righteousness because of the passing over of sins previously committed **26** in the forbearance of God, in order to display his righteousness in the present time, so that he himself would be just even as he justifies a person by the faith[fulness] of Jesus.

I agree wholeheartedly with Stanley Stowers's judgment that, in Rom 3:21ff., Paul continues the diatribe with the fictive interlocutor he first introduced in 2:17. In fact, I doubt we can understand 3:21–26 unless we appreciate that Paul is still explaining why a gentile who takes on the full yoke of Torah-observance to pursue the righteousness of God cannot succeed. Even more importantly, this passage almost *necessitates* that Paul imagines a gentile interlocutor (rather than a Jewish teacher/ missionary to gentiles). One cannot read texts like Deuteronomy 28–32 and *not* get the impression that God intended his people Israel to embody his righteousness and to do so precisely by keeping Torah's ordinances and commandments. Hence the difficulty with traditional readings of Paul and Romans, which interpret Paul as saying that Torah obscures rather than reveals God's righteousness. However, if Rom 3:21ff. addresses a gentile

---

but the participatory conception that this formula expresses does not occur until as late as 6:11, 23 and especially 8:1.

who has taken on the yoke of Torah, and if Paul insists that gentiles are not reconciled with Israel's God by keeping Torah, then his explanation of the righteousness of God revealed apart from Torah [*chōris nomou*] takes on different connotations. Paul explains how gentiles who worship the Creator God of Israel can keep Torah's righteous commandments [*dikaiōmata tou nomou*; see 2:26] without observing its more salient precepts (circumcision, Sabbath observance, *kashrut*, etc.).[3] Despite his adamance that gentiles should not submit to Torah observance, Paul clearly expects his gentile readers to know and value Torah as the word (or oracles) of God, and even "to enter the symbolic universe of the Scriptures."[4]

Paul has already explained that sin is a problem for both Jew and gentile (Rom 3:9–20). Since Torah has not been able to keep Israel situated within the blessings of the Creator God, Torah clearly cannot be the answer to the problem of the gentiles' estrangement from God (see 3:19–20). At this key moment in Paul's rhetoric, Paul begins, "But now..." [*nyni de*; 3:21]. "But now the righteousness of God is being revealed apart from Torah." "But now" clearly marks an important transition in Paul's rhetoric, from the revelation of God's wrath (see 1:18) to, now, the revelation of his righteousness. However, this transition does not negate what Paul has already said; the revelation of God's righteousness "now," "apart from Torah," is directly related to the problem of sin that plagues "everyone" (3:23). "The gospel that reveals God's righteousness (1:16–17) is a word of judgment (Rom 1:18–3:20) before it is a word of grace (3:21ff.). In this sense, the 'but now' of 3:21 is an affirmation of 1:18 and 3:9, 19–20 before it is their antithesis."[5]

---

3. NT scholarship should probably abandon its proclivity to speak of Paul's "law-free gospel." This phrase is ubiquitous among the secondary literature. For example, Eung Chun Park essentializes two different gospels, "the Torah-free *gospel of the uncircumcision* (*to euangelion tēs akrobystias*, Gal 2:7) vis-à-vis the Torah-bound *gospel of the circumcision* ([*to euangelion*] *tēs peritomēs*, Gal 2:7)," and situates Paul within the tension between these two gospels (see Park, *Either*; pp. 1–2 quoted). The righteousness of God that Paul proclaims may be revealed "apart from Torah," but he nevertheless clearly explains its effects in terms of the gentiles keeping Torah's righteous commandments. Andrew Das uses the more appropriate phrase, "Paul's *circumcision-free* mission to the Gentiles" (*Paul*, 1, my emphasis), though see Garroway's argument ("Circumcision") that Paul portrays his gentile converts as circumcised by Christ.

4. Ehrensperger, "Scriptural Reasoning."

5. Linebaugh, "Debating," 118. Linebaugh's entire essay is relevant here and worth consulting; for example, "The objects of the divine saving action implied in the passive verb *dikaioumenoi* (3:24) are the sinners of 3:23.... In other words, words that would scandalize the Epistle [of Enoch]'s author, the objects of divine judgment are also the objects of divine justification" (ibid., 124).

The Revelation of Dikaiosynē Theou

In a now-classic essay, Sam Williams wrote, "most Pauline scholars now agree that in the OT and in Paul 'righteousness' designates conduct or activity appropriate to a relationship rather than an inherent quality, static attribute or absolute moral norm."[6] In Romans, Williams argues, the phrase refers to the fidelity and faithfulness of God to his promises to Abraham and his descendants.[7] This understanding—that "the righteousness of God" refers to the trustworthiness of God's promises to Abraham and the confidence his people can have in those promises[8]—differs strongly from the view that "the righteousness of God" refers to the righteousness that God requires from his people (an *ethical* righteousness in contrast to the moral depravity Paul described in Rom 1:18–32) or that God grants to his people (righteousness as a *status* that God grants his people despite their inability to maintain the ethical righteousness already mentioned).[9] When Paul discusses "the righteousness of God," "its primary and most important meaning in Romans is God's covenant fidelity to Israel. God's righteousness means that the gifts and calling of God to Israel are irrevocable."[10] We could paraphrase Rom 3:21a: "Despite the fact that God's people were unfaithful to Torah and so merited the curses described therein (i.e., they did *not* merit Torah's blessings), God has been faithful to his promise to Abraham, even apart from the terms laid out in Torah."[11]

---

6. Williams, "Righteousness of God," 241.

7. For example, "When we recognize the conceptual ties between Rom 1:16–17 and Galatians 3/Romans 4, there is nothing fantastic about the suggestion that a leading connotation of *dikaiosynē theou* in Romans in God's faithfulness in keeping his promise to Abraham" (ibid., 265).

8. As an analogy, consider a couple's marriage vows on their wedding day. A man and a woman promise they will be for each other and each other only for the rest of their lives. If they keep those vows, they are said to have been "faithful" to their spouse. I mean the same thing when I speak of God's "faithfulness" to his promises to Abraham. More than that, God's faithfulness to Israel is comparable to the situation in which one spouse is unfaithful to their marital vows and the other spouse nevertheless stays faithful (cp. Hos 1:2—3:5; Ezek 16:1–63; passim). God's faithfulness—*the righteousness of God*—is akin to the faithfulness of a spouse who discovers that their wedding vows have been desecrated and defiled and nevertheless remains faithful to those vows.

9. See Grieb, *Story*, 36–38.

10. Ibid., xii.

11. Similarly, Furnish helpfully summarizes Rom 3:19–20: "The apostle has said that God's power to put things right does not work through the law" ("Living to God," 188). "God's power to put things right" is an appropriate way to refer to the righteousness of God.

The prepositional phrase "apart from Torah" describes *the revelation* of God's righteousness and not the righteousness of God itself.[12]

Despite the fact that Paul envisions the revelation of God's righteousness—his *faithfulness*—apart from Torah, that revelation has not lost all mooring to Torah, the Mosaic covenant and tradition.[13] The righteousness that Paul says is revealed by means of the gospel he proclaims (see 1:16–17) "was attested to by the Law and the Prophets" [*martyroumenē tou nomou kai tōn prophētōn* (3:21b)]. This is not as surprising a claim as we might imagine. The Hebrew Bible heralds God's divine faithfulness at every turn, so the idea that his faith-ful-ness would overshadow his people's faith-less-ness (and the curses that faithlessness merits under Torah's terms) finds expression in multiple and diverse traditions throughout.[14] We might, then, infer two ideas from Rom 3:20–21: (i) Torah points out and condemns humanity's sin; (ii) Torah also makes evident God's faithfulness, even in light of his people's *un*faithfulness.[15] For Paul, this "making evident" climaxes and receives its clearest interpretation in the message of Jesus' crucifixion and resurrection. "With the mission of Christ accomplished ... the genuine meaning of the scriptures has at last been revealed and the historic advantage enjoyed by the Jews has accordingly lapsed."[16]

---

12. That is, we should render the passage, "But now, the righteousness of God is being revealed apart from Torah." We misunderstand Paul if we translate this phrase, "But now, the righteousness of God apart from Torah is being revealed" (*pace* KJV, NIV, NLT).

13. Watson, in an effort to explain away the second half of Rom 3:21, says Torah and the prophets bear witness to the righteousness of God "indirectly, by showing that the righteousness of which it speaks—in the form of a way of life wholly shaped by its prescriptions and prohibitions—does not actually exist" ("Law in Romans," 103). Paul, of course, says no such thing anywhere. Torah and the prophets attest the righteousness of God actively, especially insofar as they "promised [the gospel] beforehand" (see Rom 1:3).

14. See, e.g., the overarching narrative embodied in the books of Isaiah and Ezekiel. Numerous particular texts speak to the same issue (Deut 32; Jer 31; Ps 51; 2 Kgdms 7:14–15; passim).

15. *Pace* Watson, "Law in Romans," 103.

16. Garroway, *Gentile-Jews*, 98. (In the passage quoted, Garroway is commenting on Rom 3:2, 9. His point, however, applies again to Rom 3:21–22.)

More on the Revelation of Dikaiosynē Theou

As we move on to v. 22, we encounter a second, relatively simple but important, problem. As we have already seen, Rom 3:21 describes "the righteousness of God" in two ways: (i) it is revealed apart from Torah, and (ii) it is attested to by the Law and the Prophets. Paul restates the subject of his sentence in v. 22: "the righteousness of God." He does not, however, restate the verb. Traditional interpretations have often supplied some form of the verb "to come." For example, the NIV starts a new sentence at 3:22: "This righteousness from God comes through faith in Jesus Christ to all who believe."[17] The NIV is doubly wrong. First, Paul is not speaking of a righteousness *from* God. Second, nothing in Romans 3 suggests that Paul has in mind how this righteousness *comes* to or from anywhere. Commentators and exegetes have also succumbed to this problem. Furnish, for example, suggests: "For Paul, the righteousness that the law *cannot impart is bestowed* as a gift of God's grace," even though Paul consistently refers to the *revelation* rather than the *impartation* or *bestowal* of the righteousness of God.[18]

How, then, does Paul expect his readers to understand v. 22, given that he has not included a verb? The answer is near at hand: Paul has already used the verb in 3:21:[19] "the righteousness of God is being revealed [*pephanerōtai*; 3:21] through faith."[20] Paul, of course, has already said pre-

---

17. Other translations awkwardly leave the sentence without any verb (see ESV, NASB, NRSV). Francis Watson refers to "righteousness (that) is by faith" without explaining what verb he would supply (i.e., "the righteousness that is [*what?*] by faith"; "Law in Romans," 98 [2x], 103). When he does supply a verb, he opts for one that Paul never uses: "the righteousness that is right relation with God is *associated* with faith rather than law, for law is to be associated not with righteousness but with its opposite, sin" (ibid., 103; my emphasis). Watson misreads Rom 3:21–22 on two fronts: (i) righteousness is "revealed by"—not "associated with"—faith[fulness], and (ii) Torah ("law") bears witness to that righteousness and is not restricted to its "association" with sin.

18. Furnish, "Living to God," 189; my emphasis. A few sentences later, Furnish rightly describes "Christ's death as a 'sacrifice [*or* place] of atonement' that *reveals* [my emphasis] God's 'righteousness' and 'forbearance' in dealing with sins" (ibid.; see also pp. 194–95).

19. In arguing another point (concerning the significance of *pantas* ["all"] in 3:22), Stowers says off-handedly, "God's righteousness has been manifested through the faithfulness of Jesus Christ . . ." (*Rereading*, 203). See also Campbell, "Faithfulness," 57–71, esp. pp. 62, 63–64, 67–71; Elliott, "Political Christology," 47; Jewett, *Romans*, 268; Witherington and Hyatt, *Romans*, 101; Wright, "Romans," 469–70.

20. Robert Jewett is surprisingly confused here. Despite clearly affirming, "the expression, 'in regard to all who have faith' modifies the ellipsed [*sic*] 'manifested'"

cisely this sort of thing in Rom 1:16–17.[21] Therefore, I have translated Rom 3:21–22a: "But now the righteousness of God is being revealed apart from Torah, although it is attested to by Torah and the Prophets. The righteousness of God [is being revealed] through faith[fulness] . . . ." In my reading, Paul continues to explain to his gentile interlocutor the mechanics of the revelation of God's righteousness.

Translating Pistis Iēsou Christou

We immediately encounter a third—and more complex—interpretive problem. Paul says God's righteousness is revealed *dia pisteōs Iēsou Christou* (lit. "through faith of Jesus Christ"). *Pistis [Iēsou] Christou* occurs at a number of key places in Paul's letters and is the subject of intense academic discussion.[22] There are two broad interpretive options: the objective genitive reading ("through faith *in* Jesus Christ") and the subjective genitive reading ("through the faith[fulness] *of* Jesus Christ"). The differences between these readings matter, though perhaps not as much as some commentators claim. If we opt for the objective reading, this passage takes on an anthropological emphasis, focusing on the person who exhibits "faith in Jesus." Once a person exhibits (or receives) faith in Jesus, that person becomes privy to the righteousness of God that is manifested to him by God. If we opt for the subjective reading, this passage takes on a theological emphasis, focusing on God and the revelation of his righteousness within creation. Once God's people failed to manifest God's righteousness within creation by means of Torah, God took it upon himself to reveal his righteousness apart from Torah. This he did through Jesus Christ, who exhibited *pistis* in/toward God.[23] And "through the faithfulness of Jesus Christ" to Israel's God, God reveals his righteousness.

(*Romans*, 278), he nevertheless claims, "The nature of 'God's righteousness' *is defined as coming* 'through faith in Jesus Christ'" (ibid., 275; my emphasis). Similarly, I disagree with Thomas Schreiner, who thinks that this passage is concerned with *obtaining* the righteousness of God, even though Paul makes clear that he is explaining the *revelation* of God's righteousness (Schreiner, *Romans*, 180).

21. Paul uses different verbs in 3:21[–22] and 1:17. In Rom 3:21 he uses *phaneroō* ("I make known"), whereas in 1:17 he uses *apokalyptō* (I disclose; I make known"). Louw-Nida discusses both verbs in close proximity to one another (see L&N §§28:36; 28:38).

22. Rom 3:22; Gal 2:16 [twice], 20; 3:22; Phil 3:9; Eph 3:12. See the essays in Bird and Sprinkle, eds., *Faith of Jesus Christ*.

23. The Greek term *pistis* is broader, in some ways, than the English term "faith." The

However, we can find room to accommodate Paul's ambiguity, whereby he just might say both things at once. Daniel Wallace proposes a *plenary genitive*, in which an author intends both the objective and subjective genitive connotations simultaneously.[24] I think the connotations of the subjective genitive are dominant in this passage,[25] especially in light of the prepositional phrase that follows: "The righteousness of God [is being revealed] through the faithfulness of Jesus Christ *to everyone who believes*" [*eis pantas tous pisteuontas*; 3:22]. If *dia pisteōs Iēsou Christou* at the beginning of v. 22 meant "by faith in Jesus Christ," then the prepositional phrase at the end of v. 22 would be redundant. The only people who have "faith in Jesus Christ" *are* "those who believe"! But if *dia pisteōs Iēsou Christou* means "by the faithfulness of Jesus Christ," then it makes sense to add the prepositional phrase: only those who believe/trust in the gospel message perceive in Jesus' life—his faithfulness to Israel's God—the revelation of the righteousness of God.

The Universal Scope of Pas

Finally, Paul goes on to explain the significance of a word he has just used: *pantas* ("everyone"). The end of Rom 3:22, in conjunction with v. 23, unpacks *pas* ("all, every") and echoes the idea of 3:19–20 (which uses *pas* three times). According to the popular interpretation of 3:23, every individual human being has sinned, and every individual human being falls short of the glory of God. This reading picks up on a narrowly literal understanding of the catena earlier in Romans 3 ("There is no one righteous, not even one . . ."). Perhaps Paul would agree with this idea; perhaps not.[26] Regardless, that simply is *not* what Paul is saying here. Instead, when he says, "For there is no distinction, for all [*pantes*] sinned and are falling short of the glory of God" (3:22b–23), he is telling the interlocutor that

---

point here is not that Jesus "believed in" God more (or better) than Israel; rather, Jesus exhibited more steadfast confidence in the truth of God's word and promises. Hence, we might translate *pistis* as "faithfulness, confidence, trustworthiness," or similar.

24. "The noun in the genitive is *both* subjective and objective. In most cases, the subjective produces the objective notion" (see Wallace, *Greek Grammar*, 119).

25. Recall Wallace's caveat: "In most cases, the subjective produces the objective notion" (ibid.; see the previous note).

26. Famously, Paul describes himself as "blameless" [*amemptos*] with respect to the righteousness that is circumscribed by Torah [*dikaiosynēn tēn en nomō*; Phil 3:6]. Interpreters have had to engage in hermeneutical contortions in order to harmonize this verse with the popular reading of Romans 3.

everyone, Jews as well as gentiles, have not attained to the righteousness of God that was revealed to Israel in Torah. While this "falling short" may be understandable for gentiles, it poses a special problem for Israel.

But no matter. God has stepped beyond the terms of Torah to reveal his righteousness through the faithfulness of Jesus Christ, which everyone who believes can now perceive in the gospel. Both Jew and gentile—"for there is no distinction"—benefit from this revelation of God's righteousness apart from Torah. Jews and gentiles may have taken different routes to their current position "under sin,"[27] but both now find themselves reconciled to Israel's Creator God as a result of Jesus' faithfulness (in contrast to Israel's *un*faithfulness). All—Jew as well as gentile—sinned, and all—Jew as well as gentile—are falling short of the glory of God.

Jesus, the New Hilastērion

But all—Jew as well as gentile—are also "being justified freely by his grace through the redemption that is in Christ Jesus" (3:24). Commentators often understand the language of "being justified" [*dikaioumenoi*] in its legal sense: "being acquitted" or "declared innocent" despite the fact that the law [*nomos*] makes sin known (see Rom 3:20). This is probably right, but we need to be cautious to remember that *nomos* in Romans 3 is not a legal term ("law") but a covenantal term ("Torah").[28] Within the terms of the covenant (= Torah) God's people are guilty and have merited the curses prescribed in the covenant. However, they have been acquitted of that guilt because God is faithful to the promises that preceded Torah, even in light of his people's unfaithfulness (3:3–4).[29] This faithfulness, which is made evident "apart from Torah" [*chōris nomou*; 3:21], is offered "freely," "by his grace" (3:24). The description of the redemption God offers as "that which is in Christ Jesus" [*tēs en Christō Iēsou*] picks up on the idea we encountered in v. 22, that the righteousness of God is revealed

---

27. "The courses of Israel and the Gentiles through history have been quite different, and continue to be different (as witnesses also the argument in Romans 9–11); but it is God's unswerving integrity that guides them both and determines them both" (Elliott, *Rhetoric*, 223); see Rom 3:9 and my comments on that verse, above.

28. This is why I have avoided the translation "law" or "Law"; this word in English is simply too legal and insufficiently covenantal to convey Paul's use of *nomos* in Romans.

29. My phrase "God is faithful to the promises" picks up on our interpretation of *dikaiosynē theou* ("righteousness of God") in 3:21. That 3:24 continues the idea of God's righteousness from 3:21 is clear from the first word of 3:24, *dikaioumenoi* ("being justified"), which is built on the same stem as *dikaiosynē*.

through (or by) the faithfulness of Jesus. In vv. 21–22 Paul identified Jesus' faithfulness as the means of the revelation of God's righteousness. Here in v. 24 he identifies Jesus as the sphere circumscribing the redemption God offers.

Paul says, first, that God put forward Christ Jesus "as a covering" [*hilastērion*].[30] This word is as perplexing in Greek as it is in English.[31] Since *hilastērion* is a Pauline hapax legomenon, we cannot appeal to other instances where Paul uses this word to get a sense for what Paul means here. Hebrews 9:5—the only other use of *hilastērion* in the NT—clearly refers to the covering of the ark of the covenant, the "mercy seat" that served as the throne of YHWH prior to the destruction of the first temple.[32] According to Colin Brown, "[t]he LXX uses *hilastērion* 22 times for the Heb. *kappōret* which may be rendered 'propitiatory' or 'mercy seat.'"[33] In twenty-two of the LXX's twenty-eight uses of *hilastērion*, it refers to the lid of the ark of the covenant, the throne of YHWH and the location of the atonement ritual at the heart of Yom Kippur. This usage agrees with the only use of *hilastērion* (other than in Rom 3:25) in the NT (see Heb 9:5).

Our first inclination, therefore, must be that Paul also uses *hilastērion* in this traditional, Hellenistic Jewish sense. In non-biblical literature *hilastērion* often referred to a *propitiatory gift*, a sacrifice or offering that wins or gains favor, especially from a deity.[34] In Romans 3, Paul does not focus on the wrath of God (cf. 1:18), and he does not emphasize the "propiatory," appeasing actions people must take in order to satisfy God's wrath. Instead, Romans 3 focuses on God's faithfulness to his promises

---

30. Commentators often identify creedal or hymnic material in Rom 3:25–26 (see the discussion in Jewett, *Romans*, 270–71; 283–93; Meyer, "Pre-Pauline Formula," 198–208; Sumney, "Christ Died for Us," 161–62). Certainly Paul is capable of quoting early Christian material (e.g., Phil 2:6–11). I am not, however, persuaded that scholars have been able (i) to conclusively differentiate what comes from Paul's source and what Paul adds to his source material, or (ii) to convincingly explain how Paul incorporates and/or transforms the significance of the material he takes over from his source. As a result, I will interpret the final form of these verses within their context in Romans 3 even as I grant that Paul may allude to or incorporate pre-Pauline material in vv. 25–26.

31. Many translations use the English word "propitiation," which seems hardly any clearer than if they had just transliterated *hilastērion*! For a helpful and accessible discussion, see Matera, *Romans*, 94–95; for a brief but more technical discussion, see Bailey, "Mercy Seat," 155–58.

32. "But above it the cherubim of glory overshadowed the mercy seat [*to hilastērion*]" (Heb 9:5; v. 4 describes the contents of the ark of the covenant).

33. Colin Brown, "ἱλάσκομαι" (part), 3:156.

34. See Bailey, "Mercy Seat," 157.

and the faithfulness of Christ by which God brings those promises to fulfillment.[35] Paul says God put Jesus forward as the locus—or place—of salvation, just as the *kappōret* provided that location during the Yom Kippur ritual. "God's open setting out of Jesus as the new *hilastērion*—the centre of the sanctuary and focus of both the revelation of God ([Exod] 25:22; [Lev] 16:2; [Num] 7:89) and atonement for sin (Leviticus 16)—fulfils this tradition."[36] Bailey identifies two functions of the *hilastērion*: atonement and revelation, both of which are apropos to Romans 3.

At this point we can see the interpretive gain to be had by our decision to understand Paul's interlocutor as a proselyte to Judaism rather than an ethnic Jew. Like a number of contemporary Romans commentators (Stowers, Das, *inter alios*), I read all of Romans as aimed at an explicitly gentile audience. But unlike most commentators, I think Paul is still speaking *to* a gentile interlocutor (as well as *for* a gentile audience). If so, we can understand why Paul reacts so violently to the notion that gentiles had to take on the full yoke of Torah (including circumcision, Sabbath observance, etc.) in order to fulfill the righteous commandments of Torah (see Rom 2:26). Torah identified the lid of the ark of the covenant (Heb. *kappōret*; Grk *hilastērion*) as the location in which God's people found atonement for their sins. Paul placed the location of atonement on Christ and his faithfulness to YHWH. More than that, Paul identified the entire mechanism of atonement with Jesus:

> Jesus Christ represents Israel and therefore also represents the world for which Israel was chosen to be God's servant. As the Anointed One, the Messiah, he is the designated representative of Israel (like the high priest; see Hebrews for a corresponding argument). Like the mercy seat, he is the place where God will deal with the covenant violations of Israel. Moreover, he is himself the sacrifice for sin. So Jesus is the person who offers

---

35. I want to underscore this point: a propitiation is a sacrifice or gift that a penitent party offers an angry or offended party, like a dozen roses from a husband for a wife. It makes no sense, as far as I can tell, to suggest that Paul here refers to Christ as the gift that penitent humanity offers an offended God. Indeed, Paul says explicitly, "*God put [him] forward*" [*proetheto ho theos*; 3:25]. Bailey rightly notes, "Yet no one has ever succeeded in showing how God is supposed to have presented humanity (or himself?) with a gift that people normally presented to the gods" (ibid.). Sensing this problem, a number of exegetes have preferred the translation "expiation." This, however, would be a singularly unbiblical use of *hilastērion*.

36. Ibid.

the sacrifice, the place where the sacrifice is performed, and the sacrifice itself.[37]

The gentile proselyte has missed the mechanism God offers for reconciliation with himself, and the proselyte's influence over other gentiles (see Rom 2:19–21) threatened the heart of Paul's mission to the gentiles.

As Paul continues, he employs two prepositional phrases to further explain how Jesus becomes this "locus of atonement":

- "by means of faithfulness" [*dia tēs pisteōs*];
- "in his blood" [*en tō autou haimati*].

Both of these phrases present difficulties. Regarding the first, Whose faithfulness? Does God put Jesus forward as a *hilastērion* through/by *humanity's* faith in his blood? If so, Jesus' followers appropriate atonement through/by faith in the power of his blood.[38] This seems the most straightforward reading of v. 25's syntax. However, so far in Romans 3 "faithfulness" [*pistis*] has always been followed by a genitive noun and referred to "the faithfulness" of a person (either of God [3:3] or of Jesus Christ [3:22]). If possible, we ought to understand Paul's use of *pistis* here in v. 25 the same way. I would therefore suggest that *dia tēs pisteōs* refers, as in 3:22, to the faithfulness of Jesus to Israel's God. It was through/by Jesus' faithfulness that God put him forward as a *hilastērion*.

If this is the correct reading of the first prepositional phrase, what does the second ("in his blood") mean? I doubt Paul is saying that Jesus exhibited "faith in his [own] blood." If "faith in his blood" is the right way to interpret 3:25, then Paul must surely be talking about humanity's faith in the atoning power and efficacy of Jesus' blood. Reading *pistis* as a reference to humanity's faith, however, runs into the problem we discussed in the previous paragraph. "In [*en*] his blood," however, is not the only way to translate this phrase. The preposition, *en*, in addition to identifying a location ("in"), can also communicate the means by which a verbal idea is accomplished.[39] We might translate Rom 3:25: "whom God put forward as the *hilastērion* (the locus of salvation) through his faithfulness, achieved by means of his blood." In this reading, Jesus' will-

---

37. Grieb, *Story*, 41.

38. See Matera, *Romans*, 98.

39. BDAG (s.v., §8): "marker denoting the object to which someth[ing] happens or in which someth[ing] shows itself, or by which someth[ing] is recognized," for which they offer the glosses, "*to, by, in connection with*." If we translate *en* in this manner, Jesus' blood is the object "by which" God put Jesus forward as the *hilastērion*.

ingness to face death on a cross according to God's will demonstrates his obedient faithfulness to God.[40]

Jesus' death, then, reveals God's righteousness, which is exactly the point Paul introduced in Rom 3:21–22. Paul now explains God's righteousness in terms of "the passing over of sins previously committed," another difficult phrase. What does it mean to say that God "passed over" [*paresin*] previous sins? How does this relate to the Jewish cult, whose systems of sacrifices and offerings were meant to address the people's sins and restore their relationship to God?

Once again our decision to understand Paul's interlocutor as a gentile proselyte offers a way forward. Paul is certainly aware of the Jerusalem temple and its mechanisms for dealing with (= atoning for) Israel's sin. But God did not put any such system in place to deal with (= atone for) the sins of the gentiles.[41] The righteousness of God—the key theme of this entire paragraph—requires that God acknowledge and judge gentile sin rather than simply brush it aside. After all, "[God] will repay each person according to their deeds. . . . For there is no favoritism with God" (Rom 2:6, 11). But now, in the present time [*en tō nyn* kairō; 3:26], God's forbearance has resulted in the opportunity for the nations to find peace with the Creator God on account of Jesus' faithfulness. The proselyte's submission to Torah has missed the actual mechanisms by which, according to Paul, God reveals his righteousness, to the Jew first as well as to the gentile.

Fielding Objections (Rom 3:27–31)

> **27** "Where, then, is boasting?" It is excluded. "By means of what understanding of Torah? One of works?" No, but by means of Torah understood through faith. **28** For we reckon a person is justified by faith apart from works of Torah. **29** Or is God [the God] of the Jews only? "No; [he is God] also of the gentiles." Yes, [he is God] also of the gentiles, **30** since God is one, and he will justify the circumcision by faith and the uncircumcision through faith. **31** "Do we, then, nullify Torah by our faith?" By no means! Rather, we establish Torah.

---

40. I am reading the words "his blood" as a synecdochical reference to Jesus' death.
41. See Jewett, *Romans*, 291; Matera, *Romans*, 99.

If You Call Yourself a Jew

We have not heard Paul speak as the interlocutor since Rom 3:9.[42] Now, in 3:27, after Paul makes clear that the gentiles are made right with God on the basis Jesus' faithfulness to God, the interlocutor asks, "Where, then, is boasting?" Though "boasting" carries a strongly negative connotation in English, that was not necessarily true of the Greek word, *kauchēsis*. In the LXX, *kauchēsis* describes God's name (lit. "the name of your boasting"; 1 Chr 29:13) or the crown that comes with old age (Prov 16:31; Ezek 16:12) and so means something like "glory" or "honor." *Kauchēsis* can also mean "prize" or "beauty" (see Ezek 16:17, 39; 23:26, 42; 24:25). Sirach 31 even refers to the reward for the person who is not driven by gold as *kauchēsis*: "Who has been tested by it and been made perfect? So it will be as a boast [= prize, reward; *kauchēsin*] for him. Who was able to transgress and did not transgress, and to do evil and did not do so? Therefore his good things will be confirmed, and his acts of charity an assembly will recount" (Sir 31:10–11 NETS). In only one of its ten occurrences in the LXX does *kauchēsis* have similar negative connotations as "boasting" (see Jer 12:13).[43] So when the interlocutor asks, "Where, then, is boasting?" he is asking a question about the positive benefits of observing Torah. We might paraphrase, "Where, then, is the value, the beauty, of me—a proselyte—observing Torah?"[44]

---

42. *Pace* Matera (*Romans*, 99), Paul does not "return to the form of the diatribe" in v. 27. Rather, he has been engaged in diatribe, but speaking in his own voice, since 3:9.

43. See Hahn, "καύχημα," 1:227–28. Jewett inexplicably says, "While Paul uses *kauchēsis* only here and in [Rom] 15:17, the negative connotation is consistent with LXX usage (Sir 31:10; Prov 16:31; etc.)" (*Romans*, 295 n.10). This is exactly wrong. As I have shown, only once in the LXX is *kauchēsis* used negatively. Moo is even less helpful: "'Boasting,' of course, is a sin common to all people—it reflects the pride that is at the root of so much human sinfulness" (*Romans*, 246). The LXX's use of *kauchēsis* offers absolutely no support for this comment, though we should recognize that Moo seems to be taking care to avoid the implication that Jews were any more inclined toward "boasting" than other nations. This concern is exactly right, even if it does not reflect Paul's discussion here at the end of Romans 3.

44. *Pace*, Matera, *Romans*, 100. Despite his more traditional construal of Paul's rhetoric in Romans 2–3, Simon Gathercole rightly explains "boasting": "[T]he Jewish boast is defined neither as a legalistic, self-centered self-confidence which is negative by definition, nor as a confidence based merely on divine election. Rather, it is a conviction of God's gracious election of Israel, and that the nation (or a particular individual or group within the nation) was fulfilling the Law and would be vindicated at the eschaton on that basis. Thus another element of boasting is that it is not a generalised confidence, but is usually oriented toward God's vindication. It is also, then, not merely a feeling of superiority in relation to gentiles (thus Stendahl), but a confidence that God will act on Israel's behalf" (Gathercole, "After the New Perspective," 306).

The Righteousness of God apart from Torah

At this point in Romans 3, traditional interpretations of Romans get very confused. Commentators too often arbitrarily decide that, sometimes, when Paul uses *nomos*, he is not referring to Torah. Instead, sometimes he just means "principle," or "rule," or "law" with a lower-case *l*.[45] This may be possible, in which case Paul would be playing with the word *nomos* since he has usually if not always used *nomos* up to this point to refer to "Torah." But if we suppose that Paul is playing with *nomos*, then we put ourselves in the position of saying that Paul uses this one word twice in a very short span (v. 27) with two very different meanings. When Paul qualifies *nomos* as being "of works," he means "Torah." But when he qualifies *nomos* as being "of faithfulness," he cannot mean "Torah." This reading imports a conviction from outside the text (*viz.* that "Torah" has something to do with "works" but not with "faith"), a conviction that, as we will see, Paul clearly does not share.

Others have argued, convincingly, that Paul consistently uses *nomos* to refer to Torah. When Paul, speaking as the interlocutor, asks, "Through what kind of law? Of works?" [*ergōn*], the question focuses on the approach to Torah that excludes boasting. Paul's response excludes works. Instead, Torah understood in terms of "faith" [*pisteōs*] excludes boasting. Robert Jewett offers a clear expression of this reading:

> The Jewish concept of law is thus rendered ambivalent. Having distinguished in 2:17–24 between true and false uses of the law and in 3:21 between the law as a power that demands righteousness that humans cannot achieve and law as Scripture that affirms righteousness through faith, Paul now creates a distinction between the "law of works" that demands good works but produces only the awareness of sin, and the "law of faith" derived from Christ. This is a distinction between an interpretation of law that enhances boasting and an interpretation of law that excludes boasting.[46]

Dunn paraphrases Paul's question in 3:27, "What kind of understanding of the law is this?"[47] Jewett and Dunn (and others) offer a better understanding of v. 27, which I modify by reading v. 27 in terms of Paul's gentile

---

45. See Moo, *Romans*, 249–50. Matera avoids the issue with a breath-taking, "Whatever the precise nuance of the text, its fundamental meaning should be evident" (*Romans*, 100). This is a failure of commentary; *nomos* is one of the key terms in this section of Romans, and Matera dismisses it with a rhetorical wave of the hand!

46. Jewett, *Romans*, 297.

47. Dunn, *Romans*, 1:186.

interlocutor.[48] Paul denies any value [*kauchēsis*] to the proselyte's submission to Torah's distinctive ordinances (especially circumcision). Instead, Paul enjoins "trust" or "faith" [*pistis*] in Torah's testimony to the righteousness of God that has been revealed apart from Torah (see 3:21). This, Paul tells his interlocutor, is the appropriate response to Torah, "for we reckon a person is justified by faith apart from works of Torah" (3:28).

Paul now goes on the offensive, posing a question for his interlocutor: "Or is God [the God] of the Jews only?" The interlocutor, having already been persuaded that Israel's God is God of the whole world, can only answer, "No; [he is God] also of the gentiles." Paul then pushes the conclusion aggressively: "Yes, [he is God] also of the gentiles, since God is one, and he will justify the circumcision by faith and the uncircumcision through faith." Paul clearly alludes to the Shema (Deut 6:4–9): "Listen, Israel: The Lord your God, the Lord is one" [*kyrios heis estin*; Deut 6:4 LXX]. This one God justifies both the circumcision and the uncircumcision by faith, and so the gentile proselyte's submission to circumcision comes to naught (recall Rom 2:25–29 and my comments there).

The interlocutor has one final question, though the first-person plural form of the question ("Do *we* nullify . . .") may suggest that Paul portrays his dialogue partner as one who understands and concedes the force of his argument. "Do we, then, nullify Torah by our faith?" Paul answers with the strong negative, "By no means!" [*mē genoito*], and explains, "Rather, we establish [*histanomen*] Torah." I interpret the verb *histanomen* as a synonym of Matt 5:17's *plēroō* ("fulfill"). Torah's *intention* was to fulfill the promises given to Abraham and his offspring; its *result*, however, was the knowledge of sin (Rom 3:20). The gospel, Paul's proclamation of the righteousness of God revealed by Jesus' faithfulness, "establishes" or "fulfills" Torah's intention. This gospel results in the Abrahamic blessing for all nations (see Gen 12:3). Gentiles, then, ought not submit to Torah's yoke. The way is open for them to fulfill "Torah's righteous commandments" (see 2:26) without literally keeping all its ordinances.

---

48. Similarly, see Garroway, *Gentile-Jews*, 100: "Asked about the enduring validity of the boast previously available to Jews, Paul explains that it has been eliminated, not by the Law *as it is fulfilled through works*, which was the source of the boast, but by the Law *as it is fulfilled by the faith made possible in Christ and now accessible to all*" (my emphases).

The Righteousness of God apart from Torah

Abraham, Father of Many Nations (Rom 4:1–25)

1 "What then? Shall we claim to have found Abraham [to be] our forefather according to the flesh? **2** For if Abraham was justified by works, he has a boast (but not before God)." **3** For what does Scripture say? "But Abraham believed God, and it was reckoned to him for righteousness" (Gen 15:6). **4** For the one who works, [his] pay is not considered as a favor but as a debt. **5** But for the one who does not work, but rather sets his faith upon the one who justifies the ungodly, his faith is reckoned for righteousness. **6** In the same way, David speaks of the blessing of the person for whom God reckons righteousness apart from works:

> **7** "Blessed [are those] whose lawless acts are forgiven,
> and whose sins have been covered over.
> **8** Blessed is the man whose sin the Lord does not reckon"
> (Ps 31:1–2 LXX).

9 Is this blessing, then, for the circumcision or also for the uncircumcision? For we are saying "The faith was reckoned to Abraham for righteousness." **10** How, then, was it reckoned? After he had been circumcised or when he was still uncircumcised? **"Not while he was circumcised but when he was still uncircumcised."** **11** Then he received the sign of circumcision as a seal of the righteousness [he experienced] while he was still uncircumcised, so that he might be the father of everyone who believes through uncircumcision (so that righteousness might be reckoned to them also) **12** as well as the father of the circumcision, for those who, not by circumcision alone, but also by following in the footprints of the faithfulness of our father Abraham, which he had while uncircumcised.

13 For the promise—that he would be the heir of the world—was not spoken to Abraham or to his offspring through Torah but through the righteousness [that is revealed] by faithfulness. **14** For if they are heirs on the basis of Torah, then faithfulness is void and the promise is nullified. **15** For Torah produces wrath, but where there is no Torah neither is there transgression. **16** For this reason, [righteousness is revealed (or reckoned)] by faithfulness in order that [it might be considered] as a favor, so that the promise would be secure for all [his] offspring, not only those [who are offspring] on the basis of Torah but also for the offspring on the basis of the faithfulness of Abraham, who is the father of us all. **17** As it is written, "I have set you the father of many nations" (Gen 17:5), in whose sight he trusted in God, who makes live those who are dead and calls things that are not as though they were. **18** He trusted against hope—and upon hope!—that he would become the father of many nations, just as it had been said: "In such a manner will your offspring be" (Gen 15:5). **19** And without growing weak in faithfulness, he considered his own body [already] dead (since he was about a hundred years old) and the necrosis of Sarah's womb. **20** But for the sake of the promise of God, he did not hesitate in unfaithfulness, but rather he was invigorated by faithfulness, thereby giving glory to God. **21** And he was fully convinced that [God] is able even to do that which had been promised. **22** Therefore, it was [also] reckoned to him for righteousness. **23** But "it was reckoned to him" was not written for his sake alone **24** but also for our sake, for whom it is about to be reckoned, we who have set our faith upon the one who raised Jesus, our Lord, from the dead, **25** who was handed over for our transgressions and was raised for our justification.

After his very dense and complicated argument through Romans 3 (esp. 3:21–31), Paul finally arrives at the point to which he has been aiming since 1:16–17: Abraham, not Moses, provides Paul his clearest glimpse of God's intentions and plans for the nations (including Israel). Moses spoke with God and received from him Torah, the oracles of God (3:2). Torah was inextricably linked with the Abrahamic promise.[49] "Part of Paul's goal for his mainly gentile communities was to ground them in the heritage of Abraham not as Jews but as legitimate gentile heirs of the promises."[50] But the promise was not just land and numerous descendants; the promise included the blessing of YHWH to all the nations of the earth [*pasai hai phylai tēs gēs*; Gen 12:3 LXX]. As a result, in Paul's explanation about how *pistis* ("faith" or "trust") in God results in the justification of all nations and their salvation, the Jew first as well as the gentile, it was always inevitable that Paul was going to appeal to the story of Abraham.

My translation of v. 1 follows Hays's argument that Paul is asking whether "we" (Paul and his interlocutor, but also the Christians in Rome) have found Abraham our forefather "according to (or in the manner of) the flesh."[51] The question arises naturally, given that Paul imagines himself speaking with a proselyte to Judaism. This proselyte has submitted to circumcision (literally, in his flesh), but Paul argues that Abraham was already the father of many nations even before his circumcision. His descendants

---

49. The theme of God's oath to the patriarchs is ubiquitous throughout the Books of Moses; e.g., Gen 50:24; Exod 32:13; 33:1; Deut 1:8; 6:10; 9:5, 27; 29:12; 30:20; 34:4.

50. Ehrensperger, "Scriptural Reasoning."

51. See Richard Hays's essay, "Abraham as Father of Jews and Gentiles" (*Conversion*, 61–84). Unlike Hays, however, I punctuate the text so that the first question is *ti oun* (What then?), and *eroumen* begins the second question ("Shall we claim to have found ... ?").

are not "according to the flesh" [*kata sarka*; 4:1].⁵² Abraham's relationship with the Creator God was not "on the basis of works" [*ex ergōn*]. If it had been, he would have had something to be proud of. Instead, Paul reads the Scripture at face value: "But Abraham believed [or trusted] God, and it was reckoned to him for righteousness" (Rom 4:3). Paul draws a sharp contrast between two verbs in the next two verses: "working" [*ergazomai*] and "believing" [*pisteuō*]. Abraham's circumcision did not "produce" (another translation of *ergazomai*) righteousness; instead, righteousness was credited to him on account of his faith, his trust, his believing in the Creator God.

Paul enlists David as further support of his case (4:6–8). David—an ethnic as well as religious Jew, who lived fully under the systems of atonement provided by Torah—experienced the atonement offered by Torah as God's grace (or "blessing" [*makarismos*]), just as Abraham did. David's example might confirm the gentile proselyte's view that Torah provides the terms of (or appropriate response to) the atonement and forgiveness God's people receive from him. But Paul asks about the conditions of Abraham's reckoning of righteousness; was it "[A]fter he had been circumcised or when he was still uncircumcised?" (see Rom 4:9–10a). The interlocutor, aware of the narrative of Genesis—in which the promise was given in Genesis 12, the notice of Abraham's credit of righteousness happens at 15:6, and the covenantal seal of circumcision does not appear until Genesis 17—can only answer, "Not while he was circumcised but when he was still uncircumcised" (Rom 4:10b).

This exchange between Paul and his proselyte interlocutor gives us an insight into the earlier passage, Rom 2:25–29. Abraham's circumcision was the sign (or seal) of a covenant that God made with Abraham beforehand. As a sign/seal of a preexisting covenant, Abraham's circumcision was significant only on the basis that Abraham had already believed the Creator God and exhibited faith (or trust) in him. This is the inward/secret/spiritual dimension of being "a Jew" that Paul referred to there. Abraham exhibited this inward/secret/spiritual dimension to being "a Jew" (remember 2:17!) *prior to* bearing the outward/visible/fleshly marks

---

52. Though see Garroway, *Gentile-Jews*, 101–9. According to Garroway, Paul's point is precisely that even his uncircumcised, gentile converts may lay claim to that most Jewish of epithets, "descendant of Abraham," and that despite the foreskin on their penises, they have received the circumcision of Christ. Grieb, on the other hand, answers Paul's rhetorical question in Rom 4:1 with an emphatic, "No! Of course not" (Grieb, *Story*, 46).

of the covenant. The gentile proselyte who accepts those outward/visible/ fleshly marks has missed the basis on which God offers his blessing and displays his righteousness. Both Jew and gentile must walk, then, in the footsteps of "the faithfulness of our father Abraham,"[53] which faithfulness he exhibited even while he was uncircumcised.

Paul generalizes from Abraham's faithfulness to the relationship between the promise [*hē epangelia*; 4:13], Torah, and faith in Rom 4:13–25. Paul does not seem too concerned that his Roman audience in particular or Second-Temple Judaism in general thought Torah enabled a person to *earn* God's blessing, whereas the promise offers God's blessing only by faith. Instead, the point is that Torah came after the promise and resulted in neither the blessing of Israel (remember, she chose death and curse rather than the life and blessing God placed before her; see Deuteronomy 28–32) nor of the nations (see Rom 1:18—2:16).[54] Now, the righteousness of God revealed apart from Torah confirms and fulfills the promise to Abraham. If Torah had been God's last word, "faith"—both Abraham's confidence in God and YHWH's trustworthiness—would have been void and the promise nullified (4:14). Paul draws this conclusion not because Torah is "not-faith" but because Israel, historically, failed to keep the terms God laid down in the Torah itself. In the years between Abraham and Moses, when Abraham's seed did not keep the terms of Torah (which had not yet been given), there was no transgression [*parabasis*; 4:15]. Once God had given Torah to Israel, and he set before them the choice between blessing/life, on the one hand, and curse/death, on the other, Torah brought about the wrath of God against Israel's transgressions (4:15). As a result, in order to make the promise secure for all of Abraham's seed [*bebaian tēn epangelian panti tō spermati*; 4:16], the basis of the promise must be faithfulness (such as Abraham exhibited) rather than Torah.

Paul then reiterates the point he implied in the question he posed back in v. 1: God has made Abraham the father of many nations, not just of the Jews (Rom 4:17). As a result, the gentile proselyte's endeavors to bear the label "Jew" (see 2:17) prove inappropriate. Paul returns to the

---

53. Notice the clearly subjective genitive construction, *pisteōs tou patros hēmōn Abraam* ("faithfulness of our father Abraham"; 4:12); it would be nonsensical to suggest that Paul might be speaking of faith *in* our father Abraham (an objective genitival reading)!

54. In his discussion of Romans 2, Akio Ito rightly insists on reading Romans within an emphatically covenantal context: "In a sense we can regard Romans 2 as a Pauline version of the list of blessings and curses in Deuteronomy 27–30 where the covenantal overtones are apparent" ("Romans 2," 25).

theme of the Creator God in v. 17, which theme figured prominently in Rom 1:18–32. God makes the dead live, not simply by restoring life after death, but even by the initial giving of life (see Gen 2:7) and calls things that are not as if they were. Abraham set his hope in this Creator God. Paul highlights Abraham's faithfulness to (= Abraham's confidence in) God, which is a parallel example to the faithfulness of Jesus that Paul described in Rom 3:21–26. Abraham exhibited total confidence in God's faithfulness (= God's reliability), despite the absurdity of the promise, namely that a man so old he might as well be dead (not to mention his old, dead wife) would become the father of many nations (4:18–21). Abraham's confidence in God's reliability was reckoned as righteousness, and this apart from Torah (4:22)!

Finally, Paul generalizes beyond Abraham's faithfulness to God—and God's faithfulness to Abraham—to make the point that the Scripture was not written for Abraham alone but also for us [*alla kai di' hēmas*; 4:24]. (Remember, Paul is speaking to a gentile proselyte and making the point that Abraham's faithfulness, reckoned for him as righteousness, is described "also for us," i.e., for Paul [a Jew] and his interlocutor [a gentile].) Now, however, God is not described in Abrahamic terms (as the one who can reinvigorate the elderly) but in terms of Jesus Christ: God is "the one who raised Jesus, our Lord, from the dead" [*ton egeiranta Iēsoun ton kyrion hēmōn ek nekrōn*; 4:24]. The link with Abraham's faith, who believed in a God "who makes live those who are dead" [*zōopoiountos tous nekrous*; 4:17], is clear and even co-opts Abraham's faithfulness for Jesus: What Abraham believed God *could* do for him, God *did* do for Jesus. This Jesus was handed over [*paredothē*; 4:25 (a reference to the crucifixion)] on account of our transgressions, and he was raised on account of our justification (see Rom 3:26).

∽

This brings the first major section of Romans (1:18—4:25) to a close. Paul has established the universal wickedness of the nations/gentiles, who indulge in depraved debauchery (1:18–32) or self-righteous moralism (2:1–16) without any recognition of the Creator God of Israel. Those gentiles who do worship Israel's God have been compelled—whether internally (on their own accord) or externally (by Jews who proselytize gentiles)—to bend their necks to the full yoke of Torah (2:17ff.). Paul objects even more fiercely to this gentile than he did to the immoral gentile and the self-righteous gentile.

Notice, though, that *nowhere* in Romans 1–4 have we read Paul as critiquing, arguing with, or finding any fault whatsoever with "Judaism" or with Torah. And *nowhere* have we found Paul opposing a legalistic "works-righteousness" with righteousness by faith. The question of grace versus works has dominated our reading of Romans for too long, and the reading of Romans 1–4 that we have put forward in these last four chapters has hopefully demonstrated that this just is not the question Paul is answering.[55] If Paul is not addressing the issue of works versus grace, what issue have we found at the heart of Romans to this point? Paul has been addressing the issue of Torah (not works) versus Jesus (not grace). The problem with Torah is not that it presents a works-based system of atonement. The problem with Torah is that God's people—the Jews—have been unfaithful [*apistia*; 3:3] to the grace God offers them through Torah. But God has been faithful [*hē pistis tou theou*; 3:3] to his promises, and Jesus, rather than Torah, is the means of his faithfulness. This, I think, is the heart of the message of Romans, or at least of the first four chapters of Romans.

---

55. Elliott rightly challenges reading Romans 1–4 as a "debate with Judaism" (*Rhetoric*, 167–223). Despite insight in some important areas (e.g., Romans' exclusively gentile audience), Elliott misses the texture of Paul's rhetoric as a diatribe with a gentile interlocutor.

6

Christ, the New Adam

Undoing the Curse of Death

Paul, I suggest, is telling the story of the people of the Messiah in terms of the new exodus. Jesus' people are liberated people, on their way home to their promised land. . . . Paul, like many other Second Temple Jews, longed for the day when God would fulfill the promises made to Abraham by bringing Israel back from exile, repeating what had been done at the exodus. Only this time, through the work of the Messiah, it would be on a different scale. This time the whole cosmos would be involved. This would be the revelation of the righteousness of God before the whole world. Paul's mind has already been moving in this way in chaps. 2 and 4; now he will develop the picture far more extensively. If he is talking about salvation, he is talking about the new exodus.[1]

Unlike Wright, I am not so confident that Paul "is talking about the new exodus," though he is talking about a larger theological pattern of which the exodus is one instance. In light of Paul's appeal to Adam as a "pattern" or "type" [*typos*; see 5:14] of Jesus ("the one about to come"; *tou mellontos*), Paul is appealing to creation motifs as much as, if not more than, to exodus motifs. But the biblical account of the exodus itself appeals to creation motifs, in which God brings forth through the water a

---

1. Wright, "Romans," 510, 511.

people for himself and undoes the estrangement from God that resulted in Genesis 3.[2]

The two paragraphs of Romans 5 provide an important transition from Paul's discussion in Romans 1–4 and the rest of the letter. When read from the perspective of systematic theology, Romans 1–4 sets a schema for the justification of all individuals, and Romans 5–8 moves on to address the sanctification of individuals.[3] We have offered a significantly different reading. Romans 1–4 has focused not so much on the justification of individuals as on the righteousness of God, his faithfulness to his creation and the promises he made on its behalf to Abraham. The topic/theme of justification has arisen at key points, but it has not been the main focus at any point thus far. This new perspective will continue to open the way for a coherent and compelling reading of Romans as Paul finally begins to focus intently on the center of his gospel: Jesus, the Christ.

Reconciliation with God, and More (Rom 5:1–11)

> **1** Therefore, since we are justified by faithfulness, we have peace with God through our Lord Jesus Christ, **2** through whom we have received access [by faith(fulness)] to this favor, in which we are standing, and we boast in the hope of the glory of God. **3** And not only this, but we also boast in our afflictions, because we know that affliction produces endurance, **4** and endurance [produces] testing, and testing [produces] hope. **5** *And hope does not disappoint, because the love of God is poured out in our hearts by the Holy Spirit, which is given to us.* **6** For while we were still weak, Christ died at the right time for the ungodly. **7** For rarely will someone die for a righteous person; though perhaps a person might dare to die for a good person. **8** But God demonstrates his own love for us, because while we were still sinners, Christ died for us. **9** Therefore, since we have now been justified by his blood, how much more shall we be saved, through him, from his wrath. **10** For if, while we were his enemies, we were reconciled to God by the death of his son, how much more, now that we are reconciled, will we be saved by his life. **11** And not only this, but we also boast in God through our Lord Jesus Christ, through whom we now have received reconciliation.

---

2. Similarly, see Grieb, *Story*, 56–84. For another reading of Romans that emphasizes resonances with Israel's exodus traditions, see Keesmaat, "Intertextual Transformation," 29–56.

3. Wright, "Romans," 509; for a detailed reading of Romans by a systematic theologian, see Cottrell, *Romans*.

Christ, the New Adam

In Rom 3:21—4:25, Paul taught his proselyte interlocutor that being made right with God—justification [*dikaioō*]—happens by means of faithfulness, both the faithfulness of Jesus to the Creator God (which faithfulness contrasts with Israel's *un*faithfulness) and the response of faith, first from the Jew and also from the gentile. This double action *vis-à-vis* "faithfulness" recalls Rom 1:17, where Paul spoke of the righteousness of God revealed "by faith for faith" [*ek pisteōs eis pistin*]. That is, Paul refers to the revelation of the righteousness of God *by* Jesus' faithfulness to the Creator God [*ek pisteōs*] and *to* the one who demonstrates confidence or trust in the gospel [*eis pistin*].

Paul now explains the result of justification by faith: "we have peace with God [*eirēnēn echomen pros ton theon*] through our Lord Jesus Christ."[4] The theme of "peace" puts us in touch with one of the Bible's key concerns: the resolution of the enmity between the Creator God and his rebellious creation, epitomized by (but not limited to) the sin of Adam in the Garden of Eden. Dunn rightly resists spiritualizing "peace" (i.e., as inner peace) and insists that "peace" is a covenantal concept.[5] This "peace" stands in antithetical relation to the "wrath of God" [*orgē theou*; 1:18] that is being revealed from heaven against gentile idolatry and depravity. Sin results in estrangement and brings the wrath of God. Faithfulness results in justification and brings peace with God for those who respond in faith to the message of the gospel.

Paul identifies this peace as "access" [*prosagōgē*] to the favor (or grace) of God. *Prosagōgē* occurs only two other times in the NT, both in Ephesians:

- ... because through him we have access [*tēn prosagōgēn*], both [i.e. those who are far and those who are near] by the one Spirit, to the Father. (Eph 2:18)

- ... in whom we have boldness and access [*prosagōgēn*], with confidence, through the faithfulness of him (or in him). (Eph 3:12)

According to Liddell and Scott, *prosagōgē* means "*approach, access to* a person, esp. to a kings [*sic*] presence" in both Xenophon and the NT.[6] This

---

4. Stowers (*Rereading*, 248–49) argues for the subjunctive *echōmen* ("let us have") as the original reading (see also Jewett, *Romans*, 344, 348). For more information, see Metzger's discussion in *Textual Commentary*, 452, as well as the commentaries.

5. Dunn, *Romans*, 1:247.

6. LSJ, s.v. BDAG (s.v.) agrees: "A status factor is implied (cp. X[enophon], *Cyr.* 7, 5, 45 of access to Cyrus for an audience)." The LXX does not use *prosagōgē* (or the related adjective, *prosagōgos*, "attractive").

last nuance—the particular connotation of access to a *king's* presence—is especially interesting in light of Paul's reference to this access being "through" [*dia*] the Lord Jesus Christ.[7] J. R. Harrison, in his exploration of Paul's apocalyptic language in 1 Thessalonians, explains,

> From the time of Augustus onwards, *kyrios* was transferred as an honorific from the eastern ruler cult to the imperial cult. So thoroughly had the Julian-Claudians eclipsed their political rivals that talk of "another Lord," without any deference to or incorporation into their power base, was inconceivable.[8]

This approach to Paul's reference to Jesus as "Lord" [*kyrios*] argues that Paul denies this title to Caesar and insists that Jesus—*and only Jesus*—is Lord.[9] In a world in which the worship of the deified emperor was everywhere (and everywhere enforced), the proclamation and worship of another *kyrios* in place of Caesar stood out as conspicuous, even treacherous.[10] Harrison is probably right, though Denny Burk rightly cautions us to remember that "Paul's selection of terms is driven in large part by his interface with the LXX Scriptures."[11] More importantly, however, Paul

---

7. The reference to "the Lord Jesus Christ" comes at the end of Rom 5:1. The preposition *dia*, however, takes the relative pronoun *hou* ("whom") as its object. The relative pronoun's antecedent is obviously "the Lord Jesus Christ." See, e.g., Jewett, *Romans*, 349.

8. Harrison, "Imperial Gospel," 78. For cautions regarding the appeal to imperial uses of key terms in Paul's gospel (*kurios*, *euangelion*, *parousia*, etc.), see Burk, "Paul's Gospel."

9. Remember the unusual (for Paul) formulation at Rom 1:3–4, which explicitly portrays Jesus as the Davidic King and "son of God" [*huiou theou*; 1:4]. For the imperial (and specifically Augustan) dynamics of this phrase, see Kim, "Anarthrous."

10. Wright identifies the imperial cult, the means by which Rome's subjects experienced Caesar as a god and subjected themselves to him, as more than simply "one new religion among many in the Roman world": "[The cult of Caesar] was actually the means (as opposed to overt large-scale military presence) whereby the Romans managed to control and govern such huge areas as came under their sway. The emperor's far-off presence was made ubiquitous by the standard means of statues and coins (the latter being the principal mass communication of the ancient world), reflecting his image throughout his domains; he was the great benefactor, through whom the blessings of justice and peace, and a host of lesser ones besides, were showered outwards upon the grateful populace—who in turn worshipped him, honored him, and paid him taxes" ("Paul's Gospel," 161). See also Stegemann, "Coexistence and Transformation."

11. Burk, "Paul's Gospel," 317. He continues, "With respect to *kyrios* in particular, Paul's primary motivation for using this term would have been his desire to link Messiah Jesus with the 'Lord' of the Greek OT, where the divine name 'Yahweh' is frequently rendered as *kyrios*. These observations should at least give us pause before concluding too quickly that Paul was trolling around Greco-Roman cults in order to find linguistic grist for his Christology" (ibid., 317; see pp. 315–19).

Christ, the New Adam

does *not* say we have "access" *to* the Lord Jesus Christ. Rather, we have access *through* the Lord Jesus Christ "to this favor" [*eis tēn charin tautēn*], which itself offers "hope" for access to "the glory of God" [*tēs doxēs tou theou*; 5:2].

Paul reminds his readers that we "are standing and we boast [*kauchōmetha*] in the hope of the glory of God" (5:2) and declares to them that "we boast [*kauchōmetha*] in our afflictions" (5:3). Remember that Paul has already declared that "boasting" [*kauchēsis*] is excluded by means of faith (Rom 3:27). Now Paul affirms the appropriate use of boasting, only now in the hope of [beholding] God's glory and the afflictions he and his readers endure because of that hope. How can Paul both exclude and affirm boasting in the span of just over one chapter? We have already encountered the answer in our comments on 3:27: despite the wisdom of so many commentators, *kauchēsis* did not have the same negative connotations in Hellenistic Jewish Greek as our English word "boast."[12] Paul informed his proselyte interlocutor in 3:27 that the *kauchēsis* (= value, prize, beauty, boasting) of keeping Torah by works (circumcision, etc.) was excluded by virtue of keeping Torah by faith (worshipping the Creator God). And even though the works of Torah, which Paul insists were restricted to Israel, have lost their *kauchēsis*, Paul nevertheless boasts (= finds value in, cherishes, prizes) in his hope of beholding God's glory and the suffering he undergoes as his eyes are set on the object of his hope.

The chain of virtues in vv. 3-5 builds from "the afflictions" [*tais thlipsesin*; 5:3] of which he boasts. The individual items in the chain escalate logically until the climactic term, "the love of God" [*hē agapē tou theou*; 5:5] poured out in our hearts by the Holy Spirit:

- *We also boast in our afflictions, because we know that affliction produces [katergazetai] endurance.* Paul has already referred to "endurance" [*hypomonē*] at 2:7: "those who persistently [*kath' hypomonēn*] seek the glory and honor and immortality of a good deed [shall receive] eternal

---

12. *Pace* Jewett (*Romans*, 351), who reads the verb as a subjunctive ("*let us* boast ..."') on the basis that "[t]he indicative is particularly inappropriate in this instance, because it places both Paul and the Romans in the position of continuing to act contrary to his previous critique of boasting." Jewett then has to argue that Paul "recommend[s] *a revolutionary new form of boasting* to replace the claims of honorable status and performance that mark traditional religion in the Greco-Roman world" (my emphasis), though nothing about Paul's language in Rom 5:2 suggests he is using *kauchasthai* ("to boast") in an unusual way. (Note, however, the irony of *kauchasthai* in 5:3, in which Paul explains that we also "boast" in afflictions.) Besides, even Jewett's subjunctive interpretation does not escape the criticism that it contradicts his (i.e., Jewett's) interpretation of 3:27.

life."[13] In Romans 2, Paul's point was the just and impartial judgment of God on the basis of works, "for the Jew first as well as for the Greek" (2:9, 10). Paul expands the idea of endurance in Rom 5:3, anchoring to both the "suffering" (or "affliction"; *thlipsis*) that "endurance" presupposes, on one end, and to "testing," on the other.

- *And endurance [produces] testing.* Paul's only reference to "testing" [*dokimē*] in Romans occurs in 5:4, but every other use of the word in the NT also occurs in Paul's writings.[14] In 2 Corinthians, Paul describes his purpose for writing to the churches of Corinth in terms of ascertaining their "proof [*dokimēn*], if in all things you are obedient" (2 Cor 2:9). In the same letter he uses both *dokimē* and *thlipsis* in the same context to refer to the Macedonian Christians' "extreme testing of affliction" [*pollē dokimē thlipseōs* (8:2; see also 9:13)]. Finally, Paul uses *dokimē* to refer to "proof of character" or perhaps "proof of authority," whether of Paul himself (2 Cor 13:3) or of Timothy (Phil 2:22). Here in Romans, the status of being "proven" or "approved" comes on the far side of afflictions [*thlipseis*], trials that have been endured [*hypomonē*].

- *And testing [produces] hope.* Paul had already spoken of Abraham "hoping against hope" [*par' elpida ep' elpidi*] and believing God's promise that he would be father of many nations (4:18). The tested, vetted, approved character that is produced by enduring afflictions has hope in the justice of a God who reveals his wrath against injustice and evil. Even more recently, Paul spoke of his readers ("we") standing and boasting "in the hope [*elpidi*] of the glory of God" (5:2). What does it mean to hope "in the glory of God"? The most likely answer is that Paul hopes to see the glory of God, the Shekinah presence of God that descended upon the Tabernacle (Exod 40:34–38) and Solomon's temple upon their respective dedications (3 Kgdms 8:10–11; 2 Chr 5:13–14). The presence of the glory of God was fearsome in biblical tradition and was carefully managed so that the people did not come into contact with God.[15] However, Paul, convinced that faith makes us

---

13. Remember Paul's praise ("[the] glory and honor and immortality . . .") for "a good deed" [*ergou agathou*], or "a good work" in Rom 2:7. This praise should reinforce for us our conclusion, esp. in 3:27–28, that Paul is not addressing the problem of "works" [*erga*] but of "law," or Torah [*nomos*].

14. See 2 Cor 2:9; 8:2; 9:13; 13:3; Phil 2:22. Dunn suggests that Paul himself coined the word and that "the metaphor on which he draws . . . would have been familiar enough" (*Romans*, 1:251).

15. Even Moses and the priests were prevented from coming into contact with God's physical manifestation in a cloud of glory (see Exod 40:35; 3 Kgdms 8:11; 2 Chr 5:14)!

Christ, the New Adam

right with God [*dikaiōthentes*; 5:1] and results in peace with God, sets his hope in the prospect of beholding the glory of God.

- *And hope does not disappoint, because the love of God is poured out in our hearts by the Holy Spirit, which is given to us.* This is the first of nine references to "love" [*agapē*] in Romans, which is primarily love "of God" (5:5, 8; 8:39) but also "of Christ" (8:35) and "of the Spirit" (15:30). The remaining four uses of [*agapē*] prescribe appropriate behavior for the people of God (12:9; 13:10 [twice]); 14:15). In Romans 5, the love of God focuses our attention onto Israel's God, whose righteousness (= faithfulness) is on display "apart from Torah." Paul links the pouring out of God's love with "the Holy Spirit" [*pneumatos hagiou*]. The promise of God's Spirit upon his people was potent in the Hebrew Bible. The Lord promises through the prophet Joel that he "will pour out my Spirit upon all flesh" (3:1-5 LXX). The two terms *ekcheō* ("pour out") and *pneuma* ("Spirit") occur in both Rom 5:5 and Joel 3:1 LXX.[16] Paul will return to Joel 3 (LXX) in Romans 10, though here in Romans 5 the prophetic resonance remains implied rather than explicit.[17]

The remainder of the paragraph (Rom 5:6-11) expands on the final and climactic term of this ascending chain (affliction → endurance → testing → hope → love of God). The *agapē* of God is most clearly evident in his righteousness, his faithfulness to unfaithful humanity (the Jew first and also the Greek). And so Paul points to Jesus' death on behalf of humanity "while we were still weak" [*eti ... ontōn hēmōn asthenōn*; 5:6]. The language of "weakness" plays a key role in Romans. Paul has already described Abraham's faith in terms of him "not growing weak" [*mē asthenēsas*; 4:19]. Here he uses all-inclusive language ("*we* were weak") to describe the predicament in which all peoples, Jew as well as gentile, find themselves. Later, especially in Romans 14-15, Paul will employ the language of "weakness" to negotiate divisions among the Roman Christians. For now, however, all of Paul's readers are (or were) "weak," and while "we" were in this state "Christ died for the ungodly."[18]

---

16. Joel 3:1-5 LXX (= 2:28-32 MT). Dunn (*Romans*, 1:253) suggests that *ekkechytai* "had already become fixed within Christian terminology as a reference to the founding event of Pentecost." For a broader discussion of *ekcheō*, see Jewett, *Romans*, 356.

17. James Dunn also argues that "Paul's sequence of thought here [*viz.* Rom 5:3-5] was prompted by Joel 2:26-29" (*Romans*, 1:253).

18. Paul equates (or at least likens) "weakness" [*asthenōn*] with "ungodliness" [*asebōn*]. This is an interesting connection that we should perhaps explore later. Stowers (*Rereading*, 248) understands *asebōn* here in v. 6, as well as "sinners" [*hamartōloi*; 5:8]

If You Call Yourself a Jew

Paul ponders a hypothetical situation in Rom 5:7-8 that, quite frankly, makes little sense in English.[19] Paul contends that "rarely" [*molis*] would anyone die "for a righteous person" [*hyper dikaiou*], while it seems more likely [*tacha*; "perhaps"] to Paul that someone would die "for a good person" [*hyper tou agathou*]. Certainly this strikes us as exactly backward. In English, "righteous" is always a higher status—is always more deserving—than "good." The Greek word *agathos* ("good [man]"), however, differs from the English word *good*. For one thing, in addition to its moral sense (which mirrors the moral connotations of "good"), *agathos* has a secular sense on which Paul capitalizes in 5:7.

Andrew Clarke, citing A. W. H. Adkins, explains that *agathos*, "was amongst the most valued words of praise that could be attributed to a man in Greek society from Homeric days onwards. It described one who was valued because he was of considerable benefit to his immediate society."[20] The social value of being *agathos* appears to have been very important to the ancient Greeks, so that it even "took precedence over some of the other moral values, such as, for example, *dikaiosynē*" ("righteousness").[21] Adkins provides a helpful explanation why:

> To be *agathos* had always been more important than merely to be *dikaios*, and one's injustice did not traditionally—nor, it is clear, in the Athenian courts—impair one's *arete* ["goodness, virtue"]. Again, to be *agathos* was to be a specimen of the human being at his best, making to society the contribution that society valued most; and the poorer citizens could not deny this, nor yet that they were not *agathoi* themselves. In accepting *arete* as more important than *dikaiosune* they were of course not letting their hearts run away with their heads, but treating the well-being of the city as more important than the injustice of an individual: a calculation of advantages.[22]

---

and "enemies" [*echthroi*; 5:10], as ciphers for "gentiles." I find this an attractive proposal, except that I cannot see how it accounts for the first-person plural verbs and pronouns that Paul uses in this section (e.g., "while we were weak" [*ontōn hēmōn asthenōn*]. Paul clearly includes himself alongside his gentile readers under these negative labels (see Dunn, *Romans*, 1:254–55).

19. Matera (*Romans*, 134) offers almost no discussion of 5:7; he sweeps the difficulties of Paul's comparisons off the table with a simple (but unexplained), "this distinction is primarily for rhetorical effect." According to Andrew Clarke ("Good and Just," 128 n.2), this may be typical of Romans commentators.

20. Clarke, "Good and Just," 134. Clarke provides a helpful historical ("diachronic") survey of the connotations of *agathos* and *dikaios* ("righteous [man]"; see pp. 134–37).

21. Ibid., 135.

22. Adkins, *Moral Values*, 124 (cited in Clarke, "Good and Just," 135–36).

Christ, the New Adam

The social value of being *agathos* tapped into the cultural script of *benefaction*, in which the wealthy and élite members of a city provided goods and services to the city's population in exchange for public recognition, honor, and praise. The technical terms for a city's benefactors were *euergetai* and *agathopoioi*, both of which mean, literally, "doers of good." Clarke demonstrates "a definite connection in Hellenistic Greek between the *agathos* and the benefactor."[23] Paul's hypothetical scenario suggests that, though there is little or no likelihood that someone would voluntarily die for the sake of a just and upright person, it is more likely that a person would die on behalf of "the good man," the benefactor who had contributed real and concrete benefits for a city or community.[24] Paul moves *up to the top* of the social scale to find a person for whom someone might possibly give his life; in 5:8 he moves *down to the bottom* of that scale to find the person for whom Jesus Christ did in fact give himself. While "we" were yet sinners, Jesus—whose faithfulness reveals the righteousness of God (see 3:21–22)—died for "us."

Paul then draws the conclusion of vv. 1–11, a conclusion that we need to hold up against the beginning of the letter (1:18–32) to understand it properly. At the start of the body of Romans, Paul pointed to the revelation [*apokalyptetai*] of the wrath of God [*orgē theou*; 1:18] from heaven against the stark and depraved sinfulness of idolatrous gentiles. In Romans 1, Paul's rhetoric clearly pointed toward a gentile target: idolatrous gentiles, who failed to recognize the Creator as God and instead honored images of created beings, bore in their bodies, their minds, and their social structures the marks of God's wrath. Here in Romans 5, however, Paul has explained how "we" have been justified "by his blood" [*en tō haimati autou*; 5:9[25]], and he concludes that, if this is how we have been treated when

---

23. Clarke, "Good and Just," 140. Jewett approvingly cites Clarke's reading, though he also leans (unjustifiably, in my view) toward identifying all of Rom 5:7 as a later interpolation (see *Romans*, 359–60).

24. I find this reading significantly more plausible, historically and rhetorically, than Troy Martin's proposal that *tou agathou* in v. 7 refers to God ("Good," 55–70). Martin dismisses Clarke's reading as "less than conclusive" simply on the basis that *agathos* ("good man") is not synonymous with *euergetēs* ("benefactor"; see ibid., 56 n.2). However, Clarke's reading does not depend on the two terms being synonymous; it is enough that the two terms can, under certain conditions, refer to the same things (like "rocky" and "troubled," though not synonymous, both describe an imperfect childhood in the same way). Ironically, Martin's own proposal depends on the semantic overlap of *ho agathos* (and/or *to agathon*) and *ho theos*, even though these are certainly not synonymous!

25. See Rom 3:25 and my comments on *dia* [*tēs*] *pisteōs en tō autou haimati* ("through [the] faithfulness by his blood").

we were sinners, "how much more [*pollō mallon*] ... shall we be saved, through him, from his wrath [*apo tēs orgēs*]." The article *tēs* points back to his earlier references to wrath (1:18, but also 2:5, 8; 3:5; 4:15). God's wrath, which is revealed from heaven against the gentiles (1:18) and was the result—*but not the purpose!*—of Torah (4:15), no longer targets those for whom Christ died. Rather than being abandoned to the depravity that awaits idolatrous gentiles or the judgment that awaits the Jews, "we" have been reconciled to God [*katēllagēmen tō theō*]. Torah, on the basis of faith, excluded boasting (3:27). Jesus, on the basis of his faithfulness, opens up the way for us to boast in God (5:11; cf. 5:3).

Adam of Eden vs. Jesus of Nazareth (Rom 5:12–21)

> **12** For this reason, just as sin entered the world through one man, and death [entered] by means of sin, so in this way death was spread to everyone (in that everyone sinned). **13** For sin was in the world up until Torah, but it was not accounted because there was no Torah. **14** But death reigned from Adam until Moses, even over those who did not sin in the likeness of the transgression of Adam (who is a type of the one to come). **15** **"But isn't the gift just like the transgression?"** Yes. For since many died by means of one man's transgression, how much more did the favor of God—as well as the gift by means of his favor that is given by the one man, Jesus Christ—abound to the many. **16** **"And didn't the gift abound in the same way as sin abounded by the one who sinned?"** Yes. For, on the one hand, judgment abounded from the one man to the point of condemnation. But, on the other hand, the gift abounded from the transgression of the many to the point of justification. **17** For if, on the basis of the one man's transgression death reigned through the one man, how much more will those who receive the abundance of the grace and of the gift of righteousness reign in life through the one man, Jesus Christ. **18** So then, just as through one transgression [sin abounded] to all people for condemnation, in the same way through one righteous act [grace abounded] to all people for the justification of life. **19** For just as through the disobedience of the one man the many were rendered sinners, so also through the obedience of the one man the many will be rendered righteous. **20** But Torah came alongside so that transgression might increase. And where sin increased, grace abounded all the more, **21** so that just as sin reigned in death, so also grace might reign through righteousness for eternal life through Jesus Christ our Lord.

Christ, the New Adam

Paul's tone changes in Rom 5:12. His relatively straightforward writing in vv. 1-11 becomes dense and compacted in v. 12. In this section the themes of creation and rebellion (Genesis 1-3), which moved just under the surface of Paul's rhetoric ever since Rom 1:18, come to the fore as Paul brings Adam and Jesus alongside one another. His treatment of Adam and Jesus is largely symbolic and mythic rather than historical. That is, Paul understands both men as the embodiment of larger vices or virtues (sin and death, or grace and life, respectively), and most importantly, he treats them in stark, binary terms.[26] Though Paul does not use the name "Adam" until 5:14—and in fact he *only* uses Adam's name in v. 14—Paul clearly refers to Adam as early as v. 12: "sin entered the world through one man [= Adam], and death [entered] by means of sin, so in this way death spread to everyone (in that everyone sinned)."[27]

Paul goes on to explain how sin and death operated prior to the giving of Torah at Sinai (see 5:13-14). With Adam's transgression of God's commandment, "sin" [*hamartia*] entered the world but was "not registered" [*ouk ellogeitai*] before Torah was given.[28] Even so, "death reigned [*ebasileusen*] from Adam until Moses" (5:14). (The idea of *reigning* explains the "typology" Paul refers to at the end of v. 14: Adam's legacy was the reign of death through sin, just as Jesus' legacy was the reign of life through faithfulness.[29]) We need to appreciate that Paul says *both* (i) that sin was not registered before Torah (i.e. between Adam and Moses), *and* (ii) that death was king in the time between Adam and Moses. Unlike Adam, however, those who sinned (and died) between Adam and Moses did so in the absence of any covenantal commandment. Adam was told not to eat the fruit of the tree of the knowledge of good and evil. Moses and the people of Israel were told . . . well, lots of stuff.[30] Between

---

26. Paul reduces Adam to the singular trait, *sin*, even though Genesis does not portray Adam as a singularly and totally disobedient person. But Paul, here in Romans 5, uses *Adam* as if it were synonymous with *sin*, *disobedience*, even *death*.

27. This last phrase, "in that everyone sinned" [*eph' hō pantes hēmarton*] presents multiple difficulties. Why does Paul use the preposition *epi* ("upon, on, at")? What does the relative pronoun *hō* refer to? Is *hō* masculine or neuter? I have opted for an explanatory interpretation: the relative clause, "in that" explains the earlier claim that "death spread to everyone." Death spread to everyone because everyone sinned. Notice the link with Rom 3:23 (for detailed discussion, see Jewett, *Romans*, 375-76).

28. See Rom 3:25-26, and cf. 4:3-10, where Paul focuses on the "registration" (*elogisthē*) of righteousness as opposed to sin.

29. Jewett, *Romans*, 378. Jewett rightly continues, "In other regards, as the pericope goes on to show, Adam and Christ are more antithetical than similar" (ibid., 378-79).

30. As a result, Israel's sin was like Adam's sin and unlike the sin between Adam and

Adam and Moses, however, humanity continued to sin and to succumb to the authority of death, but their sin, Paul says, was not registered.

Paul introduces a complicated series of comparisons in Rom 5:15, which Matera describes as "one of the most confusing passages in Scripture."[31] Matera finds three asymmetrical comparisons at work in vv. 15–17. Robert Jewett, however, follows Chrys Caragounis and Stanley Porter and reads Rom 5:15a "as a rhetorical question posed by Paul to the audience."[32] I agree, though I put the question in the mouth of Paul's interlocutor. We would then translate v. 15a: "But isn't the gift just like the transgression?" The answer, clearly implied by the question's syntactical structure, is: "Yes, it is."[33] This reading is exactly opposite the interpretation of many commentators and translators.[34] Paul likens Adam and Jesus, as Jewett explains, in that both figures embody the same principle.[35] On the basis of Adam's disobedience, sin and death came to rule over all people. On the basis of Jesus' obedience (or faithfulness),[36] those who receive the abundance of God's gracious gift of his righteousness will reign. Adam and Jesus both affect "the many" [*hoi polloi*] and so evince very real similarities. But at the same time Paul draws stark and clear—*and total!*—contrasts between them. Adam sins; Jesus is obedient. Adam brings death; Jesus brings life. Adam brings condemnation; Jesus brings justification (5:18).

In all of this, Paul has been contrasting the situation between Adam and Moses (see 5:14)—the time before Torah—with the current situation—the time after Messiah. At the end of Romans 5 Paul explains the relation

---

Moses. "Paul does not mean . . . that since Moses all sinning the world over has the character of 'transgression.' The inference here, as in 3:20 and 4:15, is that 'transgression' is something of which Israel in particular is guilty, since Israel in particular has the law (so 2:1–3:20)" (Dunn, *Romans*, 1:276).

31. Matera, *Romans*, 138.

32. Jewett, *Romans*, 379; see Caragounis, "Romans 5:15–16," 142–48; Porter, "Argument," 655–77. *Pace* Jewett, Porter reads the question as posed by the interlocutor, with Paul's answer given in v. 15b (ibid., 673–74).

33. See ftn 29 (p. 54), above; BDF §427.

34. See Dunn, *Romans*, 1:279; Matera, *Romans*, 138–39; Moo, *Romans*, 334–35; Schreiner, *Romans*, 283–84; Witherington and Hyatt, *Romans*, 148–49. See also all of the English translations of Rom 5:15, without exception, listed on the NET Bible's website (https://lumina.bible.org/bible/Romans+5).

35. Matera, *Romans*, 140; see also n. 29, above.

36. Paul does not refer to Jesus' "faithfulness" [*pistis*] or his "obedience" [*hypakoē*] in 5:15–17. Even so, he clearly has these in view when he uses various words in this passage that mean "the gift." See v. 19, where Paul explicitly contrasts Jesus' *hypakoē* with Adam's *parakoē* ("disobedience").

of Torah to this situation: "But Torah came alongside so that transgression might increase" (5:20). We have argued that Torah was given in order to bring blessing and life to Abraham's descendants and, through them, to the rest of the world (see Deuteronomy 28–32; Gen 12:1–3). Before God gave Torah to Israel, death reigned. Torah was meant to bring an end to this situation. However, Israel did not keep Torah, something Paul could assume not because Jews were inherently sinful but because they had been exiled from the land and were now under Roman rule. Torah itself anticipated this result if (or better, *when*) Israel failed to keep Torah's terms (Deut 30:17–18; 31:24–30). The point here is not that the revelation of God's Law (= Torah) caused people to sin more frequently. Paul is saying that the severity or seriousness of the transgression increased [*pleonasē*] in the aftermath of Torah. After the giving of Torah, Israel's worship of other gods, for example, did not necessarily increase. But it did get worse, because now Israel was violating an explicit commandment.

Despite the increase in Israel's guilt—their sin, like Adam's, was now *disobedience*—God's gift of grace [*charis*] "increased all the more" [*hypereperisseusen*]. After laying out Torah's terms before the people and clearly establishing the results of both obedience and disobedience, God "increased all the more" the favor he bestows in that he forgives both the sin and the disobedience. The result—and this is the point Paul began to express back in 5:12, but which has been left incomplete until now—is the final contrast of the chapter: "just as sin reigned [*ebasileusen*] in death, so also grace might reign [*basileusē*] through righteousness for eternal life through Jesus Christ our Lord."[37] As a result of Adam, sin came to reign through death. As a result of Jesus, grace reigns through righteousness. And the result of grace's enthronement is "eternal life."

---

37. Matera suggests that Paul began a comparison in v. 12 and returns to complete that comparison in vv. 18–19 (*Romans*, 139–40; similarly, see Dunn, *Romans*, 1:272). I am suggesting that Paul does not complete that comparison until v. 21. The difference is probably not that great, but Paul does not use the comparative *hōsper* ("just as") in v. 18, as he does in vv. 12, 21. If this word signals Paul's return to the idea he began in v. 12, then both Matera and I should probably look to vv. 19, 21 (which both use *hōsper*) as the completion of v. 12.

7

Baptized, Buried, Raised

Freed from Sin, Enslaved to Righteousness

> *If baptism is a kind of analogy, for what is it an analogy? A Platonic reading of metaphor and personification allows for an interpretation of sin as a representation of the irrational passions and "death to sin" as a call to master the passions. On these terms, Rom 6:1–11 construes baptism as an analogy for a moral-psychological transformation brought about by God's work in Christ, and 6:12–23 explains how the transformation restores the capacity for self-mastery, obedience to God, and acquittal at the coming judgment. Romans 6:12–23 further develops the language of dying to sin and living to God in moral-psychological terms.*[1]

Despite the importance of baptism in the NT and Christian theology in general, Paul has surprisingly little to say about the definitive rite that mediated entrance into the assembly of believers [*ekklēsia*].[2] Though we might wish it otherwise, Paul does not say very much about baptism

---

1. Wasserman, "Paul," 403.

2. Paul uses the verb *baptizō* ("dip, baptize") ten times in 1 Corinthians (1:13–17 [six times]; 10:2; 12:13; 15:29 [twice]) without ever explaining or reflecting on the rite. The same pattern holds for Rom 6:3 (twice) and Gal 3:27, which extract real significance from the fact of baptism "into Christ" [*eis Christon*] without ever explaining baptism explicitly. Perhaps unsurprisingly, the same holds true of the rarer nouns, *baptisma* ("baptism"; Rom 6:4; Eph 4:5) and *baptismos* ("baptism"; Col 2:12). Paul never uses *baptistēs* ("baptist") or *baptō* ("dip").

here.³ In fact, Romans 6 is not "about" baptism any more than Romans 1–5 has been "about" justification by faith. Commentators have read Romans 1–5 in precisely these terms, but we have seen that Romans 1–5 has concentrated on the righteousness of God—his faithfulness to his creation and the promises he made to Abraham and his descendants—despite the *un*faithfulness that both Jews and gentiles have exhibited toward him as Creator. Romans 6 continues this discussion, now with the focus on how, as a result of God's faithfulness, people can be set free from their enslavement to "the lusts of their hearts" [*epithymias tōn kardiōn autōn*; 1:24], to "dishonorable passions" [*pathē atimias*; 1:26], and to the "worthless mind" [*adokimon noun*; 1:28] to which God had formerly "handed them over" [*paradidōmi*; 1:24, 26, 28].

Death to Sin, Newness of Life (Rom 6:1–14)

> **1** "What then? Shall we say, 'Let us remain in sin so that grace might increase'?" **2** Certainly not! How will those of us who died to sin continue to live in it? **3** Or are you ignorant that, as many of us who were baptized into Christ, into his death we were baptized? **4** Therefore, we were buried with him through our baptism into death, so that—just as Christ was raised from the dead by means of the glory of the Father—we also might walk in newness of life. **5** For if we are identified with the likeness of his death, then we also will be [identified with the likeness] of his resurrection. **6** For we know this, that our old person is crucified with Jesus so that our body of sin would be rendered null and void, in order that we would no longer serve as sin's slaves. **7** For the one who died is justified from sin. **8** Now if we died with Christ, we believe that we will also live with him **9** because we know that Christ, after being raised from the dead, no longer dies. Sin no longer reigns over him. **10** For that which he died, he died once [and for all] to sin; that which he lives, he lives for God. **11** Similarly, you also consider yourselves dead, on one hand, with respect to sin, but on the other hand, alive with respect to God in Christ Jesus. **12** Sin, therefore, ought not reign in your mortal body, so that you obey [the body's] desires.

---

3. *Pace* George R. Beasley-Murray, who refers to "Paul's exposition of baptism in Romans 6" ("Baptism," 60). Hans Dieter Betz also assumes that Paul offers his "interpretation of baptism" (Betz, "Transferring," passim). Paul's comments in Romans 6 cannot in any meaningful way be said to "expose" the *meaning* or *significance* of baptism; instead, Paul exploits the *imagery* of baptism in order to make a point about the Christian experience (*viz.* that the Christian is dead with respect to sin). Thus, we might refer to "Paul's exposition of a Christian lifestyle in Romans 6," but we should avoid assuming that Paul must be *speaking about* baptism in Romans 6 just because he *mentions* baptism.

> **13** Do not present the members of your body to sin as instruments of unrighteousness; instead, present yourselves to God, as those who live from the dead, and [present] the members of your body to God as instruments of righteousness. **14** For sin shall not reign over you, for you are not under Torah but under grace.

In Romans 6, Paul explains the transferal of believers from the dominion of sin and death to that of righteousness and life (see Rom 5:14, 17, 21).[4] Paul clearly sees baptism as a useful metaphor for his efforts to explain this transferal, and we should perhaps not dismiss the apparently powerful role baptism played in Paul's theological imagination.[5]

Paul resumes the diatribe in Rom 6:1, which presents the interlocutor's objection. The interlocutor does not seriously propose "remaining in sin"; rather, he reacts incredulously to Paul's claim at the end of Romans 5: "Where sin increased, grace abounded all the more" (5:20).[6] Paul's interlocutor, who exhibits a conspicuous interest in pursuing righteousness (remember, he has submitted to the full yoke of Torah, even to the point of circumcision!), cannot believe his ears! "What, then? Shall we say, 'Let us remain in sin so that grace might increase'?" Paul agrees with the interlocutor's premise: this conclusion is preposterous. However, Paul denies that the gospel leads to this conclusion.[7] "Certainly not! How will those of us who died to sin continue to live in it?" This rhetorical question introduces the binary pair death|life, one of the main themes of this section of Romans. The problem, however, is that Paul has not yet explained *that* (or *how*) he and his readers have died to sin, let alone what it means not to live in sin. At the end of Romans 5, death was the means by which sin exercised its rule.[8] There is, then, some irony that the means by which sin

---

4. Hellholm, "Enthymemic," 140–41.

5. And so, despite my disagreement with Beasley-Murray (see ftn 3, above), I think Dunn goes too far in restricting the imagery of baptism to 6:3–4. What Dunn describes as "different elaborations of the death/life theme (vv 5–6) and . . . a rationale in which baptism is not mentioned again (vv 7ff.)" (*Romans*, 1:308) pertain also to the logic of baptism-as-metaphor. Betz ("Transferring," 110–11), however, refers to the whole of Romans 5–8 as "[the interpretation] of baptism as the Christian initiation ritual," which certainly applies the baptism-as-metaphor too broadly.

6. "This wording in the mouth of an imaginary interlocutor would likely strike the Christian audience in Rome as risible, unless a serious antinomian threat were present in the congregations, which seems unlikely" (Jewett, *Romans*, 394).

7. See Hellholm, "Enthymemic," 143–46.

8. *ebasileusen hē hamartia en tō thanatō* ("sin reigned in death"; Rom 5:21); see BDF §219.

exercised dominion over humanity (*viz.* death) also provides the means for the escape from sin: "we died to sin" [*apethanomen tē hamartia*].⁹

Paul broadens his focus in Rom 6:3. Rather than addressing his fictive interlocutor, he addresses his audience directly through the second-person plural verbs (v. 3) and pronouns (v. 11), and he consistently includes himself by means of the first-person plural verbs and pronouns throughout.¹⁰ Paul asks, "Or are you ignorant that, as many of us who were baptized into Christ, into his death we were baptized?" Paul's question takes a chiastic structure:

A	as many of us who were baptized
B	into Christ Jesus
B'	into his death
A'	we were baptized

Paul's point focuses not on baptism directly but on identification with [see *symphytoi*; 6:5] Christ Jesus and, specifically, with his death. "The association of baptism and death is probably distinctively Christian. Jesus himself was remembered as having made the link (Mark 10:38–39; Luke 12:50), that is, explicitly using baptism as a metaphor for his own death."¹¹ Sin results in death (see 6:23), and death has already had its result for those who identify with Jesus and the gospel. Thus Paul's question earlier in 6:2: "How will we continue to live in [sin]?"

The mechanics of baptism, in which a person is metaphorically "buried" beneath the water, provides Paul an opportunity to expand his point regarding the believers' identification with Jesus' death. In this light, the "raising" up of the baptizand out of the water becomes an identification with Jesus' "raising" up from death. Paul, however, does not say this explicitly. That is, he does not use the verb *egeirō* ("raise") in the first-person plural here in 6:4. Instead, he likens Christ's "raising" [*ēgerthē*] with the result that "we also might walk [*peripatēsōmen*] in newness of life." Dunn,

---

9. Dunn (*Romans*, 1:307) notes the ambiguity of Paul's "death"-language: "died, so that the sinful act is no longer possible; but again the context (5:21) implies more strongly that what Paul had in mind is a death which puts the individual beyond the power of sin (as in 6:7, 10), and so unable (because dead!) to live 'in' it, that is, in its realm, under its authority."

10. Thus I agree with Dunn that Paul considers both Jews and gentiles to relate to YHWH in the same terms (i.e., "grace" [*charis*]), even if I emphasize that Jews and gentiles came to that relation via different routes. Nevertheless, we can agree that "Israel's failure is of a piece with the sin of humankind as a whole; God's faithfulness to Israel is no different from his grace open to all" (ibid., 1:306).

11. Ibid., 1:312; see also Jewett, *Romans*, 398 n.70.

who speaks of being "buried with Christ, but not yet raised with him," misses how Paul creates a link between Christ's "raising" and the Christian's "walking."[12]

Paul repeats the comparison of the "newness of life" with Christ's "raising" in v. 5, only this time he uses the word "resurrection" [*anastasis*] to make the point: "For if we are identified with the likeness of his death, then we also will be [identified with the likeness][13] of his resurrection." The future-tense verb *esometha* ("we will be") extends the comparison with Christ's raising; Christ's literal resurrection results in a metaphorical resurrection, a "walk in newness of life." But that result does not change the fact, for Paul, that Christ's literal resurrection will also result in a literal resurrection one day (see 1 Cor 15). Paul applies the "likeness" [*homoiōma* (6:5)] of both Jesus' death and his resurrection to the baptized believer. He has already used *homoiōma* twice (see Rom 1:23; 5:14), and he will use it again at 8:3. In both of its previous uses, Paul refers to something that conforms to the pattern of something else, or that takes on the appearance of something else by means of imitating it. So the objects of pagan worship assume the appearance of corruptible humanity, birds, four-footed creature, or reptiles (Rom 1:23), while the sin of humanity from Adam to Moses did not conform to the pattern of Adam's sin (because Adam disobeyed a direct command; Rom 5:14). At the most obvious level "the likeness" of Christ's death to which Paul refers applies to the action of being lowered beneath the water, as Christ was buried underground.

But, given Paul's emphasis on "the faithfulness of Christ" earlier in the letter (esp. 3:22, 26), I think we can say more. Christ's death provided for Paul the epitome of Jesus' faithfulness to YHWH: Jesus was obedient "to the point of death, even death on a cross" (Phil 2:8). As a result, conforming "to the likeness of his death" also strongly implies a willingness to be faithful to God in the likeness of *pistis Christou* ("the faithfulness of Christ"), even to the point of death. That is, Paul does not compare only baptism with Jesus' Passion; he compares the entire manner in which believers live their lives with Jesus' death, burial, and resurrection. "The likeness [*homoiōmati*] of his death" refers to both the metaphor of immersion beneath the baptismal waters as well as the metaphor of uncompromising faithfulness to the Creator God.

---

12. Dunn, *Romans*, 1:316.

13. "Almost all commentators agree that *symphytoi tō homoiōmati* has to be supplied to complete the balance of the clauses and the sense" (ibid., 1:318).

Baptized, Buried, Raised

This identification with the death of Jesus, and especially his faithfulness to YHWH, precludes the possibility of remaining in sin so that grace might continue to increase (cf. 6:1). Quite the contrary, the gospel results in the knowledge that "our old person is crucified with Jesus."[14] This phrase holds within itself a striking tension. On the one hand, Paul's reference to "our old person" (or "our old self") is obviously pejorative; *palaios* stands in clear contrast with the "newness of life" [*kainotēti zōēs*] to which Paul referred in v. 4. On the other hand, we have already seen that Christ's death is the epitome—the clearest instance—of his faithfulness to God, and so "being crucified with" [*synestaurōthē*] Jesus suggests our faithfulness to God in imitation of Jesus' faithfulness. "Our old self" (= bad) participates in the experience of Jesus' faithfulness (= good), namely co-crucifixion with Christ. Both aspects of this tension support the twin-purpose of our co-crucifixion:

1. our co-crucifixion renders the sinful body "null and void" [*katargēthē*].[15]
2. our co-crucifixion frees us from bondage to sin [*mēketi douleuein hēmas tē hamartia*].

The verb *douleuō* ("to be or serve as a slave") conveys the flipside of a verb Paul used in Romans 5 to describe the status of sin (and of death) vis-à-vis Adam's legacy. Paul said that death/sin "reigned as king" [*basileuō*; see 5:14, 17 (of death); 5:21 (of sin)]. As part of Adam's legacy, death/sin "reigned as king." Now, those crucified with Christ no longer "serve [death/sin] as slaves."[16]

Paul goes on to carry the positive connotation of "death" (= the extent of Christ's "faithfulness") forward into 6:8. If we identify with Christ's

---

14. We should interpret *ho palaios hēmōn anthrōpos* ("our old person" or even "our old self") corporately rather than individualistically: "While *palaios anthrōpos* means 'the aged person' in classical Greek, here it is the obsolete human in the generic sense, with all of its corrupt relationships, that is put to death with Christ. The 'obsolete self' is the one that 'belongs to the old aeon, the self dominated by sin and exposed to wrath.' This old 'self' should not be interpreted in an individualistic manner, as almost all commentators have done" (Jewett, *Romans*, 402–3; citing Fitzmyer, *Romans*, 436).

15. Paul has already used the verb *katargeō* ("to nullify, render void") on three previous occasions (Rom 3:3, 31; 4:14), all three of which raise (and refuse) the possibility that something thought permanent (the faithfulness of God [3:3], Torah [3:31], or God's promise to Abraham [4:14]) might come to naught. This is the first time in Romans that Paul affirms that a thing would actually pass into non-existence; that "thing" is "the sinful body" [*to sōma tēs hamartias*; lit. "the body of the sin"].

16. Or, to switch from a political to a legal metaphor, "The one who died is justified from sin" [*dedikaiōtai apo tēs hamartias*; Rom 6:7].

faithfulness so that we can say "we died with Christ," then the result, not yet realized but nevertheless assured [*pisteuomen*; "we believe"], will be life with him. The assurance of this result, however, does not hang solely on the reliability conveyed by means of the *pist-* stem ("faith") in v. 8. Paul's confidence in the promise of life is also rooted in the knowledge that Jesus being raised from the dead means he is not subject to death, that death "no longer reigns as lord [*ouketi kyrieuei*] over him." In Romans 5 Paul said three times that death/sin "reigned as king" [*ebasileusen*; 5:14, 17, 21]. Now death/sin has lost its authority over Jesus and, through him, over those who have become identified with the likeness of his death (6:5).

Up through vv. 8–9 Paul has primarily used first-person plural verbs and pronouns. In v. 11 he turns to address his audience directly and draws out the moral-ethical consequence of the gospel's logic for his readers.[17] Paul instructs them to consider themselves [*logizesthe heautous*][18] dead with respect to the sphere of sin's influence and, as part of their participation "in Christ Jesus" [*en Christō Iēsou*], alive with respect to the sphere of God's influence. Remember, however, that this moral imperative stands as Paul's response to his interlocutor's question, "What then? Shall we say, 'Let us remain in sin so that grace might increase'?" (6:1). If that were the result of Paul's gospel, then we would not be able to claim identification with Christ's death—both the liberation from death's (and/or sin's) rule and the full extent of Christ's faithfulness to YHWH—and life with respect to God.

At this point we might profitably consider a biblical text we have mentioned a number of times already: Deuteronomy 28–32. These chapters, as the climax and conclusion of God's covenant with Israel, establish in crystal-clear terms the stakes of obedience or disobedience.

> 19 I call both heaven and earth to swear to you today: I have set before your face both life and death, blessing and curse. Choose life, so that you might live, you and your seed. 20 Love the Lord your God. Listen to his voice and hold to it, because this will be

---

17. "The opening three words *houtōs kai hymeis* ('so also you') are argumentative, explicitly drawing the inferences from Christ to believers" (Jewett, *Romans*, 408).

18. The verb *logizesthe* is certainly an imperative command or instruction ("consider yourselves") rather than an indicative statement of fact ("you consider yourselves"). Dunn helpfully points out, "*logizesthe*, here certainly imperative, recalls the prominence of the word in 3:28 and chap. 4 (this is the first use of it since then). The believer's reckoning himself dead to sin and alive to God *answers to God's reckoning him righteous*" (*Romans*, 1:323; my emphasis). Jewett (*Romans*, 408) takes a minority position and reads *logizesthe* as an indicative, though he is almost certainly wrong.

your life and the length of your days, for you to dwell in the land, which the Lord promised your ancestors—Abraham, Isaac, and Jacob—to give to them. (Deut 30:19-20 LXX)

Given the stark opposition between life and death and the exhortation for his readers to consider themselves "dead, on the one hand, with respect to sin, but on the other hand, alive with respect to God in Christ Jesus" (Rom 6:11), Paul likely has the end of the Mosaic covenant—Torah—in mind here. But even if Paul did not intend the allusion to the end of Deuteronomy, the death|life binary common to both Deuteronomy and Romans functions in the same way in each (*viz.* as covenantal markers).

Paul continues his binary thinking in 6:12ff., but now, instead of death|life, the binary opposition is sin|righteousness (6:16, 18, 20; cf. 6:22).[19] Whereas baptism provided the controlling metaphor in 6:1-11, in the second half of Romans 6 Paul uses the socio-political metaphor of slavery and lordship. As we have seen, Paul exhorts his readers, "consider yourselves dead, on one hand, with respect to sin, but on the other hand, alive with respect to God in Christ Jesus" (6:11). The grammatical (and moral) imperatives continue in v. 12: "Sin, therefore, ought not reign in your mortal body, so that you obey [the body's] desires." Paul's reference to his readers' "mortal body" [*tō thnētō hymōn sōmati*] provides a link with the reference to "dying" [*apothnēskō*] to sin earlier in the paragraph. However, Paul yields no ground whatsoever to sin. While the body might indeed be mortal (= subject to death), Paul instructs his readers to ensure that sin does not exercise authority with respect to [*en*] their mortal body. Moreover, Paul urges his readers in Rom 12:1: "present your bodies [*ta sōmata hymōn*] as a sacrifice—living, holy, and pleasing to God." Even the physical, fleshly body, subject as it is to death (sin's ultimate result; see Rom 6:23), should not be given over to sin's reign. The body presents special dangers. "The desires" [*tais epithymiais*] that must be avoided are specifically the body's desires; they are not sin's desires.[20] Rather than succumbing to the body's desires or presenting the parts of the body to sin, Paul exhorts his readers to "present yourselves to God, as those who live

---

19. In his comments on v. 2, Jewett explains helpfully, "Paul's assumption, like that of the rest of the NT, is imperial: no one can serve two empires or masters simultaneously. Dying to the realm of sin means living in the realm of Christ; the two realms are as incommensurate as the antithesis between 'life' and 'death'" (*Romans*, 396).

20. Paul refers to "obedience to its desires" [*hypakouein tais epithymiais autou*; 6:12], but the pronoun *autou* is either masculine or neuter (here, neuter) and so cannot refer back to the feminine noun, "sin" [*hē hamartia*]. The point: Paul is not warding off *sin's* desires but rather *the body's*!

from the dead, and [present] the members of your body to God as instruments [*hopla*; lit. "weapons"] of righteousness" (6:13; see also 12:1).

Paul begins to explore the metaphor of *reigning* in earnest in Rom 6:14, which metaphor he introduced in Romans 5 (see vv. 14, 17, 21). The future-tense verb *kyrieusei* ("will/shall reign as lord") takes on an imperatival force: "For sin *shall not reign* over you." In addition to the clear exhortational implication, commentators also rightly see a genuine future sense, the promise of an eschatological reality yet to be realized: "For sin *will not reign* as lord over you."[21] We should not impose a sharp distinction between these two readings; both may be operative at the same time. If Paul considers this promise for the future valid for and operative in the present, it makes sense that he also exhorts his readers to live according to this promise. The preponderance of imperatival verbs in the immediate context makes it all the more likely that at least *some* imperatival force attaches to the future-tense verb, *kyrieusei*.

We should, perhaps, be surprised by the reason Paul gives his readers to resist sin's hegemony: "for you are not under Torah but under grace" (6:14). The dichotomy between Torah (or "law") and grace, while not surprising in a Christian-theological context, requires some explanation. Paul has already made extensive references to Torah, using the language of "the oracles of God" [*ta logia tou theou*; 3:2], as first among the "advantages" [*perisson*] of being a Jew and the "benefits" [*ōpheleia*] of circumcision. In just a few chapters (see Rom 9:4) Paul will include "the Torah-giving" [*hē nomothesia*] among the marks of honor that attach to being an Israelite. So while *we* may be used to thinking of Torah as an ineffectual covenant, or perhaps a covenant that was never supposed to result in peace with God (cf. Rom 5:1), *Paul* seems perfectly comfortable with the notion that Torah was a blessing from God and a point of pride for Israel. Why, then, does Paul seem to place Torah and grace in antithetical relationship to one another?

Romans 6:14 finds its most satisfying interpretation in light of the audience Paul envisions for his letter: gentile converts to faith in Christ.[22] Paul does not dichotomize Torah and grace as fundamentally opposed to one another. Instead, he instructs his *gentile audience* that the basis for their relationship with the Creator God is grace, expressed in the gospel of Jesus' life, death, and resurrection, rather than Torah, the Mosaic

---

21. See Dunn, *Romans*, 1:339; Jewett, *Romans*, 411.

22. See our discussion in chap. 1, above; see also Rom 1:5–7, 13–14; 11:1; 15:16.

covenant that structured *Israel's* relationship with YHWH.²³ The problem in Rom 6:14 is not Torah. The problem is gentiles attempting to relate to God by means of Torah.²⁴ Paul everywhere resists vociferously the notion that gentiles should take on Torah's yoke. So, again, the problem is not Torah. The problem is that God never intended Torah for gentiles.²⁵ We would do well to remember Rom 3:19: "What Torah says, it says to those in Torah." Note the third-person language here: "*those* in Torah." But when Paul turns and addresses his (gentile) audience in the second-person, he tells them, "*You* are not under Torah but under grace" (6:14). Paul clearly makes a distinction between his audience—gentile Christians in Rome— from "those in Torah" (Jews).

---

23. See n. 30 (p. 120), below.

24. Jewett, apparently solely on the basis of the anarthrous *nomos*, reads Rom 6:14 in terms of "every form of law in the Greco-Roman world" (*Romans*, 411); "[The restriction of *nomos* to the Jewish Torah] fails to account for the lack of a definite article; in the context of Rom 6, it must include law in every form available to Paul's audience in Rome" (ibid., 412 n.230). This is too flimsy a basis to ignore the fact that Paul has used *nomos* to refer predominantly (even unanimously) to Torah up to this point in Romans. James Dunn (*Romans*, 1:339-40) correctly reads *nomos* as Torah but then for some reason argues that Paul critiques *Israel* for "putting themselves so fully under the law as peculiarly theirs"! This leads Dunn to equate "under the law" with "a general characterization of the old epoch of Adam," though I suspect that Paul, in the previous chapter (5:14), makes an important distinction, at least for Israel, between Adam and Moses (= Torah). Dunn recognizes at the very least "a goodly proportion or preponderance of Gentiles . . . who had (previously) been attracted to Judaism, that is, attracted by the customs and standards embodied in the law, and so were in danger of thinking they could only participate in the covenant promises by 'judaizing,' living like the Jews, that is, by putting themselves 'under the law'" (ibid., 1:340). I agree, but I would go further and argue that Paul *only* has in mind gentiles who might otherwise submit themselves *hypo nomon* ("under Torah").

25. Despite misreading *nomos* as "law" in general rather than as Torah (see the previous note), Jewett rightly reads 6:14 in relation to Paul's gentile audience: "Submission to law's commands was usually motivated in part by the desire to gain honor as a decently submissive citizen or slave, a decent respecter of the gods, or in the Jewish case, *a proper God-fearer*" (*Romans*, 412; my emphasis). "God-fearer" is a technical term that refers to gentiles who "were linked in some formal way to the Jewish community, without being proselytes" (Trebilco, "Diaspora Judaism," 292). However, Jewett's reference to "a proper God-fearer" does not fit Paul's construction of his interlocutor in 2:17-29, who submitted to Torah's *full* yoke (including circumcision; see 2:27). As a result, Jewett misses the full force of Paul's statement, "*you* are [*este*] not under Torah but under grace." Here Paul generalizes from his interlocutor—a gentile proselyte whom he has employed to flesh out his argument—to his Roman audience, which consisted of gentile Christians, whom he likewise insisted ought not submit to Torah's yoke.

If You Call Yourself a Jew

Slaves, but Whose Slaves? (Rom 6:15–23)

> **15** "What then? [Shall we say,] 'Let us sin, because we are not under Torah but under grace'?" Certainly not! **16** Don't you know that whatever you present yourselves to as slaves for obedience, you are slaves to that which you obey, whether of sin (for death), or of obedience (for righteousness)? **17** But thanks be to God that you were slaves to sin, but you obeyed from the heart the pattern of the teaching to which you were entrusted, **18** and now that you are freed from sin, you are enslaved to righteousness. **19** (I am speaking humanly because of the weakness of your flesh.) For just as you presented your members [in the past] as slaves to impurity and to lawlessness, which resulted in lawlessness, so now, in the same way, you are presenting your members as slaves to righteousness, which resulted in consecration. **20** For when you were slaves of sin, you were free with respect to righteousness. **21** What fruit, then, were you bearing? Now you are ashamed by them, for the result of those things is death. **22** But now that you have been set free from sin and are now serving God, you are bearing fruit that results in consecration, whose result is eternal life. **23** For the wages of sin is death, but the gift of God is eternal life in Christ Jesus our Lord.

At this point, perhaps almost predictably, the proselyte interlocutor speaks up. The interlocutor, of course, found value precisely in being "under Torah," though Paul insists that gentiles are not "under Torah" [*hypo nomon*]. So the interlocutor asks, "What then? [Shall we say,] 'Let us sin, because we are not under Torah but under grace'?" The question picks up exactly the terms of Paul's assertion in v. 14, and Paul's response should be predictable by now. "Certainly not!" [*mē genoito*]. Paul has already answered this objection earlier in Romans 6 (see vv. 2–11), though his earlier answer assumed the language of death|life. I interpret the interlocutor's question in 6:15 as virtually synonymous with the question in 6:1, but now Paul's answer will take the language of enslavement to sin|righteousness. "Do you not know that whatever you present yourselves to as slaves for obedience, you are slaves to that which you obey, whether of sin (for death), or of obedience (for righteousness)" (6:16). So when Paul continues, "But thanks [*charis*][26] be to God that you were slaves to sin" (v. 17), we should appreciate that this language ("you were slaves to sin" [*ēte douloi tēs hamartias*]) clearly identifies Paul's audience as gentiles *and not Jews*,

---

26. This is the same word Paul used in 6:14: "for you are not under Torah but under grace" [*hypo charin*].

whom Paul never describes in this way.²⁷ The gentiles, who were formerly [ēte; "you were"] slaves to sin, now have "obeyed from the heart the pattern [typon; see 5:14] of the teaching to which you were entrusted" (6:17).²⁸ The result of this obedience "from the heart" [ek kardias] is freedom (redemption, liberation [eleutherōthentes]) from sin and enslavement (bondage, captivity [edoulōthēte]) to righteousness (v. 18).

At this point we should return to Stanley Stowers's important book, *A Rereading of Romans*. Stowers presents his central thesis in terms of the moral-philosophical context of Paul's original audience(s), and he contrasts that context with "traditional readings" of Romans in Western Christianity.

> The theme of self-mastery would have loomed very large for ancient readers of Romans but is scarcely noticed by modern readers. It has receded deeply into the background for contemporaries because the concept of self-mastery has none of the powerfully loaded social and cultural meaning for us that it did for people in Paul's day.... The rhetoric of Romans pushes the theme of self-mastery, or the lack of it, into the foreground in three ways. First, Romans tells the story of sin and salvation, problem and solution, punishment and reward at its most basic level as a story of the loss and recovery of self-control. Second, the letter represents the readers as characters in this basic story that concerns self-mastery. Third, Romans relates this story of loss to the story of God's righteous action through Jesus Christ

---

27. Contrast the description of Paul's interlocutor (Rom 2:17-22); similarly, note Paul's contrast between "Jews by nature" [physei Ioudaioi] and "gentile sinners" [ex ethnōn hamartōloi; Gal 2:15]. Similarly, of the eleven times in the Pauline corpus where *Ioudaios* ("Jew or Judean") and *Hellēn* ("Greek") are brought together for comparison or contrast, three times a similar contrast is drawn between *doulos* ("slave") and *eleutheros* ("free person"). If *slave* and *free* are as categorically exclusive of one another as *Jew* and *gentile*, then "slaves of sin" in Rom 6:17 clearly encodes Paul's readers in Romans as gentiles *and not Jews*. Paul's use of the adjective *hamartōlos* ("sinful") is ambiguous but can be understood in these terms. However, note Rom 3:9; 1 Cor 1:22-24; 10:32; 1 Thess 2:14, all of which, in various ways, liken rather than distinguish Jews and gentiles.

28. Jewett (*Romans*, 417-19) tentatively argues that v. 17b is a later interpolation. While v. 17a flows nicely into v. 18, this hypothesis has no textual support. The only textual variant in v. 17 is found in A, which adds the adjective *katharas* ("clean, pure") to the prepositional phrase *ek kardias* ("from [the] heart"). I am not persuaded that Paul always wrote in nice, tight, balanced rhetorical structures (in fact he very often did not!), and so I do not think we can use infelicities in Romans' rhetorical structure as evidence of later, non-Pauline interpolations.

> so that Christ becomes an enabler of the restored and disciplined self.[29]

A little later, Stowers makes a claim that resonates especially well with Paul's rhetoric in Romans 6: "The letter establishes the audience's relation to the theme of self-mastery also by making Christ an enabler of the mastery over self that the readers are already depicted as having by virtue of their new lives."[30] The issue at hand is not simply whether or not Paul's readers considered themselves (and/or actually were) self-disciplined and controlled. The value of self-mastery enabled a person to place himself in relation to others in society (especially women and slaves). "Clearly people with any ambition in life got the message that they had to acquire mastery of their passions and desires in order to achieve their social aspirations. Since the vast majority of slaves and women were denied such aspirations and thought to exemplify weakness, *to fail in this inner contest was to act slavishly or womanishly with regard to passions and desires*."[31]

Late Second-Temple-era Jews were well aware of the social value of and pervasive concern for self-mastery in the Hellenistic and Roman world. Moreover, they participated in the cultural conventions of self-mastery, and of course they put forward Torah as an effective (or even *the* effective) means to self-mastery. Philo uses *enkrateia* ("self-control or self-mastery") sixty-two times in his extant writings.[32] Perhaps predictably, Philo postures aspects of Torah as either the embodiment of[33] or the means to attain[34] self-mastery. Later, Philo describes the most peculiar

29. Stowers, *Rereading*, 42.

30. Ibid., 44. Stowers continues, "The arguments in chapters 5–8 aim to change the readers' understanding of how they have attained mastery over their passions and desires: not through the law but through their identification with Jesus Christ." This, I think, applies in particular to 6:14.

31. Ibid., 49; my emphasis.

32. According to Borgen, *et al.*, *Philo Index*, s.v. All translations are taken from the LCL edition of Philo's works; I will note where I have modified the translation.

33. See *Spec. Laws* 1:172–76. Philo describes the placement of twelve loaves of sacred bread, in "two sets of six loaves" [*hai dittai tōn . . . artōn hexades*], in the temple each seventh day, which he explains in terms of the productive annual cycle (i.e., the spring bloom and the autumnal harvest). Philo likens these loaves to "that most profitable of virtues, self-mastery" [*enkrateian*; 1:173; modified]. Also, when he describes how frankincense and salt are placed on the loaves, he interprets the frankincense as "a symbol that in the court of wisdom no seasoning is judged to be more sweet-savoured than frugality and self-mastery" [*enkrateias*; 1:175; modified].

34. See *Spec. Laws* 1:190–93. Philo explains how Moses foresaw and curtailed the danger of licentious and extravagant behavior at religious festivals. The prescribed

Baptized, Buried, Raised

Jewish "feast," Yom Kippur, which involves abstaining entirely from food or drink [*nēsteia*; "fast"]. Why would Moses call for a "feast" [*heortē*] with no food?

> He gave it this name for many reasons. First, because of the self-mastery [*enkrateian*] which it entails; always and everywhere indeed [Moses] exhorted them to shew this in all the affairs of life, in controlling the tongue and the belly and the organs below the belly, but on this occasion especially he bids them do honour to it by dedicating thereto a particular day.[35]

Moses enjoins *enkrateia* in all areas of life, especially on Yom Kippur, a festival that Philo puts forward as the very embodiment of self-mastery.

Philo was not only very aware of the virtue and value of *enkrateia* in Hellenistic and Roman moral-philosophical discourse; he lived within that discourse and participated in it.[36] Philo, according to Stowers, offered Torah to the Roman world as "superior because it better produces self-mastery. In contrast, the idolatry-promoting laws of other peoples 'nourish and increase' the passions and vices (*Sacr. Abel* 15)."[37] Torah, for a broad cross-section of Jews in the Hellenistic and Roman eras, provided freedom from the ever-present dangers posed by pleasure, which lurked in the shadows and was ever ready to pounce on any opportunity afforded by means of hunger, desire, or lust.

> All of this helps one to understand what Jews meant when they described their law and way of life as a *politeia* and when they stressed the virtues that the [sic; their] law and way of life would produce. ... When gentiles heard Jews talk about the advantages of and virtues produced by the law of Moses, they were

---

sacrifices "are accompanied on each day of a feast by the sacrifice of a kid called the sin-offering [*peri hamartias*] offered for the remission of sins," by which sacrifices the people are to "make themselves pure by curbing the appetites for pleasure [*hēdonēn*]" and, by participating in the offerings, the hymns, and the prayers, may be "enamoured of self-mastery [*enkrateias*] and piety" (1:190, 193; modified).

35. *Spec. Laws* 2:195; modified.

36. See Stowers, *Rereading*, 58-65.

37. Ibid., 59. Interestingly, Philo advocates Torah-observance for all nations (*Mos.* 2:18-20). As Stowers argues, "Jews inhabit the whole civilized world because they have a mission to be to the whole world as a priest is to the whole Jewish people. ... [T]he Jewish people have this office because they 'corrected' the worship of many false gods that the other peoples adopted ([*Spec. Laws*] 164-67)" (ibid., 58-59). Thus Philo and Paul think in very nearly exactly the same terms about Israel's relation to the rest of the nations ("gentiles") of the world, but Philo attributes to Torah the very same functions that Paul attributes to the gospel (ibid., 60).

hearing a familiar topic. . . . The works of Philo and Josephus and other Jewish writings from the period of the second temple, but especially the sources from the early empire, provide vital evidence for Jews who wanted to attract gentiles into a sympathetic relation with Jewish communities by advertising Judaism as a superior school for self-mastery. Such attraction did not normally mean becoming a naturalized citizen of the Jewish commonwealth. Rather, Jewish teachers encouraged gentiles to learn applicable moral teachings and practices from the law of Moses.[38]

~

In sum, both Paul and his Roman readers lived in a world in which self-mastery [*enkrateia*] functioned as one of society's chief virtues. Both Paul and his Roman readers would have known of the presentation of Torah as the most effective means to achieve *enkrateia*, such as we find in Philo.[39] In contrast to all of this, however, Paul offers grace [*charis*; Rom 3:24; 4:4, 16; 6:14; passim], the favor of the Creator God, as the efficacious means for achieving self-mastery. More than this, Paul has already made clear that Torah does *not* actually lead to self-mastery. Instead, Torah produces knowledge of sin (3:20) and even *increases* transgression and facilitates the reign of sin and death (5:20–21). So when Paul says, "Now that you are freed from sin, you are enslaved to righteousness" (Rom 6:18), he must have expected his readers to recall his argument about the righteousness of God, manifested apart from Torah (3:21), and to relate that argument to the common cultural currency of Torah among Diaspora Jews and gentiles interested in self-mastery.

Romans takes a bit of a jarring turn in v. 19. Without any warning, Paul claims to be "speaking humanly" [*anthrōpinon legō*], but without explaining what he means. One option is that Paul claims to be "speaking humanely" or gently, which interpretation finds support from Paul's reasons for speaking *anthrōpinon*, namely "the weakness of your flesh." How, specifically, Paul has softened his rhetoric and how he might have spoken more harshly, we will never know. If this is the right reading, Paul seems to expect that his readers understand he is using kinder, gentler words than he might otherwise have used.[40] However, almost exactly the

38. Stowers, *Rereading*, 63, 65.

39. Besides the above discussion (and references), see the texts Stowers cites (ibid., 338 n.62).

40. Galatians, which Paul had already written when he wrote Romans, might provide

same phrase appears in Gal 3:15, a letter in which Paul has not really used gentler or more humane language.[41] So, despite how well the translation "I am speaking humanely" seems to work in Romans 6, this does not seem to be Paul's intention. Instead, Paul seems simply to call attention to the fact that he is speaking metaphorically in Romans 6, likening a theological truth to a human analogy, namely the sociocultural institution of slavery.[42]

Even more interesting, however, is the reason Paul gives for speaking humanly (= figuratively): "because of the weakness of your flesh" [*dia tēn astheneian tēs sarkos hymōn*]. This is the third time we have encountered "weak[ness]" language in Romans, and once again Paul attributes weakness to his readers (see also 5:6). In light of the common suggestion that Paul writes Romans in order to put his best foot forward and appeal for Roman support for an upcoming mission to Spain,[43] these references to his readers "having weakness" or "being weak" might seem counterproductive. This language makes better sense in terms of Das's proposal that Paul writes to the Roman gentile Christians because, as the "apostle to the gentiles" (Rom 11:13), he sees them as falling under his apostolic authority and commission. Paul does not, then, appear to be *appealing* to his audience so much as taking an authoritative posture toward them. Why their "weakness" motivates Paul to speak figuratively, we do not know. For whatever reason, Paul clearly flags that he is speaking figuratively.

As we mentioned in the first part of Rom 6:19, the second part of v. 19 clearly identifies Paul's intended audience as gentile (and not Jewish)

---

us one possibility. Paul opens that letter expressing his consternation that the gentile Galatian Christians, much like Paul's imagined gentile proselyte interlocutor, were deserting the one who called them by grace [*en chariti*; Gal 1:6; cp. Rom 6:14]. Later he chastises the Galatian gentile Christians, referring to them as "You foolish Galatians" [*ō anoētoi Galatai*; 3:1]. By the end of the letter Paul has settled down and once again refers to his readers using friendlier language ("brothers" [*adelphoi*; 3:15]). However, he continues to use harsh language regarding those who persuade gentiles to observe Torah, even going so far as to wish that those who are disturbing the Galatian gentile Christians would "emasculate themselves" [*apokopsontai*; Gal 5:12].

41. Galatians 3:15a reads "Brothers, I am speaking humanly" [*kata anthrōpon legō*], almost exactly the same phrase in Romans 6. For details regarding Paul's harsh language in Galatians, see the previous footnote.

42. Jewett, *Romans*, 416; 419. Similarly, in Galatians 3, immediately after Paul says he is speaking humanly, he turns to the metaphor of a "humanly ratified covenant" [*anthrōpou kekyrōmenēn diathēkēn*; Gal 3:15].

43. See Longenecker (*Introducing*, 109–10) for a helpful discussion of this perspective. While Paul clearly hopes to solicit the Romans' support for his planned missionary activities, he also clearly takes an authoritative stance *vis-à-vis* his Roman audiences, despite never having met them.

believers in Jesus. "For just as you presented your members [in the past] as slaves to impurity and to lawlessness, which resulted in lawlessness, so now, in the same way, you are presenting your members as slaves to righteousness, which results in consecration." The next three verses unpack further the concept of the transfer of gentile slaves from the sphere (or ownership) of sin to the sphere (or ownership) of righteousness. Paul's audience, in their former state, produced fruit that is now a source of shame for them. But now [*nyni de*; 6:22], in their present state of slavery to God, they are producing fruit whose *telos* ("result, end, goal, completion") is eternal life.

Romans 6 ends with the famous verse, "For the wages of sin is death, but the gift of God is eternal life in Christ Jesus our Lord" (6:23). "In [Paul's] view there is nothing whatsoever that anyone can do to deserve such a gift; *life eternal is the very opposite of the death the children of Adam have earned*. This antithesis strikes at the heart of much of the religious motivation in Paul's time."[44] We can agree fully with Jewett here, and we can go even further: the eternal life Paul mentions in v. 23 is the very opposite of the depravity that leads to futility and the wrath of God in Rom 1:18–32. Whereas God, in Romans 1, delivers the wicked over to the results of their choices (see 1:24, 26, 28), God intervenes in Romans 6 to give the "free gift" [*charisma*] of eternal life to those who identify with Christ's death, his faithfulness, and his resurrection.

---

44. Jewett, *Romans*, 426; my emphasis.

8

Nomos, Flesh, Spirit

The War Waging Within

> *We cannot presuppose the introspective Christian conscience of late antiquity or the middle ages. Nor can we assume the much later Christian stereotypes of the legalistic Jew who attempts the impossible task of keeping the law. The picture of Paul the Pharisee who attempted that impossible task clearly comes from reading the narratives of his conversion in Acts through the lens of later Christian constructions of Judaism and the law. Types and assumptions for reading will have to be those that readers in Paul's time could have made.*[1]

The standard reading of Romans 7 in terms of Paul's angst over his inability to keep Torah and the futility of his efforts to do what he knows to be right makes no sense in light of what Paul says about himself elsewhere or what he has said up to this point in Romans. This chapter, therefore, will read Romans 7 in rather different terms.

A Legal Analogy (Rom 7:1–6)

> **1** Or are you ignorant, brethren (for I am speaking to those who know Torah), that Torah reigns over a person for as long a time as that person lives. **2** For a married woman is bound to her husband by the marriage

---

1. Stowers, "Romans 7," 191.

> decree while he lives. But if her husband dies, she is released from the decree [and] from her husband. **3** Therefore, as long as the husband lives, she will be called an adulteress if she marries another man. But if her husband dies, she is free from the decree. As a result, she would not be an adulteress if she married another man. **4** So then, my brethren, you also were executed by the *nomos*, through the body of Christ, so that you might marry another, that is, the one who raised him from the dead, so that we might bear fruit for God. **5** For when we were in the flesh, the sinful passions that were [made known] through Torah were brought into effect in our members, so that we bore fruit for death. **6** But now we are released from Torah, since we have died to that in which we were confined, so that we might serve in newness of spirit and not in oldness of letter.

Let me start with what may be an obvious point: in order to rightly understand Romans 7, we have to remember Romans 1–6. Up to now Paul has been addressing his audience of gentile Christians in Rome (see 1:5–6), and as part of that address he has been employing a rhetorical character—a gentile proselyte to Judaism who has fully accepted the yoke of Torah-observance, including circumcision—as a dialogue partner. In Romans 6, Paul portrayed his gentile audience as formerly enslaved to sin (i.e., to their passions and desires), but now after their baptism into Christ and into his death, they have died to sin and are now enslaved to God (i.e., to righteousness and obedience).

Paul begins Romans 7 by addressing his readers as "brethren" [*adelphoi*] for the first time since the letter's opening (1:13): "Or are you ignorant, brethren (for I am speaking to those who know Torah), that Torah reigns [as lord; *kyrieuei*] over a person for as long a time as that person lives" (7:1). Paul's parenthetical statement in v. 1 suggests considerable overlap between his fictive interlocutor and his actual gentile audience;[2] that is, Paul portrays his Roman audience as gentiles who, like his interlocutor, have exhibited considerable interest in, and have substantive knowledge of, Torah. This is the first time Paul has used *nomos* since 6:14–15, that strange passage where Paul tells his audience, "you are not under Torah but under grace." Paul's interlocutor then wondered if sin had therefore lost its consequence (*viz.* death).

---

2. See Thorsteinsson's "general principle of identity," whereby the interlocutor "represents or speaks for the letter's recipient(s), thus functioning as an object of identification for the latter" (*Interlocutor*, 140–44; p. 144 quoted).

Interestingly, up to this point Paul has only used *kyrieuō* ("reign as lord") with either death or sin as its subject.[3] Paul has used the near-synonym *basileuō* ("reign as king") similarly, with death or sin exercising sovereign authority (5:14, 17, 21; 6:12), though twice Paul has referred to the future or contrasting reign of grace and/or those who receive God's grace.[4] By way of contrast, *Torah* exercises sovereign authority in 7:1, and it does so as long as a person lives. Under normal circumstances I would expect Paul to be addressing a Jew here. Nowhere does Paul subject gentiles to Torah's authority, and in fact in 6:14 he explicitly denies that his readers fall under Torah's rule. In light of Paul's dialogue with a proselyte since Rom 2:17, however, I suggest that Paul imagines himself addressing a gentile audience that is positively disposed toward Torah.[5] With respect to *this* audience, Paul needs to nail home the point that Torah cannot deliver gentiles from the power of their passions—Torah cannot deliver self-mastery—and that freedom from sin comes through some other means.

First, Paul turns to a secular metaphor, using the legal analogy of a marriage decree and the extent of its authority (Rom 7:2–3). He provides four rhetorically balanced phrases that exhibit a remarkable degree of parallelism.

> A   2 For a married woman is bound to her husband by the marriage decree while he lives.
>
> > B   But if her husband dies, she is released from the decree [and] from her husband.
>
> A' 3 Therefore, as long as the husband lives, she will be called an adulteress if she marries another man.
>
> > B' But if her husband dies, she is free from the decree. As a result, she would not be an adulteress if she married another man.

Each phrase is progressively longer than the one before. Phrases A and A' center on the decree's authority over the woman, with both phrases emphasizing that the husband "lives" [*zōn*]. Conversely, phrases B and B' explore the space beyond the decree's authority, with both beginning with the conditional phrase, "But if her husband dies" [*ean de apothanē*

---

3. Rom 6:9, 14, respectively.

4. Rom 5:21, 17, respectively.

5. Remember Paul's clarification: "... for I am speaking to those who know Torah" (7:1).

ho anēr]. More importantly, Paul uses the crucial word *eleuthera* ("free") to describe the woman after her husband's death. This, in fact, is the point of the analogy. The marriage decree [*nomos*] holds sway over the woman's identity and her fate as long as her husband lives, but death—*his* death—releases her.

In light of the Hebrew Bible's frequent use of marital imagery to describe the relationship between Israel and YHWH (with, of course, YHWH as husband),[6] the metaphor in Rom 7:2–3 takes on additional significance. Paul is addressing more than simply the *extent* of the authority of the *nomos* ("marriage decree"). He is also making the point that the nations, who have found themselves under the authority of sin and death (whether as slaves [Romans 6] or as wives [7:2–3]), have been released by Jesus' death "under the *nomos*" to take another husband (see Gal 4:4–5).[7] "So then, my brethren, you also were executed by the *nomos*, through the body of Christ, so that you might marry another, that is, the one who raised him from the dead, so that we might bear fruit for God" (Rom 7:4). The [dead] body of Christ has secured the freedom of Paul's readers from their marriage decree [*nomos*] to sin (and death). And remember that Paul has already told his readers that Torah [*nomos*] results in knowledge of sin (3:20). This is why I have left *nomos* untranslated in 7:4; Paul here engages in a wordplay in which *nomos* refers to both the marriage decree (7:2–3) and Torah (7:1) at the same time. Just as death releases the wife from the *nomos* of her marriage, so Christ's death releases humanity from the obligation and the consequences of Torah and frees her to become a productive [*karpophoreō*] wife of God.[8]

We need to remember, however, that Paul does not normally subject "humanity" to Torah. Torah structured *Israel's* covenant with YHWH, and Paul put the failure to observe Torah solely at *Israel's* feet. The nations, however, had been handed over [*paradidōmi*] to enslavement to their passions and desires (Rom 1:24, 26, 28) because they abandoned the Creator God

---

6. Most famously, see Hosea; see also Ezekiel 16; Isaiah 54; Jer 3:1–13, among others.

7. Paul says that Jesus "was born under Torah" [*genomenon hypo nomon*] and that he "redeemed those who were under Torah" [*tous hypo nomon exagorasē*] (Gal 4:4–5). Although he does not explicitly describe Jesus' death as being "under Torah," the context—especially the reference to Jesus "redeeming" those under Torah—clearly includes Jesus' death. See also Gal 3:13.

8. Wright correctly points out that *hina karpophorēsōmen tō theō* ("so that we might be fruitful to/for God") "picks up the image of fruitbearing from 6:21–22, but sets it now within a context where its meaning is more precisely childbearing" (Wright, "Romans," 559; original emphasis); see also Jewett, *Romans*, 435–36.

Nomos, *Flesh*, *Spirit*

in favor of worshipping images of created beings. As a result, Paul claims in v. 5 that both Jews (*viz.* Paul) and gentiles (*viz.* Paul's readers) belonged "in the flesh" [*ēmen en tē sarki*], and both Jews and gentiles were enslaved to the "sinful passions" [*pathēmata tōn hamartiōn*] which were brought into effect "within our members." Most remarkable, however, is the means by which the sinful passions came to effect "within our members" [*en tois melesin hēmōn*]: namely "through Torah" [*dia tou nomou*]! Jewett wrongly assumes a verb of *coming* ("sinful passions *that came* through the law") and refers to "the extraordinary role of law in promoting sinful passions rather than, as traditionally believed, holding them in check."[9] But Paul does not say Torah "promotes" one's sinful passions; rather, he says Torah points out, names, and/or identifies sin (see 3:20) and then condemns the sinful passions present in the person who falls under Torah's authority.[10] As we saw in the previous chapter, Paul's Hellenistic Jewish contemporary, Philo of Alexandria, postured Torah as the primary vehicle for attaining self-mastery, surely a standard position among Hellenistically-oriented Jews in the Roman era. Here in Rom 7:5, Paul takes exactly the opposite position and postures Torah as a vehicle of both Israel's and the gentiles' enslavement to their passions.

Paul therefore rejects categorically and absolutely any suggestion that gentiles should observe Torah. Freedom from the passions and desires of the flesh comes via a different route. "But now [*nyni de*] we are released from Torah, since we have died to that in which we were confined, so that we might serve [as slaves; *douleuein*] in newness of spirit and not in oldness of letter" (Rom 7:6). The opposition of spirit to letter picks up again the same opposition from the end of Romans 2, where Paul explains the "circumcision of the heart" [*peritomē kardias*] in terms of being "in spirit and not in letter" [*en pneumati ou grammati*; 2:29]. In both Rom 7:6 and 2:29, we have to decipher whether Paul uses *pneuma* to refer to the human spirit or to God's Spirit. In light of our decision to read Rom 2:17–29 in terms of Paul's efforts to dissuade gentiles from submitting to Torah's yoke, Rom 2:29 refers to the sphere of their observance of God's commandment (spirit versus written regulation, which would involve their

---

9. Jewett, *Romans*, 436.

10. Wright rightly and repeatedly stresses Paul's positive evaluation of Torah throughout this section of Romans; for example: "All the blame attaches once more to sin itself. Sin was at work in 'me' through the law ('the good thing'); and that work of sin, not of the law itself, produced death. This is the basic explanation that goes behind the dense statement of 7:5, and exonerates Torah from willing complicity in the process" ("Romans," 565).

flesh).[11] The same contrast surfaces again in Rom 7:6. By means of our release [*katērgēthēmen*] from Torah's strictures, punishments, and curses, we are freed to serve as slaves with renewed vigor [*kainotēti pneumatos*] rather than on account of the previously written regulation [*palaiotēti grammatos*]. Romans 7:1–6, therefore, tells much the same tale and makes much the same point as Romans 6: Rather than providing the means for achieving self-mastery and freedom from sin, Torah confirmed the gentiles' enslavement and sentenced them to death. Grace, however, intervened by means of Christ's death, and his death nullified not Torah itself (see Rom 3:31) but rather their subjection to its authority (Rom 7:6). As a result of Christ's death, they are freed from the power of their passions and desires and set under a new authority: God himself.

The Gentile Proselyte Finds His Voice (Rom 7:7–13)

> 7 "What then? Shall we say, 'Torah is sin'?" Certainly not! "But I did not know what sin is except through Torah. For example, I did not know covetousness, except that Torah said, 'You shall not covet.' 8 But sin, taking advantage of the occasion afforded by the commandment, produced in me all manner of covetousness. For apart from Torah, sin was dead. 9 I once lived apart from Torah, but when the commandment came sin sprang to life.[12] 10 So I died, and the commandment was found in me, which was intended for life, this only resulted in death. 11 For sin took advantage of the occasion afforded through the commandment and deceived me, and through that occasion sin killed me. 12 So then, Torah is indeed holy, and the commandment is holy and just and good.[13] 13 So did that which is good for me become death? Certainly not! But sin, so that it would clearly be seen as sin, by means of what was good for me produced death, so that sin might be exceedingly sinful through the commandment."[14]

---

11. As I will mention presently, in Romans 8 Paul will contrast "s/Spirit" not with "letter" but with "flesh." But given the consequence of the written code of circumcision—"letter"—for the literal flesh, I understand the binary pairs s/Spirit|letter and s/Spirit|flesh as rhetorical synonyms.

12. In my reading, Rom 7:9 does not give a general principle that is universally applicable; instead, Paul, by means of the gentile proselyte persona he inhabits here, is addressing the Hellenistic Jewish posturing of Torah as an auspicious avenue toward self-mastery. Far from it, Paul points out that Torah only highlights the problem of enslavement to one's passion and desires and does not solve that problem.

13. Recall Paul's use of "just" [*dikaios*] and "good" [*agathos*] in Rom 5:7.

14. Notice the fit between the sentiment in 7:13 and Paul's point at 3:20: Sin becomes

The interlocutor speaks up again in v. 7, immediately after Paul has just contrasted the *pneuma* ("spirit") with the *gramma* ("letter"). Paul has already explained that Christ's death has freed us from sin (6:10), and he has strongly implied that Christ's death has also freed us from Torah (7:4-6). The interlocutor, therefore, asks, "What then? Shall we say, 'Torah is sin'?" Paul, of course, vehemently denies this; he has already referred to Torah as "the oracles of God" [*ta logia tou theou*; Rom 3:2]. Even the condemnatory function Paul attributes to Torah at Rom 3:19-20 is nevertheless of a piece with the subordination of the whole of creation [*pas ho kosmos*; 3:19] to the Creator God. The interlocutor echoes the same sentiment from Rom 3:19-20 again in 7:7: "But I did not know what sin is except through Torah." Notice Paul's consistency: Torah has never been the problem. Torah has only pointed out the problem, which has always been us and our sin. Even so, I am struck by how starkly Paul has explained what is and what is not made known through Torah:

- "the knowledge of sin [is revealed] through Torah" [*dia nomou*; Rom 3:20];
- "the righteousness of God is revealed apart from Torah [*chōris nomou*] ... through the faithfulness of Jesus Christ" [*dia pisteōs Iēsou Christou*; Rom 3:21, 22];
- "But I did not know what sin is except through Torah" [*dia nomou*; Rom 7:7].

This gets us to the heart of Paul's theologizing about Torah and its consequences: Torah identifies sin as such and confirms the subjection of those under its authority to God's judgment against sin. Moreover, this explains why Paul so vehemently insists that gentiles ought not submit to Torah's yoke. The gentiles were already so plainly under the power and rule of sin and death (1:18-32; 6:19-21) that Torah would only point out and exacerbate their obvious depravity.

As an example, Paul—speaking as the interlocutor[15]—turns to the tenth commandment, "You shall not covet [*ouk epithymēseis*] your neighbor's wife. You shall not covet [*ouk epithymēseis*] your neighbor's house,

---

known through Torah (3:20) and/or the commandment (7:13). The primary difference between these two verses, other than the word *nomos* ("Torah") in the former and *entolē* ("commandment") in the latter, is that Romans 7 describes from within, in experiential terms, the point Paul makes more objectively (i.e., from the outside) in 3:20.

15. It is not yet clear that Paul is speaking as the interlocutor, but it will become so in the course of the chapter (see my discussion of Rom 7:7-8, immediately below).

nor his field, nor his servants (male or female), nor his ox, nor his donkey, nor any of his herd, nor anything that belongs to your neighbor" (Exod 20:17 LXX). Twice the commandment instructs the people not to covet; the only other similarly repetitious idea in the Decalogue is YHWH's insistence against his people worshipping and serving other gods (see Exod 20:2-6). Indeed, Jews in the Second Temple era often saw the tenth commandment as the summary and heart of the Decalogue.[16] But Paul deconstructs the commandment, claiming instead that he did not know what coveting was except that Torah gave the commandment, "You shall not covet" (7:7).[17] As a result, the commandment provided an occasion for sin, which produced all manner of covetousness [*pasan epithymian*] where previously there had been only contentment. After all, "apart from Torah sin is dead" [*chōris gar nomou hamartia nekra* (7:8)].[18]

At this point we have some fairly significant interpretive problems that we need to deal with before moving on to the rest of Rom 7:7-13. Not long ago we noted Paul's considerable consistency across a large section of Romans as he explained what Torah does and does not reveal. But now, in the very same passage (Rom 7:7-8), Paul risks being so *inconsistent* that he loses all coherence and becomes completely self-contradictory. Note the following data:

---

16. See Dunn, *Romans*, 1:380; Jewett, *Romans*, 447-49; Moo, *Romans*, 435; Schreiner, *Romans*, 369; who variously cite Philo, *Creation* 152; *Decalogue*, 142-43, 173; *Spec. Laws* 4:84-94; 4 Macc 2:6; L.A.E. 19; Apoc. Mos. 19:3; Apoc. Abr. 24:9, 10; Tg. Neof. 1 on Exod 20:17, as well as Jas 1:15.

17. I want to point out (but then leave aside for the moment) that I am not fully convinced by Paul's point here. We often have fairly clear ideas about right and wrong even before we have similarly clear ideas about what rules or laws might be in place that might pertain to a particular situation. Why else would we say (perhaps too often), "Better to ask for forgiveness than permission"? But, as I will explain presently, Paul is not *actually* affirming that we do not know where the boundaries lie until God puts up a fence.

18. Paul uses the same phrase here as he did in Rom 3:21, where the righteousness of God was being revealed "apart from Torah" [*chōris nomou*].

Paul has already said, "The knowledge of God is evident among them (for God made it evident to them). ... Although they knew the righteous requirement of God, they not only practice such things but also approve of those who do them" (Rom 1:19, 32) ...	... but now he says, "I did not know covetousness except that Torah said, 'You shall not covet'" (Rom 7:7).
Paul has already said, "Sin was in the world up until Torah, but it was not accounted because there was no Torah. But *death reigned from Adam until Moses*" (Rom 5:13–14) ...	... but now he says, "Apart from Torah sin is dead" (Rom 7:8).

The passages on the left (Rom 1:19, 32; 5:13–14) represent significant moments in Paul's rhetoric. If Paul contradicts those moments here in Romans 7, the coherence of the letter as a whole begins to unravel![19] How is it that sin reigned in death (5:21), and death reigned between Adam and Moses (5:14), and yet Paul can claim sin, apart from Torah, is dead?! How can Paul argue that humanity's exchange of the glory of the Creator God for graven images (1:23) and the truth of God for a lie (1:25) resulted in a deplorable deepening of depravity, and yet seriously suggest that covetousness was unknown prior to Torah?! More than that, if humanity would not have coveted had God not given the command not to covet, why did God give the command in the first place?! Even half-decent parents do not tell their curious children not to jam a knife into the toaster until it looks like they might do so on their own. Is Paul *really* suggesting God was more naïve than a half-decent parent? *mē genoito*!

These contradictory statements may simply be a feature of Paul's complex—some would say inconsistent—logic. But these contradictory statements might also suggest that Paul is not speaking in his own, authorial voice. That is, Paul does not *actually* think that sin apart from Torah

---

19. Commentators struggle to explain the contradiction between Rom 7:8 and his comments elsewhere. For example, "Romans 7:8, 'Apart from the law, Sin lies dead,' is more difficult to place in Paul's retelling of Genesis 3, but if 'dead' is understood metaphorically as 'inactive' or 'unable to act' (as in Abraham's old body and Sarah's dead womb, 4:19), it could describe the situation that existed before God gave the specific commandment, when the serpent had nothing to work with" (Grieb, *Story*, 72). Unfortunately, Rom 7:8 cannot describe this situation because Paul does *not* say "Apart from the *commandment*, Sin lies dead," but rather, "Apart from *Torah* sin is dead." Grieb, however, is forced into this strained reading because she has chosen, along with Dunn and Ernst Käsemann, to read Paul's speech-in-character in terms of Adam's voice.

If You Call Yourself a Jew

is dead. After all, the gentiles, who are not subject to Torah, are especially under the power and rule of sin and death. And Paul does not *actually* think that no one would have known what coveting was had God not given any commandment against covetousness. Paul has already made clear that these ideas are not his own, and so their appearance in Romans 7 suggests that Paul is not speaking in his own voice.

Stanley Stowers has argued that Paul employs a rhetorical technique, called "speech-in-character" [*prosōpopoiia*], "in which the speaker or writer produces speech that represents not himself or herself but another person or type of character."[20] Speech-in-character can take two forms; it "consists of cases where one invents the *ēthos* (i.e., character by means of words) of a known person (*prosōpon*) and also of cases where one invents both the *ēthos* and the person."[21] Romans 7:7–25 takes Stowers's second form, in which Paul speaks in the voice of the gentile proselyte with whom he has been dialoguing since at least 2:17.[22] Paul's speech-in-character begins immediately after the exclamation in v. 7, "Certainly not!"[23] Stowers argues that ancient readers, who regularly encountered speech-in-character in various genres of oral and written communications, looked for certain clues that signaled the author's change from his own, authorial voice to the character he portrays.[24]

The contradictions between Rom 7:7–8 and Paul's earlier rhetoric would have signaled for his readers that something was afoot. If any of his readers were not able to make the link between the speech-in-character in Romans 7, on the one hand, and the multiple dialogic exchanges Paul has constructed with his interlocutor, who "calls himself a Jew" (2:17), on the other, Paul explicitly states in v. 9 whose voice he employs here: "I once lived apart from Torah [*chōris nomou pote*], but when the commandment

---

20. Stowers, "Romans 7," 180.

21. Ibid., 181.

22. Thorsteinsson (*Interlocutor*, 175) goes even further: Romans 7 presents not just Paul's speech-in-character but also represents his actual audience. "The addressees' weakness spoken of in 6:19 comes to further expression in 7:7–25. Here, a certain individual, who probably is meant to represent the gentile readership, describes and laments over his inability to follow the Jewish Law, because of the very weakness of the flesh."

23. "The section begins in v. 7 with an abrupt change in voice following a rhetorical question that serves as a transition from Paul's authorial voice that has previously addressed the readers explicitly described by the letter in 6:1—7:6" (Stowers, "Romans 7," 191).

24. "These ancient readers would next look for *diaphōnia* ['discord, disagreement, inconsistency'], a difference in characterization from the authorial voice" (ibid.).

came sin sprang to life." Commentators have noted the problem of how Paul, who self-identified as a Jew even in his later years,[25] could claim to have ever lived "apart from Torah." James Dunn rightly finds it "most unlikely . . . that a Jewish male of Paul's day could ever think of a period of is life when the law was absent."[26] Instead, Dunn thinks Paul speaks as Adam, that Paul has in mind "the childhood of man, the mythical period of the human race's beginnings."[27] Robert Jewett argues that "Paul depicts himself as the person prior to his conversion, a zealous fanatic who *obeyed the Jewish law perfectly* but with such eagerness to achieve honour that he produced evil results."[28] Douglas Moo argues that Paul speaks not as himself but as Israel as whole, and so "*egō* ('I'), while referring to Paul, refers to him in solidarity with the Jewish people and therefore with the experience of the coming of the law at Sinai."[29] Thomas Schreiner, however, insists on reading v. 9 autobiographically, as though "the primary reference is to Paul himself," arguing that "Paul relays his own experience because it is paradigmatic, showing the fate of all those under the law."[30]

---

25. See Phil 3:5-6; cp. also Gal 2:15; Rom 9:1-5; Acts 22:3; 23:6.

26. Dunn, *Romans*, 1:382. See also Stowers ("Romans 7," 192): "If one asks whether Paul gives his readers any clues at all elsewhere in the letter that this might be his autobiography, the answer is clearly 'no'. Nor does this picture even fit with what he says about himself in other letters."

27. Dunn, *Romans*, 1:382 (see also Dunn, "Adam and Christ," 133-35; similarly, see Grieb, *Story*, 71-76). Dunn goes so far as to suggest that we might translate *pote* ("formerly, once") here as "once upon a time," as in, "Once upon a time I lived apart from Torah" (*Romans*, 1:382). I find this suggestion utterly implausible.

28. Jewett, "Anthropological Implications," 32; my emphasis; see Jewett, *Romans*, 444-45.

29. Moo, *Romans*, 437. Wright ("Romans," 549-57) approaches all of Rom 7:1—8:11 in terms of Paul "telling the story of Israel under one particular guise" (549).

30. Schreiner, *Romans*, 363-65 (p. 365 quoted). Jewett (*Romans*, 441-43), citing Engberg-Pedersen ("Reception," 37; see also Engberg-Pedersen, *Paul*, 243-44), argues for an autobiographical reading of Romans 7 as one of the "established" and "important exegetical advances made in recent years." Obviously I disagree, but then Jewett makes the baffling move of trying to incorporate Stowers' work on speech-in-character into his autobiographical reading: "Despite the fact that the depiction does not fit any of the stock characters known to Greco-Roman rhetoric, Paul nevertheless assumes that his hearers in Rome will have an instant grasp of who this character is. The most obvious alternative is that this character is Paul himself" (Jewett, *Romans*, 443-45 [p. 445 quoted]). If Paul speaks as himself, he is no longer speaking "in character"! The more plausible response is that Paul speaks as the interlocutor he has regularly invoked in the letter up to this point.

If You Call Yourself a Jew

There are problems with all four readings. Schreiner's, of course, simply cannot make sense of the text.[31] Paul does not claim that "the meaning and import of [Torah's] moral norms" *formerly* [*pote*] did not "strike home," as Schreiner claims.[32] Schreiner inappropriately psychologizes the passage, assuming that Paul has in mind his *perception* of Torah's authority over him rather than its *actual* authority over him. Paul says he "was living apart from Torah," which can only mean that, in whatever mode Paul is speaking here, Torah was not always normative. Moo offers a better reading that at least takes the text seriously, but it misses the disagreements [*diaphōniai*] between Rom 7:7–8 and the previous parts of Romans. More importantly, I cannot see anywhere in the text where Paul signals that he speaks here as Israel, especially since Israel's "life apart from Torah" [*ezōn chōris nomou*; lit. "I was living apart from Torah"] consisted primarily of slavery in Egypt. Paul would have had to ignore this aspect of Israel's foundation narrative if he wanted to portray Israel's life "before Torah"—which is not quite the same as "apart from Torah"—as in any sense better off.[33] Jewett never explains how perfect obedience to Torah, even "with such eagerness to achieve honour," produces evil results.[34] Moreover, nothing in Romans 7 suggests Paul's character "obeyed the Jewish law perfectly"; if anything, that character expresses exasperation at *not* being able to do the good he wants to do, despite his agreement, "in my innermost being" [*ton*

---

31. In this connection, both Stowers (*Rereading*, 270; see 363 n.47) and Wright ("Romans," 553) correctly refer to Krister Stendahl's seminal essay, "The Apostle Paul and the Introspective Conscience of the West." Stendahl himself rightly pointed out that, contrary to contemporary Western angst about the impossibility of human perfection, Paul seems not to have hesitated to describe himself, with respect to righteousness as circumscribed by Torah, as "blameless" [*amemptos*] ("Introspective Conscience," 200–201).

32. Schreiner, *Romans*, 365.

33. Stowers rightly characterizes the *ethos* of the current passage: "Like the handbooks recommend, the person speaks of his 'happy' past before he learned about the law (7:7b–8 and esp. 9), his present misery, and his future plight (7:24)" ("Romans 7," 192). The obvious point here, of course, is that Torah is not just "law" or even "Law"; Torah is Israel's covenant with YHWH. And so any reading that portrays Paul—autobiographically or figuratively as Israel—nostalgically and romantically portraying Israel's pre-Torah days and diminishing the gracious gift of Torah suffers an inherent risk of historical improbability.

34. Jewett refers to Gal 1:13–14, but the parallel between Galatians and Jewett's explanation of Romans 7 does not work. Jewett proposes the character of "a zealous fanatic who obeyed the Jewish law perfectly" ("Anthropological Implications," 32). Galatians 1, however, does not portray the problem with Paul's "former conduct in Judaism" as perfect obedience to Torah but rather as extraordinary persecution [*kath' hyperbolēn ediōkon*] of the church of God.

esō anthrōpon; Rom 7:22] that Torah is spiritual and the commandment is holy and just and good (7:14, 12). Dunn's reading also lacks conviction; Paul only mentions Adam once in the whole of Romans (see 5:14), and he has not alluded to Adam since 5:19.[35] If Paul, thirty-two verses after his last reference to Adam, suddenly begins to speak in Adam's voice, how would he expect his audience to follow him?

Another explanation lies nearer to hand, and a simpler one to boot. Paul has repeatedly raised the specter of a gentile proselyte who has submitted himself to Torah's authority as a means to achieve self-mastery. Now, Paul speaks as that character, and he provides two different signals for his audience to follow his rhetorical move: (i) the *diaphōniai* in 7:7–8, and (ii) the portrayal of his fictional *prosōpon* ("character") as one who formerly lived "apart from Torah." Both signals point in the direction of the *prosōpon* of Rom 7:7–25 being a gentile proselyte, one who once lived without any reference to Israel's Torah but who no longer does so. Paul has already given his judgment of such a character-type: Such a person should be only too aware of his or her sinfulness, "for knowledge of sin comes through Torah" (3:20). Stowers reads this passage similarly: "The speaker in 7:7–25 speaks with great personal pathos of coming under the law at some point, learning about his desire and sin, and being unable to do what he wants to do because of enslavement to sin and flesh."[36] Given that some Jews (e.g., Philo, *4 Maccabees*) postured Torah as an (even *the*) effective means for achieving self-mastery, Paul dons the *persona* of a gentile who has taken on Torah only to find that, rather than self-mastery, Torah has led him to a deeper, more vivid awareness of his enslavement to his passions and desires. This character—the gentile proselyte—agrees with Jews that Torah deserves to be highly regarded, but he has found it powerless to deliver what he truly seeks: freedom from sin and death.[37]

---

35. Thus I disagree with Wright ("Romans," 560), who thinks "the flesh" in 7:5 "is another way of saying 'in Adam.'"

36. Stowers, "Romans 7," 191–92.

37. *Pace* Wright, who sees in Romans 7 a paradox, namely that "[t]he exodus both has and has not happened. This is exactly Paul's analysis of the plight of Israel under Torah. In terms of the original exodus, Israel is the free people of God. In terms of the new one, the exodus from sin and death, Israel is still in slavery. The very Torah that spoke of the original freedom reminds Israel daily of that continuing servitude, and its consequences" ("Romans," 551). While I find much to agree with here, this just is not what Paul is talking about in Romans 7. The entire context of Paul's dialogue with the gentile proselyte since Rom 2:17 pushes the speech-in-character here in 7:7–25 away from Israel and toward gentiles interested in (and even observant of) Israel's Torah.

The gentiles, according to Paul, already languished under their bondage to "the lusts of their hearts" and to their "dishonorable passions" and to their "worthless mind" (Rom 1:18–32; vv. 24, 26, and 28 quoted). Those who turned to Torah to remedy the situation, however, find that Torah only confirms their bondage and cannot rescue them from it. This is not a weakness—or still yet a *failure!*—of Torah.[38] The speech-in-character in Rom 7:7–13 portrays Torah in utterly positive terms and laments the speaker's inability to keep Torah. In light of the ladder Torah offers by which the gentile proselyte might climb up out of the muck and mire of enslavement to sin, the proselyte's inability to do so only reinforces and clarifies the awe-inspiring (and desperate) extent of sin's reign over humanity. Sin, now revealed as exceedingly sinful [*kath' hyperbolēn hamartōlos*], even prevents the well-intentioned gentile from employing Torah, God's covenant with his people Israel, as a means for self-mastery.[39] Paul attributes weakness not to Torah but to the gentile moral agent who endeavors to attain self-mastery by means of Torah.

Sin's Enslavement, Viewed from Within (Rom 7:14–25)

14 "For we know that Torah is spiritual, but I am fleshly (given that I have been sold under sin). 15 For I do not know what I am doing, because I don't do what I desire to do, but that which I hate, this I do. 16 But if I do that which I do not want to do, I agree with Torah about what is good. 17 But now, *I* am no longer doing the thing [I do not want to do], but rather sin that dwells in me. 18 For I know that the good does not dwell in me (that is, in my flesh). The *desire* is present in me, but *doing* the good is not. 19 For I am not doing the good that I desire to do, but the evil that I do not desire, *this* I am doing. 20 But if I am doing what I do not desire to do, I am no longer the one doing it; rather, sin, which dwells within me! 21 Therefore, here's what I discover about Torah,[40] which I discovered because I wanted to do good: evil dwells in me. 22 For I delight in the

---

38. *Pace* Dunn, "Adam and Christ," 113, who refers to "the law's weakness."

39. Despite our very different readings of Romans 7, I agree with Wright that, here in Rom 7:13b, we find "the key . . . [to] Paul's whole mature thinking about the purpose of Torah, or, better, the purpose of God in giving Torah" ("Romans," 565).

40. Romans 7:21 opens: *heuriskō ara ton nomon* (lit. "I find, therefore, the law"). But Paul's (or, more accurately, Paul's persona's) point is not that he has found "the law" (= Torah) but rather that he has found something *about* "the law." Hence my translation, "Therefore, here's what I discover about Torah"; similarly, see ibid., 569.

> Torah of God in my innermost being, 23 but I see a different Torah at work in my members, which wages war against my mind's Torah and takes me captive by means of Torah's judgment in my members against sin. 24 Wretched person that I am, who will deliver me from this body of death?! 25 Thanks be to God, through Jesus Christ, our Lord! So then, on the one hand I myself, in my mind, am enslaved to the Torah of God, but on the other hand I am enslaved, in my flesh, to the Torah of sin."

I agree with Stanley Stowers that Paul's speech-in-character continues beyond 7:13.[41] This has one very dramatic consequence for the interpretation of both Paul and his letter to the Romans: Paul does not exhibit the inner psychological angst at the enormity of God's righteous requirements and his inability to bear them.[42] Paul does *not* say that, although he knows what is good and what he ought to do, he—Paul of Tarsus—finds that he cannot do it and instead does the evil that he knows he ought not do. (This, of course, is precisely the significance drawn from 7:14-25 in much popular Western [and especially American] exegetical tradition.[43])

Instead, Paul continues to speak in character as the gentile proselyte who, desiring to attain self-mastery, turned to Israel's Torah only to find himself more aware of sin's reign over him. And, as before, Paul-as-gentile-proselyte has only good things to say about Torah and only bad things to say about himself. "For we know that Torah is spiritual, but I am fleshly (given that I have been sold under sin)" [*pepramenos hypo tēn hamartian*; 7:14]. This last phrase makes patently clear that Paul is speaking as a rhetorically portrayed character and not in his own voice. Only one chapter earlier Paul, in his full authorial voice, declared to his readers, "For you

---

41. Similarly, see Jewett, *Romans*, 455.

42. See esp. Stendahl's monumental essay, "Introspective Conscience" (see n. 31 [p. 136], above).

43. Cottrell is certainly wrong to discuss Rom 7:14-25 under the heading, "The Christian Continues to Struggle against Sin" (*Romans*, 1:441-54). Paul nowhere mentions "the Christian" in Romans. Worse, Cottrell forces a dichotomy of regenerate|unregenerate upon the text and argues that Paul could only be expressing the inner struggle of the regenerate, because "the things Paul says about the law of God and about his own inner life are completely incompatible with the heart and life of an unregenerate man as described elsewhere in the Bible" (ibid., 1:443). Cottrell not only misses the rhetorical texture of Romans 7 (i.e., speech-in-character), but he completely misses that Paul portrays himself here as a gentile attempting to master his passions and overcome sin by means of Torah. "Regeneration," if it really is an issue in Romans 7, does not appear on stage until 8:1! Wright ("Romans," 552-53) offers a powerful explanation of why Paul simply *cannot* be speaking as the typical or "normal Christian."

are not under Torah but under grace" (6:14). If Paul declares his readers free from the penalties and consequences laid out in Torah, penalties and consequences that accrued because of sin, he would be thoroughly incoherent if he now declared himself—rather than a rhetorically contrived character—as being "under sin."

Paul's speech-in-character continues in vv. 15–17, and it portrays in dramatic terms the proselyte's utter failure to gain mastery over his passions and desires. Even with such a powerful tool as Torah, which is spiritual (7:14), the only benefit the gentile derives from Torah-observance is a clearer understanding of his plight. He is utterly and completely under sin's rule! We might opt to read Paul's personification of sin and his portrayal of it as an active moral agent—even one that takes control and acts independently of human moral agents—as if it mitigates a person's responsibility for sinful behavior. Paul even goes so far as to say, "But now I am no longer doing it [*ouketi egō katergazomai auto*], but rather sin that dwells within me."[44] In light of the ancient cultural scripts of self-mastery and the shame and dishonor that attached to being enslaved by one's passions, Paul's speech-in-character actually *exacerbates* rather than mitigates the problem of sin dwelling within and acting in place of the human will.[45] The power of sin to overpower and control a person might be understandable—never excusable, but perhaps *understandable*—for barbarians and for women. But men—*real men!*—were expected to control rather than be controlled by anything that might make a bid for power over their moral agency, as Stowers explains at length:

> Aristotle notes that softness and lack of mastery are sometimes innate, as, for example, in the royal house of Scythia or in the female sex. In Greek constructions of the ethnic other, as in Jewish constructions of the gentile, barbarians often lack self-control because of either innate weakness or inferior laws and constitutions. Gender hierarchy lies close to the heart of the discourse of self-mastery. *Life is war, and masculinity has to be achieved and constantly fought for. Men are always in danger of*

---

44. The neuter singular personal pronoun, *auto*, in 7:17 refers back to the neuter singular relative pronoun, *ho ou thelō* ("that which I do not want [to do]"), in v. 16.

45. Wright has missed this point completely; he reads v. 17 as "a remarkable statement of *not just diminished but abrogated responsibility*" ("Romans," 567; my emphasis). In light of the considerable cultural currency that attached to self-mastery, I cannot think that any reader in antiquity would have excused a person mastered by sin, or would have concluded that Paul "has exonerated Israel whose 'I' can say, 'It was Sin's fault' (Sin dwelling within me)" (*pace* Grieb, *Story*, 75), on the basis of what he says in Rom 7:17.

succumbing to softness, described as forms of femaleness or servility. In the ancient Mediterranean construction of gender, the sexes are "poles on a continuum which can be traversed." To achieve self-mastery means to win the war; to let the passions and desires go unsubdued means defeat, a destruction of hard-won manliness.[46]

Paul's gentile proselyte *persona* comes across as weak, womanly, slavish, unable to exert himself in the manner of a true man. Unfortunately, commentators often miss that Paul portrays the speaker *and not Torah itself* as overpowered by sin. For example, Katherine Grieb suggests, "Paul also sees another law, a shadow law, *the law taken over by Sin in his flesh*, that is, in the members of his physical body."[47] But Paul, speaking as the interlocutor, clearly says that evil dwells "in me" [*moi*; Rom 7:21], and he portrays himself—again, speaking as the interlocutor—*and not the law* (= Torah) as divided (see 7:22–23, 25).

The power of the speech-in-character's critique of unmanliness comes across when we contrast it with the manliness with which the author of 2 Maccabees describes the mother (!) of seven Jewish men who faced torture and death for holding fast to their ancestral traditions:

> But the mother was especially incredible and worthy of being remembered nobly. Although she watched her seven sons murdered within the span of one day, she bore it courageously [*eupsychōs epheren*] because of her hope in the Lord. She encouraged each of them in their ancestral language, having been filled with a noble mind and bolstering her womanly reason with a manly fury [*ton thēlyn logismon arseni thymō diegeirasa*; 2 Macc 7:20–21].[48]

We might read Romans 7 in terms of letting Paul (or whomever we imagine speaking) "off the hook" for being overwhelmed by sin's power.[49] We need to consider the possibility, however, that the very feat of being

---

46. Stowers, *Rereading*, 45 (quoting Winkler, *Constraints*, 50); my emphasis.

47. Grieb, *Story*, 76; my emphasis.

48. The description of the mother in 2 Maccabees 7 provides a positive illustration of Winkler's point, which Stowers cited in the block quote above, that the sexes are "poles on a continuum *which can be traversed*" (my emphasis). Typically, the danger was that men would behave womanly, but there was always the possibility, rare though it may have been, that a woman would behave manly.

49. As does, for example, Wright ("Romans," 567–68); see n. 45, above.

overwhelmed by sin—and Torah's impotence to forestall it—presents the very problem for which the gospel provides the solution.

This possibility—that enslavement to sin *exacerbates* the problem (even *is* the problem!) rather than *excuses* the problem—provides a useful perspective from which we can continue to read Paul's speech-in-character. Again, v. 20 does not excuse sinful behavior among well-intentioned people who *want* to do good but find themselves unable. Rather, it condemns the weak who cannot master the sin that dwells within them, even with the aid of Torah, the very "oracles of God" [*ta logia tou theou*; 3:2], by which God set before his people Israel two options: life and blessing, on the one hand, or death and curses, on the other (Deut 30:19–20). Paul's rhetorical character offers personal testimony about the pathetic and woeful consequences for any gentile who would attempt to master sin and his passions by turning to and taking up Torah-observance.

At this point, Paul, still inhabiting his rhetorical *persona*, begins to draw the conclusion that Torah was always going to fail to lead to self-mastery, not because Torah was an ineffective instrument but because it was wielded by an ineffectual moral agent. The syntax of vv. 21 and 23 is quite dense and requires considerable massaging to make sense in English, and how I have massaged these two verses differs markedly from other translations. Most contemporary English translations provide basically the same translation of 7:21: "So I find it to be a law that when I want to do right, evil lies close at hand" (ESV). I have a number of problems with this translation:

- First, this translation arbitrarily decides that *ton nomon* ("the law, principle") does not refer here to Torah, even though Paul has consistently used *nomos* to refer to Torah throughout Romans.[50] Moreover, the very same word in v. 22 clearly and obviously refers to Torah.

- Second, this translation begins the thing that Paul says he has found at the wrong place. Notice the placement of the word *that* in the ESV's translation (which I quoted above; the NIV uses a colon to the same effect). This word [*hoti*] regularly functions as a "marker of narrative or discourse content," especially when "[u]sed after verbs that denote mental or sense perception . . . or an act of the mind, to indicate the

---

50. The only exception, other than possibly 2:12–13, is at 7:2–3, where Paul has clearly signaled for his readers that he is referring to a marriage decree rather than Torah. But even here, *nomos*-as-marriage-decree provides a metaphor for *nomos*-as-Torah (see 7:1, 4–6).

content of what is said, etc."[51] What Paul's *persona* has discovered about Torah, according to v. 21, is simply, "evil dwells in me" [*hoti emoi to kakon parakeitai*].[52]

- Third, this translation misunderstands the dative participial phrase, *tō thelonti emoi poiein to kalon*. Most English translations understand this phrase *temporally*, as if Paul is describing *when* or *the moment in which* he discovers the presence of evil. This is certainly a possibility.[53] However, given the context that has guided our reading of Paul's speech-in-character, this particular dative phrase should be rendered *causally*: "I discover this about Torah *because* I desire to do good."[54] That is, the gentile proselyte, motived by a desire to do good, turned to Israel's Torah, and as a result discovered that sin dwells inside him.

Romans 7:23 is a similarly difficult verse, and again I have rendered this verse substantially differently from most contemporary English translations. As I explained above, *nomos* in v. 23 consistently refers to Torah rather than to some general, nondescript "principle" or "law" in Paul's mind versus an antagonistic but equally nondescript "principle" or "law" at work in Paul's members. Rather than two different *nomoi* ("laws or principles"), Paul's *persona* describes *himself* as divided.[55] His mind delights in Torah (v. 22), but he cannot even control his body so that it obeys the will and desires of his mind. Having lost all self-control and self-mastery, he succumbs to sin's power, so that, whatever his mind might choose, his body rebels against [*antistrateuomenon*; lit. "waging war against"] his mind.

Torah has some very specific things to say about sin and establishes some very specific consequences for it. Those consequences begin as far

51. BDAG, s.v. The "verb that denote[s] mental or sense perception . . . or an act of the mind" in Rom 7:21 is *heuriskō* ("find, discover").

52. See the NASB, which renders 7:21, "I find then the principle that evil is present in me, the one who wants to do good" (i.e., the "principle" Paul discovers is simply, "evil is present in me").

53. See BDF §200, or even §201 (which would result in a translation more like, "as long as I desired to do good, [. . .] evil dwells in me"). For a similar reading, see Wright, "Romans," 570.

54. See BDF §196; Wallace, *Greek Grammar*, 167-68: "The dative substantive indicates the cause or basis of the action of the verb. *This usage is fairly common*" (my emphasis).

55. Engberg-Pedersen differentiates the "I-whole" ("the whole human being, which Paul then goes on to divide into different parts") from two "I-parts" (a good one, which is "identical with 'the inner man' [7:22] and the 'mind' [*nous*, 7:23, 25]," and a contrasting one, identified "with the 'limbs' [*melē*, 7:23] and the 'flesh' [*sarx*, 7:25]"), both of which Paul refers to as "I" (*Paul*, 244-45).

back as Genesis 2,[56] and Paul has repeatedly affirmed Torah's judgment on sin.[57] As a result, despite his mind's delight in Torah and what it says about self-mastery, righteousness, and "the good" [*to agathon*], Paul's *persona* finds himself under Torah's judgments against him *because he has been defeated and emasculated by his passions and desires.*[58] That is, Torah relates to his extremities [*tō onti en tois melesin mou*] by virtue of its authority over sin.[59] Torah condemns sin, but Paul's *persona* is enslaved by sin. So then, despite his agreement with Torah in his mind (7:22, 23), this proselyte finds himself condemned by Torah. According to Paul, "the Law actually brings judgement to Gentiles who try to keep it."[60]

Once we properly recognize Paul's rhetorical technique (speech-in-character) and work through the text carefully, always keeping in mind Paul's *persona* (a gentile proselyte frustrated by the results of his submission to Torah's yoke), Romans 7 comes into crisp focus. And so the *persona*'s exclamation, "Wretched person that I am!" stems from his awareness of the good he ought to do and his inability to do it because he has been enslaved by sin. Torah has only confirmed in his mind what is good and noble; it has provided no help in bringing his members in line and under control. I am reminded once again of Stowers's discussion of the cultural currency of self-mastery in antiquity: "Aristotle says there are two forms of unrestraint (*akrasia*), recklessness and weakness. Weakness (*astheneia*) . . . *is worse than recklessness.* 'The weak deliberate, but then fail to keep their resolution because of their passions' ([*Eth. nic.* 7.]1150b 20)."[61] Paul's *persona*—and so perhaps also his audience, at least potentially—is not

---

56. "You shall eat from every tree that is in the Garden, for food. But from the tree of the knowledge of good and evil, you shall not eat from it. On the day in which you eat from it, *you shall surely die*" [*thanatō apothaneisthe* (Gen 2:16–27 LXX; my emphasis)].

57. See, e.g., Rom 6:23; 7:5, 10, 13.

58. Our reading of this distinction—the "Torah of my mind/the Spirit" and the "Torah of sin/death" in 7:23 and 8:2—is compatible with Calvin Roetzel's argument: "Like Philo, Paul affirmed the surpassing importance of the inward law *without denying the importance of the palpable expression of that unwritten imperative*" ("Messianic Age," 124; my emphasis). That is, the "Torah of my mind" affirms the inward law, but Paul's persona finds he is not able to bring that inward law to "palpable expression" in his members. See p. 125, where Roetzel cites Rom 8:1 [*sic*; 8:2].

59. I am reading the genitive case, *en tō nomō tēs hamartias*, as a "genitive of subordination" (Wallace, *Greek Grammar*, 103–4), which, as Wallace recognizes, is related to the objective genitive (see ibid., 116–19; see also BDF §163; Porter, *Idioms*, 92, 94).

60. Campbell, "Rationale," 24.

61. Stowers, *Rereading*, 46; my emphasis.

reckless, as were the gentiles described in 1:18–32. Paul's persona is *weak*! And this is worse.

Hence his *persona*'s self-identification as *talaipōros* ("miserable, wretched, distressed"[62]). He is so weak, so unable to master his passions even with the power of Torah as his guide, that he cries out, "who will deliver me from this body of death?!" Of course, *death* [*thanatos*] has featured prominently throughout this section of Romans; eighteen of the twenty-two references to *thanatos* in Romans occur in chapters 5–7.[63] The Pauline *persona* experiences the full wages (6:23) of his enslavement to sin, and he cries out in his weakness, looking for someone more manly in his ability to conquer sin and, moreover, to rescue others from its power.

In the closing verse Paul's *persona* recognizes and proclaims that Torah was ineffectual for delivering a person from the power of sin—of the passions and desire—and turns instead to the power of the gospel.[64] The proselyte's mind may have recognized and agreed with Torah's ordinances, but the body's members proved too weak to overcome the passions that Torah condemns as sinful. The emphatic personal pronoun *autos egō*, which I have translated "I myself" (v. 25), emphasizes the unity of the moral subject who finds himself divided, mind against members. This division represents the catastrophic results of the loss of self-mastery: though he mentally concedes Torah's rightness, he *at the same time* finds himself under Torah's judgment on sin.

The speech-in-character ends with the stark phrase, *douleuō ... nomō hamartias* ("I am enslaved ... to the Torah of sin"). The Septuagint nowhere describes Torah as being "of sin" or "of transgression." In the NT, only Paul describes Torah this way. Back in 7:23 we translated *en tō nomō tēs hamartias* as "by means of Torah's judgment against sin." In light of this translation, we might render v. 25: "in my mind I am enslaved to Torah's praise of God, but in my flesh I am enslaved to Torah's judgment against sin." Perhaps a similar idea appears at 1 Cor 15:56: "Torah is the power of sin" [*hē de dynamis tēs hamartias ho nomos*].[65] Regarding this phrase, Anthony Thiselton explains, "The law, in spite of its being 'holy and good' (Rom 7:12, 13) and designed to bring life, comes to perform the very opposite effect in the context of human fallenness, sin, and bondage.

---

62. BDAG, s.v.

63. Outside Rom 5–7, *thanatos* appears only in Romans 1 (v. 32) and 8 (vv. 2, 6, 38).

64. Recall Rom 1:16–17, which commentators often identify as the thesis statement for the whole letter.

65. Wright ("Romans," 570) also refers to 1 Cor 15:56 in his discussion of Rom 7:25.

Rom 1:18—2:29 and 5:12–21 underline human culpability, which the law appears to intensify as a kind of slavery (Rom 3:20; 6:20; cf. 7:7)."[66]

Readers will have to decide for themselves whether I have offered a compelling defense of my expanded translation of 7:25. Either way, the relation of Torah [*nomos*] to sin and the flesh, on the one hand, and life and the s/Spirit, on the other, will be an important feature of Romans 8. And even if the difficulties of the relation between Torah and sin in Paul's perspective and Roman's rhetoric remain unexplained, to some extent, we can be fairly confident that Paul does not identify a second *nomos* ("law or principle"). Throughout the entire passage he has been focused on Torah, the Law of God given to Moses on Sinai.[67] Torah has not made known the righteousness of God (cf. Rom 3:21); it has only increased the evidence of sin (see 3:20). Here in Romans 7, Paul explains in greater depth why this is so.

∼

But if Romans 7 focuses so starkly on the predicament caused not by Torah but by the failure of gentile self-mastery, with or without Torah, Romans 8 focuses on the solution to the predicament. Torah has not been able to elevate the nations above their base and senseless desires, but Paul, the herald and apostle of the gospel, the power of God for salvation (Rom 1:16), is about to explain how Christ, the paragon of faithfulness to the Creator God, has achieved what Torah did not. We now turn to Romans 8.

---

66. Thiselton, *Corinthians*, 1302.

67. See Wright, "Romans," 552: "'The law' here, to repeat, is the Mosaic law, the Torah, and this [*viz.*, Rom 7:1—8:11] is one of Paul's fullest discussions of it. And those who are 'under the law' are, basically, Jews, and, by extension, those who attach themselves to Israel, i.e., God-fearers and proselytes."

9

Creation Renewed by the Spirit

Security in the Presence of God

The absence of the Spirit in Rom 7:7–25 proves a decisive difference from the Pauline texts that refer to the struggle in the Christian life. No one denies that the Christian is caught up in the transition from the present age, which is characterized by the ongoing activity of sin, to the full manifestation of the age to come. The imperatives of Rom 6 and 8 are necessary because of sin's continuing influence on the believer, but those imperatives follow from the indicative of a changed status in Christ. The contrast between Rom 7:7–25 and Rom 8 could not be more striking. Nineteen times Paul mentions the Spirit in chap. 8! The contrast between these two sections of the letter is therefore intentional.[1]

We saw in the previous chapter that the traditionally difficult rhetoric of Romans 7 comes into fairly clear focus when we recognize (i) that the *egō* ("I") that speaks in Rom 7:7–25 is not Paul himself (i.e., it is not autobiographical); (ii) that Paul speaks in the voice of a rhetorical *persona* ("speech-in-character"); and (iii) that Paul portrays that *persona* as a gentile who has taken on Torah-observance as a means to achieve self-mastery. A gentile, who lacks the Spirit of God, finds himself unable to keep Torah "in his limbs" [*en tois melesin mou*; 7:23], or "in his flesh" [*tē sarki*; 7:25], and so the holy and just and good commandment (7:12) results in death rather than life (7:13). Andrew Das, in the epigram to this

---

1. Das, *Solving*, 207.

chapter, rightly focuses on the centrality of the Spirit [*pneuma*] in Romans 8—and its absence from Romans 7!—as the key difference between the gentile who hopes to but cannot attain self-mastery through Torah, on the one hand, and the gentile who has been adopted into the Father's family (see 8:15). As Das explains,

> The Spirit nowhere factors into the struggles of the "I" against sin in 7:7–25 (cf. 7:6!). The absence is conspicuous and renders likely the conclusion that Rom 7:5–6 functions to an extent as a thesis for both 7:7–25 and 8:1–17. . . . A new era has opened up and stands in full view. With the emphatic "now" of Rom 8:1 (echoing the turn in 7:6) the Christian no longer experiences condemnation or "death" (cf. 7:10, 13).[2]

Paul's *persona* cried out in Romans 7, "Wretched man that I am, who will deliver me from this body of death?!" (7:24). Paul's authorial voice expresses total confidence that his current sufferings do not compare to the glory that awaits him (8:18) and that nothing can separate him from the love of God (8:39). Paul shifts his tone radically as he moves from Romans 7 to Romans 8, and the central role of the Spirit explains this shift.[3]

Sin's Condemnation, Not Ours (Rom 8:1–11)

> **1** Therefore, there is now no condemnation for those who are in Christ Jesus. **2** For the Torah of the Spirit of life in Christ Jesus has set you free from the Torah of sin and of death. **3** For the impossibility of the Torah—in that it was weakened by the flesh—God condemned sin in the flesh by sending his own son in the likeness of sinful flesh (even as an offering for sin), **4** so that Torah's acquittal might be fulfilled among us who walk not according to the flesh but according to the Spirit. **5** For those who are [walking] according to the flesh think about the things of the flesh, but those who [walk] according to the Spirit [think about] the things of the Spirit. **6** For the mind of the flesh is death, but the mind of the Spirit is life and peace, **7** for the mind of the flesh is enmity toward God, for it does not

---

2. Ibid.

3. L. Ann Jervis opens her essay with the observation, "The Spirit appears prominently in Romans, particularly in the central part of the letter—chapters 5–8" ("Spirit," 139). Although Paul uses *pneuma* ("spirit, Spirit") in Rom 5:5 and 7:5, the Spirit's "prominence" does not actually start until Romans 8, where Paul uses *pneuma* twenty-one times (out of thirty-four for the entire letter!). Her claim, then, that "the majority of references to the Spirit in Romans are found in chs. 5–8" is somewhat misleading (ibid., 140–41).

> submit to the Torah of God, for neither is it able [to submit]. **8** But those who are [walking] in the flesh are not able to please God.
>
> **9** But you, you are not in the flesh but in the Spirit, since the Spirit of God dwells among you. **10** But if Christ is among you, the body is dead because of sin, but the Spirit is life because of righteousness. **11** But if the Spirit of the one who raised Jesus from the dead dwells among you, the one who raised Christ from the dead will bring life even to your mortal bodies through his indwelling Spirit among you.

Paul has just explored the pitiable state of the gentile who attempts to achieve self-mastery by observing Israel's Torah. On the one hand, his mind assents to the inherent goodness and worth of Torah, but, on the other hand, his body disobeys his mind and does sin's bidding. The situation is dire; after all, "the wages of sin is death" (6:23). Paul has already explained the solution to this problem (repeatedly, actually; e.g., see 3:21–31; 5:18–21).[4] But Romans 8 provides the climactic and final exposition of how God has kept his promise for people who find themselves unable to keep Torah. Romans 8 begins by declaring in sharp, contrasting terms the results of Torah versus the results of being "in Christ" [*en Christō*]. Whereas Torah results in "this body of death" (7:24), "there is now no condemnation for those who are in Christ Jesus" (8:1).

The clear change in tone from Romans 7 is clear not just from the sudden appearance of and emphasis on God's Spirit in Romans 8. Just as importantly, *nomos* ("Torah"), to which Paul made fifteen references in nineteen verses (see Rom 7:7–25), only appears five times in all thirty-nine verses of Romans 8. Moreover, *nomos* completely disappears after Rom 8:7. When the Spirit comes onto the rhetorical stage, Torah moves off-stage. Paul identifies the reason for his change in tone in v. 2: "For the Torah of the Spirit of life in Christ Jesus has set you free from the Torah of sin and of death."[5] Paul has already introduced the two different means

---

4. So also Matera, *Romans*, 185.

5. The second-person singular pronoun, *se* ("you" [sing.]), signals the change from Paul's speech-in-character back to his authorial voice and suggests that, in Romans 8, Paul is addressing his gentile proselyte interlocutor. Wright ("Romans," 575) employs a logical argument, pertaining to the structure of syllogisms, to explain how Rom 8:1 follows on from 7:7–25. I find the change in voice, from "speech-in-character" to Paul's speaking in his own authorial voice, a more helpful way to explain the text.

of relating to Torah in Rom 7:23, 25: "Spirit/life" on the one hand; "sin/death" on the other.[6]

Those same ways of relating to Torah continue in Romans 8. But whereas Paul's *persona* in the previous chapter found himself enslaved by sin's power and unable to master his passions, in 8:2 Paul explains that Torah (!) has "set you free" [*ēleutherōsen se*] from the Torah of sin and death. Wright comments on 8:2, "When God acts in Christ and by the Spirit the Torah is somehow involved as well, somehow present and active. . . . Though Paul has spoken with eloquent passion of the way in which Torah locks the door on those who are imprisoned within Adamic humanity, *he has never forgotten its promise of life*."[7] What a surprising development! But then again, Paul already used contrasting terms to provide two different explanations of a singular event. In the opening to the letter, Paul described Jesus as "his [= God's] son—who was from the seed of David according to the flesh [*kata sarka*] and was declared son of God with power according to the Spirit of holiness [*kata pneuma hagiōsynēs*] by the resurrection from the dead" (Rom 1:3–4). Just as Paul could present Jesus' "sonship" from two different angles in Romans 1 ("according to the flesh," "according to the Spirit of holiness"), here in Romans 7–8 he presents Torah from two different angles.[8]

When Torah was first offered to Israel prior to crossing the Jordan into Canaan, God couched the terms of the covenant in the language of life|death.[9] That was for Israel. The gentiles had been offered blessings (or curses) through Abraham's descendants (see Gen 12:3), which blessing has been postponed because Abraham's descendants chose death and curses instead of life and blessing. But now, through the faithfulness of one of Abraham's seed, God offers life and freedom to the gentiles, not by keeping Torah's commandments, but by the Spirit of life in Christ Jesus. If Paul no longer posits Torah-*observance* as the key to life, he nevertheless still reserves a role for Israel's covenant with God in the offer of life to

---

6. Cp. ibid., 576–77; *pace* Matera, *Romans*, 190–91.

7. Wright, "Romans," 577 (my emphasis). Wright continues: "The Torah, then—why, after all, should we be surprised at being surprised by Paul?—is the hidden agent of what God has achieved, which is the life of which the Spirit is the personal giver."

8. *Pace* Jervis: "Paul speaks of the 'law' of the Spirit of life (8:2). This 'law' is not, of course, the Mosaic law, but, as a wise scholar has written, 'the dynamic "principle" of the new life, creating vitality and separating humans from sin and death.' The Spirit, being of God, is all about life" ("Spirit," 146, citing Fitzmyer, *Romans*, 482–83). As we will see presently, Torah itself was "all about life," even if Israel failed to choose it.

9. Deuteronomy 28–32, which we have already mentioned on multiple occasions.

the nations. "What surprises us is that we do not hear, 'the *Spirit* of life in Christ Jesus has freed us, but 'the *law* of the Spirit of life in Christ Jesus has freed is from the law of sin and death.'"[10] Torah offered the promise of life and freedom beforehand (see Rom 1:2–4).[11] This is the righteousness of God, revealed apart from Torah and yet attested to by Torah (see 3:21–22).

Verse 3 is difficult, if only because Paul does not clearly explain what he means by "the impossibility of the Torah" [*to adynaton tou nomou*]. Most translations render the phrase along the lines of, "what the law could not do" (see NRSV), and they add the idea that God himself did what the law (or Torah) could not do. Technically, this is not what Paul says, though it could be what he means. His language here is too incomplete for us to be sure. Perhaps we should first recognize what Paul *does* clearly say: "God . . . condemned [*katekrinen*] sin in the flesh." Paul's *persona* has already discovered sin dwelling inside him (see 7:21), and his mind, which assents to Torah's holiness and rightness and goodness, finds itself under siege and taken captive by Torah's judgment against the sin that dwells "in his members" (7:23). But here in Rom 8:3, God has condemned sin in the flesh, and sin can no longer take his mind captive. Paul then explains the means by which God accomplished sin's condemnation: "by sending his own son in the likeness of sinful flesh (even as an offering for sin)."[12]

Therefore, the main thrust of Rom 8:3 is clear enough: "God condemned sin in the flesh by sending his own son in the likeness of sinful flesh (even as an offering for sin)." However, we still need to return to the beginning of the verse and its syntactic ambiguities. Paul describes Torah as "weakened" [*ēsthenei*], which should perhaps cause some surprise. The language of "weakness," in Romans and throughout the Pauline corpus, always describes people.[13] As Jewett notes, the attribution of weakness

---

10. Dillon asks whether Paul *actually* uses Torah as the subject of *ēleutherōsen*, but he never actually resolves the issue ("Spirit," 691–92). In my view, Dillon's doubts could be assuaged by a more robust appreciation for Paul's nuanced application of Torah to the gentiles (i.e., that they keep its righteous requirements simply by worshiping God as Creator [Rom 2:26]—and so it offers life to the nations—though they do not observe its terms "in letter" [2:29]).

11. Paul refers to "the Holy Scriptures" [*graphais hagiais*], in which he found the gospel "promised beforehand" (Rom 1:2–4).

12. For the translation of *peri hamartias* as "an offering for sin," see Moo, *Romans*, 480; Wright, "Romans," 579; Jewett, *Romans*, 484; *pace* Matera, *Romans*, 192.

13. Abraham "did not weaken [*asthenēsas*] in faith" (4:19), though "while we were still weak [*asthenōn*], Christ died at the right time for the ungodly" (5:6). Later, Paul writes metaphorically to the Romans "because of the weakness [*astheneian*] of your flesh" (6:19). The remaining four references to "weakness" or "the weak" (see 8:26; 14:1,

to Torah here in 8:3 would be "unique to the NT."[14] Given the prominence of the conceptual apparatus of self-mastery and weakness in our interpretation of Romans 7, where the human moral agent found himself overwhelmed and defeated by sin and, consequently, under Torah's judgment, I would expect weakness to afflict the gentile proselyte rather than Torah itself. That is, the gentile was "weakened" and unable to achieve self-mastery, even with Torah's help. How strange, then, that Paul appears to describe Torah as "weakened"! Whatever Paul's precise meaning, the broad strokes are relatively clear: Torah results in God's judgment brought against the weak and powerless in the face of sin's reign-as-king, but now God, by sending his son in the likeness of sinful flesh, has condemned sin in the flesh. As a result, God opens up the possibility of life and victory over sin even for the weak moral agents who just one chapter ago found themselves mastered by their passions. "God's indwelling Spirit ... empowers believers with the inner dynamism to *fulfill* a law they could not *do* because of the overriding power of sin."[15]

In contrast to its apparent weakness in Rom 8:3, Torah seems alive and well (and without weakness!) in v. 4: "so that Torah's acquittal might be fulfilled among us who walk not according to the flesh but according to the Spirit." Once again, the flesh seems to have been affected by weakness, and Paul, speaking in his authorial voice, leaves the flesh behind and affirms the fulfillment of Torah's penalty [*dikaiōma*] among those who walk according to the Spirit. *Dikaiōma* can mean "regulation, requirement, commandment";[16] it can also refer to the action that fulfills or meets a requirement. However, according to BDAG, *dikaiōma* can also be used as a synonym for *dikaiōsis* ("justification, vindication, acquittal"). In Romans 8, Paul contrasts Torah's *dikaiōma* with the "condemnation" [*katakrima*; 8:1] that previously harangued gentiles who sought to keep Torah's covenantal terms. For this reason, Wright argues, "*to dikaiōma tou nomou* here refers to the verdict that the law announces rather than the behavior which it requires. And, in the light of 5:16, 18 and the argument of the present passage, this is clearly (unlike 1:32) the *positive* verdict."[17]

2; 15:1) also refer to people.

14. Jewett, *Romans*, 483.

15. Matera, *Romans*, 185 (original italics). I would specify that Paul is writing not to "believers" but to gentile believers, and the "law" they fulfill with the Spirit's aid is Israel's Torah.

16. BDAG, s.v. ("a regulation relating to just or right action").

17. Wright, "Romans," 577 (original emphasis).

In other words, here in 8:4 Paul affirms that Torah offers an acquittal—a verdict of "not guilty"—for those who walk according to the Spirit.

Daniel Kirk disagrees. In his analysis of *dikaiōma* in Rom 5:16, which commentators overwhelmingly translate "justification" or "acquittal," Kirk argues that, "contextually, the stronger argument can be made for reading *dikaiōma* in v. 16 not as the justifying verdict but rather as the just action that allows the judge to justify the defendant: 'The gift, coming from many transgressions, led to reparation.'"[18] Kirk offers a compelling lexical discussion of *dikaiōma*; however, the difference between "the just action that allows the judge to justify the defendant" and "the justifying verdict" is not great. For this reason, I translate *dikaiōma*, "acquittal": Torah's verdict on sin—and its acquittal of sinners—is "fulfilled among us who walk not according to Torah but according to the Spirit." This happens on the basis of the accomplishment of v. 3: that God has condemned sin in the flesh. Or, in Kirk's words, "Paul creates a context in Romans in which *dikaiōma* refers to a legal requirement of death, a requirement met in the cross of Christ."[19]

The fulfillment of Torah's verdict on sin does not conflict with Paul's binary language in Romans 8, because the opposite of "Spirit" is not "Torah" but rather "flesh." Rather than overcoming Torah and/or its weakness, the Spirit overcomes the flesh and enables the whole body to participate in the mind's judgment that Torah is spiritual, holy, just, and good. The self-mastery that proved so elusive in Romans 7 appears here in the language of "walking according to the Spirit." "The flesh" [*hē sarx*] and its opposite, "the Spirit" [*to pneuma*] produce exactly what we would expect: death for the former; for the latter life and peace. Paul has already written extensively in Romans on *thanatos* ("death"), with eighteen references in Romans 5–7 alone. "Life" [*zōē*] has figured a little less prominently, with eight references in the same three chapters. Paul has referred to "peace" [*eirēnē*] even less frequently, but of course the most important reference came in 5:1, where Paul explains that faith has resulted in justification, our reconciliation with God, and as a result "we have peace with God" [*eirēnēn echomen pros ton theon*]. This peace, Paul now explains, represents "the mind of the Spirit" (8:6).

---

18. Kirk, "Reconsidering," 790.

19. Ibid., 791; *pace* McFadden, who argues that "the fulfillment of Torah's *dikaiōma*" refers "to Christian obedience by the empowering Spirit" ("Fulfillment," 486). In Romans 8, Paul does not have the fulfillment of Torah-as-a-whole in view but rather the fulfillment of Torah's *verdict* on sin (which verdict, of course, is death).

Paul continues the flesh|Spirit dichotomy in Rom 8:7, but he also adds an interesting nuance. Paul identifies the mind of the flesh as "enmity," or "hatred" [*echthra*], toward God.[20] More importantly, he declares why the flesh is at such odds with God: "for it does not submit to the Torah of God, for neither is it able [to submit]" (8:7). Here we find Torah, not weakened as so many translators and commentators have supposed Paul to say in 8:3, but rather quite effective at keeping God and the flesh in opposition to one another. In fact, Paul identifies the very same problem with the flesh here in 8:7 that we ran into in 7:7–25: Despite whatever the mind might desire, the flesh of Paul's *persona* in Romans 7 was unable to keep Torah in his body. In contrast to the discovery that Paul announced in his speech-in-character (*viz.* that evil dwells within him; 7:21), Paul tells his readers that the Spirit of God dwells [*oikei*] among (or within) them. Thus the enslavement to sin that featured so prominently in Romans 7 no longer characterizes the person "in Christ Jesus" (see 8:1).

Quite the contrary, the indwelling Spirit becomes a point of focus in vv. 9–11, a text which blurs the distinctions between the Spirit of God and the Christ, both of whom Paul locates *en hymin* ("in or among you").[21] Paul's use of participatory language ("in, among" [*en*]) in vv. 9–11 is striking. This language clearly contrasts Paul's readers with the pathetic *persona* of the previous chapter. With the opening paragraph of Romans 8, Paul's rhetoric has turned a real corner. Paul leaves behind the depravity of the gentiles so vividly portrayed (1:18–32) and the captivity of the gentile proselyte who wants to but cannot keep Torah (7:7–25). With Romans 8, the gentiles have had the Spirit of God poured out even on them. They are in Christ and Christ is in/among them (8:1, 10, respectively). The problem of the barrier between the peoples of the earth and the Creator God has been dealt with definitively, and the promise of God to Israel's famous forefather has been fulfilled: "I will bless those who bless you, and those who curse you I will curse. And in you all the tribes of the earth will be blessed" (Gen 12:3).

---

20. "The mind of the flesh" in 8:7 lacks precisely what Paul says we now have because of our "justification by faith" [*dikaiōthentes ek pisteōs*; 5:1]; the flesh is *enmity* [*echthra*] *toward God*, but we have *peace* [*eirēnēn*] *with God*.

21. Jewett, *Romans*, 491.

A New Metaphor (Rom 8:12–17)

> **12** Therefore, brethren, we are indebted not the flesh (to live according to the flesh), **13** for if you live according to the flesh, you are about to die. But if by the Spirit you put to death the practices of the body, you will live. **14** For as many as are led by the Spirit of God, these are children of God. **15** For you did not receive a spirit of slavery again unto fear, but you received a Spirit of adoption by which we cry out, "Abba! Father!" **16** For the Spirit itself testifies with our spirit that we are children of God. **17** But if children, then we are also heirs, heirs of God as well as coheirs of Christ, since we are suffering with [him] so that we will also be glorified with [him].

Our reference to God's promise of blessing to Abraham in Genesis 12 is appropriate, not least because that promise focused on Abraham's family. In particular, Abraham received the promise of God when he did not and could not have his own descendants, even though "growing, multiplying, and filling the earth" was a significant feature of God's purpose for humanity (see Gen 1:28). Paul will now turn to a new metaphor to explain how God has blessed and restored the gentiles to their right minds (cf. Rom 1:28) and to a proper relationship with the Creator God. Now, instead of being put to death by Torah (Rom 7:4), Paul promises life for those gentiles who "by the Spirit put to death the practices of the body" (8:13; cf. 7:15–23); he says: "You will live" [*zēsesthe*]. At this point Paul introduces a new image, the metaphor of the family of God, which guarantees the reality of life for those who are led by the Spirit. "For as many as are led by the Spirit of God, these are children of God" [*houtoi huioi theou eisin*; 8:14].[22] This metaphor provides the real power of Paul's rhetoric, especially concerning Torah. Remember that some Jews in the late Second Temple period (e.g., Philo, *4 Maccabees*) put Torah forward as an efficacious means to achieve self-mastery. But Paul has opposed this view and argued that

---

22. The Greek word *huios* often means "son," as opposed to *thygatēr* ("daughter") and distinct from *teknon* or *paidion* ("child"). I have opted for a gender-neutral translation because the male-ness of the English word "son" is not in play in v. 14. Paul will go on in v. 17 to discuss the inheritance of the sons/children of God. In antiquity *inheritance* concerned sons in particular, and so *huios* might have been especially appropriate for Paul to use here. Today, however, a child's gender has little—if anything—to do with whether or not they will receive a share of their parents' inheritance, and so the gender-neutral term "child" (or plural, "children") seems more appropriate than "son" (or plural, "sons"). Paul uses "children" [*tekna*] in Rom 8:16, 17, 21, which confirms this interpretation. See ibid., 500–501.

Torah, rather than reconciling gentiles to the Creator God, points out their sinfulness and condemns them as slaves of sin. The Creator God, rather than abandoning his creation to judgment, bestows upon sinful humanity "a Spirit of adoption [*pneuma huiothesias*] by which we cry out, 'Abba! Father!'" (8:15).

Given the rhetorical texture of the earlier parts of Romans—especially Romans 5–7, which prominently featured the language of reigning as king or as lord as well as serving as slaves[23]—I find it significant that Paul contrasts this Spirit of adoption with a (or the) "spirit of slavery" [*pneuma douleias*]. Up to this point Paul has stressed humanity's enslavement to its passions, to sin, and to death; he has also emphasized Torah's role in shutting up the whole world to sin and magnifying by distinction the glory of God (see 3:5–8). But now, "apart from Torah" (as it were), God has undone our slavery and welcomed us into his family. As a result, we echo the characteristic cry of Jesus, *abba*, the Aramaic word for "father." This is not characteristic language for Paul; his only other use of the Aramaicism *abba* comes at Gal 4:6, which also features the ideas of gentile adoption, the Spirit of God or of Christ, crying out to God, and the contrast between being a child and being a slave. The only other time *abba* appears in the NT comes in Jesus' prayer in the Garden of Gethsemane (Mark 14:26), when Jesus addresses God, "Abba! Father!" [*abba ho patēr*], exactly the same phrase Paul uses in Romans and Galatians. Despite the rarity of this Aramaicism, scholars generally draw a number of conclusions from its usage in the NT:

> First, Jesus referred to God in a highly personal way (e.g., "my Father") and, especially in prayer, characteristically used the Aramaic term "*abbā*" to address God. Second, "*abbā*" constituted an unusual (perhaps unique) form of direct address to God for Jesus' day. Third, Jesus' use of this unusual and rather intimate form for addressing God in prayer suggests strongly that Jesus' religious life was characterized by relating to God in a very intense and personalized way that is not fully paralleled even in other examples of very devout spirituality in the ancient Jewish setting. "Jesus seems to have thought of himself as God's son in a distinctive sense."[24]

---

23. In Romans 5–7, Paul uses *basileuō* ("reign as king") four times (5:14, 17, 21; 6:12), *kyrieuō* ("reign as lord") three times (6:9, 14; 7:1), and *douleuō* ("serve as slave") three times (6:6; 7:6, 25).

24. Hurtado, "God," 275, citing Dunn, *Jesus and the Spirit*, 38.

As a result of Jesus' distinctive usage, we have here one of the stronger links between the teachings and language of the historical Jesus and Paul's letters. In other words, Paul appears to be quoting the Jesus tradition here in Romans 8.

The power of Paul's new metaphor is not simply our new status as children of God rather than as slaves to sin and subjects to its power to produce death. Paul explicitly identifies the consequences of this new status, though before we get to Paul's explicit point I would like to draw out something he implies. Back in v. 2 Paul signaled the end of his speech-in-character by saying that God "freed *you* [*ēleutherōsen se*] from Torah of sin and death." The second-person singular pronoun *you* represents Paul's response to his *persona*, whose voice he employed in 7:7–25.[25] That is, Paul's gentile *persona* discovered sin dwelling within him and cried out for deliverance (7:21, 24), and Paul announces that Torah, operative through the Spirit, has set him free. Up until this point in Romans 8, Paul has used the second-person pronoun (usually plural) regularly to make clear that he is talking *to* as well as *about* his readers (and perhaps even distancing himself from his comments *to* and *about* them):[26]

- The Torah of the Spirit of life in Christ Jesus set *you* [singular] free from the Torah of sin and of death. (8:2)
- But *you, you* are not in the flesh but in the Spirit, since the Spirit of God dwells among *you*. (8:9a)
- But if Christ is among *you*, the body is dead because of sin, but the Spirit is life because of righteousness. (8:10)
- But if the Spirit of the one who raised Jesus from the dead dwells among *you*, the one who raised Christ from the dead will bring life even to *your* mortal bodies through his indwelling Spirit among *you*. (8:11)

---

25. Some ancient manuscripts (A D and a large number of miniscules and Fathers) read "he freed me" [*ēleutherōsen me*] here, and an even fewer number read "he freed us" [*ēleutherōsen hēmas*]. However, an impressive list of manuscripts, including Sinaiticus [א] and Vaticanus [B] read "he freed you (sing.)" [*se*]. According to Metzger (*Textual Commentary*, 456), the first-person pronoun *me* "harmonizes better with the argument in chap. 7." As I have argued in this lesson and the previous one, *me* harmonizes better with a *misreading* of Romans 7, while the second-person pronoun *se* ("you") fits better with a reading that recognizes Paul's speech-in-character and his *persona* as a gentile proselyte to Judaism.

26. As Matera (*Romans*, 195) notes, though he does not seem to comment on the switch to first-person plural pronouns in 8:15. In fact, after v. 15 Paul *never* uses second-person pronouns though the rest of the chapter!

If You Call Yourself a Jew

- For if *you* live according to the flesh, *you* are about to die. But if by the Spirit *you* put to death the practices of the body, *you* will live (8:13)

- For *you* did not receive a spirit of slavery again unto fear, but *you* received a Spirit of adoption by which we cry out, "Abba! Father!" (8:15)

These are all the second-person references in Romans 8. Until the end of v. 15, Paul only uses second-person pronouns (with two exceptions[27]). The effect on Romans' rhetoric is to distance Paul from the text; in Rom 8:1–15 Paul talks *to* and *about* his Roman readers *and not about himself*.[28]

But all that changes in Rom 8:15, when Paul announces that his gentile readers have received a (or the) Spirit of adoption.[29] Now, having been adopted into the family of God, the gentiles are no longer "you." Now they are "us."[30] From Rom 8:15a through the end of the chapter, Paul uses *only* first-person plural pronouns and verbs ("*we* cry out"; "the Spirit itself testifies along with *our* spirit that *we are* children of God"; etc.). The implication of Paul's use of pronouns in Romans 8, then, is that the gentiles, who were not part of God's family but have nevertheless received the Spirit of Israel's God ("the Spirit of adoption"), now belong to the people of God. And, just as importantly, they belong by virtue of receiving the Spirit of

---

27. The exceptions are, first, in 8:4 ("so that Torah's acquittal might be fulfilled among us" [*en hēmin*]) and then in 8:12 ("Therefore, brethren, we are indebted [*esmen opheiletai*] not to the flesh").

28. I am making a very narrow claim here. The things Paul says *to* and *about* his readers in Rom 8:1–15 might also be true of himself (e.g., that Paul is not "in the flesh but in the Spirit"; Rom 8:9), but he is not saying these things *to* or *about* himself. In Romans 8, from v. 1 until the end of v. 15, Paul focuses solely and narrowly on his readers as distinct from himself. But this makes very good sense within the whole context of Romans, in which Paul is explaining the reconciliation between gentiles and the Creator God of Israel. Paul, as a Jew, is not part of this reconciliation, except for his (priestly) role as the apostle to the gentiles.

29. "Adoption"—and so a new identity in and relation toward the Creator God—is the primary effect Paul attributes to the Spirit in Romans 8. As Ann Jervis rightly recognizes, "being 'in the Spirit' is not an occasional or necessarily ecstatic or extraordinary experience. Being 'in the Spirit' is a stable way of life for believers" ("Spirit," 143).

30. Keesmaat ("Intertextual Transformation," 38–39) helpfully reminds us, "a careful look at the Old Testament and intertestamental literature reveals that by far the most common image associated with the 'son of God' terminology is *Israel* as son of God. ... God is Israel's father, who created them ([Deut 32] v. 6) and begot them (v. 18)" (original italics). The "Spirit of adoption" of which Paul writes, then, incorporates the gentiles—to whom Paul writes—into the people of God, Israel, which fulfills the original Abrahamic promise! Similarly, see Paul's deployment of the metaphor of the olive tree in Romans 11.

God (notice that *reception* is a passive idea) rather than by keeping Torah's commandments (an *active* idea).

This implication brings us back to Paul's explicit point in Romans 8. The gentiles, now fully embraced within the "we" of God's family, enjoy the supporting testimony [*symmartyrei*] of God's Spirit that "we are the children of God" [*tekna theou*]. Certain consequences follow from being included within God's family, and Paul lays these out in v. 17: "But if children, then we are also heirs [*klēronomoi*], heirs of God as well as coheirs [*synklēronomoi*] of Christ." We should not let two millennia of Christian tradition blunt the radical quality of Paul's claim here: *gentiles*, people who never enjoyed a covenantal relationship with Israel's Creator God, now relate to God as a son relates to his father. Andrew Das has seen this "radical quality" well, though we will have to qualify Das's expression of it: "The people of Israel were God's 'children.' Paul now applies this title to Christians."[31] Not quite. Rather, Paul applies this title to *gentiles*. Moreover, Paul brings his gentile readers on a par, not with "the Jews," as if they were coheirs with Israel; he says they are coheirs *of Christ*! This is the good news [*euangelion*] that Paul proclaims. In this light, the end of v. 17 offers a promise rather than a threat. That is, Paul does not mention "suffering with" Jesus [*sympaschomen*] as the cost of being coheirs with Christ. Instead, he extrapolates from the current experience of suffering to the promise (or the result [*hina*]) of that suffering: "we will also be glorified with [him]" [*syndoxasthōmen*].[32]

The [W]holistic Plan of God (Rom 8:18–30)

> **18** For I suppose that the sufferings of the present time are not worthy in the face of the glory that is about to be revealed for us. **19** For the excited expectation of creation eagerly awaits the revelation of the children of God, **20** for creation was subjected to futility—not voluntarily but because of the one who subjected it for hope— **21** because even creation itself will be set free from the slavery of corruption for the freedom of the glory of the

---

31. Das, *Paul*, 79.

32. By "current experience of suffering," I am not necessarily implying that the Roman Christians were experiencing any sort of persecution around 57 CE. Whether or not they were persecuted, they lived in the shadow of Rome's Empire—in its heart, even!—and devoted themselves to a different *kyrios* ("lord"). In this context, "suffering" can refer even to the social ostracization and marginalization the members of a minority subculture might experience in the midst of a very different, even oppositional, dominant culture.

> children of God. **22** For we know that the whole creation is groaning and suffering together until now. **23** Not only this, but so do those who have the guarantee of the Spirit; we also groan inwardly as we await adoption, that is, the redemption of our body. **24** For we were saved by hope, though hope that is seen is not hope. (For who hopes for that which they see?) **25** But if we hope for that which we do not see, we wait eagerly, with perseverance. **26** In the same way, the Spirit joins in helping with our weakness, for we do not know what we ought to pray for, though the Spirit itself intercedes with unspeakable groanings. **27** But he who searches [our] hearts knows what is the mind of the Spirit, because he intercedes according to God on behalf of the saints. **28** But we know that all things work together for good for those who love God (those who are called according to his purpose), **29** because those whom he foreknew, he also chose beforehand to be conformed to the image of his son, so that he would be the firstborn among many brethren. **30** And those whom he chose beforehand, these he also called; and those whom he called, these he also justified; and those whom he justified, these he also glorified.

In the first half, roughly, of Romans 8 Paul has explained how gentiles, frustrated in any efforts they may have exerted toward keeping Torah's covenantal terms, have now received the Spirit of God, the adoption into the people and family of God. When Paul uses first-person plural pronouns in Rom 8:15ff., he brings gentiles and himself into a single group. He has already explained, "for there is no distinction" [*ou gar estin diastolē*; 3:22], that is, no distinction between Jews and gentiles (see also 10:12). On the one hand, "all have sinned and fall short of the glory of God" (3:23); but on the other hand, "we are children of God" (8:16). In other words, the scope of God's plan transcended Israel and included the whole of humanity, all of whom were created in God's image (Gen 1:26–27). The universal blessing of God upon all peoples—not just Israel—is a keystone in Christian theology, and so we should not be too surprised to find this idea here in Romans.

What might be a little more surprising, however, is the creation-wide scope of Paul's vision of the family of God in Romans 8. We discover in Rom 8:19 that Paul has "the entire cosmos . . . in view."[33] Paul goes well beyond universalizing from Israel to all of humanity; he universalizes from Israel to all of humanity *to the whole of creation*! That movement begins in 8:18: "For I suppose that the sufferings of the present time are not worthy in the face of the glory that is about to be revealed for us." Paul refers to

---

33. Wright, "Romans," 596.

"the present time" [*tou nyn kairou*] in precisely the same manner here as he did in Rom 3:26, when he referred to "the demonstration of his righteousness in the present time" [*tō nyn kairō*]. In Romans 3, "the present time" refers to the occasion in which God reveals his righteousness, "to the Jew first as well as for the Greek." In Romans 8, however, "the present time" refers to a period characterized by suffering. Despite initial appearances, these two ideas make sense together. The restoration of God's plan for creation is hidden in this present age, when suffering and death (rather than blessing and life) afflict people everywhere. But now, via the message of Jesus' faithfulness to the Creator God, the righteousness of God is being made known even in the present age. Paul, in other words, perceives a "turn of the ages" in the present time, a turn in which the blessings of God's covenant are waxing and the suffering caused by sin and rebellion is waning.

Humanity, however, does not await the final revelation of the age to come on its own. Creation itself exhibits "eager expectation" [*apokaradokia*] as it awaits the revelation of God's family. Romans 8:19 presents a unique perspective on creation's anticipation of God's activity. We might normally have expected Paul to refer to his readers' eager anticipation of the revelation of God's son, or perhaps of God's kingdom or power or glory. In other words, we might be a little surprised that Paul did not write something more like, "For creation's eager expectation awaits the revelation of God's son, descending from heaven and bringing with him his holy angels and the new Jerusalem." Instead, Paul makes an astonishing claim: creation awaits the revelation of . . . *us*, Jews as well as gentiles, filled with and propelled by the Spirit of God within (or among) us.[34] Until then, creation has sort of lost its point; it has "been subjected to futility" [*mataiotēti hypetagē*] and can only wait in the hope [*eph' helpidi*] that God will restore not just humanity but the entire created *kosmos* back to order. Paul then describes creation [*hē ktisis*] in Rom 8:21 using language that resembles terms he used in relation to his gentile readers:[35]

1. creation, like the gentile believers in Rome, will be set free [*eleutherōthēsetai* (cp. 8:2)];

---

34. Eastman, "Whose Apocalypse?" 263–77.

35. This may be an appropriate time to remind ourselves that Paul is not addressing "the gentiles," *all* gentiles everywhere *qua* gentiles. I agree with Runar Thorsteinsson's conclusion, "Paul was writing not to gentiles at large but to a certain group of gentiles whose knowledge of Jewish writings and experience of Jewish ways of life was substantial. Every aspect of Paul's message in Romans must be read in light of this particular audience" (*Interlocutor*, 122).

2. creation, like Paul's gentile readers, will find freedom "from slavery" [apo tēs douleias (cp. 8:15)];

3. creation, like the gentiles, will enjoy "the freedom of the glory of the children of God" [tēs doxēs tōn teknōn tou theou (cp. 8:17)].

In all of these things, then, creation—*the whole of creation* [*pasa hē ktisis*]—eagerly awaits the fulfillment of God's plan. It waits so eagerly, in fact, that it groans and suffers in its expectation.

These two words—groans [*systenazei*] and suffers [*synōdinei*]—suggest the image of a woman in the throes of childbirth.[36] The first word, a compound of *syn-* ("with, together") and *stenazō* ("sigh, groan"), occurs in a number of contexts and can mean little more than crying out, groaning, or sighing in the face of difficulty, oppression, or hardship in general.[37] But, as Johannes Schneider points out, this word group can be used to describe "sighing at child-birth," as it does at Jer 4:31 LXX.[38] The second word, a compound of *syn-* ("with, together") and *ōdinō* ("be in labor, have pains"), refers more specifically to the pains of labor and childbirth.[39] In fact, these two roots occur together at Jer 4:31 LXX, which confirms that Paul's language in Rom 8:22 suggests the single image of childbirth (as opposed to suggesting two different images, or types, of suffering). The whole of creation enters into and shares in [*syn-*] the birth pains associated with the "birth" of God's children. "As knells of the old world's passing and portents of the redemption that is underway but is not yet completed, they are testimonies of the suffering which the Spirit shares with the creatures whom it must constantly remind of their distance from the goal."[40]

---

36. Wright refers to "[t]his (essentially female) image of the birth pangs of the new age" ("Romans," 597). Braaten ("Groaning," 21) argues, "these terms [*viz., systenazei* and *synōdinei*] have different spheres of meaning." The terms certainly *can* "have separate spheres of meaning," but Braaten misses the effect of Paul using these two words in such close proximity. By using both words together, the two terms become mutually interpreting and work together to suggest the image of creation in labor. By way of comparison, the English words "sick" and "tired" certainly mean very different things, but bringing them together—"sick and tired"—results in a very specific and identifiable emotional state.

37. See Harris's comments on *stenazō* ("groan, sigh") in "Appendix: Prepositions and Theology in the Greek New Testament," 3:1195. For more information, see also Schneider, "στενάζω, στεναγμός, συστενάζω," 7:600–603.

38. Ibid., 7:600.

39. See Harrison, "ὠδίνω," 3:857–58.

40. Dillon, "Spirit," 699.

Creation Renewed by the Spirit

Paul expands the point in Rom 8:23: "Not only this, but so do those who have the guarantee [*aparchēn*; lit. "first-fruit"] of the Spirit; we also groan inwardly as we await adoption, that is, the redemption of our body." The solidarity Paul portrays between the created order as a whole and the human race in particular, as both cry out like a woman in labor, emphasizes the truly broad scope of God's intention for the gospel. The purpose of God is not to save individuals or even to redeem humanity; the purpose of God is to restore creation itself, including humanity (as the apex of creation) and, of course, individual humans (as individuated embodiments of the image of God). If creation waits in hope (see 8:20), we, too, are saved by hope for the restored creation (which we currently do not and cannot see). We wait patiently [*di' hypomonēs*; lit. "by endurance"], which picks up a theme from earlier in Romans, in which Paul referred, first, to those who persist [*kath' hypomonēn*] in good work as they seek glory, honor, and immortality (2:7) and, second, to development from affliction to endurance [*hypomonē*], proven character, and hope (5:3-4). In all of these texts (Romans 2, 5, and 8), the ideas of endurance, hope, and life appear in rather close proximity.

In a crescendo that has been building steadily since v. 18, Paul turns to the function of the Spirit and its participation in the co-groaning and co-laboring of creation and humanity as they await the restoration of the *kosmos* and the fulfillment of God's plan.[41] Verses 26-30 highlight the role of the Spirit of God in the anticipation of the eschatological renewal of the family of God within a renewed creation. The Spirit "joins in helping with our weakness" [*tē astheneia hēmōn*], which is now the second time Paul has referred to *us* being weak (see also 5:6; cf. the reference to the weakness of *your* flesh in 6:19).[42] Given the cultural revulsion for weakness, Paul's reference to "*our* weakness" is striking, but we should also notice that Paul has identified the Spirit of God as the solution for weakness throughout Romans 8. The cooperation between God, the Spirit, and believers engaged in prayer that Paul portrays in vv. 26-27 contrasts sharply with the division of the previous chapter, in which the human moral agent, Paul's gentile *persona*, discovered a division cutting between his mind, on the one hand, and the members of his body, on the other.

---

41. I owe the musical metaphor of "crescendo" to Johannes Schneider ("στενάζω, στεναγμός, συστενάζω," 7:601): "In R. 8:22-27 the apostle speaks of a triple sighing, that of all creation, that of Christians and that of the Spirit. This sequence is a crescendo."

42. See Jewett, *Romans*, 522.

Finally, Paul explains that "all things work together for good for those who love God" (8:28), a famous phrase that, we should notice, incorporates a number of important terms from elsewhere in Romans.

- Paul refers to his readers as "those who love God" [*tois agapōsin ton theon*]. Although this is the first time he uses the verb *agapaō* ("love"),[43] Paul has already used the similar adjective "beloved by God" [*agapētois theou*; 1:7]. He has also emphasized that the Spirit has poured out the "love of God" [*agapē tou theou*] into our hearts and that God has demonstrated that love for us through Christ's death (5:8). Up to this point, then, God has been the agent of love and people have been the object. For the first time in Romans, Paul now refers to people as the active agents who show love and God as the object who receives that love.

- The word that I translate "work together" [*synergei*] is another compound word [*syn-* ("with, together") and *-ergeō* ("work, accomplish")]. James Dunn identifies about forty *syn*-prefixed terms in the NT, "more than half [of which] appear only in Paul" and "which form a characteristic and distinctive feature of Paul's style and theology."[44] Dunn goes on to suggest that the implicit subject of this verb is not "all things" [*panta*], as I have translated it, but rather the Spirit of God.[45] The difference would not matter much (which Dunn also acknowledges). But if Paul does imply that the Spirit works in all things to produce "the good" (see immediately below), then the striking cooperation we saw in 8:26–27 between God and humans, who now enjoy a state of peace together (see 5:1), continues into v. 28.[46]

- We saw in our discussion of Romans 5 that "the good" [*to agathon*] taps into the larger social value of benefaction, the cultural practice of contributing to the well-being of society as a whole through the giving of food, infrastructure, festivities, or other goods. Bruce Winter has argued that Paul, when he refers to "the good" in Rom 13:3–4, tells

---

43. Paul will use *agapaō* a total of eight times between now and the end of the letter. Despite our current discussion of Rom 8:28 and how Paul picks up themes from earlier in the letter, *agapaō* in this verse arguably *introduces* a theme that will prove important in the rest of the letter.

44. Dunn, *Romans*, 1:313 (where Dunn is commenting upon Rom 6:4, though he also mentions the prevalence of *syn*-prefixed words at 8:16–28).

45. Ibid., 1:481; similarly, see Wright, "Romans," 600.

46. Jewett rightly argues that Paul "claims a divine-human synergism in the midst of disadvantageous circumstances, because the Spirit works 'with' those who love God. . . . Paul's wording implies divine and human co-responsibility in the face of adversity" (*Romans*, 527).

the Roman Christians to provide "public benefactions."[47] If a similar connotation attaches to *agathon* here as did in Romans 5 and will in Romans 13, then Paul would be saying that God, like the civic benefactors that would have been familiar in any major Mediterranean city, guarantees the welfare and well-being of all those who love him. If so, the language of "loving God" might also take on resonances with the client/patron system of Hellenistic and Roman culture, which David deSilva has described as "the basic building block of Greco-Roman society."[48] God, as our patron, is both faithful and trustworthy to provide for his clients.[49]

- Finally, Paul refers to "those who are called [*klētois ousin*] according to his purpose." This is the last of four uses of the adjective *klētos* in Romans. At the very beginning of the letter Paul identifies himself as "called [to be] an apostle" [*klētos apostolos*; 1:1]. Immediately following from his self-identification, Paul refers to his readers as "called by Jesus Christ" [*klētoi Iēsou Christou*; 1:6] and "called [to be] holy" [*klētois hagiois*; 1:7]. Notice, then, that in Rom 1:1, 6–7, Paul describes both himself and his readers as "called," with the strong implication in vv. 1, 7 that God (or Jesus Christ) has called them.[50] *Paul and his readers have this in common!* Here in Romans 8, now that Paul has emphasized the adoption of gentile believers into God's family (8:15, 23) and shifted from using second-person to first-person pronouns, he once again implies the unity of "those who love God," Jews as well as gentiles. For these, all things work together to produce, ultimately, "the good."

~

Popular or pastoral references to Rom 8:28 often fail to notice that, in vv. 29–30, Paul unpacks what "good" he has in mind when he affirms that "all things"—which at least includes "the sufferings of the present time" (see 8:18)—work together to produce the good for those who love God. Paul signals the link between the good of v. 28 and the catena of blessings

47. Winter, *Welfare*, 33–34; see also Winter, "Christian Benefactors."

48. See David A. deSilva's helpful discussion in "Patronage," 766–71 (p. 766 quoted).

49. We need to remember that Paul has made considerable use of a different metaphor, that of the family of God (in which we are God's children), which conflicts with the client/patron metaphor that might be operative here. Paul, however, would be neither the first nor the last writer to mix his metaphors.

50. I read the genitive *klētoi Iēsou Christou* as a subjective genitive. If this is right, then 1:6 identifies his readers specifically as called *by Jesus Christ*.

in vv. 29-30 with the conjunction *hoti* ("because"), which identifies "the cause or reason" of the assertion in 8:28.⁵¹ Romans 8:29-30 explains Paul's confidence back in Rom v. 18; the sufferings of the present age cannot compare to the glory about to be revealed to us because [*oti*; 8:29] God's foreknowledge and fore-choosing (i.e., "predestination") the conformity of Jews and gentiles into the image of his son guarantees God's gifts of call, justification, and glorification.

One final thought on this passage. Paul mentions the promise that we would be "conformed to the image [*tēs eikonos*] of his son." Paul does not often use the word "image."⁵² But when he does, he is usually, if not always, resonating with the creation tradition of Gen 1:26-27, in which God creates humanity "in our image" [*kat' eikona hēmeteran*]. We saw that resonance in Rom 1:23, where Paul critiques humanity—the image of God—for worshiping the image of created beings (people, birds, four-footed creatures, and reptiles). Here in v. 29, when Paul says we will be conformed into the image of his son—"who is the image of God" (2 Cor 4:4)—he clearly implies that we have lost or failed to reflect the image of God in which we were created. But the restoration of that image happens as God returns us to his original plan, visible in Jesus (and especially Jesus' faithfulness to the Creator God), and he becomes the "firstborn among many brethren" (Rom 8:29). Again, the mandate of Genesis, given to both Adam (1:28) and to Abraham (12:2; 15:4-5) is fulfilled in Jesus. Adam and Abraham were commanded or promised to be fathers of many; this commandment/promise is fulfilled in Jesus (not in Cain [!] and not in Isaac), the firstborn of God's very-large family, which includes Jews as well as gentiles.

The Assured Results of the Plan of God (Rom 8:31–39)

> **31 "What, then, shall we say about these things? If God is for us, who [is] against us?" 32** Indeed, he did not spare his own son but gave him up for us all; how, then, would he not freely give all things to us who are with him. **33** Who will bring charges against those who are chosen by God? God is the one who justifies; **34** who is the one who condemns? Christ [Jesus], who died and, moreover, was raised and is seated at God's right hand, who also intercedes for us. **35** Who will separate us from the love of Christ?

51. LN, s.v.

52. *hē eikōn* ("image") appears seven times in Paul's undisputed letters (Rom 1:23; 8:29; 1 Cor 11:7; 15:49 [2x]; 2 Cor 3:18; 4:4) and twice more in Colossians (1:15; 3:10).

> [Will] affliction or distress or persecution or famine or nakedness or danger or sword? **36** Just as it is written,
>
> > "For your sake we are put to death all day long;
> > we are considered as sheep for the slaughter" (Ps 43:23 LXX)
>
> **37** But in all these things we more than overcome through the one who loved us. **38** For I am persuaded that neither death nor life nor angels nor rulers nor things present nor things to come nor powers **39** nor heights nor depths nor any other created thing will be able to separate us from the love of God that is in Christ Jesus our Lord.

The final section of Romans 8 concludes Paul's discussion of the effects and consequences of God's pouring out his Spirit upon his people (not just Jews, but *also gentiles*). Gentiles, *all* gentiles, may have been enemies of God at one point (see Rom 5:10), but now those gentiles who respond in faith to the gospel of Jesus' faithfulness to the Creator God find that "God is for us" (not just Jews, but *also gentiles*). There is, then, confidence that no one— or no one who ultimately matters—can be against us (8:31). Paul's gentile *persona* in Romans 7 found he could not escape the power of sin because it was at work in his very members. But now, having received the Spirit of adoption that God offers to everyone who responds in faith (not just Jews but *also gentiles*), "we" have confidence that God will freely give [*charisetai*] all things to us. The interlocutor asks Paul, "What, then, shall we say about these things? If God is for us, who [is] against us?" (Rom 8:31).

The answer, which Paul gives in his authorial voice, highlights the guarantee of God's love that Paul (and his gentile readers) finds in Christ. If God gives his son "while we were still sinners" (Rom 5:8) in order to reconcile humanity—the Jew first as well as the Greek—to himself, how much more will he freely give all things to those who have been adopted into God's family. The description of Christ as "the one who condemns" [*ho katakrinōn*; 8:34] might seem surprising at first, but we need to remember the object of God's condemnation.[53] Paul does not emphasize that God (or Christ) will judge sinners. Rather, God has condemned *sin* itself in the flesh (8:3), and now there is no risk or threat of condemnation for those in Christ.[54] For-

---

53. *Pace* Wright ("Romans," 613), who thinks the answer to Paul's question, "Who is the one who condemns?" is implicitly, "No one."

54. Matera (*Romans*, 206) rightly links Paul's question here in v. 34 with the beginning of Romans 8. And though he rightly says, "No one can condemn those for whom Christ died, rose, and intercedes at God's right hand," he misses that Paul has also

merly, the gentiles exhibited weakness in the face of their passions, lusts, desires, and emotions; they found themselves unable to attain self-mastery, even with Torah's help. The gospel, however, has bestowed the Spirit of God even upon the gentiles, and the Spirit has overcome (even "more than overcome"! [*hypernikōmen*; 8:37]) the power of sin over our members (or our body). As a result of the gospel, instead of being under the condemnation of Torah's judgment against all sin, "the one who condemns" now intercedes [*entunchanei*; 8:34] on our behalf.

The intercession of Christ, "who died and, moreover, was raised and is seated at God's right hand" (8:34), explains Paul's amazing confidence in the power, persistence, and permanence of God's love. "For I am persuaded that neither death nor life nor angels nor rulers nor things present nor things to come nor powers nor heights nor depths nor any other created thing [*tis ktisis hetera*] will be able to separate us from the love of God that is in Christ Jesus our Lord" (Rom 8:38–39). At this point Paul has come full circle. Romans began, in 1:18–32, with a devastating attack on sinful humanity's willingness to worship the image of any created thing (see 1:23). Now, having forsaken that willingness and, by God's grace, received the outpouring of God's love in their hearts (see 5:5), no created thing will be able to separate the gentile believers in Rome from God's love.

The reciprocity of the relationship between God and his people is evident simply by placing 8:28 alongside 8:37 and noting (i) the promise of "good" for those who love God [*tois agapōsin ton theon*; 8:28], and (ii) that we are granted the power and strength to "more than overcome" precisely "through the one who loved us" [*tou agapēsantos hēmas*; 8:37]. We love God. God loves us. The rhetoric of the letter has come a long way from the pathetic "I" who could not even do the good he knew in his heart that he ought to do (7:15–20). By the end of Romans 8, Paul and his readers seem to have largely shed the weakness that Paul has mentioned on multiple occasions.[55] In fact, Paul will not mention "weakness" or "the weak" again until 14:1—15:6.

But before we get ahead of ourselves, we need to attend to the dramatic turn that Paul's rhetoric takes in Romans 9–11.

---

affirmed that God *has* condemned sin in the flesh.

55. Rom 5:6; 6:19; 8:3 (?); 8:26.

10

Israel and Christ

Paul's Pathos *for the People of God*

Through scripture, foot-race imagery, and agricultural metaphors, Paul reiterates several points in [Romans 9–11]: Gentiles have been included through Christ; many in Israel have not recognized this as God's plan; and this lack of understanding was planned by God in the first place. The tension created between these two peoples propels them both toward this salvation. The larger goal is not the creation of the church or Christianity, but the salvation of Israel.[1]

Chapters 9–11 have been perennially difficult chapters in Romans, which, as we have seen, is itself a particularly difficult letter. In previous generations, the danger has been that commentators would approach Paul's comments on Israel and the place of her election within God's larger plan as an appendix clumsily tacked on to his exposition of the gospel of Jesus Christ and justification by faith.[2] In post-Holocaust scholarship commentators have begun to identify these chapters as a climactic moment—even as *the* climax—of the letter. Our reading to this point has emphasized the covenantal basis upon which gentiles find themselves adopted into God's family (see Rom 8:12–17), and so we are now in a strong position to appreciate how Paul explains the covenantal basis of Israel's uninterrupted presence in the family of God. If the gentiles' rec-

---

1. Johnson Hodge, "Light to the Nations," 169.

2. Ibid.

onciliation with Israel's Creator God results "apart from Torah" [*chōris nomou*], has the Mosaic covenant gone out of effect? Given what Paul has already said about Torah (e.g., at Rom 3:21, 31; 7:12, 14), we might expect him to respond, *mē genoito* ("Certainly not!"). To find out, let us turn to Romans 9.

Sorrow for Israel (Rom 9:1–13)

1 I am telling the truth in Christ—I am not lying—as my conscience testifies on my behalf in the Holy Spirit, **2** that my sorrow is great, and the distress of my heart is unceasing. **3** For I myself would pray that I would be accursed from Christ for the sake of my brethren, my kin according to the flesh, **4** who are Israelites, whose are the adoption and the glory and the covenants and the Torah-giving and the ministration and the promises, **5** whose are the patriarchs and from whom is the Christ (according to the flesh), who is God over all, blessed be he forever. Amen.

6 It is not as though the word of God has failed, because not all those who are from Israel are Israel. **7** Not all the children [of Abraham] are the Seed of Abraham, but, "your Seed will be invoked through Isaac" (Gen 21:12). **8** That is, the children of the flesh, these are not the children of God, but rather the children of the promise are reckoned as "the Seed." **9** For this is the account of the promise: "At this time next year I will return and Sarah will have a son" (Gen 18:14). **10** And not only this, but Rebekah also conceived children in one act of intercourse with Isaac, our ancestor. **11** Before they were born—even before they had done anything good or evil, so that the plan of God, according to his choice, might remain, **12** not on the basis of deeds but on the basis of the one who calls—it was said to her, "The older will serve the younger" (Gen 25:23), **13** just as it is written, "I loved Jacob, but I hated Esau" (Mal 1:2–3).

Immediately on the heals of his impassioned expression of confidence in the reliability and permanence of God's love, Paul changes tone dramatically and without warning. Paul swears on oath, invoking the same "Holy Spirit" that poured out the love of God in our hearts (5:5) and brought about the adoption of the gentiles into God's family (8:14–17). Paul's oath formula takes on a particularly emphatic tone: certainly Paul expects his readers to assume he has been speaking the truth all along, but now, as he begins speaking about his fellow Jews/Israelites, he feels compelled to draw attention to and solemnly attest that his words communicate his heart.

Israel and Christ

Whatever we *might* have expected from Paul—for example, that he is not lying about the permanence of God's love—he takes a dramatic turn in v. 2: "my sorrow [*lypē*] is great, and the distress [*odynē*] of my heart is unceasing." The chapter division before the previous verse ought not mitigate the force of the change in tone from 8:35-39 to 9:1-9.[3] Paul has just portrayed all of creation writhing in labor pains, "groaning and suffering together [*synōdinei*] until now" (8:22). Paul uses the same root in Rom 9:2 to describe his unceasing distress for his fellow Israelites. Just as creation writhes in anticipation of the revelation of the children of God (!), so too does Paul writhe in the hopes that Israel would submit herself to the fulfillment of God's promises. His desire for his people is so strong that he wishes himself even to be cursed [*anathema*] for his people's sake. Dunn may be right when he expresses skepticism that "Paul could conceive of such a martyr-like death as having the same effect or being more effective than Christ's."[4] But he risks missing the point that both Paul's powerful emotional impulses and the force of his will are patterned after Christ, who was willing to let himself become a curse for the sake of God's people and in obedience to his will.[5] In light of the rhetoric of self-mastery pervading Romans, especially Romans 6-7, we should recognize that Paul's emotional outcry here strongly contrasts him with the weak, whose emotional desires run counter to rather than along the same lines of Christ's love for Israel.

Paul's "great sorrow and unceasing distress" are aimed directly at "my kin according to the flesh," which he immediately identifies as "Israelites" [*Israēlitai*; 9:4]. All of vv. 4-5 are taken up with a very positive description of the Jews—the Israelites—in terms of their distinctive covenantal identity.

- *They* received from God the adoption and the glory and the covenants.
- *They* received from God the legislation and the ministration and the promises.

---

3. "The *autos egō* increases the pathos, especially coming so soon after the glowing assurance of 8:38-39" (Dunn, *Romans*, 2:525).

4. Ibid.

5. "Christ purchased us from Torah's curse [*kataras tou nomou*] by becoming a curse [*kataras*] for our sake, because it is written, 'Cursed [*epikataratos*] is everyone who hangs upon a tree'" (Gal 3:13). Even though Paul uses different words for curse in Gal 3:13 and Rom 9:3, the ideas operative in both texts are the same, *viz*. that a benefactor might take up and take away the curse of his people-group. For a very good discussion of *kataras tou nomou* and the larger issues of Israel's restoration in Galatians, see Morales, *Spirit*, esp. pp. 105-9.

If You Call Yourself a Jew

- *Theirs* are the patriarchs.
- From *their* lines of descent the Christ was born.

Paul's list of Israel's blessings appears all the more striking in light of his earlier flattening of the differences between Jews and gentiles (esp. Romans 2–3). The judgment of God applies to all—both Jews and gentiles—on the basis of their deeds (see 2:6–16), "*for there is no distinction*" (3:22)! Nevertheless, Paul can still admit Israel's special relationship with the Creator God and describe that "special relationship" in robustly Jewish terms. Even here, in this "robustly Jewish" section of Romans, Paul makes the universal claim that the Christ (= Messiah) is "God over all [*ho ōn epi pantōn theos*], blessed be he forever. Amen."[6]

In a very short span of text Paul expresses exceeding confidence in the reliability of God's love for those who are characterized by the Spirit, on the one hand, and also found it necessary to defend "the word of God" against any accusation of failure (9:6).[7] But why? Why does Paul follow up the sublime vision of God's love in Romans 8 with a defense of God's word in Romans 9? This only makes sense if Romans 1–8 has focused narrowly and exclusively on the *gentiles'* reconciliation with God. Paul has *not* addressed the Jews' reconciliation with God at any point so far in Romans. Whenever Paul has been talking about Torah, he has been focused narrowly and exclusively on whether or not gentiles should observe Torah. Paul argued that gentiles should not submit to Torah's yoke because they have already received the Spirit of adoption into God's family. Now, nothing can remove the gentiles from God's love; the internal war of Romans 7 no longer threatens the person whose spirit is joined by the Spirit in prayer to God (8:26–27). Paul's confidence in the *gentiles'* reconciliation with God raises fairly naturally the question of God's faithfulness to *Israel*.[8] Has God abandoned his people, Israel, in favor of the gentiles? Have the Jews' transgressions against the covenant—against Torah—separated them from the love of God, the very thing that Paul exclaims neither "affliction

---

6. For a very good discussion of the problems associated with the end of Rom 9:5, see Jewett, *Romans*, 567–69.

7. See ibid., 557.

8. Wright offers a similar interpretation: "Why Paul needed to make such a powerful affidavit, with its triple emphasis (I'm telling the truth; I'm not lying; my conscience agrees) and its invoking of both Christ and the Spirit, we can only guess; but the guess must surely be that he knew he had an uphill struggle to persuade the Gentile Christians in Rome to concern themselves now, after the last exhilarating chapter, with the plight of Israel according to the flesh" ("Romans," 627). See also Das, *Paul*.

nor distress nor persecution nor famine nor nakedness nor danger nor sword" could do to gentiles, neither "death nor life nor angels nor rulers nor things present nor things to come nor powers nor heights nor depths nor any other created thing" (8:35, 38–39)?!

When Paul asserts, "it is not as though the word of God has failed" (9:6), the word of God [*ho logos tou theou*] must refer at least to the covenants and the promises in 9:4, and probably to the entire table of Israel's blessings in 9:4–5, rather than to the gospel of Jesus as Israel's Messiah.[9] The singular *logos* ("word") does not stand off from the plural terms *diathēkai* ("covenants") and *epangeliai* ("promises"). Instead, the singular *logos* encompasses those plural terms. The distinction matters. Jewett reads 9:6–18 as a defense of the gospel against the accusation of failure, failure because the Jews have not believed the message. Given Paul's confident tenor throughout Romans 8, which only became more confident as the chapter progressed, I cannot see how we could read Romans 9 as Paul's defense of the gospel despite Israel's failure. Instead, *the gentiles' adoption into the family of Israel's Creator God itself vouchsafes Paul's gospel!* Jewett has missed the very problem Paul addresses in Romans 9, in which Paul defends the reliability of God's promises *to Israel* rather than the reliability of the gospel. "[I]f God welcomes Gentiles into the church without requiring them first to become Jews, then what are we to say of God's covenantal relationship with Israel?"[10] Israel's rejection of Paul's gospel, along with the widespread acceptance of the message among the gentiles, calls into question the reliability of God's promises *to Abraham for his descendants*, not the reliability of God's adoption of the gentiles announced by the gospel.

If God gave the blessings and promises mentioned in 9:4–5 to Israel, has God's word for them failed? Now that the gentiles have received the Spirit of adoption, now that the gentiles cry out to God, "Abba! Father!," now that the gentiles find themselves the objects of God's favor and even election, has Israel been rejected? No. Why? "Because not all those who are from Israel [*hoi ex Israēl*] are Israel." Paul draws a distinction within Israel

---

9. Pace Jewett (*Romans*, 573–74), who identifies *ho logos tou theou* in v. 7 as the gospel (so also Dunn, *Romans*, 2:538–39; Moo, *Romans*, 572–73; Morales, "Promised," 118–22). Das rightly identifies the question(s) driving Paul's discussion in Romans 9–11: "If God is so faithful to the elect in Christ, of what value is God's prior election of ethnic Israel? Were not all these blessings originally Israel's? Romans 9–11 is a natural extension, then, of Romans 8. How can Christians find solace in their special place and election by God when God's historic, elect people are not benefiting from their blessings?" (Das, *Paul*, 82).

10. Johnson, "Covenant Faithfulness," 157.

on the basis of the very promise to Abraham.[11] Stated plainly, not every child born of Abraham is "the Seed of Abraham"[12] [*to sperma Abraam*; see Gen 15:4–5 LXX; Gal 3:16, 29], the object of YHWH's promise to Abraham. The distinction between Abraham's sons and Abraham's Seed was not new with Paul.[13] The second-century BCE book of *Jubilees* narrates the birth of Ishmael to Abram through Sarai's maid, Hagar (*Jub.* 14:21–24). Then, immediately after that pericope, the Lord appears to Abram and confirms the covenant with him by giving him the sign of circumcision. As part of the covenant's confirmation, the Lord says to Abraham, "Sarai, your wife, will therefore not be called Sarai because Sarah is her name. And I will bless her and I will give you a son from her. And I will bless him. And he will become a people. And kings of nations will come from him" (*Jub.* 15:15–16).[14] Despite Abraham's intercession for Ishmael, the Lord insists that the promise to Abraham will be fulfilled through Isaac. "Sarah will bear a son for you and you will call him Isaac. And I shall raise up my covenant (as) an eternal covenant with him and with his seed after him. . . . But my covenant I shall establish with Isaac, whom Sarah will bear for you in another year during these days" (*Jub.* 15:19, 21).[15]

Similarly, according to *Biblical Antiquities* (Pseudo-Philo), a text roughly contemporary with Paul's letter to the Romans,

> since Sarai was sterile and had not conceived, then Abram took Hagar his maid and she bore him Ishmael. Now Ishmael became the father of twelve sons. . . . And God appeared to Abram, saying, "To your seed I will give this land, and your name will be called Abraham, and Sarai, your wife, will be called Sarah. And *I will give to you from her an everlasting seed, and I will establish*

---

11. Wright ("Romans," 635–36) makes an interesting connection between Paul's differentiation of "Israel" from "Israel" here in 9:6 and Paul's differentiation of the "I" who affirms Torah's holiness, righteousness, and goodness, on the one hand, and the "I" who cannot do the good it knows it ought to do, on the other (7:7–25).

12. I translate *to sperma Abraam*, "the Seed of Abraham" (with a capital S) in order to highlight the covenantal significance of *sperma* in this context.

13. Jewett (*Romans*, 575) rightly refers to "the more traditional path of Jewish exegesis, claiming that the line of Abraham, Isaac, and Jacob received the promised inheritance."

14. Citations of *Jubilees* come from O. S. Wintermute's translation in Charlesworth, *Pseudepigrapha*, 2:35–142.

15. In the account of Abraham's near-sacrifice of Isaac, *Jubilees* calls Isaac "your firstborn son" (*Jub.* 18:11, 15) and therefore overlooks and dismisses Ishmael. Josephus similarly calls Isaac "his only child" [*monogenē onta*; *Ant.* 1:222]; for discussion, see Feldman, *Antiquities*, 84 n. 676.

my covenant with you." And Abraham knew Sarah, his wife, and
she conceived and bore Isaac. (*L.A.B.* 8:1, 3; my emphasis)[16]

Josephus, another near-contemporary of Paul, says that Sarai gave Hagar
to Abram "at God's command" (*Ant.* 1:187).[17] But Josephus immediately
curtails any thought that Hagar's son might be God's vehicle to fulfill the
Abrahamic promise: "And becoming pregnant, the maidservant dared to
show insolence to Sarra, assuming queenly airs, *as though the rule would
pass over to her son about to be born from her*" (*Ant.* 1:188; my emphasis).[18]
Instead, when he appears again to Abram, God "announced that he would
have a child by Sarra. And He bade him to call him Isakos ["Isaac"], revealing that there would be great nations and kings from him" (*Ant.* 1:191). All
of this suffices to demonstrate that Jews in the Second Temple era were
already used to having to distinguish Abraham's *children* from Abraham's
Seed. The distinction between *children* and *Seed* ran between Isaac and
Ishmael. Both were children of Abraham, but only the former was the son
of promise (= Seed).

Paul, however, draws his distinction not *between* Abraham's two
sons (or even between Abraham's grandsons, Jacob and Esau) but directly
through Israel (= Isaac's son, Jacob): "For not all those who are from Israel
[*hoi ex Israēl*] are Israel" (9:6). Jewett says that Paul's quotation of Gen
21:12 in Rom 9:7 proves "that the patriarchal tradition supports the kind of
distinction Paul wishes to draw *between the various children of Abraham*."[19]
But this reading fails to notice that Paul radically reconfigures the traditional distinctions between Abraham's sons and Abraham's heirs by drawing a boundary not between Ishmael and Isaac but rather right through

---

16. Citations of *Biblical Antiquities* come from Daniel J. Harrington's translation in Charlesworth, *Pseudepigrapha*, 2:297-377. According to Harrington, *Biblical Antiquities* was written sometime between 135 BCE and 100 CE, though "A date around the time of Jesus seems most likely" ("Pseudo-Philo," 2:299).

17. Feldman explains, "Gen 16:2 says nothing about God's commanding Sarai at this point, though perhaps this is an anticipation of Gen 21:12. Josephus' version serves to legitimate what might appear an act of adultery as instigated by Sarai herself. However, midrashic tradition (*Midrash Gen Rabbah* 45:2), in the name of the fourth-century Palestinian Rabbi Yose, asserts that Abram listened to Sarai because she was inspired by the holy spirit. Josephus, by remarking that Sarai acted on God's command in giving Hagar to Abram, is in effect presenting her as a prophetess (so also in rabbinic literature [*Megillah* 14a]) and is thus giving to Sarai's deed a greater weight" (*Antiquities*, 71 n.587).

18. Citations of Josephus, *Ant.* 1-4 come from Feldman, *Antiquities*.

19. Jewett, *Romans*, 576; my emphasis.

the middle of Isaac's son, Israel![20] Paul makes this distinction precisely by appealing to the well-known (and well-used) tradition of Abraham's two sons by two mothers. Ishmael and Isaac demonstrated the difference between physical descent, or "children of the flesh" [*ta tekna tēs sarkos*], and connection with the promise, or "children of God" [*tekna tou theou*] and "children of the promise" [*ta tekna tēs epangelias*]. Paul, however, takes that difference and applies it directly to Isaac's own descendant(s), Israel/the Jews. Remember also that Paul has just declared exuberantly that the gentiles were now offered the status "children of God" (see 8:14–17). Paul's declaration helps explain his claim that not all of Israel's (= Jacob's) descendants are Israel/the children of God/the children of promise.

Paul follows his reference to Abraham's two-sons-from-two-mothers with the very different story of Rebekah, who "conceived children in one act of intercourse with Isaac, our ancestor" (9:10) but nevertheless gave birth to two sons.[21] Here Paul finds textual support for his argument that not every physical descendant, even of the child of promise (Isaac), is himself a child of the promise. Paul's emphasis on the pre-[s]election of Jacob and not Esau ("before they were born, even before they had done anything good or evil"; Rom 9:11) simply makes the point that God does not operate according to accepted cultural practice, according to which a father would name his firstborn son his heir. God, solely on the basis of his election [*kat' eklogēn*], works his purpose [*hē prothesis*]. In this case, the older son [*ho meizōn*; lit. "the greater"] will serve the younger (= "the lesser" [*tō elassoni*].[22] When Paul cites Mal 1:2–3, "I loved Jacob, but I hated [*emisēsa*] Esau," he certainly does not mean that God *hated* Esau. The Hebrew root *sana'*, which the LXX translates with *miseō*, is not as strong

---

20. Joshua Garroway offers a better reading (than Jewett; see the previous note). In Romans 9–11, Paul addresses the question, "Does Jewish unbelief mean God's word is unreliable?" Garroway explains Paul's response: "Paul's apology is revealing: he does not defend God's honor by insisting, as he is thought to do in Rom 15:8, that God held up his end of the bargain by sending Christ as a servant to the Jews; rather, he vindicates God by proposing that Israelites, as they are construed on the standard reckoning by physical descent, Law observance, and other such factors, are *not* the intended recipients of the patriarchal promises" ("Circumcision," 308; original emphasis).

21. I have adopted Moo's translation (*Romans*, 570), despite our very different interpretations of this section of Romans. For his explanation of Rom 9:10, see pp. 578–80; see also Dunn, *Romans*, 2:542.

22. I am avoiding questions about unconditional election, predestination, or other issues between Calvinist and Arminian theology. As important as such questions are for contemporary Christians, they belong to later church history and never occurred to Paul.

as the English word "hate."[23] A more appropriate translation would render both Mal 1:2–3 and Rom 9:13: "I chose (or favored) Jacob, but I refused (or rejected) Esau." But we must remember Paul's larger point: God acts not only as an independent moral agent but, indeed, as a *sovereign* moral agent who is not bound by social or cultural norms. God chose Jacob according to his act of election and not on account of birth order, behavior, or any other criterion.

A Defense of God's Sovereignty (Rom 9:14–29)

14 "What, then, shall we say? Is there unrighteousness with God?" Certainly not! **15** For he says to Moses, "I will show mercy to whomever I show mercy, and I will show compassion to whomever I show compassion" (Exod 33:19). **16** Therefore, consequently, not of the one who wills nor of the one who runs, but of the who shows mercy, God. **17** For the Scripture says to Pharaoh, "For this very reason I raised you up, so that I might demonstrate in you my power, and so that my name might be proclaimed throughout the whole world" (Exod 9:16). **18** Therefore, he shows mercy to whom he wants and he hardens whom he wants. **19** Therefore, you will ask me, "Why, [then], does he still find fault? For who is able to oppose his will?" **20** On the contrary, sir, who are you to answer back to God? "Shall what is molded say to the one who molded it, 'Why did you make me like this?'" (Isa 29:16; 45:9).[24] **21** Or does the potter not have authority over the clay, to make from the same lump one noble vessel and one ignoble? **22** But what if God, wanting to put his wrath on display and to make his power known, bore with great patience vessels of wrath that are prepared for destruction, **23** so that he might also make known the richness of his glory upon vessels of mercy, which he prepared beforehand for glory, **24** those of us whom he called, not only from the Jews but also from the gentiles? **25** Thus he says in [the book of] Hosea,

"The son named, 'Not-my-people,' I will rename, 'My-people,'
and the daughter, 'Not-loved,' I will rename, 'Beloved'" (Hos 2:23).

---

23. In its entry for *miseō*, BDAG (s.v.) says, "depending on the context, this verb ranges in [meaning] from 'disfavor' to 'detest'. The Eng. term 'hate' generally suggests affective connotations that do not always do justice esp. to some Semitic shame-honor oriented use of μισέω = שָׂנֵא (e.g., Dt 21:15, 16) in the sense 'hold in disfavor, be disinclined to, have relatively little regard for.'" The NET translators, in a note at Mal 1:3, similarly note, "The context indicates this is technical covenant vocabulary in which 'love' and 'hate' are synonymous with 'choose' and 'reject' respectively (see Deut 7:8; Jer 31:3; Hos 3:1; 9:15; 11:1)" (n. 3).

24. See also Wis 12:12; Job 9:12 (cited in Jewett, *Romans*, 592).

> **26** "And so it will be in the place where it was said to them, 'You are not my people,'
> there they will be called, 'Children of the living God'"
> (Hos 2:1 LXX)
>
> **27** But Isaiah cries out for Israel,
> "Though[25] the number of the children of Israel is like the sand of the sea, the remnant will be saved,
> **28** for by bringing the account to an end and cutting it short, the Lord will do this upon the earth" (Isa 10:22–23).
> **29** In the same way Isaiah said beforehand,
> "If the Lord of Hosts had not left behind for us a seed,
> we would have become as Sodom, and we would have been rendered as Gomorrah" (Isa 1:9).

On its surface, Romans 9 appears to portray God as arbitrary and capricious, as one who chooses to show favor to one person and to damn another for no reason other than that he can.[26] For no reason at all, God chose Isaac's son, Jacob, and did not choose Isaac's son, Esau. Paul takes up once again the interlocutor's voice (which he has not done since Rom 7:7–25): "What, then, shall we say? There is no unrighteousness with God, is there?" (9:14).[27] If God distinguishes between people simply on the basis

---

25. According to BDAG (s.v.), *ean* can function as a "marker of the prospect of an action in a point of time coordinated with another point of time." Given that the action "coordinated" by *ean* in Rom 9:27 is, on the one hand, the expansion of Israel "as the sand of the sea," and the salvation of only a remnant, on the other hand, the concessive conjunction "though" seems appropriate in this context.

26. Paul's question in v. 14 ("What, then, shall we say? There is no unrighteousness with God, is there?"), according to Jewett, "relates to the entire preceding argument in vv. 6–13, but is particularly provoked by the harsh arbitrariness of the quotation from Malachi" (Jewett, *Romans*, 581). Jewett rightly sees the connections joining Rom 9:14–23 with the preceding passage (i.e., 9:1–13), *pace* Moo, who calls this section "a detour from the main road of Paul's argument" (Moo, *Romans*, 589). We might observe, hopefully not uncharitably, that whenever Paul's argument has turned in a direction commentators did not expect, they call that turn a "detour" or "digression" rather than questioning whether their reading of Roman's flow might have gotten off on the wrong foot.

27. Unless the text provides reasons otherwise, I will continue to read Paul's interlocutor as a gentile proselyte to Judaism. Moreover, this interlocutor likely speaks as (or for) Romans' intended readers, at least as far Paul is able to anticipate their response to his argument. "[T]he sources available give ample support to the general principle of identity, *viz.* that, unless otherwise stated or implied, the epistolary interlocutor represents or speaks for the letter's recipient(s), thus functioning as an object of identification

of his own choice and not through any trait or characteristic of the people involved, how can Paul defend God's justice? Or is Paul's theology here inconsistent, given that he earlier affirmed that God "repays each person according to their deeds" (2:6) and that, indeed, "there is no favoritism with God" (2:11)? Is Paul not saying, in other words, that God judged Jacob and Esau *before* there were any deeds for him to repay? Did God show favoritism to Jacob?!

The interlocutor has asked the wrong question. The problem is not simply that he asks, perhaps indirectly, whether God is unjust.[28] The problem is his focus on God's hatred (= rejection) of Esau rather than his love for Jacob. Paul has already vividly portrayed the revelation of God's wrath against "all the ungodliness and *unrighteousness [adikian]* of people who by their *unrighteousness [en adikia]* suppress the truth" (Rom 1:18); God's judgment against *adikia* ("injustice; unrighteousness") is already assured. From the perspective of Romans 1, the surprise of the quotation from Mal 1:2–3 does not come from God's rejection of Esau. Instead, the real shocker is God's declaration of love for Jacob, especially for anyone familiar with the facts of Jacob's biography![29] But precisely this declaration of love proves useful for Paul's defense of God's promises to Israel, which, as he already explained, have not failed [*ouk ekpeptōken*; 9:6]. In other words, the issue in Rom 9:14 is not, "how can God justly hate (= reject) Esau even before birth?" The issue, instead, is: "how can God justly love Jacob even before birth?" The recognition of this problem in v. 14—that the interlocutor's focus was drawn to God's hatred (= rejection) of Esau rather than his love for Jacob—has a further and more important effect for our understanding of Romans 9: Paul's rhetoric does not explain how God relates to humanity as a whole (i.e., that he shows mercy on those whom he chooses and pours out wrath on those whom he rejects). Instead, *Paul focuses solely on Israel and Israel's standing before God*, and so Paul's de-

---

for the latter. It may be assumed on this basis also that *in any given letter an interlocutor remains the same unless otherwise indicated*" (Thorsteinsson, *Interlocutor*, 140–44 [p. 144 quoted; my emphasis]). Pace Jewett (*Romans*, 590), who comments on 9:19, "This person is different from the interlocutor in chap. 2 and fits perfectly into the stereotype in the wisdom literature of the wily scoffer."

28. On the significance of the noun *adikia* ("injustice or unrighteousness") rather than the adjective *adikos* ("unjust or unrighteous"), see Jewett, *Romans*, 581; Morris, *Romans*, 359.

29. Wright rightly catches the tenor of this passage and the truly shocking aspect of the text, *viz.* God's *mercy*: "The surprise . . . is not that some were allowed to fall by the wayside, but that any at all were allowed to continue as God's covenant people, carrying the promises forward to their conclusion" ("Romans," 638).

fense in this section of Romans is solely of God's relationship with Israel.[30] In Rom 9:14–29, Paul addresses Israel's election, and the language of hate (= rejection) in v. 13 or of hardening in v. 17 serves as a foil to set into sharper relief God's love *for Israel*.

As strange as this reframing of Rom 9:14 might sound, we should notice that this is precisely the question Paul goes on to answer in v. 15: "For he says to Moses, 'I will show mercy to whomever I show mercy, and I will show compassion to whomever I show compassion'" (Exod 33:19). Rodrigo Morales rightly emphasizes Paul's focus on God's redemptive grace and election of Israel:

> On the surface, this citation seems to confirm rather than to refute the charge of caprice. ... The broader context of the citation, however, tells a different story. God's self-description appears shortly after Moses's intercession on behalf of Israel following the people's act of idolatry. God responds to Moses's intercession by showing mercy to Israel. The statement is not a simple descriptor of what God is like, but rather is a part of a story of God's fidelity to Israel.[31]

Paul's focus is squarely—even solely—on God's mercy/compassion rather than his wrath, which does not come into view until v. 17.[32] As Paul explains God's favor for those whom God chooses, he turns to the climactic moment in the story of Moses' relationship with Israel's God, in which Moses asks to see the glory of the Lord.[33] Why should God grant Moses' request? Why should Moses be granted a vision of God's glory? The answer: because God wills it. He will show mercy and compassion to those for whom he grants mercy and compassion. Moreover, God's mercy in

---

30. See the excellent discussion of Paul's view of God's mercy in Barclay, "Have Mercy."

31. Morales, "Promised," 118.

32. Similarly, see Garroway ("Circumcision," 308): "The promises to Abraham, Isaac and Jacob are determined by faith, by grace, and as Paul says explicitly in Rom 9:15–18, by *God's merciful election* (cf. Rom 15:9) (original emphasis)."

33. Moses requests from God, "If, then, I have found favor before you, reveal yourself to me, so that I might see you clearly" (Exod 33:13 LXX). In a striking passage with no real parallel within the biblical canon, the Lord consents, saying, "Even this, your word, which you have spoken, I will do, for you have found favor before me, and I know you better than all things" (33:17 LXX). Moses, in response to YHWH's assent, asks, "Show me your own glory" [*deixon moi tēn seautou doxan*; 33:18 LXX]. Verse 19, which Paul quotes in Rom 9:15, is part of the Lord's concession to reveal himself uniquely to Moses.

Israel and Christ

Exod 33:19 is not directed solely at Moses. In Exodus 32–34, Moses intercedes on Israel's behalf in light of the people's idolatry in the Golden Calf incident. The Lord relents from his plan to destroy the Israelites and begin anew with Moses and his children. As Paul reads Exodus 32–34, God in his mercy *recreates* the covenant people by his grace, solely as an act of his sovereign election.[34]

The syntax of v. 16 is too complicated and ambiguous to provide firm and reliable support for any reading of this passage. The best we can hope for is to offer a reading of Rom 9:14–16 that makes sense of the entire passage. In light of our decision to reframe v. 14 in terms of God's love rather than his hate (= rejection), our reading of v. 16 will have to focus on the central role of God's mercy/compassion at this point in Paul's rhetoric. A literal translation of v. 16 might read, "Therefore, consequently, not of the one who wills nor of the one who runs, but of the one who shows mercy, God." Robert Jewett says rightly, "[Paul] wishes to insist on the absolute freedom of divine mercy as the basis not only for understanding predestination but also for understanding the first eight chapters of the letter."[35] Though Jewett wants to understand this verse as part of Paul's defense of the gospel (hence his reference to Romans 1–8), I find it more likely that this verse explains the basis of *Israel*'s election and God's sovereign choice to "love Jacob." No act of human volition [*ou tou thelontos*] or striving [*oude tou trechontos*] resulted in Jacob's election in God's plan. Rather, it was solely on the basis of God's act of mercy [*alla tou eleōntos theou*].

Paul then appeals in v. 17 to Israel's history and her historic encounter with Pharaoh to flesh out the dynamics of God's sovereign mercy. More importantly in light of our reading's emphasis on God's love for Jacob, rather than on his hatred (= rejection) of Esau, we might be somewhat surprised to see Paul refer to God hardening "whom he wants" in v. 17. Some commentators interpret Paul's rhetoric as if it evenly balanced God's mercy with his wrath. Douglas Moo offers exactly this approach to 9:15–18: "In vv. 15–16 Paul reiterates and expands the positive side of God's sovereignty in election that he alluded to in vv. 10–13 ('Jacob I have loved'). Now Paul will do the same with respect to the 'negative' side ('Esau I have rejected')."[36] At the very least, according to Moo's comments on

---

34. See Barclay, "Have Mercy," 100. In contrast to Paul's reading of Israel's story, which focuses squarely and intensely on this, the nadir of Israel's relationship to YHWH, Josephus's account of the biblical history "omits all reference to the Golden Calf" (ibid., 88).

35. Jewett, *Romans*, 582.

36. Moo, *Romans*, 593.

9:17, Paul has in mind *both* God's election and his judgment, rather than the narrow focus on God's election that we have been proposing.

Two factors, however, give us reason to think God's raising up of Pharaoh and hardening his heart also serve to demonstrate the extent of God's love for Jacob (rather than function as a parallel to God's hatred [= rejection] of Esau). First, Paul has already explained that God gave over [*paradidōmi*] the gentiles to the lusts of their hearts, to their shameful passions, and to their senseless mind (Rom 1:24, 26, 28). God did not give the gentiles over to depraved hearts except as a consequence of their ungodliness and injustice (1:18), their exchange of God's glory—*the very thing Moses insisted on seeing!* (see Exod 33:18)—for the likeness of created beings (1:23). So when Paul says that the gentiles "were rendered foolish in their thoughts and their senseless heart was darkened" (1:21), readers could be forgiven for remembering the story of Pharaoh, who hardened his heart and so, as a result, had his heart hardened by YHWH.[37] We should not, then, rush to the interpretation that Paul depicts God arbitrarily hardening Pharaoh's heart. Instead, in light of Romans 1, God handed Pharaoh over to the desires of his heart.[38] Second, in light of the Abrahamic promise in Gen 12:1–3, in which God promises, "I will bless those who bless you, and those who curse you I will curse" (12:3 LXX), the cursing of Pharaoh provides a striking example of the fate of those nations that oppose Israel, the Seed of Abraham and the children of God (see Rom 9:7–8).

These two factors make it unlikely that Paul is saying God, in his sovereignty, arbitrarily hardened Pharaoh's heart. If this were the case,

---

37. Thirteen times the LXX refers to the hardening [*sklērynō*] of Pharaoh's heart (Exod 4:21; 7:3, 22; 8:15; 9:12, 35; 10:1, 20, 27; 11:10; 14:4, 8, 17).

38. *Pace* Moo (*Romans*, 597), who concludes, "We have seen that Paul has insisted that God bestows his mercy on his own initiative, apart from anything that a person is or does (v. 16). The strict parallelism in this verse suggests that the same is true of God's hardening: as he has mercy on 'whomever he wishes,' so he hardens 'whomever he wishes.'" Moo acknowledges that other exegetes liken Paul's comments here in Romans 9 with what he has already said in Romans 1, but he dismisses them with a rhetorical wave of the hand ("the assumption that Paul expects his readers to see behind God's hardening a prior self-hardening on the part of the individual is questionable"; ibid., 598) and a brief argument about the narrative function of "hardening" in Exodus 1–14. Moo's reading of Romans 9, however, *utterly fails to cohere with what Paul has already said in Romans!* If Moo is right, then the stark depravity Paul described in 1:18–32 does not apply to Pharaoh in 9:17–18, and the just God who does not show favoritism in Romans 1–2 becomes utterly erratic and unpredictable. If Moo is right about Romans 9, then Paul's most famous letter becomes an incoherent mess undeserving of the prominence it has enjoyed throughout Western culture and history!

Israel and Christ

perhaps we could in fact argue that God did act unjustly. Wright offers a helpful comment here:

> Paul is not, then, using the example of Pharaoh to explain that God has the right to show mercy, or to harden someone's heart, out of mere caprice. Nor is it simply that God has the right to do this sort of thing when someone is standing in the way of the glorious purpose that has been promised.... God's action upon Pharaoh was part of the means, not only of rescuing Israel from slavery, but of declaring God's name to the world.[39]

If the hardening of Pharaoh's heart resulted from his own unwillingness to submit to the Creator God, then the way is opened for us to see in the hardening of Pharaoh's heart an expression of God's love and compassion for Israel, whom he loved (see 9:13).[40]

And this is exactly what Paul says when he cites Exod 9:16: "For the Scripture says to Pharaoh, 'For this very reason I raised you up, so that I might demonstrate in you my power, and so that my name might be proclaimed throughout the whole world'" (Rom 9:17). Robert Jewett provides a helpful discussion of the subtle but significant differences between Exod 9:16 (LXX) and Paul's citation of that verse, which "is somewhat closer to the MT."[41] One of those changes, where Paul says, "For this very reason ..." [*eis auto touto*], connects the citation directly to the divine display of mercy at the end of Rom 9:16. Another of those changes, in which God's purpose is to "display my power" [*endeixōmai ... tēn dynamin mou*], picks up a key theme in Romans, in which the gospel is "the power of God [*dynamis theou*] for salvation." Moreover, the verb "display" in the quotation has a parallel in Rom 3:25, where God set forth Jesus as a *hilastērion* precisely as "a display [*eis endeixin*] of his righteousness." The goal of this display is to spread the fame of God's name "throughout the whole earth" [*en pasē tē gē*], which phrase reminds us of God's promise that "all the tribes of the earth [*pasai hai phylai tēs gēs*] would be blessed" by Abraham (Gen 12:3 LXX). As Elizabeth Johnson has nicely explained, "God's power is always power to save."[42] Paul's statements in v. 18 are significantly

---

39. Wright, "Romans," 639.

40. Dunn (*Romans*, 2:553) similarly finds that "*God's* mercy is the central motif" (original italics).

41. Jewett, *Romans*, 584.

42. Johnson, "Covenant Faithfulness," 161.

off-balance, despite the superficial appearance of symmetry.[43] When Paul writes, "Therefore, he shows mercy to whom he wants and he hardens whom he wants," God's display of mercy is truly arbitrary and a function of God's sovereignty. On the other hand, as we have seen, God's hardening is not arbitrary, but rather (i) is a response to human ungodliness and injustice (see 1:18) and (ii) serves the purpose of demonstrating his mercy.[44]

The interlocutor does not pick up on the imbalance, and so he objects, "Why, [then], does he still find fault? For who is able to oppose his will?" (Rom 9:19). These questions not only make sense as a misunderstanding of what Paul has just said in v. 18; they also make sense coming from Paul's proselyte interlocutor, who struggled vividly but unsuccessfully with his weakness to do the good he knew Torah required of him (7:7–25). In 9:18, the interlocutor sees a different explanation for his moral failure: not his own weakness but God's own hardening. We should already be prepared to answer this objection. After all, it was precisely those who oppose God's will who found themselves handed over to their depraved hearts and minds (Rom 1:24, 26, 28). Paul, however, does not defend God's justice (at least, not directly); instead, he defends God's sovereignty. Romans 9:20 quotes Isaiah 29 and introduces the prophetic tradition of God-as-potter and his authority (sovereignty) over the products formed on his wheel.[45] However, it also picks up the theme of God-as-Creator from Romans 1, as Jewett explains nicely:

> The story of God making Adam in Gen 2:7–8 is phrased with the same language: … "And God molded the human of dust

---

43. I like Jewett's discussion here: "the truly scandalous form of selectivity was that God 'has mercy on whom he wills,' namely, on those who did not deserve it.... Well-meaning theologians have expended far more ink in dealing with the hardening side of this antithesis, even though that was widely accepted throughout biblical literature.... It would be more appropriate to conclude that Paul applies the widely shared teaching about Pharaoh's hardening in order to make the much more controversial case that God's mercy is sovereign" (*Romans*, 585, 586).

44. We cannot reverse these terms. That is, God's hardening Pharaoh's heart served the purpose of showing his mercy for Israel. But nothing in either the Exodus story or in Romans suggests that God's mercy for Israel served the purpose of hardening Pharaoh's heart. This observation confirms our hermeneutical decision to focus on God's love for Jacob rather than to keep it in balance with his hatred (= rejection) of Esau. Mark Nanos's formulation of this point strikes me as awkward but nevertheless exactly right: "Instead of eliminating Pharaoh, God is represented as making him stubbornly resistant to God's will so that the people of Israel would be freed" ("Temporary Protection," 53).

45. In addition to Isaiah 29, see Jer 18:1–11. Morales ("Promised," 119) offers a brief but helpful discussion of the image of the potter and the clay.

from the earth.... And the Lord God planted a garden ... and placed there the person he had molded." This terminology is widely used by other biblical writers to describe God's shaping of humans in general, or the prophet in particular, the earth and all within it, Israel and its destiny, as well as the other nations. The assumption of this usage is the absolute sovereignty of the molder over what is molded to provide whatever shape God desires.[46]

However, unlike Jewett, we need to keep in mind that Paul is offering a defense of Israel's election rather than an explanation of her disbelief in the gospel.[47] Paul does not cast Israel in the role of the sass-talking vessel. Throughout Romans 9 he has emphasized that God shows mercy and compassion on his people, that he loved Israel, and so on. Moreover, Paul is addressing the interlocutor's misperception of 9:18, in which he (i.e., the interlocutor) focused his attention on the hardening of Pharaoh's heart. Instead, Paul is making his way to drawing the interlocutor's (and his readers') focus back onto God's mercy for Jacob (= Israel). After all, the demonstration of God's wrath (see 9:22; cp. 1:18) and the preparation of "vessels of wrath" serves the purpose of [*hina*] making known the richness of his glory (9:23).

Paul's emphasis the entire time has been on the mercy, kindness, and love of God, and so our reading of Romans 9 should not succumb to the temptation to emphasize God's hatred (= rejection) and wrath.[48] We can even say, on the basis of Paul's statements about God's power [*dynamis*] and glory [*doxa*] since Romans 1, that "vessels of wrath" [*skeuē orgēs*] and "vessels of mercy" [*skeuē eleous*] *refer to the very same vessels!*[49] That is, since the gospel is the power of God for the salvation of everyone who believes (1:16), the manifestation of God's power in 9:22 *transforms the vessels of wrath into vessels of mercy*. "By using this image [*viz.* of the potter and the clay] Paul does not simply condemn Israel to destruction; rather,

---

46. Jewett, *Romans*, 593.

47. Again, see Das, *Paul*, 82.

48. Again, *pace* Jewett, who has been reading this entire section of Romans as a response to "the issue of Israel's rejection of the gospel" (*Romans*, 595). Instead, Paul's purpose here is to defend the trustworthiness of God's word, in particular his promises to Israel.

49. Similarly, see ibid., 595–96: "In this instance the ultimate purpose of divine wrath and power, as Rom 9:23 and 11:26–32 will show, is to *change 'vessels of wrath' into 'vessels of mercy'* through the power of the gospel" (my emphasis). Pace Moo, *Romans*, 604–7.

he holds out hope for repentance."[50] Jonathan Linebaugh makes a similar point *vis-à-vis* Rom 3:21–24, that "the judgment of the sinner contains within it, *not as its complement but as its consequence*, the justification of the judged."[51] Or, in the language of Romans 9, the consequence of God's judgment against the vessels of wrath is justification and transformation into vessels of mercy.

This interpretation finds support in Paul's only reference to God's "patience" [*makrothymia*] other than here in Rom 9:22. Earlier Paul asked his interlocutor, "Or do you despise the richness of his kindness, his forbearance, and his *patience*, being ignorant that the kindness of God leads you into repentance" (Rom 2:4).[52] If the patient expression of God's kindness leads sinners ("vessels of wrath") into repentance, that patience must surely play a central role in transforming them into "vessels of mercy."[53] As we have already said, Paul is not defending God's sovereign—even arbitrary—election of individuals to either mercy or wrath. He is defending God's sovereign—even arbitrary—display of mercy upon "those whom he prepared before hand" [*ha proētoimasen*], a phrase that recalls the beginning of the string of verbs in 8:29–30:

> foreknew → predestined (or "fore-chose") → called → justified → glorified[54]

The connection with the end of Romans 8 continues in v. 24, where Paul brings the argument back around to the justice (or better, the righteousness) of God. That God "called" [*ekalesen*] the vessels of mercy certainly recalls 8:30, where God "called" those he foreknew and predestined. Paul uses the first-person plural pronoun [*hēmas*; "us"], which he has not done since 9:10, to identify the "vessels" in v. 23 as himself together with his readers: vessels of mercy, "those of us whom he called, not only from the Jews but also from the gentiles" (9:24).[55]

Paul's reference to "the Jews" [*hoi Ioudaioi*] in 9:24 represents a significant shift from his use of the label "Israel" earlier in the chapter (see 9:4,

---

50. Morales, "Promised," 119.

51. Linebaugh, "Debating," 119; my emphasis.

52. The word "richness" [*ploutos*] provides another link between Rom 9:22–23 and 2:4.

53. See Dunn's discussion of *makrothymia* (*Romans*, 2:558–59).

54. The first two words in this chain, *proegnō* and *proōrisen*, feature the *pro-* ("pre-" or "fore-") prefix that appears also in 9:23 [*proētoimasen*; "prepared in advance"].

55. So also Jewett, *Romans*, 598.

6). The labels *Israēl* and *Israēlitēs* ("Israelite") are "the most pregnant of the theological concepts consistently used within the community. . . . [They refer] to Jews as members of the people of God."[56] When Paul said, "not all those who are from Israel are Israel" (9:6), his meaning was clear: not all the descendants of Abraham's grandson, Israel, belong to the covenantal community of the people of God, the children of promise (9:8). Paul's discussion (and defense) of the covenantal status of the Jews in Rom 9:1–23, using the label *Israel*, addresses the question raised in v. 6 by affirming that the word of God has had its effect, that Israel has received its blessings from God. This is what it means, after all, to be Israel! Israel's historic unfaithfulness to her covenant with YHWH—to Torah—has not frustrated the fulfillment of YHWH's promises to Abraham and to his Seed. Paul has already exclaimed, "Let God be true and every human being a liar" (Rom 3:4). God's faithfulness, in other words, outlasts and overcomes the faithlessness of his people. As a result, even the contemporary fact of Jews who do not believe the gospel does not call God's promises to Israel into question, in part because large numbers of Jews *did* believe the gospel!

Therefore, when Paul lays aside the covenantal term, *Israel*, and resumes using the geo-political term, *Jews*, the change matters. When God called "us" his "vessels of mercy," the people comprising that "us" came "not only from the Jews but also from the gentiles" (9:24). This is the new make-up of *Israel*, the covenantal people of God.[57] Although Paul's focus throughout Romans has been the basis for the inclusion of *gentiles* in the promises of God, his focus throughout Romans 9 has shifted onto the continued inclusion of the Jews. Paul's exuberant exposition of the inclusion of the gentiles into the family of God has raised the possibility, if only implicitly, that the historic people of God—the Jews—have found themselves disinherited.[58] When Paul writes "not only from the Jews, but also from the gentiles," the emphasis is on the former rather than the latter for the first time in Romans. The citations from Hosea and Isaiah in vv. 25–29 bear this out. In Rom 9:26, Paul quotes the tradition of Hosea's children, which his prostitute-wife, Gomer, bore him. Hosea's marriage to

---

56. Mayer, "Ἰσραήλ," 2:310; see also Das, *Paul*, 83; Johnson, "Covenant Faithfulness," 158; Moo, *Romans*, 560–61, esp. n. 30.

57. "Paul redefines Israel 'by *in*cluding believing Gentiles rather than *ex*cluding unbelieving Israel'" (Jewett, *Romans*, 599; original italics; citing Johnson, *Function*, 149). While I appreciate the sentiment, Paul's discussion of the olive branches in Rom 11:17–24 clearly depends on *both* the grafting in *as well as* the breaking off.

58. Das takes this possibility seriously in his exposition of Romans 9–11 (see *Paul*, 78–113).

a woman of questionable faithfulness was a prophetic symbol of Israel's unfaithfulness to YHWH. Similarly, the naming of each of his children provided a prophetic symbol of the Lord's rejection of the people of Israel.[59] The *re*-naming of Hosea's children also symbolized the reversal of *Israel's* fortunes.[60]

Precisely where Paul's rhetoric places a question mark against God's fidelity to his promises to Israel in light of the adoption of the gentiles into the family of God, he reminds his gentile readers that God reversed his judgment against Israel by changing the names of Hosea's children.[61] Paul cites a particularly relevant text, Hos 2:1 LXX, which restores Israel's status from "Not-my-people" to "children of the living God." As Paul moves from Hosea to Isaiah, his *pathos* deepens. Whereas Hosea simply speaks [*legei*], Isaiah "cries out for Israel" [*krazei hyper tou Israēl*].[62] Numerous difficulties, both exegetical and textual, plague Rom 9:27–28.[63] But in this context, the best reading is that Paul cites Isaiah's promise that God's judgment against Israel will come to an end before the people are completely wiped out. The judgment of God upon the numerous people of Israel will end while a remnant remains, which remnant will be saved. Paul has already explained the process by which gentiles, despite their former estrangement from the Creator God of Israel, are now adopted into his family (see 8:12–17). Paul's references to Hos 2:1 and Isa 10:22b–23 LXX similarly explain the Jews' continued presence in God's family. Even though the Jews found themselves under Torah's curses rather that its blessings, the way nevertheless remains open for their reconciliation with God.

Our reading of Rom 9:27–28 finds confirmation in v. 29, where Paul cites another Isaianic passage to explain that, had God not cut short his judgment and preserved a remnant for Israel, they would eventually have

---

59. Hosea 1 narrates Hosea's marriage to Gomer and his three children with her, whom he names "Jezreel" (a son), "Not-pitied" (a daughter), and "Not-my-people" (a son). The children's names all incorporate prophetic oracles against the people of Israel, which oracles are reversed when the Lord finishes punishing his people (see Hos 1:10—2:1; 2:14–23).

60. So rightly Ehrensperger, "Scriptural Reasoning."

61. *Pace* Jewett (*Romans*, 599); Morales ("'Promised,'" 119); Wright ("Romans," 642–43), who read the citations from Hosea in 9:25–26 as references to the *gentiles'*—rather than *Israel's*—reversal of fortunes.

62. Jewett calls Paul's use of *krazein* ("call out, cry out") an "unusually powerful term" (*Romans*, 601).

63. See Metzger's brief discussion (*Textual Commentary*, 462).

Israel and Christ

been left utterly bereft, just like the legendary objects of God's total judgment, Sodom and Gomorrah.

∼

We have come nearly one-third through a very difficult passage. To this point in Romans 9–11, we have made one primary point: Paul offers a defense of God's fidelity to the Jews and to his promises to Israel. Some readings of these chapters (e.g., Jewett) argue that Paul is defending the authenticity of his gospel. In this latter reading, the gospel's rejection by the lion's share of Jews (especially the Jewish religious and political leadership) purportedly presents a challenge to Paul's proclamation of Jesus as Israel's Messiah.[64] I cannot see that this reading makes sense of the text, however, since Romans 8 absolutely brims with confidence in the gospel's efficacy among the gentiles without even a hint of concern that the Jews' response to the gospel might call his message into question. How, then, does Paul's confidence in Romans 8 lead to his sorrow in Romans 9?

Instead, the inclusion of the gentiles (over which Paul positively exults in Romans 8) raises the question, if the gentiles now have the Spirit of God, what is the status of God's promises to his historic people, Israel? Our reading of Rom 9:1–29, therefore, has focused on how Paul positions the gospel as not only the mechanism by which the gentiles take on the status, "children of God," but also the means by which Israel's promises find their fullest and most satisfying fulfillment. If this reading gets us on the right track, it will have to continue to make good sense of the remainder of Romans 9–11. With that, let us continue reading.

---

64. Similarly, Moo thinks (along with a plurality of commentators) that Paul is responding to suspicions that he has abandoned his fellow Jews, that "his passionate and well-known defense of the law-free Gentile mission had earned him the reputation—in Rome, as elsewhere—of being anti-Jewish" (*Romans*, 556). But I find it much more likely that Paul is anticipating and responding to a potentially anti-Jewish inference *on the part of his gentile readers in Rome*. Even Paul's emphatic and emotional defense of his "kinsmen according to the flesh" does not sound like a defense of his own identification with Israel. For one thing, had Paul been concerned in Romans 9–11 to defend his Jewish *bona fides*, I would have expected him to identify the accusations made against him (see, e.g., Rom 3:8). But nowhere in Romans 9 does Paul complain that he is being slandered or otherwise misrepresented; neither does he say explicitly he is setting the record straight.

11

Israel and Christ, Pt. II

Torah's Telos

> *The discussion from 9:6 onward, the whole theme that concludes in 11:28–36 is ultimately about God's own character and actions; and, thus far, it has all circled around the question, Has God been faithful to his promises? In doing so, has he been guilty of ἀδικία (adikia, "unrighteousness")? This, as we have seen, sends us back to 3:1–8, where the main subject is God's own "righteousness."*[1]

Up to this point, we have focused on Paul's concern for Israel and his defense of the reliability of God's word (9:6), his promises to Abraham and his descendants. However, we have also stressed that Paul presents this defense for the benefit of his gentile readers in Rome, gentiles upon whom God has poured out his Spirit of adoption (8:12–17) and who may now find themselves asking what happened to God's historic people, Israel. In other words, Paul, the apostle to the gentiles, explains to the gentiles that God has not abandoned his promises to the Jews. Far from it, the very same means by which the gentiles now find themselves reconciled with the Creator God have also brought YHWH's promises to Israel to fulfillment. Nowhere does Paul advocate a "two covenant" approach to the salvation of both Jews and gentiles.[2] "Paul would find such a solution

---

1. Wright, "Romans," 646.

2. Andrew Das provides an excellent and devastating critique of the "two covenant" reading of Romans 9–11, according to which Paul critiques Israel for resisting

highly unacceptable because it excludes Christians from their God-given identity as Israel and it deprives Israel of its own Messiah."[3] By the end of Romans 8 Paul has finished his argument that the gentiles have been brought fully within the family of God apart from taking on the yoke of Torah-observance. Here in Romans 9–11, then, the presence of the gentiles among the people of God can be taken as given. Paul's focus now is on the possibility of Israel finding their own "peace with God" (see Rom 5:1).

Israel's Missed Mark (Rom 9:30–33)

> 30 "What then? Shall we say that the gentiles, who did not pursue righteousness, nevertheless obtained righteousness, that is, the righteousness [that is revealed] by faithfulness? 31 But Israel, who did pursue Torah—which is righteousness—did not attain Torah?" 32 Why? "Because they did not [pursue Torah] from faith but as from deeds." They stumbled upon the stumbling stone, 33 as it is written,
>
> "Look! I am placing in Zion a stumbling stone, even a rock of offense, and the one who trusts in it shall not be put to shame" (Isa 8:14; 28:16).

These four verses do not mention "sin" [*hamartia*],[4] but Paul's discussion of "obtaining righteousness" certainly makes the concept of *hamartia* relevant here. Perhaps the most common thing people say about *hamartia* is that it means, "missing the mark." The related verb *hamartanō* ("I sin") "originally meant to miss, miss the mark, lose, not share in something, be mistaken," and the noun, *hamartia*, means "mistake, failure to reach a goal

---

the inclusion of the gentiles, but he anticipates the salvation of the Jews by means of the Mosaic covenant (see Das, *Paul*, 96–106). Park offers a variation of the "two covenant" approach to Paul (*Either*), but his reconstruction of Paul in particular and Christian origins as a whole is inadequate. For example, he emphasizes the mention of "the 'saints' in Jerusalem" (ibid., 68) in Rom 15:30–32 and neglects Paul's explicit concern that he would be "delivered from those who are disobedient [*apo tōn apeithountōn*] in Judea" (15:31). "Those who are disobedient" clearly refers not to Jewish followers of Jesus but to non-believing Jews. As a result, Park's entire interpretation of Paul's collection for the Jerusalem church as evidence that Paul's "theological horizon had broadened" and that Paul now accepted two gospels, one of circumcision and one of uncircumcision, collapses in on itself (ibid., 73).

3. Johnson, "Covenant Faithfulness," 166.

4. Paul uses the noun *hamartia* forty-eight times in Romans; by Rom 9:30–33, we have encountered all but two of those uses (see 11:27; 14:23). The lion's share of references (thirty-six, exactly 75 percent) occurs in 6:1—8:3.

If You Call Yourself a Jew

(chiefly a spiritual one)."[5] In one of the most famous verses from Romans, Paul has already explained, "there is no distinction [i.e., between Jew and gentile], for all have sinned [*hēmarton*] and fall short of the glory of God" (Rom 3:22–23). Paul is still thinking in these terms in 9:30–33, as James Dunn helpfully demonstrates,[6] and in just a little while Paul will return to the lack of distinction between Jews and Greeks (see 10:12).

All of this raises the question, what "mark," specifically, might Paul think both Jew and gentile have missed? The first candidate must surely be Torah, the *nomos* Paul has mentioned so frequently throughout Romans. But two factors make it unlikely that Paul would say that both Jew and gentile have "missed the mark" of Torah. First, Paul argues throughout Romans 2–8 that gentiles were not under Torah's authority and so should not take on the yoke of Torah-observance (see esp. Rom 6:14). It would make no sense whatsoever for Paul to claim, "there is no distinction, for all have sinned [= missed the mark] and fall short of the glory of God" if he had missing the mark of the Torah in mind—the gentiles were never expected to aim for *that* mark. Second, Paul has already explained, "*hamartia* was in the world until Torah" [*achri nomou*; Rom 5:13], and as a result death reigned from Adam to Moses (5:14). In fact, the arrival of Torah augmented *hamartia* (= sin) and transformed it into transgression [*paraptōma*; 5:20]. Death—the consequence of missing the mark—exercised hegemony in the era leading up to Torah. These points make it extremely unlikely that Paul identifies "the mark" that has been missed in human *hamartia* (= sin) as Torah.

What, then, is "the mark" that has been missed? At this point it would be helpful for us to remember the purpose of Paul's apostolic calling, which he explained in the opening of his letter. "We received grace and apostolic vocation *for the obedience of faith* [*eis hypakoēn pisteōs*] among all the gentiles, for his name's sake" (Rom 1:5). Paul presents himself as a herald proclaiming to the nations the message of peace with God on the basis of faith: both Jesus' faithfulness to the Creator God, which distinguishes him from every other person (both Jew and gentile), and the act of believing in and behaving toward God on the basis of this peace. This "believing in" and "behaving toward" together comprise the concept *obedience* [*hypakoē*]. All of humanity has missed the mark of *obedience*,

---

5. Günther, "ἁμαρτία," 3:577–83 (p. 577 quoted).

6. See the table of key vocabulary (*dikaiosynē, pistis, pisteuō, nomos,* and *erga*) across different sections of Romans (Dunn, *Romans*, 2:577), and notice the similarities between 3:20—5:21 and 9:30—10:21.

Jews (who transgressed Torah's covenantal terms) as well as gentiles (who turned from the Creator God to worship the image of created beings; see Rom 1:23). Paul understands himself as a herald who procures this obedience from the gentiles.

As we return to Romans 9, Paul has just cited four passages from Hosea and Isaiah as part of his explanation that God reverses his judgment against Israel, whom he called "Not-my-people" and "Not-beloved" (see Hosea 1–2; cited in Rom 9:25–26), but this reversal applies only to a remnant (Isaiah 10; cited in Rom 9:27–28). Had God not relented in his punishment of Israel's transgressions, the nation would have been utterly destroyed, rendered like Sodom and Gomorrah (Isaiah 10; cited in Rom 9:29). God's judgment falls on a large part of—even the majority of—Israel. Paul's interlocutor latches onto this point and speaks up. (Remember, Paul imagines this interlocutor as a gentile who exhibits considerable interest in Israel and her Torah, even to the point of converting fully to Judaism.[7]) He asks Paul, "What then? Shall we say that the gentiles, who did not pursue righteousness, nevertheless obtained righteousness, that is, the righteousness [that is revealed] by faithfulness? But Israel, who did pursue Torah—which is righteous[8]—did not attain Torah?" Eleven times throughout Romans Paul interrupts himself with the rhetorical question, *Ti oun* ("What then?").[9] In five of those instances he follows up with a

---

7. BDAG defines *Ioudaïsmos* as "the Judean way of belief and life" and offers both *Judeanism* and *Judaism* as glosses. The related verb, *Ioudaïzō* means to "live as one bound by Mosaic ordinances or traditions" (BDAG, s.v.), or "to customarily practice Jewish patterns of behavior.... In some languages an expression such as 'to live Jewish' may be rendered as 'to live just like Jews live' or 'to do the same things that Jews do'" (LN, s.v.). However, Josephus appears to make a distinction between "the Jews" [*tous Ioudaious*] and "the Judaizers" [*tous Ioudaïzontas*; J.W. 2:463], which suggests that the verb *Ioudaïzein* has the connotation of *gentiles* who live like Jews. This would fit my reading of Romans perfectly, which has focused exclusively on the problem of *gentiles* who are attracted to Torah-observance and has not addressed at any point the question of whether Jews should continue to keep Torah. We have imagined the interlocutor with whom Paul has portrayed himself having a discussion (or better, a Question and Answer session) as one of these "Judaizers" (i.e., a gentile who takes on Jewish customs and beliefs). For a very good discussion of these terms, see Novenson, "Did Paul."

8. I translate the genitival phrase *nomon dikaiosynēs* (lit. "Law [or law] of righteousness) as a "genitive of quality" (the genitive "provides in many combinations an attributive which would ordinarily be provided by an adjective"; BDF §165) or an "attributive genitive" ("The genitive substantive specifies an *attribute* or innate quality of the head substantive. It is similar to a simple adjective in its semantic force, though more emphatic"; Wallace, *Greek Grammar*, 86–88).

9. See 3:1, 9; 4:1; 6:1, 15; 7:7; 8:31; 9:14, 19 (*v.l.*), 30; 11:7.

strong negative exclamation, usually *mē genoito* ("Certainly not!").[10] In light of Paul's impassioned defense of Israel thus far in Romans 9, we might have expected a similar response here at 9:32. Instead, he seems to affirm the premise of the question, as if to say, "Yes, the gentiles have received what they did not pursue, while Israel, with Torah (which is righteous) as their target, did not attain Torah."[11] Note what Paul says Israel did not attain: Torah itself! We might have expected Paul to say that Israel did not attain righteousness by means of Torah. Unfortunately, commentators too often talk around what Paul actually wrote in favor of what they expected him to write.[12]

Paul responds to the interlocutor with a question of his own: "why?" [*dia ti*; v. 32]. I attribute the statement of 9:32b to the interlocutor: "Because they did not [pursue Torah] from faith but as from deeds."[13] Given the number of times the interlocutor has drawn the wrong inference, we should allow for the possibility that his answer to Paul's question in 9:32 is also a wrong inference. However, given that the distinction between "faith" [*pistis*] and "deeds" [*erga*] in the context of a discussion of Torah already occurred in Rom 3:27-28, we might interpret 9:32 as the beginning of the interlocutor's successful apprehension of Paul's message.[14]

---

10. At 3:9 Paul responds to the interlocutor's question with the similar exclamation, *ou pantōs* ("Not at all!").

11. Dunn, despite getting too close to punctuating 9:30-31 as a statement rather than a question, rightly comments, "Here the following *hoti* and the content of the sentence it introduces (something Paul would want to affirm on his own part) suggests rather that he intended the sentence to be read as a statement, or, if with the suggestion of a question in the voice, at least as a question to which he would give an affirmative answer" (*Romans*, 2:580). I do not agree that we should punctuate these verses as a statement, but Dunn is correct that Paul anticipates an affirmative answer to the question.

12. For example, "Gentiles who did not engage in the race have obtained the prize of a right relationship with God, whereas the Jews, although they energetically pursued the law for righteousness, did not attain *to what the law demanded and fell short of reaching the goal*" (Schreiner, *Romans*, 536-37; my emphasis). Similarly, "Yes, Paul suggests, as a matter of fact the Gentiles did attain righteousness *whereas Israel did not!*" (Garroway, *Gentile-Jews*, 104; my emphasis). Although I agree with Garroway's affirmative response to the question in Rom 9:30-31 (see ftn 14, below), we must account for the fact that Paul portrays gentiles and Jews in pursuit of two different (but related) objects: righteousness and Torah, respectively.

13. I have carried forward the verb *diōkō* ("pursue") from 9:31, as also do most commentators (see Dunn, *Romans*, 2:582; Jewett, *Romans*, 610; Wright, "Romans," 649).

14. Garroway, in his discussion of Rom 4:1 (*Gentile-Jews*, 103-5), discusses the rhetorical question, "What then [shall we say]?": "It is true that the inference Paul introduces in the second part of the "What shall we say?" construction is usually false.

Given Paul's approval of this answer (see below), what does he mean that the Jews pursued Torah "as from deeds" [*hōs ex ergōn*] rather than "from faith" [*ek pisteōs*]? Paul is clearly not saying that the Jews circumcised their sons, abstained from certain foods, and set apart the Sabbath as holy, among other things, without exhibiting any faith in Israel's God, whether faith that God sees their actions or faith that he will reward their obedience. The Jews kept Torah's commandments, which were, of course, God's commandments, *precisely because of* their faith! According to Witherington, "The problem was not that Israel realized that God required obedience. The problem was that they pursued righteousness by works of the Law, not by faith in Christ, and therefore did not attain it."[15] Witherington is right to identify the Jews' lack of "faith in Christ" as Paul's primary complaint (see the discussion of 9:32–33, below), but he misses that the Jews did not attain Torah itself (rather than righteousness)! What, then, might Paul have thought was lacking in the Jews' pursuit of Torah? He does not provide an explanation here, so we will have to wait and see if Paul clarifies this point in the subsequent discussion.[16]

Romans 9:32c–33 picks up again Paul's authorial voice. Paul not only approves of the interlocutor's response in v. 32; he also expands on it. Yes, Israel pursued Torah mechanically rather than by faith. But he goes on to add, "They stumbled upon the stumbling stone, as it is written, 'Look! I am placing in Zion a stumbling stone, even a rock of offense, and the one who trusts in it shall not be put to shame'" (Rom 9:32–33, quoting Isa 8:14; 28:16). The contexts of the Isaianic passages Paul cites are complicated.[17] Isaiah 8:14, in the LXX, explicitly *denies* that the people will encounter YHWH "as a stone for stumbling" [*hōs lithou proskommati*] or "as a rock for falling" [*hōs petras ptōmati*]. However, according to the Hebrew text of

---

On at least two occasions, however, the inference is correct. Paul makes it absolutely clear, too, when the inference is correct. Whenever Paul introduces a false inference with the "What shall we say?" construction, he always indicates its falseness with an expression of unequivocal dissent" (ibid., 103–4). Garroway goes on to point out that, in both Rom 4:1 and 9:30, "Paul indicates that the inference is correct by offering no dissent" (ibid., 104).

15. Witherington and Hyatt, *Romans*, 259. Paul does not say, as Witherington seems to suppose, that Israel did not attain *righteousness*; rather, he says Israel "did not attain Torah" [*eis nomon ouk ephthasen*; 9:31; see also n. 12 (p. 194), above]. Jewett provides a more helpful comment: "The focus here is on law, which Israel failed to achieve despite zealous striving" (*Romans*, 609–10).

16. We will return to this point in our comments on Rom 10:3–4, below.

17. See the discussions in the commentaries, esp. Dunn, *Romans*, 2:583–85; Jewett, *Romans*, 612–14.

Isa 8:14, the Lord will become "a stone one strikes against and a rock one stumbles over for both houses of Israel."[18] Paul's citation agrees with the MT against the LXX; however, when Paul cites Isa 28:16, where the MT and the LXX agree, he cites the LXX's reading nearly verbatim.

The Masoretic text of Isa 8:14 is an oracle of judgment against "both houses of Israel." Israel and Judah have fallen short of the mark of obedience to YHWH, and so the Lord sets in Zion a stumbling stone and a rock of offense, which stone will bring about the Lord's judgment against the people. Given Paul's references in the immediately preceding verses (see 9:27–29) to the Lord's judgment against Israel, which judgment would have been all-consuming had he not brought it to an end, the reference to the same judgment in 9:33 makes good sense and continues the central theme. Israel failed to obey the word of the Lord (recall 9:6), and the Lord levied his judgment against Zion. Paul's real rhetorical achievement, however, is to pair the judgment of the Lord in Isa 8:14 together with Isa 28:16, where "the one who places his trust" [*ho pisteuōn*] believes "in it," that is, in the precious cornerstone God established as the foundations of Zion.[19] The personal pronoun "in it" [*ep' autō*] is masculine and refers back to the "precious cornerstone." This cornerstone is the object in which the Lord calls the people to put their trust.

In Romans 9, however, the referent of the *masculine* personal pronoun "in it" [*ep' autō*] is blurred because of the *feminine* noun "rock of offense" [*petran skandalou*]. Paul *cannot* be saying, "whoever believes in the rock of offense," though perhaps he is saying "whoever believes in the stumbling stone."[20] This ambiguity allows Paul to imply, without saying overtly, "whoever believes in *him*," that is, in Jesus. The stumbling stone that God places in Zion—that is, Israel's Messiah, Jesus of Nazareth—brings to effect God's judgment against the people (recall Isa 10:22b–23; 1:9, cited in Rom 9:27–29) *but also results in the vindication of the remnant of Israel, those Jews who acknowledge Jesus and "put their trust in him."* Paul identifies those Jews who stumble over or are offended by the gospel as those who receive the Lord's judgment. But the very fact that some Jews

---

18. NRSV (slightly modified).

19. The LXX of Isa 28:16 reads, "For this reason, thus says the Lord: 'Look! I myself am putting in place, as the foundations of Zion, a stone both valuable and chosen, a precious cornerstone [*akrogōniaion entimon*] as her foundations, and whoever puts his trust on it will certainly not be put to shame" [*kai ho pisteuōn ep' autō ou mē kataischynthē*].

20. Unlike "rock of offense," the Greek noun "stumbling stone" [*lithon proskommatos*] is masculine, just like the personal pronoun "in it" [*ep' autō*].

Israel and Christ, Pt. II

call upon Jesus in faith is evidence enough for Paul that the Lord has preserved a remnant for Jacob, just as he said.

The Prayer of the Remnant (Rom 10:1–13)

> 1 The desire of my heart, brethren, and [my] prayer to God for them is for salvation. 2 For I am testifying to them that they have a zeal for God, but not in accordance with knowledge. 3 For they are ignorant of the righteousness of God, and seeking to establish their own righteousness, they did not subject themselves to the righteousness of God. 4 For Christ is the fulfillment of Torah unto righteousness for everyone who believes. 5 For Moses writes concerning the righteousness that is [revealed] by Torah, that "The person who does them shall live by them" (Lev 18:5). 6 But the righteousness [that is revealed] by faithfulness speaks in this way: "Do not say in your heart, 'Who will ascend into heaven?'" (Deut 30:12). (That is, to bring Christ down.) 7 Or, "Who will descend into the abyss?" (Deut 30:13). (That is, to bring Christ up from the dead.) 8 But what does it say? "The word is near you, in your mouth and in your heart" (Deut 30:14), that is, the word of faithfulness, which we are proclaiming. 9 Because if you confess with your mouth, "Jesus is Lord," and you believe in your heart that God raised him from the dead, you will be saved. 10 For with the heart it is believed unto righteousness, and with the mouth it is confessed unto salvation. 11 For the Scripture says, "Everyone who believes in him shall not be put to shame" (Isa 28:16). 12 For there is no distinction between Jew, on the one hand, and Greek, for there is one Lord over all, and he is rich toward all those who call upon him. 13 For "everyone who shall call upon the name of the Lord shall be saved" (Joel 3:5 LXX).

Paul begins Romans 10 by identifying his readers as "brethren" [*adelphoi*], which he has done at key points in the letter (1:13; 8:12). Just as significantly, Paul has already explained that God conforms his fore-chosen people to the image of his son "so that [Jesus] would be the firstborn among many brethren" [*en pollois adelphois*; Rom 8:29]. When Paul referred to his "brethren" in 9:3, he explicitly excluded his gentile readers because he was expressing sorrow for his "kinsmen according to the flesh." Here in 10:1, Paul recalls and re-affirms his bond with gentile believers in Rome, calling them "brethren" and circumscribing them and him within a single boundary *while expressing intense sorrow for those with whom Paul should have affirmed this connection: the Jews.* "Paul places the entire Roman audience ... within a rubric of solidarity as his siblings while introducing the divisive issue of Israel's rejection of the gospel."[21] Paul acknowledges that the Jews have intense zeal for God [*zēlon theou*; 10:2],[22] but he denies that this zeal was informed by knowledge, saying instead that the Jews "are ignorant of the righteousness of God" (10:3). Paul has already explained that the righteousness of God, which is also "the power of God for salvation" (1:16), is now being revealed "apart from Torah ... through the faithfulness of Jesus Christ." The Jews' ignorance of *this* righteousness has tragic consequences: "seeking to establish their own righteousness, they did not subject themselves to the righteousness of God" (10:3).[23]

Here we get an explanation of the distinction Paul affirmed back at the end of Romans 9, in which the interlocutor offered the explanation that the Jews pursued Torah "not from faith but as from deeds" (Rom 9:32b). The Jews expressed and embodied their faith by means of Torah's commandments (or "by deeds"). The problem, however, is that many of them did not recognize that Torah bore witness to the righteousness of God that was revealed apart from Torah by Jesus' faithfulness (3:21–22), and so their rejection of the gospel—the proclamation that Jesus is Israel's Messiah—is tantamount to a refusal to "subject themselves to the righteousness of God" (10:3).[24] The Jews' problem, then, is not that they have

---

21. Jewett, *Romans*, 614.

22. Contemporary Christian readers might also grant that Jews in the Roman era were intensely zealous for the Lord; after all, we are used to attributing the Jewish-Roman War (66–70 CE) to the Jews' refusal to compromise their adherence to Torah. We should remember, however, that Roman pagans often accused both Jews and Christians of atheism: "Christians refused to worship Roman gods, representing them as either nonexistent or demonic, and would not even acknowledge that others ought to do so. To the Romans this was atheism" (Kruse, "Persecution," 776). As one example, in the mid-second-century CE text *Martyrdom of Polycarp*, the crowds respond to the Christians' willingness to face death by calling for Bishop Polycarp's arrest, saying "Away with the atheists [*Aire tous atheous*]! Get Polycarp!" (*Mart. Pol.* 3:2). So we should not assume that, in Paul's world, the Jews' "zeal for God" would have been universally acknowledged among gentiles.

23. The following strikes me as incoherent: "There is an issue of [the Jews'] not submitting to the righteousness of God. Here *dikaiosynē* certainly does not mean 'right standing with God,' for they already had that. The issue lies elsewhere. As those who were already God's people, they were standing in the wrong place and not submitting to the right righteousness" (Witherington and Hyatt, *Romans*, 260). Were the Jews submitting to the *wrong* righteousness?! What would this mean? If Witherington had brought Paul's explanation of the righteousness of God in Romans 3 to bear on his comments on Rom 10:1–3, he might have had a better chance of helpfully explaining the relationship of Torah and God's righteousness in the latter passage.

24. Dunn (*Romans*, 2:588) also refers back to Romans 3, though he refers to v. 31 (twice). In his first reference to 3:31, I wonder if he meant v. 21, which better makes his

kept Torah's commandments; their problem is that they sought to keep Torah's commandments *while refusing to accept Torah's testimony on Jesus' behalf.* "Works without faith (in Jesus)," in other words. In this reading, Paul does not level any criticism against Jews who observe Torah; his critique aims squarely (and solely) against Torah-observant Jews who reject Israel's Messiah, Jesus.

At this point we encounter one of the most puzzling and vexing phrases in all the New Testament. Romans 10:4 reads: "For Christ is the *telos* of Torah unto righteousness for everyone who believes." *Telos* has a broad range of meanings; Louw and Nida provide five glosses: "end, result, purpose, completely, and tax."[25] Liddell and Scott add other semantic possibilities, including "fulfillment, completion, death, final decision, perfection," and others.[26] Paul, however, offers little guidance as to which sense he has in mind. How we choose to read 10:4 matters quite a bit. Consider the following translations, each of which might legitimately render the Greek, *telos gar nomou Christos*:

> For Christ is the *end* of the Law . . .
>
> For Christ is the *death* of the Law . . .
>
> For Christ is the *completion* of the Law . . .
>
> For Christ is the *purpose* of the Law . . .
>
> For Christ is the *perfection* of the Law . . .
>
> For Christ is the *fulfillment* of the Law . . .
>
> For Christ is the *goal* of the Law . . .

These various and equally legitimate ways of rendering *telos* demonstrate the truth of Wright's observation: "lexicography can offer us options, but exegesis must decide which better fits the flow of thought."[27] How we interpret and translate *telos* matters tremendously for our understanding of Rom 10:4, but our interpretation of v. 4, of chapter 10, and of Romans as a

---

point. Wright ("Romans," 654–55) is helpful here: Paul "does not regard his contemporaries as proto-Pelagians, trying to pull themselves up by their own moral bootstraps in order to be good enough for God and to earn 'works-righteousness' of that sort. Rather, they believed that God's covenant with Abraham was their exclusive and inalienable possession, whereas Paul had come to believe that, through the death and resurrection of the Messiah, the long covenant story as set out in the Scriptures had all along had a different shape" (ibid., 655).

25. L&N, s.v.

26. See LSJ, s.v.

27. Wright, "Romans," 655.

whole must determine how we understand this individual use of *telos*. The challenge of determining what *Paul* thought he was saying is especially difficult here.

Christian tradition has been too quick to jump at the first option, that Paul puts Christ forward as the *end* of Torah.[28] This interpretation fits Paul's rhetoric across the whole of Romans only if we restrict the meaning of *nomos* to Torah's curses, so that Rom 10:4 makes a similar point as Gal 3:10–14: Christ is the *telos* (= end) of the curse of Torah upon all those who do not keep its terms.[29] This interpretation of *nomos*, however, seems too restrictive, and it does not adequately account for Paul's carefully balanced statements about Torah throughout the entirety of the letter.[30] Yes, Paul has already explained that no flesh is justified before God by means of Torah (3:20), that God does not deliver his promises to Abraham and his Seed through Torah (4:13), and that Torah "slipped in" [*pareisēlthen*], transforming sin into transgression (5:20). However, Paul has also affirmed that Torah is spiritual (7:14), it identifies sin as sin (3:20; 7:7), and it finds its establishment [*histanomen*] by the faith that Paul proclaims (3:31). And so on. Christ cannot be the *end* of these positive facets of Torah, and so we will need to find another interpretation of *telos* to fit the context of Romans as a whole.[31]

---

28. Of the ten parallel versions listed on net.bible.org [https://lumina.bible.org/#!search/rom%2010:4], fully eight translate *telos* as "end." The NLT and The Message do not offer a clear, one-word gloss, and so the issue is less clear for these two. However, the NLT's use of "already" and The Message's "simply" push them in the same direction. For a defense of this interpretation, see Witherington and Hyatt, *Romans*, 260–61.

29. See the very insightful discussion in Morales, *Spirit*, 105–9.

30. See Adeyẹmi, "Positive," though Adeyẹmi argues for a different reading of Rom 10:4: "[R]ather than supporting a reinstitution of the Mosaic Law within the New Covenant church, Paul used the positive statements only to support his point about *the termination of the Mosaic Law* for the New Covenant participants" (ibid., 51; my emphasis). For a better approach to this question, see Eisenbaum, *Paul*, 27–29; 208–39.

31. See Jewett's helpful discussion (*Romans*, 619–20). Schreiner (*Romans*, 544–48) discounts all of the reasons offered against reading *telos* as "end," though he does acknowledge that the "translation 'goal' certainly yields a coherent sense in the context." Since he reads *telos* as "end," he struggles to understand how the conjunction *gar* ("for, because") joins v. 4 onto v. 3. "Verse 4 is attached to verse 3 with a *gar*, demonstrating that there is a logical relationship between the two verses. An implied proposition must be supplied, though, since it does not makes sense to say 'the Jews did not subject themselves to God's righteousness' *because* Christ is the end of the law" (ibid., 547; emphasis in the original). Perhaps this should have suggested that Paul does not use *telos* here in the sense of "end."

Once we get past the blind alley of Christ as Torah's "end" or "completion," we can better appreciate that Paul puts Christ forward as Torah's "goal" (perhaps) or as Torah's "purpose" or "fulfillment."[32] If we opt for interpreting *telos* as "fulfillment," this allows us both to appreciate the totality of Paul's assertions about Torah (the negative as well as the positive) and to see that Paul identifies Jesus as God's response to both Torah's blessings and its curses.[33] "When [Paul] says at 10:4 that 'Christ is the end of the law so that there may be righteousness for everyone who believes,' he means that the Christian message is the goal, the destination, the end toward which God's law, God's covenant with Israel, has always been directed."[34] The blessings God set forth in Torah's terms (see esp. Deuteronomy 38-32) are fulfilled in Jesus, and those blessings already pertained to God's promises to Abraham: that God would bless Abraham and, through him, bless all the families/peoples of the earth (Gen 12:1-3). But the curses set forth in Torah's terms are likewise fulfilled in Jesus (see Gal 3:10-14), with the result that those children of Israel who actually *are* Israel (see Rom 9:6), who respond in faith to the gospel of Jesus, Israel's Messiah, are set free from those curses. (Keep in mind that Paul's focus here is squarely and solely on Israel and the basis on which God interacts with Israel in light of the gospel.[35]) Christ cuts short God's judgment upon Israel, just as God had promised he would do (see Isa 10:22-23; 1:9, cited in Rom 9:27-29). And the result [*eis*[36]] of Christ as Torah's fulfillment is "righteousness for everyone who believes" (10:4),[37] which strongly echoes earlier passages in Romans (1:16; 3:22; 4:11).

32. Jesus says something very similar in Matthew, that he came "not to abolish but to fulfill" [*ou katalysai alla plēsōsai*] Torah (Matt 5:17). We cannot use Matt 5:17 to determine Paul's meaning in Rom 10:4 (especially since Romans was written before Matthew), but it certainly helps us to see how such an idea might be "in the air" among Jesus' followers in the first century.

33. Similarly, "the Messiah is the goal of the Torah so that there may be righteousness—the righteousness of the 'Torah of righteousness'!—for all who have faith" (Wright, "Romans," 656-57).

34. Johnson, "Covenant Faithfulness," 162.

35. Jewett, *Romans*, 608-9 (despite our different approaches to Romans 9-11 as a whole).

36. BDAG (s.v., §4.) offers the following as part of its discussion of *eis*: "marker of goals involving affective/abstract/suitability," and it offers "into, to" as potential glosses. More to the point here in 10:4, "w. the result of an action or condition indicated" (s.v., §4.e.).

37. *Pace* Dunn (*Romans*, 2:589), who translates 10:4, "for Christ is the end of the law *as a means to* righteousness for all who believe" (my emphasis; see also Schreiner,

If You Call Yourself a Jew

Paul provides extensive scriptural support for his point—which culminated in the difficult phrase, "Christ is the *telos* of Torah"—in Rom 10:5-13.[38] He begins by citing Leviticus 18, in which the Lord instructs the people to avoid the practices of Egypt, from which they had been led out, as well as of Canaan, into which they were being led. Instead, the Lord says to the people, "You will practice my judgments, and my ordinances you shall keep, to walk in them; I am the Lord your God. And you will keep all my ordinances, and all my judgments, you will practice them, *which by doing them a person will live by them*. I am the Lord your God" (Lev 18:4-5 LXX; Paul cites the italicized text, with only minor variations). The form (or shape) of righteousness that is revealed by Torah is restricted to the observance of Torah's commandments. Thus Paul cites a text (Lev 18:5) in which God emphatically calls his people to observe a distinctive lifestyle that sets them apart from the surrounding nations.

In contrast to "the righteousness that is [revealed] by Torah" (10:5), Paul finds in the end of the Pentateuch a description of "the righteousness [that is revealed] by faithfulness" (10:6).[39] In a very similar passage, Paul explained that the righteousness of God is being revealed, first, apart from Torah [*chōris nomou*] and, second, by the faithfulness of Jesus Christ [*dia pisteōs Iēsou Christou*; Rom 3:21-22], and he affirmed that the righteousness of God "was attested" [*martyroumenē*] by Torah and the prophets. When Paul returns to the idea of the righteousness that is revealed "by faithfulness" [*ek pisteōs*] here in Romans 10, he explains *how* Torah offers

---

Romans, 547 for a similar translation). BDAG does explain *eis* as a "marker of instrumentality, *by, with*" (s.v., §9), and so Dunn's translation of *eis* ("as a means to") is lexically possible. But both the sentence's word order, which inserts *Christos* between *nomou* and *eis dikaiosynēn*, and Paul's rhetoric in this chapter and throughout the entire letter make it unlikely that Dunn has rightly translated v. 4. For a better discussion, see Wright, "Romans," 655-58.

38. See my discussion of this passage in Rodríguez, *Oral Tradition*, 100-107.

39. I have added the verbal idea of revelation to both 10:5 and 10:6 on the basis of the similarity of these verses with Rom 3:21-22, where Paul was explicitly and overtly focused on how (or where) the righteousness of God was made visible or manifest to his people. I am resisting the interpretation of Romans 10 in terms of the "coming" of righteousness, whether that "coming" is achieved through Torah or through faith. Similarly, I do not see in Romans the idea that righteousness is "based" on either Torah or faith. Instead, Paul speaks of righteousness being revealed [*apokalyptetai*; 1:17], established [*synistēsin*; 3:5], and made known [*pephanerōtai*; 3:21], and he also mentions that righteousness "is reckoned" or "credited" [*logizetai*; 4:6] or, more commonly, that something else (especially "faith" [*pistis*]) is reckoned or credited "unto righteousness" [*eis dikaiosynēn*; 4:3, 5, 9, etc.]. However, Paul concerns himself in Romans with neither how righteousness "arrives" or "comes to" humanity (*pace* the NRSV) nor with its "basis" or "foundation" (*pace* the NASB; ESV).

Israel and Christ, Pt. II

up its testimony to the faith-revealed righteousness by citing the end of Torah's story.[40] The context of the text Paul cites and interprets here provides the key to understanding his comments in Romans 10. The Lord speaks through Moses to the people of Israel:

> 11 For this commandment, which I am commanding you today, it is neither excessive nor out of your reach.[41] 12 It is not up above, in heaven, so that you should say, "Who will go up for us into heaven and retrieve it for us? Then, after we hear it, we will do it." 13 Neither is it across the sea, so that you should say, "Who will go across for us, to the other side of the sea, and retrieve it for us? Then, he will make it audible for us, and we will do it." 14 The word [*to rhēma*] is very near you, in your mouth and on your heart and in your hands, for you to do it. (Deut 30:11–14 LXX)

To understand Deuteronomy 30, we have to appreciate the distance that has separated the people from YHWH throughout the exodus account. Once upon a time, the Lord appeared to and spoke with Abraham, Isaac, and Jacob. However, YHWH's self-revelation to Moses surpassed his appearance to the patriarchs, since "I did not reveal my name, 'Lord,' to them" (Exod 6:3). The Lord appeared to and spoke with Moses regularly since his encounter with the burning bush that did not (burn, that is). This closeness— with the patriarchs, and especially with Moses—stood in stark contrast with YHWH's relationship with the people of Israel. The people were commanded to stand aloof from the Lord. When the people arrived at Mt. Sinai, only Moses went up onto the mountain to speak with God. The people stayed off the mountain and were prohibited from coming

---

40. *Pace* Witherington and Hyatt (*Romans*, 261–62), who think that, "in a sense Moses is pitted against himself." This reading could only work if Paul really did mean, in Rom 10:4, that Christ was the *end* of Torah (Schreiner, *Romans*, 551–56, offers just this type of adversative reading). Since we offered a different explanation of v. 4, we can read Paul's references to Moses much more consistently throughout the entire letter, including here in Romans 10. Dunn's contrastive reading between v. 5 and vv. 6–7 (*Romans*, 2:602), is more responsible than both Witherington's and Schreiner's, though Dunn also fails to keep in view how Paul marshals Torah as a witness for the righteousness revealed *ek pisteōs* ("by faithfulness"). Wright is even better: "[I]t would be naive to think that Paul supposed, or imagined his hearers might be tricked into supposing, that Deuteronomy was not a book of Moses just as much as Leviticus was. It would also be out of character for Paul to set up one passage of Scripture against another" ("Romans," 658–59); see also Jewett, *Romans*, 624–27.

41. The phrase I have translated, "nor out of your reach," is *oude makran apo sou* (lit. "nor far away from you"; Deut 30:11 LXX). The spatial imagery is a metaphor for whether the Lord's commandments are reasonable.

onto or even touching it (see Exodus 19). The only access the people had to the God who redeemed them from slavery was through an intermediary, Moses.

As Moses' life approaches its end and the Lord wraps up the presentation of Torah to the people, he inaugurates his covenant with the people by leading them into the land he promised to Abraham, Isaac, and Jacob. Deuteronomy 30:11–14 represents a significant change in the people's relationship with YHWH. This text promises that the people would no longer require an intermediary like Moses ("Who will go up for us?" "Who will go across for us?"). The word of God would be directly available to the people by means of the written Torah. We can see Paul's understanding of this direct access to God's word in Rom 3:2, where he refers to the value of the Jews having been entrusted with "the oracles of God" [*ta logia tou theou*].

Paul refers to this passage when he finally comes around to explain how "the righteousness that is made known by faithfulness" [*ek pisteōs*] speaks. The truly fascinating thing about Paul's quotation from Deut 30:11–14 is how he has interpreted the *rhēma* of God's covenant. In Deuteronomy, the *rhēma* refers to "this commandment, which I am commanding you today." The singular term *entolē* ("commandment") in Deut 30:11 refers to Torah as a whole rather than to any single instruction. But in Romans 10, we encounter some ambiguity: what would the person ascend up into heaven or descend into the abyss to retrieve? In Deuteronomy the goal would be the commandment (= Torah) of the Lord. In Romans 10, the syntax of Paul's quotation seems to suggest that person pursues the faith-revealed righteousness, on the one hand, but also that Christ himself is the object of pursuit. Since the commandment—the *rhēma*—bridges the distance between the people and God in Deuteronomy 30, Paul brings the three entities—the *rhēma*/commandment, the faith-revealed righteousness, and Christ—together. He stops short of equating them and making them one thing, but he nevertheless blurs the distinctions between them. That is, the *rhēma* of God's covenant, the faith-revealed righteousness, and Christ all bridge the distance separating the people from God.

Paul then interprets the bodily references in Deut 30:14 (though he leaves out the hands) in terms of the mechanics of the profession of faith. Moses said the *rhēma* was "very near you, in your mouth and on your heart ... for you to do it." Paul now identifies the Mosaic *rhēma* as "the *rhēma* of faithfulness which we are proclaiming," and he unpacks that proclamation in Rom 10:9–11. We should not make too much of Paul's explicit mention of two of the three bodily references in Deut 30:14. We cannot say that Paul removes salvation completely out of the sphere of human behavior, so that only the mouth and the heart are involved in the appropriation of faith and the experience of salvation. Belief may be rooted in the heart and confession in the mouth, but the whole of Romans makes clear that a person's lifestyle and conduct ("in your hands"; see Deut 30:14) must embody and live out their belief and confession. A person who *only* believes and/or *only* confesses, but who still presents their members to sin as instruments of injustice (see Rom 6:13), calls their belief and their confession into question by means of their incongruous lifestyle. Paul clearly and obviously thinks that a person who confesses, "Jesus is Lord," will exhibit that confession in their daily living. (The question of *how* they exhibit their confession is still open, but *that* they display their confession in their actions is a given.) "To 'confess Jesus as Lord' was therefore not only to make a claim about his divine status but also to reveal one's own identity and commitment. . . . Such a confession binds the speaker to someone else in final loyalty."[42] Paul clearly expects that this loyalty would be evident in the way a person lives, as we will see.

The person who does this—who believes and confesses and so has their life transformed (see Rom 12:1–2)—this person "will not be put to shame." Paul returns to Isa 28:16, brings his interpretive comments on Deuteronomy 30 to a close, and recalls his citations from Isaiah in Rom 9:27–29, 33. The Lord announced through Isaiah that he was placing in Zion a stumbling stone and promised that his judgment against the people would not last long enough to wipe them out completely. The trustworthy word of the Lord is, "the remnant will be saved" (Rom 9:27; Isa 10:22b). And who is the remnant? "Everyone who believes in him." If any questions remained about Paul's meaning back in Rom 9:6, that "not all those who are from Israel are Israel," those questions now have been fully and clearly answered. Who are those that truly are "Israel," the people of God, whose trust in YHWH will not be put to shame? They are the remnant, those who believe in their heart and confess with their mouth; they are "everyone who believes in him." Has God, then, been faithful to his promises to Israel now that the gentiles find themselves adopted into his family? Yes he has, by cutting short his judgment against the recalcitrant nation, preserving for himself a remnant, and by sending them heralds who announce the *rhēma* of Jesus' faithfulness to God and fulfillment [*telos*] of Torah.

---

42. Jewett, *Romans*, 630.

Paul then backs out from his narrow focus on God's faithfulness to his promises *to Israel* by expanding on the significance of "everyone who believes" [*pas ho pisteuōn*; Rom 10:11]. Indeed, Paul has added *pas* ("everyone") to his quotation of Isa 28:16 LXX, so his citation was already shaped by his rhetorical agenda.[43] But here he resumes one of the main themes from Romans 1–4: there is no distinction between Jew and Greek. Paul quotes Joel 3:5 LXX and capitalizes on the universalist overtones of the adjective, *pas* ("everyone"): "Everyone who shall call upon the name of the Lord shall be saved" (Rom 10:13). Joel 3:5 [LXX; MT = 2:32] is well known from Luke's account of Peter's Pentecost sermon in Acts 2. In Acts, Peter does not yet realize that "everyone" applies not simply to "all the Jews" but to *everyone*, Jews and gentiles. Hence Peter's surprise, in Acts 10, when he realizes that God has accepted Cornelius without him converting fully to Judaism (i.e., without him undergoing circumcision).

Paul, on the other hand, cites Joel 3:5 precisely *because* of its universalist overtones, as is clear from his restatement that "there is no distinction" (Rom 10:12; see 3:22), that Israel's God and Messiah is/are God and Messiah of Jews and gentiles both (see 3:29–30). However (and this is an important point), Paul's emphasis here remains squarely on Israel.[44]

> [W]e should not miss the force of v. 13 in relation to the argument of chaps. 9–11 as a whole. If "those who call on the name of the Lord" is a regular biblical designation for "Israel," then v. 13 is an exact functional equivalent of 11:26a: "All Israel shall be saved." Verse 13 supplies Paul's initial answer to the problem of 10:1, and suggests the correct way of understanding 11:26a.[45]

Jews, no less than the gentile believers in Rome, have a place within the plan and blessing of God, and the gentiles' adoption into God's family has

---

43. Paul uses the adjective *pas* a full seventy times in sixty-one verses in just about every chapter of Romans (*pas* does not occur in Romans 6 and only occurs once in Romans 7).

44. Similarly, see my comments on 9:24 in the previous chapter. Witherington loses sight of Paul's overall argument and interprets 10:13 as if Paul were engaging the debate between Calvinists and Arminians: "Paul here is countering any notions that God has plans to save only a few or desires to bless only a few. On the contrary, anyone who responds to the gospel and calls upon and confesses the name of the Lord will be saved" (Witherington and Hyatt, *Romans*, 263). Where in Romans has this been the issue Paul addresses? The answer is clear: nowhere. Rather, Paul has everywhere been concerned with placing both Jews and gentiles together within the sphere of God's people, and in Romans 9–11 the focus has shifted from including the gentiles (the focus of Romans 1–8) toward explaining the continued presence of (at least some of) the Jews.

45. Wright, "Romans," 666.

not displaced the Jews from God's covenant.⁴⁶ Luke's report of Peter's sermon in Acts 2 confirms the appropriateness of citing Joel 3:5 in the context of arguing that *Israel* finds its restoration in the proclamation that her Messiah is Jesus.

Israel Finds Itself Provoked (Rom 10:14–21)

14 How, then, shall they call upon the one in whom they did not believe? And how shall they believe in him of whom they have not heard? And how shall they hear apart from someone proclaiming it? **15** And how shall they proclaim unless they are sent? "How timely are the feet of those proclaiming good tidings!" (Isa 52:7). **16** But not everyone has obeyed the gospel, for Isaiah says, "Lord, who believed our report?" (Isa 53:1). **17** Therefore, faith comes from hearing, and hearing through the word of Christ. **18** But I say, have they really not heard? Instead,

"The sound of their voice went out into all the earth;
 their words went out even to the ends of the world" (Ps 18:5 LXX).

19 But I say, did Israel really not know? First, Moses says,
"I, yes I will provoke you to jealousy by means of those who are
 Not-a-nation;
 I will enrage you by means of a nation that lacks understanding"
 (Deut 32:21).

20 But Isaiah is very bold, and he says,
"I was found by those who did not seek me,
 and I showed myself to those who did not ask for me" (Isa 65:1).

21 But to Israel he says,
"I spread out my hands all day long
 to an unfaithful and obstinate people" (Isa 65:2).

If we have been on the right track so far, and if Paul is indeed emphasizing Israel's presence along with the gentiles who have been adopted into God's family, then the series of rhetorical questions in 10:14–15 take on new meaning. When Paul asks, "How, then, shall they call upon the one

---

46. Dunn draws attention to the christological dynamics of this verse (in which Paul identifies Jesus as the *kyrios* of v. 13). But when he turns to Paul's "salvation-histor[ical] point," he misses that Paul's emphasis has shifted since Romans 8. Paul is no longer defending the inclusion of Greeks alongside the Jews within the family of God; he now defends the continued inclusion of (at least some of) the Jews within Israel (see 9:6) and rejects the possible inference that God's favor upon the gentiles signals his rejection of the Jews (cf. Dunn, *Romans*, 2:617–18).

in whom they did not believe?" he is asking a question about *the Jews*. We might paraphrase: "How, then, shall the Jews call upon Jesus and receive the salvation God offers, if they have not believed that Jesus is Israel's Messiah?" The series of questions progresses from there: "And how shall they believe in him of whom they have not heard? And how shall they hear apart from someone proclaiming it?" In other words, Israel's unbelief does not let Jesus' followers—Jews or gentiles—off the hook from the responsibility to proclaim Jesus as Israel's Messiah. The fact of Paul's call "to the gentiles" has not deadened him to the need for Israel to have the gospel proclaimed to them, too. Paul does not think of the gospel as a message exclusively for gentiles. Hence he asks, "And how shall they proclaim [the gospel to Israel] unless they are sent [to do so]?"

This last question brings Paul back full circle. If his gentile readers had any inclination to assume that their adoption into God's family might signal Israel's disinheritance, they now find themselves, implicitly but not subtly, challenged to consider God's call to proclaim the gospel to Israel. Such a call catches Paul's gentile readers up into Israel's story, and so Isaiah's words, first spoken of God's servant who proclaims peace to Zion, now applies even to gentile believers: "How timely are the feet of those proclaiming good tidings!" (Rom 10:15; see Isa 52:7). Isaiah saw a vision of God's herald announcing to Israel that her sins were atoned for and that she could be reconciled to her God. Paul, in an incredible hermeneutical move, maps Isaiah's vision onto his gentile readers in Rome. *They are God's herald to proclaim good tidings to Israel!*[47] The inclusion of the gentiles in the promises and plan of God has not excluded Israel; instead, the gentiles both are reconciled with God and also work to reconcile others (here, Israel) to him.

The problem, however, is that "not everyone obeyed [*ou pantes hypēkousan*] the gospel," which problem Paul explains by again citing the prophet Isaiah: "for Isaiah says, 'Lord, who believed our report?'" (Rom 10:16; see Isa 53:1). Dunn helpfully contrasts Paul's reference to "not everyone" here with his immediately earlier statement that "everyone" who calls on the name of the Lord will be saved in v. 13.[48] Paul began Romans 9

---

47. Elizabeth Johnson goes too far when she concludes, "Christian response to Jewish unbelief is therefore not more ardent proselytizing of Jews but rather concentration on the Gentile mission" ("Covenant Faithfulness," 165). Preaching to Jews and preaching to gentiles are not mutually exclusive activities, as Paul's own biography attests. However, we can appreciate that Johnson rightly sees a connection between "the Gentile mission" and the solution, in Paul's thinking, to "Jewish unbelief."

48. Dunn, *Romans*, 2:622.

Israel and Christ, Pt. II

by addressing the problem of Israel's lack of positive response, in general, to the proclamation of Jesus as her Messiah. Specifically, the widespread rejection of the gospel among the Jews called into question their status as the people of God.[49] This problem was compounded by the positive response to the gospel among the gentiles. In Rom 10:16, however, Paul has found scriptural warrant for Israel's unbelief. Isaiah posed a rhetorical question, but Paul's citation of Isa 53:1 implies a surprising answer. "Who has believed our report?" Not Israel, but the gentiles! They have heard the gospel's proclamation and responded in faith, for "faith comes from hearing, and hearing through the word [*rhēmatos*] of Christ" (10:17).

Romans 10 ends with another catena of citations from the Hebrew Bible.[50] As we look through these references, we need to remember Paul's overall purpose throughout this section: he defends the gospel as God's way of dealing with Israel and holds out hope that Israel will respond in faith to the gospel. After all, this gospel is "the power of God for the salvation of everyone who believes, for the Jew first as well as for the Greek" (Rom 1:16). Paul acknowledges that God has sent heralds to Israel to proclaim the gospel to them. Interestingly, he cites Psalm 18 [LXX; MT = Ps 19], which is the *locus classicus*, along with Rom 1:19-20, for the idea of "general revelation" or "natural theology," the knowledge about God "which is 'natural' rather than 'supernatural' or which is disclosed naturally rather than supernaturally. General revelation is communicated through nature—through the visible creation with its laws and through the moral nature of the human person."[51] Paul employed this idea—that humanity can truly know God through the testimony of creation—in his critique of pagan idolatry and sinfulness in 1:18-32. Here he employs the same idea in his critique of Israel's unimpressive response to the gospel. "The sound of their voice went out into all the earth; their words went out even to the ends of the world." Who does Paul imagine speaking here? Whose voice "went out into all the earth"?

Paul seems to have heralds of the gospel in mind here in Romans 10. Missionaries who proclaim the message of Jesus crucified and raised from the dead have gone out into all the world spreading the gospel. In the passage from Psalm 18 LXX that Paul cites, however, the situation is

---

49. Jewett (*Romans*, 641) rightly says, "It is clear from the context that the refusal of many Jews to accept the gospel is in view here."

50. In the last four verses of this chapter, Paul cites Ps 18:5 ([LXX; MT = 19:4] cp. Rom 10:18); Deut 32:21 (cp. Rom 10:19); and Isa 65:1, 2 (cp. Rom 10:20, 21). Compare the catena in Rom 3:10-18.

51. Grenz, *Theology*, 132-39 (p. 133 quoted); see also McGrath, *Theology*, 159-72.

very different. In the psalm, the heavens [*hoi ouranoi*] above the earth and its foundations [*to stereōma*] below proclaim "the glory of God" [*doxan theou*] and "the work of his hands" [*poiēsin cheirōn autou*; Ps 18:2 LXX].[52] Given the strong creation motif as recent as Romans 8, in which all of creation eagerly awaits the unveiling of God's children (see 8:19–22), Paul must have the original context of Psalm 18 (LXX) in mind. If so, then his point would be something like, "Israel cannot put their faith in Jesus unless they hear the message of the gospel proclaimed to them. But God has not left them without a witness, for the world around them tells them of God's goodness and his concern, not for their nation alone, but for all peoples, even for all of creation."

Paul seems to have been aware of the problem with the idea that Israel ought to know something of the gospel on the basis of creation.[53] "How exactly," we might reply, "can God expect the created order to communicate specifically enough to Israel that they should know that Jesus is their Messiah?" So Paul musters testimony from Moses, through whom God said to the people, "I, yes I will provoke you to jealousy by means of those who are Not-a-nation; I will enrage you by means of a nation that lacks understanding" (Rom 10:19, citing Deut 32:21).[54] God expresses exasperation at his people and their infidelity to him in Deut 32:21. The whole verse reads, "They provoked me to jealousy [*parezēlōsan me*] by means of that which

---

52. "The psalm referred to God's revelation in nature, which was clearly visible to people everywhere, but Paul applies this saying to the preaching of the gospel of Christ" (Jewett, *Romans*, 643). This is surely correct, but Jewett does not consider how the context of the psalm interacts with and affects Paul's use of the psalm here in Romans 10.

53. The double negatives in the rhetorical questions of both Rom 10:18 and 10:19 make for good Greek grammar, but rendering them effectively in grammatical English is difficult since English eschews double negatives. The questions, which both begin with the negative particle *mē*, expect negative answers. But since both questions also employ the negative particle *ouk*, the questions expect negative answers to negative questions. For example, in 10:18 Paul asks, literally, "Did they not not-hear?" We could state the negative answer thusly: "No, they did not not-hear." BDF (§427:2) explains, "In questions with *mē* the verb itself can already be negated (class. also), producing *mē* . . . *ou* with an affirmative answer implied," and they give Rom 10:18 as an example: "'have they not heard?' (Answer: 'Indeed they have')." BDF does *not* say such constructions imply an affirmative answer to the negative question! In this way, Jewett misunderstands both BDF and Paul in his comments on 10:19 (though cf. his appropriate comments on 10:18; ibid., 643) by providing an affirmative response to the negative question: "'[I]s it the case that Israel has not known[?]' . . . 'Yes, that is the case!' the audience must answer" (ibid., 644). We might better render 10:19: "Did Israel know?" to which the implied answer would be, "Yes, they did know" (or at least they ought to have known).

54. Jewett (*Romans*, 644) helpfully reads Rom 10:19 as Paul speaking in Moses' voice; the citation from Deut 32:21 "is not Paul's voice directed to his Roman audience, but Moses' voice directed to Israel."

is not a god; they enraged me [*parōrgisan me*] with their idols. Now I, too, will provoke them to jealousy by means of those who are Not-a-nation, and I will enrage them by means of a nation that lacks understanding." Paul offers a distinctive interpretation of Deut 32:21. Instead of the typical idea of God using pagan peoples to punish Israel through warfare and military and political oppression, Paul interprets the verse in terms of God shaming Israel by making himself more rightly understood by the gentiles than by his own people. But Paul also explains the positive response to the gospel among the gentiles as part of God's plea to Israel. Non-Jews turning to worship Israel's God is itself a sign and a validation of the proclamation of Jesus as Israel's Messiah. Jesus has done what Israel was supposed to do (*viz.* shine the light of Israel's God to all the nations of the earth). Paul hopes that this accomplishment—the influx of gentiles into the people of God—results in the Jews responding in faith to the gospel.

Paul finds this scheme—if that is the right word—to provoke Israel to faith by drawing the gentiles to faith in the Creator God already in the words of Isaiah. He cites Isa 65:1, 2 in Rom 10:20, 21, respectively: "But Isaiah is very bold, and he says, 'I was found by those who did not seek me, and I showed myself to those who did not ask for me' (Isa 65:1). But to Israel he says, 'I spread out my hands all day long to an unfaithful and obstinate people'" (Isa 65:2). Both Isaiah and Paul emphasize God's patient and persistent appeal to Israel, God's "unfaithful and obstinate people."[55] When God pours out his Spirit of adoption (see Rom 8:15-17) on the gentiles, he has not abandoned his historic people, Israel, in favor of a new people. Instead, God's inclusion of the gentiles within the one people of God—the *laos*—forms a piece of God's invitation to Israel to worship him as Creator and God of all nations. As the gospel of Jesus gains a foothold among gentiles, including Paul's Roman readers, Paul sees Israel's God spreading out his hands all day long to the physical descendants of Abraham, Isaac, and Jacob, calling those *from* Israel to, in fact, *be* Israel (see Rom 9:6).

∽

By the end of Romans 10 Paul has clearly explained both how God is faithful to the promises he made to Abraham and his Seed, on the one hand, and how he has poured out his Spirit of adoption onto the gentiles, on the other. God's commitment to Israel is but one instance of his commitment to "unfaithful and obstinate" humanity as a whole. God's plan was always

---

55. Witherington and Hyatt (*Romans*, 265) are helpful here: Paul portrays God "as a parent stretching out his arms toward a wayward child all day long, but the child is obstinate and wayward."

to bless "all the tribes of the earth" through the Seed of Abraham (see Gen 12:3). Now, in the gospel of Jesus, God has done just that.

12

[Re-]Grafted Olive Branches

The Persistence of Hope

> *[T]he tree is not described as Israel, and Paul does not draw the inference that non-Israelites become members of Israel. The tree appears to represent all who are in the family of God, Israelite branches as well as ones from other nations.*[1]

Paul has focused narrowly on Israel/the Jews throughout Romans 9–10 and in particular on God's faithfulness to Abraham and his descendants. Our reading differs substantially from Robert Jewett's, who reads this section as Paul's defense of the gospel despite the Jews' rejection.[2] Romans 9–11 not only *affirms* God's faithfulness to his covenantal promises; these chapters also *demonstrate how* God has maintained his faithfulness to those promises. The central idea in this section, then, is simply this: the adoption of the gentiles into God's family is a mechanism by which God fulfills his covenant with Israel and reaffirms the Jews' place within his family. God's acceptance of the gentiles in no way calls into question

---

1. Nanos, "Grafting," 276.

2. For example, in his opening comments on Romans 9, Jewett writes, "The continued opposition of zealous Jews places a question mark about [sic] the power of the gospel, which is the premise of Paul's missionary project that the letter seeks to promote" (*Romans*, 556). As we have seen, the question mark Paul addresses is placed against God's promises to Israel and not the efficacy of the gospel. If anything, the confidence Paul expresses in Romans 8 in the permanence and reliability of God's love should dissuade us of the thought that Paul perceived in Israel's unreceptiveness toward Jesus a challenge to the gospel's validity.

the Jews' continued presence among the people of God. Paul continues to develop precisely this idea in Romans 11.

Paul, a Prophet like Elijah (Rom 11:1–10)

> **1** "Therefore, I say, God didn't reject his people, did he?" Certainly not! For I myself am also an Israelite, from the Seed of Abraham, of the tribe of Benjamin. **2** "God has not rejected his people," whom he foreknew. Or do you not know that the Scripture says by Elijah, as he was appealing to God against Israel? **3** "Lord, they killed your prophets, they tore down your altars, and now I alone am left and they are seeking my life" (3 Kgdms 19:10). **4** But how did the divine response reply to him? "I have kept for myself seven thousand men, men who have not bent their knee to Baal" (3 Kgdms 19:18). **5** In the same way, then, there is also in the present time a remnant according to his gracious election. **6** But if [God's election] is by grace, it is no longer by deeds, for otherwise grace is no longer grace. **7** "What then? Did Israel not obtain that which it sought?" But the elect did obtain it. The remainder, however, were hardened. **8** Thus it is written,
>
> "God gave them a spirit of drowsiness,
> eyes that do not see and ears that do not hear,
> until the present day" (Isa 29:10; Deut 29:3 LXX).
>
> **9** And David says,
> "Let their table become a snare and a trap,
> a stumbling block and a retribution against them;
> **10** let their eyes be darkened so that they might not see,
> and render their backs perpetually bent" (Ps 68:23–24 LXX).

You will recall that Paul has just cited the Psalms, Deuteronomy, and Isaiah (see Rom 10:18–21), all in support of his argument that Israel has shown herself obstinate and that the Lord has used the gentiles to provoke Israel to repentance. At the beginning of Romans 11, the interlocutor responds to Paul's biblical citations and asks, "God did not reject his people, did he?" The premise of the question presumes a negative answer; the interlocutor himself anticipates that God has *not* rejected his people.[3] Paul emphatically agrees; he responds with the by-now-characteristic exclamation, *mē genoito* ("Certainly not!") and expands on this exclamation by recapitulating his Jewish *bona fides*: "For I myself am also an Israelite, from the Seed

---

3. The question includes the negative particle, *mē*; see the discussions of Rom 2:21–22 and 10:18–19, above.

[Re-]Grafted Olive Branches

of Abraham, of the tribe of Benjamin" (11:1). If God had rejected the Jews [*ton laon autou*; 11:1], he would have rejected Paul.

Paul appeals to a scriptural theme in which the Lord promises never to reject his people. This theme is somewhat more complicated than we might have suspected simply on the basis of Paul's comments in Rom 11:2. At a few places across the Septuagint God expresses his exasperation at his people, and he uses the very same word Paul uses: *apōtheō* ("reject; push aside"). For example, the Lord says through Ezekiel:

> 8 Therefore, this is what the Lord says: "Look! I am against you, and I will enact judgment in your midst before the nations. 9 And I will do in you things which I have not done—even things the likes of which I will not do again—in accordance with all your abominations. 10 Therefore, fathers will devour their children in your midst, and children will eat their fathers, and I will enact in you judgments, and I will scatter any of your remnant to the wind. 11 Therefore, I live," says the Lord, "and yet you have defiled my holy places by means of all your abominations, and *I will reject you* [*kagō apōsomai se*], and my eye will not spare you; neither will I show mercy." (Ezek 5:8–11 LXX)

Similarly, Jeremiah instructs the people to mourn in repentance: "Shear your head and dispose of the clippings; then, take up a lament upon your lips. For the Lord has rejected and discarded [*apōsato*] the generation that does these things" (Jer 7:29 LXX). Elsewhere, however, the prophet comforts the people as they bear the punishment for their sins: "The Lord will not reject [*ouk ... apōsetai*] his people forever" (Lam 3:31 LXX), which implies that he has rejected them for now. In fact, the promise gets stronger: "The Lord will not reject [*ouk apōsetai*] his people; neither will he forsake his inheritance, until righteousness turns to justice, with all the upright in heart holding to it [righteousness?]" (Ps 93:14–15 [LXX; MT = Ps 94:14–15]). Or, similarly, "Because of his great name, the Lord will not reject [*ouk apōsetai*] his people; for the Lord mercifully received you to himself as a people" (1 Kgdms 12:22 LXX).

Paul refers to this scriptural tradition in Rom 11:2: "'God has not rejected [*ouk apōsato*] his people,' whom he foreknew." This last phrase, "whom he foreknew" [*hon proegnō*], recalls the verbal chain in Rom 8:29–30, in which Paul says *of the gentiles*, "those whom he foreknew, he also chose beforehand to be conformed to the image of his son, so that he would be the firstborn among many brethren. And those whom he chose beforehand, these he also called; and those whom he called, these he also justified; and those whom he justified, these he also glorified." In light of our reading Romans 9–11 as Paul's defense *to* his Roman gentile readers *of* Israel and God's promises to Abraham, Paul has now come around to affirming the very same thing of Israel that he has already explained concerning gentiles: God has known them in advance, and this knowledge functions as part of God's plan ("he chose beforehand"), his invitation ("he called"), his blessing ("he justified"), and his purpose ("he glorified").

Paul continues to demonstrate this point with reference to the Elijah tradition and God's promise to preserve for himself a remnant of faithful Israelites. Paul uses the Elijah tradition as a frame that interprets his present experience [*kai en tō nyn kairō*; Rom 11:5].[4] The particular experience Paul has in mind is the general—but not total!—rejection of the gospel among Jews. By appealing to Elijah, Paul provides an explanation for the Jews' general rejection of the gospel: *Israel has always wavered in her faithfulness to God*. But more than this, God has always preserved some within Israel—"a remnant according to his gracious election" [*leimma kat' eklogēn charitos*; 11:5]—as the objects of his faithfulness to his promises to the patriarchs. As it was in Elijah's day, so it is in Paul's. "The remnant of Israel are those Jewish Christians who in Paul's day stand as proof that God's covenant faithfulness to Israel is intact."[5]

Paul expands on the description of God's election in v. 5 as "gracious" [*charitos*; lit. "of/from grace"][6] and pits that description against the notion of election based on deeds. "But if [God's election] is by grace [*chariti*], it is no longer by deeds [*ex ergōn*], for otherwise grace is no longer grace" (Rom 11:6). The temptation here is for us to revert back to the understanding that we specifically eschewed as we worked through Romans 1–4, that Paul is contrasting grace with law/Law (or Torah). But "deeds" is not a synonym for law/Law. Instead, Paul is talking about the basis of Torah (or law/Law). God gave Torah to Israel not on the basis of their deeds (whether in Egypt or in the flight to Sinai) but because he chose Israel, of his own sovereign will (or, "gracious election"), to be his people.[7]

---

4. "*Framing* is the process by which present experiences are integrated into a social group's shared symbolic universe" (Rodríguez, *Structuring*, 163).

5. Johnson, "Covenant Faithfulness," 163.

6. See BDF §165.

7. Recall the beginning of the Ten Commandments: "Then the Lord spoke all these words, saying, 'I am the Lord, your God, who led you up out of Egypt, out of the house of bondage. There shall not be for you other gods except me ...'" (Exod 20:1–3 LXX). At this pivotal moment in the story of Israel's covenant, immediately before telling Israel what he expects *them* to do, God reminds the people what *he* has already done

Torah itself was given "by grace" and not on the basis "of works." Even Israel's observance of Torah, a gift from God that marked the exodus from Egypt and from the people's bondage in that foreign land, was not about meriting or earning God's love. Torah prescribes what Israel's *response* to God's grace looks like; Torah does not define how Israel *earns* God's favor.

How, then, do Paul and his interlocutor see this grace at work in Israel's history? The interlocutor asks, "What then? Did Israel not obtain that which it sought?" (Rom 11:7a). Paul clarifies his answer in the remainder of v. 7: "But the elect *did* obtain it. The remainder, however, were hardened." Paul echoes his similar point in Rom 3:3–4, that the unfaithfulness of some does not nullify God's faithfulness. He explains how the hardness of some in Israel fits into God's plan: "Thus it is written, 'God gave them a spirit of drowsiness, eyes that do not see and ears that do not hear, until the present day'" (Rom 11:8). Paul echoes language from across biblical tradition (Isa 29:10 and Deut 29:3 [LXX; MT = 29:4]) and reinforces the point that even Israel's failures reflect and do not thwart God's will and his promises. Far from being a threat to God's promised blessing for Abraham, his Seed, and all the tribes of the earth, the gospel's lackluster reception among the Jews is par for the course of Israel's history and can even be attributed to God's own action of sending a "spirit of drowsiness" upon the fatigable people of Israel.

But the language of "eyes that do not see and ears that do not hear" makes an even more dramatic point. Paul has already described a kind of synergistic cooperation between people who worship created objects, on the one hand, and the Creator God, who hands them over to the lusts of their hearts, their shameful passions, and a depraved mind (see Rom 1:24, 26, 28). Paul's indictment in Romans 1 took aim precisely at idolatrous *gentiles*. The shocking implication in Romans 11 is that Israel, too, has been handed over to sightless eyes and senseless ears, their God-created faculties dulled by their failure to acknowledge the truth of God. This might seem a too-subtle implication in 11:8, but Paul reinforces exactly this point by citing—nearly verbatim—Ps 68:23–24 [LXX; MT = 69:22–23]:

> Let their table become a snare and a trap,
>   A stumbling block and a retribution against them;
> Let their eyes be darkened so that they might not see,
>   And render their backs perpetually bent. (Rom 11:9–10)

---

for them. This seems as good an example of God's grace as any in the New Testament.

The darkening of the psalmist's opponents' eyes and the crooking of their backs is clearly retributive. The psalmist complains that, as he waited for sympathizing friends and comforters, his enemies "gave me gall as food, and for my thirst they gave me sour wine to drink" (Ps 68:22 LXX). He even goes so far as to ask God, "Add lawlessness to their lawlessness, and do not let them enter into your righteousness" (68:28 LXX). If Paul was able in Romans 1 to take up Jewish anti-pagan polemic and explain the gentiles' depravity as the fruit of their failure to rightly worship the Creator God, here in Romans 11 he shows himself able to lay exactly the same point at Israel's feet. The Jews, no less than their gentile counterparts, find their senses dulled as a result of their rejection of the gospel of Israel's Messiah, Jesus. Perhaps we should not find this all that surprising; twice Paul has plainly denied any distinction between Jews and gentiles (see Rom 3:22; 10:12).

Branches—Natural and Grafted (Rom 11:11–24)

11 "So then, I ask you: Did Israel really stumble to the point of falling?" Certain not! Rather, by their transgression salvation has come to the gentiles, in order to provoke them to jealousy. **12** But if their transgression results in the world's riches, and their loss results in the gentiles' riches, how much more will their fullness [result in prosperity for the world/gentiles]. **13** But I am speaking to you gentiles: inasmuch, then, as I myself am an apostle to the gentiles, I glorify my service, **14** if somehow I might provoke my flesh to jealousy and save some of them. **15** For if their rejection resulted in the reconciliation of the world, what results will their acceptance be if not life from the dead?

16 But if the first portion is holy, so also is the batch of dough; and if the root is holy, so also are the branches. **17** But if some of the branches were broken off, and you, although you are from a wild olive tree, you were grafted in among them, and you were tapped into the root, along with the richness of the olive tree, **18** then you ought not boast over the branches [that were broken off]. And if you do boast, you do not support the root; rather, the root supports you. **19** But you will say, "**Branches were broken off so that I could be grafted in.**" **20** Sure. They were broken off because of their unfaithfulness, while you yourself stand because of your faith. Do not think proudly, but be afraid. **21** For if God did not spare the branches that belonged to the tree naturally, neither will he spare you. **22** Beware, then, the kindness and severity of God: severity upon those who fell, but for you, the kindness of God (if you remain in his kindness, since you also

> can be cut off). ²³ And they, too, if they do not persist in unfaithfulness, will be grafted back in, for God is able to graft them back in. ²⁴ For if you were cut off of the wild olive tree, to which you belonged naturally, and you were grafted onto the cultivated olive tree, which was contrary to nature, how much more will they who belong naturally be grafted back onto their own olive tree.

Paul continues to explain how Israel's obstinacy *vis-à-vis* the covenant (Torah) and her rejection of the gospel relate to God's preservation of a remnant and his promise to bless all the nations of the earth. The interlocutor asks: "So then, I ask you: Did Israel really stumble to the point of falling?" Paul's answer begins with the typically strong rejection: "Certainly not! Rather, by their transgression salvation has come to the gentiles, in order to provoke them to jealousy" (11:11). Somewhat surprisingly, especially given the starkness of Paul's description of sin and its consequences at every point in the letter up to now, Paul identifies a salvific function of Israel's sin. But we have seen hints—I count two—that God turns sin to positive effect. First, Paul asked his interlocutor in very pointed language, "Do you despise the richness of his kindness, his forbearance, and his patience, being ignorant that the kindness of God leads you into repentance?" (Rom 2:4). In light of 1:18–32 and its connection with 2:1–16,[8] God's *kindness, forbearance,* and *patience* must refer to God's tolerance of human sinfulness and his persistent invitation for them to repent and return to him. Second, Paul referred to the demonstration of God's righteousness—certainly a central concept across the entire letter!—which occurs "because of the passing over of sins previously committed" (3:25).

In both Rom 2:4 and 3:25, Paul has in view *gentile* sinfulness. God's patient endurance of the gentiles' depravity has created space for them to recognize their folly, come to repentance, and find themselves reconciled to the Creator God. Here Paul says that *Israel's* transgression [*paraptōma*] has created space for the gentiles' salvation [*sōtēria*]. Moreover, if gentile sinfulness provided the basis (or cause) of the demonstration of God's righteousness (see Rom 3:25), their salvation serves the purpose

---

8. Recall that the interlocutor "do[es] the same things" [*ta ... auta prasseis*; 2:1] that Paul chronicled in Romans 1. Runar Thorsteinsson argues that the logical connective *dio* ("therefore") in 2:1 closely connects 1:18–32 and 2:1–16 (see *Interlocutor*, 177–88). Unlike Thorsteinsson, who sees Paul describing a single figure across Rom 1:18–2:29, I identified three different kinds of gentiles: immoral idolatrous gentiles (1:18–32); a moralizing pagan gentile (2:1–16); and a gentile proselyte to Judaism (2:17–29).

of provoking Israel to jealousy and, Paul hopes, repentance. A considerable amount of social-scientific exegetical work with NT texts argues that Mediterranean cultures view goods, status, and so on as existing in limited supply.[9] But Paul turns limited-good thinking on its head here: "But if their transgression results in the world's riches, and their loss results in the gentiles' riches, how much more will their fullness [result in prosperity for the world/gentiles]? ... For if their rejection resulted in the reconciliation of the world, what result will their acceptance be if not life from the dead?" (11:12, 15). Paul's gentile audience may have benefitted from the Jews' failure to keep Torah's covenantal terms, but they will benefit all the more [*pasō mallon*; 11:12] from their reconciliation with the God who gave them Torah. Paul's gentile audience, then, should share Paul's *pathos*—his sorrow—for Israel (see 9:1–5), since the Jews' continued hardening delays or diminishes the full blessing of God for both Jew and gentile.

Paul specifically identifies his intended audience—those whom he imagines himself addressing—for the first time since the opening of the letter: "But I am speaking to you gentiles: inasmuch, then,[10] as I myself am an apostle to the gentiles, I glorify my service, if somehow I might provoke my flesh to jealousy and save some of them" (Rom 11:13–14). Jewett rightly notes, "In view of the divine authorization of apostolic service, it would have seemed unobjectionable that Paul glorifies his ministry."[11] Paul does not glorify himself but rather his ministry [*tēn diakonian mou*]. More importantly, given his explicit and emphatic mention of his status as "apostle to the gentiles," we should understand v. 13 in terms of Paul glorifying *God* for drawing the gentiles into his family (see, e.g., Rom 8:15–17)

---

9. For example, "[Social-scientific exegetes] argue that the culture in which Jesus lived was a 'limited good' society, meaning that 'any person's gain must come through loss by others.... Hence, if someone gains success, goods, honor or anything valued by a group, then others correspondingly perceive themselves losing worth, prestige and the like.' Honor, then, was a limited good" (Watson, *Honor*, 27; citing Hagedorn and Neyrey, "Envy," 21).

10. Jewett (*Romans*, 678), translates *eph' hoson* as "inasmuch," but he then reads *men oun* as a concessive phrase that "has the sense of 'contrary to what you may be inclined to think.'" He translates *men oun*, "notwithstanding." I follow him in my rendering of *eph' hoson*; however, I agree with Dunn, that "*men oun* probably has the force of summarizing what has been said in moving to a new subject (BDF §451:1): the following clauses (vv. 13–15) gathering up (and repeating) the point of vv. 11–12, with the point now directed firmly at Paul's Gentile audience. Cranfield's suggestion that the sense is 'contrary to what you may be inclined to think,' would have greater force if Paul had written *menounge* (see on 9:20)" (Dunn, *Romans*, 2:655–56; referring to Cranfield, *Romans*, 559).

11. Jewett, *Romans*, 679.

and using Paul to accomplish the gentiles' "drawing in." Nevertheless, even in his focus on proclaiming the gospel among the gentiles, Paul hopes his ministry will have effect on the Jews [*mou tēn sarka*[12]] and result in the salvation "of some of them." Paul's ministry to, for, and among the gentiles is simultaneously ministry to and for (if not among) the Jews![13] If Paul's gentile audience harbored any thoughts that their certain and firm adoption by God signaled the Jews' disinheritance, Paul insists that he pursues his apostolic vocation in hopes that *both* Jews and gentiles would except the gospel message he proclaims.

To the extent that either Paul or his audience perceived the status of being God's chosen people as a "limited good," Paul continues to turn that thinking on its head in Rom 11:12, 15 by bringing Jew and gentile together into a single group with a single set of interests. "But if the first portion is holy, so also is the batch of dough; and if the root is holy, so also are the branches" (11:16). If Jews and gentiles belong to the same lump of dough, or if they comprise a single tree, then they each share the fate of the other. Paul illustrates the mechanics of this "bringing together" in Rom 11:17–24 by expanding on the tree image from v. 16b. We should also mention that Paul addresses this entire section to his fictive interlocutor, as is clear from the use of second-person singular pronouns and verbs throughout vv. 17–24. Paul addresses his fictive interlocutor explicitly in v. 17 [*sy de*; "and you"] and blocks any potential boast among his gentile readers over the Jews (whether Jews who have believed the gospel or non-believing Jews). After all, even if a few (even if many!) of the branches were broken off, the tree itself is still *Israel*, the covenantal people of God, contrary to Nanos's claim (cited in this chapter's epigram). "Branches from a wild olive tree—the Gentiles—have been grafted onto this cultivated olive tree *that is Israel*, which means that, against all odds and contrary to nature (11:24), they share in the riches of Israel's heritage, God's promised redemption."[14] Bill Campbell has ably described the dynamics of Paul's manipulation of the Israel-as-olive-tree metaphor:

> It is no accident that Paul refuses to give the term "Israel" a wholly Gentile Christian or even a Gentile Christian *and* a Jewish

---

12. The genitive personal pronoun *mou* ("my, mine") is in an emphatic position; Paul stresses his relationship to ethnic Israel by calling them "*my* flesh," with emphasis.

13. I agree with the general thrust of Mark Nanos's comments, though I think he makes the point too strongly: "Israel continued to be Paul's *unmistakable priority* even through his apostleship to the gentiles" (*Mystery*, 240; my emphasis).

14. Johnson, "Covenant Faithfulness," 164; my emphasis.

> Christian content [original emphasis]. *For him it still refers to all God's people* and God determines in his election who these shall be! Likewise he refuses to allow the word Jew to be equated with unbelief. One might say that the Jew for him is still a potential Christian; more appropriately, however, we should claim that he defines the true Christian as a true Jew, i.e. he defines Christianity in terms of Judaism.[15]

The point here is not that the church "replaces" Judaism (or that Christians "replace" the Jews) as "Israel," the chosen people of God. Rather, the point is that gentiles find themselves included *alongside* Jews within the covenantal label, "Israel."

This interpretation stands in stark contrast to Das's claim that Paul "never uses the term [Israel] in a way that includes Gentiles."[16] Das argues on the basis of the logic of Paul's metaphor—that the wild and cultivated olive branches remain distinct—and insists, "Paul continues to speak consistently of 'Israel' as a group *distinct* from the Gentiles in v. 25."[17] However, Das has already acknowledged that "Paul speaks of the grafting of the Gentiles *onto the olive tree representing Israel*,"[18] which is exactly the point! Gentiles, *who are not Jews* (and so remain distinct from the cultivated branches), *are grafted into the Israel-tree*. The real problem with Das's interpretation begins precisely here:

> In the olive branch imagery, the imagery shifts from Israel as God's chosen, to their rejection and the grafting in of the Gentiles, to the restoration of the Jews, i.e. Israel—Gentiles—Israel. Verses 25-26 are drawing conclusions based on what preceded in Romans 11, and the progression remains the same: Israel—Gentiles—Israel.[19]

But this is simply *not* what Paul says. The cultivated branches that are "broken off" in v. 17 are not Israel; they are broken off from Israel, even as the uncultivated branches are grafted in. There is no "Israel—Gentiles—Israel progression." Instead, Paul offers the hope that both cultivated (Jews) and

---

15. Campbell, "Separation," 466; my emphasis. *Pace* Eisenbaum, the title of whose book (*Paul was Not a Christian*) makes a good rhetorical effect but over-emphasizes the discontinuity between Judaism and Christianity.

16. Das, *Paul*, 106.

17. Ibid., 107, italics in the original.

18. Ibid.; my emphasis.

19. Ibid.

uncultivated (gentiles) olive branches can be grafted back onto the root—
Israel!—if they find themselves removed from the root.[20]

The point of the image, then, is that God has not abandoned his "tree" in favor of a different tree. Instead, God has pruned unfruitful branches and has chosen branches from other trees to graft onto his cultivated tree. How absurd if anyone should think that, by grafting foreign branches onto the tree, the new branches renewed the health and vigor of the roots! Instead, the connection between the roots, which were always full of vitality, has brought new life to the newly grafted branches. The movement suggested by Paul's metaphor is from gentile identity toward Israelite identity. The grafted branches retain their identity as uncultivated olive branches, but they are nevertheless grafted into the tree that is Israel. "Gentiles did have to learn to relate to the God of Israel, and *thus learn from Judaism* but, even so, *they did this precisely as Gentiles.*"[21] The interlocutor accepts the point that he cannot boast over the root, but he nevertheless turns to boast over the branches that were broken off. He even imagines that the branches were broken off *in order to* [*hina*; 11:19] create space for him to be grafted in. Paul grants the point, but he rejects any idea that God had arbitrarily chosen to break off some branches and graft in others.[22] Instead, some branches were broken off "because of their unfaithfulness" [*tē apistia*], and the newly grafted branch that represents the interlocutor is successfully incorporated into the tree on the basis of faith [*sy de tē pistei hestēkas*; 11:20].

The newly grafted branch ought to respond with fear rather than hubris: fear that any branch might be removed if it proves unfruitful (= unfaithful). After all, what security does a grafted branch enjoy if the natural branches could be—and were—broken off?[23] There is no room

---

20. Nanos also rejects any suggestion that Paul has "suddenly shift[ed] his meaning of 'Israel' to that of 'true' or 'spiritual' Israel" (see Nanos, *Mystery*, 274-79; pp. 275-76 quoted). Nanos bases his interpretation, at least in part, on his understanding of Romans as "a letter that maintains throughout the distinction between Jews and gentiles (whether they be Christians or not)" (ibid., 275). Despite clear differences between Paul's expectations for and discussions of gentiles and Jews (e.g., see our reading of Romans 1-8 [gentiles] and Romans 9-11 [Jews]), Paul has twice declared "for *there is no distinction*" between Jews and gentiles (Rom 3:22; 10:12)!

21. Campbell, "Rationale," 25; original emphasis.

22. *Pace* interpretations, especially of Rom 9:10-23, that affirm precisely that God acts arbitrarily (= sovereignly) and without any basis in the human response to his call and invitation.

23. Perhaps we should balance our comments here with a reminder of Paul's exuberant confidence in the closing paragraph of Romans 8. Paul does *not* say that a

for boasting over Israel, the "root" of the tree; neither is there any room for boasting over unbelieving Jews, the "branches that were broken off." Paul offers a fairly straightforward point in Rom 11:22–24. I am especially impressed with the compassion and optimism Paul exhibits toward his fellow Jews, and in particular Jews who "were broken off because of their unfaithfulness" (11:20). Paul exhibits clear and compelling concern for Jews who have *not* responded in faith to the gospel message.

One more point before we finish this section. Paul uses "nature" [*physis*] three times in 11:24, which accounts for nearly half of its seven uses in Romans. In all seven instances, Paul refers to things that are either consonant with nature (2:14, 27; 11:21, 24 [twice]) or, on two occasions, to things that are contrary to nature (1:26; 11:24 [once]). In both of these latter instances, Paul uses *para physin* ("contrary to nature"). Other than this one phrase, however, these two verses—1:26 and 11:24—are very different. In Romans 1, Paul points to women who have "exchanged the natural function for that which is contrary to nature [*para physin*]" as evidence that "God handed them over to shameful passions" (1:26). In the context of Romans 1, the descriptor "contrary to nature" serves as a sign of the depth of the gentiles' depravity. In Romans 11, however, "contrary to nature" serves as a sign of how unexpected God's inclusion of the gentiles truly is. Here, nature dictates that some branches belong to wild olive trees and have no part among cultivated olive trees. However, God has overcome nature and brought them into connection with the root that, according to Paul's metaphor, is Israel. Jews and gentiles both and together comprise the one tree, "Israel." The Jews belong "according to nature" [*kata physin*]; the gentiles belong despite being "contrary to nature" [*para physin*].

The Mystery of Israel (Rom 11:25–32)

> **25** For I do not want you to be ignorant of this mystery, brethren—so that you might not be wise in your own sight—that a partial hardening has come upon Israel until the fullness of the gentiles arrives, **26** and in this way all Israel will be saved, just as it is written:

---

person's justification before God is in any way tenuous or precarious. After all, nothing, "not death nor life nor angels or rulers nor present things or things to come nor powers nor height nor depth nor any other created thing can separate us from the love of God that is in Christ Jesus our Lord" (8:38–39). However, at that moment when a person thinks s/he is more deserving of God's mercy and blessing than someone else, s/he needs to be reminded of God's extensive history of bringing his judgment to bear upon those he had sought to bless.

> "The deliverer will come from Zion;
>   he will remove ungodliness from Jacob.
> **27** And this will be my covenant with them,
>   whenever I remove their sins" (Isa 59:20–21; 27:9).
>
> **28** On the one hand, according to the gospel they were enemies on your account, but on the other hand, according to the election of God they were beloved on account of the patriarchs. **29** For the gifts and the calling of God are irrevocable. **30** For just as you once were disobedient to God, but now you received mercy because of their unfaithfulness, **31** so also they currently are unfaithful because of the mercy shown you, so that they, too, may [now] be shown mercy. **32** For God confined everyone to unfaithfulness so that he might show mercy to everyone.

In this next-to-last section of Romans 9–11, Paul draws his discussion about Israel to a close. For the second (and last) time in the letter, Paul emphasizes the point he is presently making by means of a disclosure formula: "For I do not want you to be ignorant of this mystery, brethren—so that you might not be wise in your own sight" (11:25). The disclosure formula signals an important point, even one that motivates the very sending of the letter. So what follows the disclosure formula? "A partial hardening[24] has come upon Israel until the fullness of the gentiles arrives, and in this way all Israel will be saved" (11:25). Understandably, some readers (scholarly as well as popular) have tried to read v. 26a as Paul's statement that all Jews would be saved. But, as we have seen, the correspondence between *Israel* and *the Jews* has been a significant issue across Romans 9–11.[25] In addition to Rom 9:6 ("For not all those who are from Israel are Israel"), we have seen how Paul uses the metaphor of the cultivated olive tree (including branches grafted in from wild olive trees) to illustrate what constitutes "Israel" and to argue that some gentiles find themselves included in Is-

---

24. BDAG (*meros*, §1.c) gives "in part" as a gloss for the prepositional phrase, *apo merous*.

25. We saw that Das maintains a strict and rigid distinction between *Israel* and the gentiles (*Paul*, 106–9). Das claims that Paul "never uses the term [*viz*. 'Israel'] in a way that includes Gentiles" (ibid., 106), and a little later re-affirms that "Paul nowhere describes Gentiles as Israel in these chapters" (ibid., 109). However, Paul has just engaged the extended metaphor of the singular olive tree of God's people—*Israel!*—from which some (Jewish) unfruitful branches had been broken off (but could later be regrafted in) and to which some (gentile) wild branches had been grafted in. In this way, Paul clearly defines "Israel" as the finished agricultural product, the olive tree from which some natural branches were broken even as some wild branches were added, the health and future of which God, as attentive caretaker, ensures.

rael while some Jews find themselves "broken off." Despite fundamental problems with his reading of Romans 11, Mark Nanos provides a helpful explanation of v. 26:

> "All Israel" was a common idiom for corporate Israel, for Israel "as a whole," that is, as a people, even if every individual was not necessarily present. . . . Paul has maintained a distinction throughout between the "remnant" and the "rest" (Rom 11:5–7, 8ff.), and his goal in provoking his brothers and sisters to jealousy was to "save *some* of them" (v. 14). So here it is some of his brothers and sisters from the "part hardened" that he sees coming back to join the "remnant" of Christian Jews in restored Israel: "and thus, in this way, all Israel shall be saved."[26]

This "all Israel" that will be saved includes both Jewish and gentile members. After all, Paul's point through the length of the letter has been that "any person baptized into Christ, whether a Jew or a Gentile originally, becomes a member of 'Israel.'"[27] Paul does not assert that the Jews, as a group or even as Jews, will be saved. Rather, despite their underwhelming reception of the gospel, the Jews' reception [= *pōrōsis apo merous*; "a partial hardening"] functions as part of God's plan and does not threaten the salvation of "all Israel" [*pas Israēl sōthēsetai*].[28]

Paul's use of *plērōma* ("fullness") deserves some attention. Here in v. 25 Paul refers to "the fullness of the gentiles," or "the full number of the Gentiles" (NET). Behind Paul's words lies some idea of "election," in which God has chosen that some gentiles would be grafted into Israel, and the "partial hardening" would continue until the full measure of gentiles is grafted into Israel. Earlier in the chapter, Paul used the same word to refer to "their [= the Jews'] fullness," which would result in the comparatively richer blessing of the world and the gentiles. "But if their transgression results in the world's riches, and their loss results in the gentiles' riches, how much more will their fullness [result in prosperity for the world/gentiles]" (Rom 11:12). Paul envisages a situation in which the gentiles eagerly

---

26. Nanos, *Mystery*, 276–77.

27. Garroway, *Gentile-Jews*, 3. Just a few sentences later Garroway says Paul "describes [his gentile audience] as branches in the family tree of Israel!" This is the primary argument of Garroway's monograph, and he is exactly right, *pace* Nanos and Das.

28. Mark Nanos argues that we should translate *pōrōsis* in Rom 11:25 as "'callused' in the sense of 'protected' rather than 'hardened'" (see Nanos, "Temporary Protection"; p. 60 quoted). While we can appreciate the tenor and especially the goal of Nanos's essay (and all his work on Romans), both the context in Romans and the other uses of *pōrōsis* in the NT (see Mark 3:5; Eph 4:18) support the harsher translation, "hardened."

await the *plērōma* ("fullness") of the Jews even as the Jews eagerly await the *plērōma* of the gentiles, with both groups realizing their full blessing when the *plērōma* of the other is fulfilled. This "full blessing" is nothing less than the salvation of "all Israel."

Paul explains his optimism *vis-à-vis* the *partial* hardening of Israel and the impending salvation of *all* Israel by quoting from (and modifying) Isa 59:20–21 and 27:9 in Rom 11:26–27. In its literary/prophetic context, Isa 59:20–21 LXX promises a deliverer that will come "on Zion's behalf" or "for Zion's sake" [*heneken Siōn*].[29] Given Paul's argument throughout Romans 9–11—that God is faithful to his promises to Abraham and that, when all is said and done, "all Israel will be saved"—Paul certainly could have cited Isa 59:20 in an unmodified form.[30] But two aspects of Paul's argument make "from Zion" more appropriate than "for Zion."

- First, Paul has just been engaged in a long and complicated effort to redefine "Israel," so that (i) not all those who are "from Israel" are Israel, while (ii) some branches were grafted into Israel's tree "contrary to nature." In other words, Israel is no longer focused on (or centered in) Jerusalem, and so "for Zion" would have been less appropriate.

- Second, and more obviously, Paul identifies "the deliverer" [*ho rhyomenos*] as Jesus. Given Jesus' ethnic and religious identity (a Galilean Jew), Jesus comes "from Zion," from historic Israel that is focused on/centered in the physical descendants of the patriarchs. Perhaps more importantly, given the specific reference of "Zion" (the Jebusite fortress, or the temple mount, or the whole city of Jerusalem) and the location of Jesus' crucifixion just outside the city walls, Jesus the Deliverer comes "from Zion," and the proclamation of his message proceeds outward from the city. As a result, "from Zion" makes good sense for Paul's argument.

Despite this change, Paul still includes the obvious element of promise *for* Israel in the Isaianic passage. When the deliverer comes from Zion, "he will remove ungodliness from Jacob," a promise that, if anything, declares the undoing of the partial hardening that Paul identified in 11:25.

---

29. The MT promises a deliverer who will come "to" or "for" [*lĕ-*] Zion, which is more accurately reflected in the LXX than in Paul's citation.

30. We should, however, recognize that we simply do not know if Paul modified the passage or if the text that he knew differed from the reading we find in our printed versions of the MT and/or the LXX.

The concluding line, which comes from Isa 27:9, promises the eventual removal of Israel's sin [*aphelōmai tas hamartias autōn*; 11:27]. Remember Paul's accusation back in Romans 3, that "everyone, Jews as well as Greeks, are under sin" (3:9) and that "there is no distinction, for everyone sinned and are falling short of the glory of God" (3:22–23). By Romans 8, Paul had explained how gentiles found themselves "set free from this body of death" (7:24), now "led by the Spirit" and declared "children of God" (8:14). Now, with the Isaianic references in 11:26–27, Paul has explained how "all Israel [*pas Israēl*] will be saved" (11:26). If Paul charged everyone—Jew as well as Greek—with being "under sin" in Rom 3:9, by the end of Romans 11 he has now explained how everyone—gentiles as well as Jews, who together comprise "all Israel"—finds salvation in the gospel of Jesus.

The final substantive paragraph of these three chapters explores the relation between disobedience and mercy. More importantly, it explains the basis and the extent of Israel's value in the new people of God and the mutuality between Jew and gentile. The enmity Paul identifies in v. 28 was not between Jews and gentiles. Remember Romans 5, where Paul explained the assurance of salvation for those who are reconciled to God: "For if, while we were his enemies [*echthroi ontes*], we were reconciled to God by the death of his son, how much more, now that we are reconciled, will we be saved by his life" (5:10). Here in Romans 11, Paul explains that the Jews were rendered enemies of God for the gentiles' sake [*di hymas*]. That is, because of Israel's failure to keep Torah's terms, God sent his son Jesus to deliver Israel from her sin and to draw the gentiles in to worship Israel's God. But Israel was not completely despised, for even as they were enemies [*echthroi*] they were simultaneously "beloved [*agapētoi*] on account of the patriarchs." This particular collocation of terms—*enemies* and *beloved*—together in the same context helps explain the complexity of Romans 9–11; Paul has had to explain how both terms apply to Israel *at the same time*!

Despite their estrangement from God, the Jews were nevertheless always going to be objects of God's compassion precisely because God had committed himself to eternal relationship with Abraham and his descendants. Thus Paul's confidence in Rom 11:29, that "the gifts and the calling of God are irrevocable," which echoes once again the remarkable confidence we noted back in Romans 8. Once again Paul is drawing to a close a topic that he first raised much earlier in the letter, especially in Romans 3. He already insisted on God's unique faithfulness, that even if everyone else be revealed a liar God would still be true (see Rom 3:4). So, even as we see Paul fully convinced that Israel had brought on themselves the covenant's curses rather than its blessings, we also see him fully convinced that God would fulfill his promises to bless Abraham's descendants (i.e., Israel).

God brought his promises to fulfillment for both Abraham's descendants and for "all the families of the earth" by means of the same mechanics: both were unfaithful (= disobedient) to God, and both have been shown mercy after their disobedience. The surprising feature of the current passage, however, is its apparent innovation *vis-à-vis* the repeated theme of "Jew first, then Greek."[31] That is, the gentiles [*hymeis*; "you" (plur.)] received mercy because of the Jews' disobedience (11:30). And in the same way, he says, the Jews presently are disobedient "because of the mercy shown you" [*tō hymeterō eleei*].[32] In other words, the Jews persist in their disobedience and await their reception of mercy *even as the gentiles are currently experiencing the mercy of God*. This sounds precariously close to "first for the Greek, then also for the Jew."[33] The discrepancy hardly matters, however, for the point of Paul's argument, here in Romans 9–11 and throughout the entire letter, centers on the equality between Jew and gentile in God's economy. As he has already explained, "there is no favoritism with God" (Rom 2:11). This equality surfaces again explicitly in 11:32: "For God confined everyone [*tous pantas*] to unfaithfulness so that he might show mercy to everyone" [*tous pantas*].[34]

---

31. See Rom 1:16; 2:9–10; 3:9; 10:12; cf. 3:29; 9:24.

32. I interpret the dative case here (as well as at the end of 11:30) as a "dative of cause" (see BDF §196, which specifically mentions Rom 11:30–31). Without exception, all of the English translations included on lumina.bible.org improperly translate *tō hymeterō eleei* ("because of the mercy shown you") *after* the *hina* ("that, so that, in order that"; see https://lumina.bible.org/#!bible/Romans+11). My translation respects the word order and keeps *tō hymeterō eleei* associated with *ēpeithēsan* ("they were disobedient") rather than with *eleēthōsin* ("they might receive mercy").

33. See Nanos, *Mystery*, 239–88 for a careful and thorough discussion of "Paul's two-step pattern."

34. Both Nanos (ibid., 275–76) and Das (*Paul*, 107, discussed above) claim Paul regularly *distinguishes* Jews (or Israel) and gentiles. For a better reading of Paul's complex use of labels, see Garroway (*Gentile-Jews*, 7–10), who recognizes that Paul uses labels (e.g., "Jew" and "gentile") in ways that both capitalize on their established meanings as well as in ways that redefine them.

Ode to the Sublime (Rom 11:33–36)

> 33 Oh, the depths of his wealth
>   and of the wisdom and knowledge of God!
> How unsearchable are his judgments;
>   how inscrutable are his paths!
> 34 For who knows the mind of the Lord,
>   or who is his advisor?
> 35 Who gives to him in advance,
>   so that he should be repaid by him?
> 36 For from him and through him and unto him are all things;
>   to him be the glory forever. Amen!

Romans 9–11 ends with a doxology. As Romans 11 comes to a close, Paul has finished his explanation of (i) how God has adopted the gentiles into his family, grafted them into his olive tree, "apart from Torah" and (ii) how God has preserved a remnant of Israel and so kept his promises to Israel. With his argument concluded, Paul pauses to express his awe and wonder at the sight of God's person and his work. The doxology marks the end of the discursive moment that comprises Romans 1–11. What follows the doxology, therefore, represents a new section, not of Paul's argument, but of the letter itself.

How might we best describe the whole of Paul's argument? First, we ought to remember that Paul has encoded an exclusively gentile audience for the letter. The various twists and turns of Paul's rhetoric throughout Romans 1–8 explained how God has revealed his righteousness to gentiles; that is, God revealed his righteousness (i) apart from Torah, (ii) through Jesus' faithfulness, (iii) by pouring out his Spirit upon all those who are "in the Spirit." These gentiles, rhetorically embodied in Paul's imagined dialogue partner, ought not submit to Torah's yoke because (i) Torah was not given to them but to Israel, and (ii) Israel found itself under Torah's curses rather than its blessings.

This argument raises the possibility that Israel, having failed to observe Torah faithfully and incurring the covenantal curses set forth in Deuteronomy 30, among other places, finds itself forsaken and abandoned by her God. But Paul finds this possibility utterly unacceptable, if for no other reason than that God is faithful to his promises to Abraham even in the face of the people's unfaithfulness (= disobedience). Therefore, having explained the adoption of gentile believers into God's family in Romans

1–8, Paul sets forth in Romans 9–11 the mechanisms by which God (i) punishes his obstinate and recalcitrant people for breaking with Torah, and simultaneously (ii) keeps faith with his promises to Abraham, to make his descendants a great nation and, through them, to bless all the peoples of the earth. We have identified a number of key aspects of this phase of Paul's argument, including (i) YHWH's sovereign and gracious decision to "love Jacob," (ii) the preservation of a faithful remnant in the midst of largely unfaithful Israel, (iii) the continued appeal to unfaithful Jews to repent and be "re-grafted" into God's covenant people, Israel, and (iv) the function of God's mercy upon gentiles to provoke the Jews to jealousy and, hopefully, to join the gentiles in finding and receiving God's mercy.

The confidence in and assurance of God's sovereignty, which we noted in Romans 9, is expressed doxologically here at the end of Romans 11 (or perhaps we should say, "... here at the end of Romans 9–11," or even, "... here at the end of Romans 1–11").

13

Living Sacrifices

One Body, Many Members

[T]here is absolutely nothing strange about the transition from Rom 12:21 to Rom 13:1ff. Believers should "conquer the bad (to kakon) by means of the good (to agathon)" (12:21): in so doing, they should be subjected to the powers of this world since these, on their side, represent God and in themselves support behavior that is good (13:1ff.). We should conclude that the movement from 12:14–21 to 13:1ff. is so smooth that it is most unfortunate that Rom 12–13 has traditionally been divided up into two separate chapters. Romans 13:1–7 is a wholly integrated part of the comprehensive and finely differentiated politics that Paul is articulating for the benefit of his Roman addressees in the two chapters taken as a whole.[1]

Paul has completed his exposition of the righteousness of God, now revealed to gentiles apart from Torah, as well as of the faithfulness of God to his historic and covenantal promises to Abraham and his descendants. Now, in Romans 12, "exposition gives way to exhortation" as Paul begins to prescribe an appropriate ethic for those who follow Jesus.[2] Paul's

---

1. Engberg-Pedersen, "Stoicizing Politics," 168.

2. Furnish, "Living to God," 193. Despite the change in focus (from exposition to exhortation), Furnish rightly insists, "Paul's subject remains the good news of the saving power of God's love revealed in Christ" (ibid.). Later, he refers to "the organic relationship of theology and ethics" (ibid., 200); this is exactly how we must read both ethics and theology in Romans.

moral instructions in these chapters apply, in broad strokes, to both Jewish and gentile believers. However, nothing in Romans 12–13 suggests that Paul has broadened his audience to include ethnically Jewish believers. Therefore, we will continue to read Paul's ethical instructions along the same lines that have governed our reading of the letter thus far: as Paul's instructions to gentile believers in Jesus residing in Rome.

In the Broadest Strokes Possible (Rom 12:1–2)

> 1 Therefore, I urge you, brethren, through the mercies of God, to present your bodies as a sacrifice—living, holy, and pleasing to God; this is your reasonable act of worship. 2 And do not be conformed to this age; rather, be transformed by the renewal of your mind, so that you might approve what is the will of God, which is good and pleasing and perfect.

Soon enough Paul will set his moral-philosophical gaze upon specific areas of concern facing the Roman communities of Jesus-followers. But in these first two verses Paul portrays the moral-ethical character appropriate to those who "walk according to the Spirit" (8:4) in the broadest strokes possible. In these two verses, Paul surveys the landscape of Christian living and attempts to describe that landscape in its entirety.[3] We might say that these two verses set forth the general principle(s) that the remainder of Paul's ethical instructions attempts to apply to various situations. For this reason, I will focus on these two verses in some detail before moving on to the moral instructions that follow.

For the first time in the letter, Paul uses the verb *parakaleō* ("urge, exhort, encourage") to lay a moral exhortation before his readers.[4] He addresses his readers using the familiar and inclusive term, "brethren" [*adelphoi*], which he has done before, though somewhat sparingly.[5] The tenor of this passage, therefore, is warm and encouraging. Unlike the early chapters of Galatians, in which Paul comes across as agitated and even antagonistic, Paul here extends his rhetorical arm across his readers' rhetorical shoulders and offers a compassionate word of advice. He then

---

3. Similarly, see Grieb, *Story*, 115.

4. Of Romans' four uses of *parakaleō*, three (12:1; 15:30; 16:17) express a moral exhortation for Paul's readers; the fourth (12:8) refers to a recipient of a particular spiritual gift (i.e., encouragement).

5. See Rom 1:13; 7:1, 4; 8:12; 10:1; 11:25 (cf. 8:29; 9:3, which do not address Paul's readers directly).

explicitly identifies the basis of his exhortation: "by the mercies of God" [*dia tōn oiktirmōn tou theou*]. These three terms—"urge," "brethren," and "mercies"—give Paul's moral instructions an encouraging and edifying tone rather than a confrontational, adversative flavor.

If Paul's encouraging tone in the opening of Rom 12:1 lowers our defenses, the content of his exhortation shocks us out of any sense of complacency. Indeed, our familiarity with this verse makes it difficult to appreciate how shocking Paul's exhortation truly is. Paul, still with his arm warmly across his readers' shoulder, urges them "to present [*parastēsai*] your bodies as a sacrifice [*thysian*]—living, holy, and pleasing to God; this is your reasonable act of worship." I offer four observations.

First, Paul links the exhortation of Rom 12:1 to the preceding material (Romans 1–11) using the conjunction *oun* ("therefore"), which "denot[es] that what it introduces is the result of or an inference" from what has gone before.[6] In other words, the exhortations we find in 12:1–2 provide the proper response to the arguments we traced through the first eleven chapters.

Second, Paul provides four descriptors in v. 1 that describe the Romans' [self-]sacrifice:

- "living" [*zōsan*];
- "holy" [*hagian*];
- "pleasing to God" [*euareston tō theō*]; and
- "your reasonable act of worship" [*tēn logikēn latreian hymōn*].

We will discuss the first and the last of these descriptors immediately below. Regarding the second, the adjective "holy" picks up Paul's identification of his audience back in the opening of the letter, in which he addressed his readers as "beloved of God, called [to be] holy [*klētois hagiois*; 1:7]." Paul has also referred to those for whom the Spirit intercedes as "the saints" [*hagioi*; 8:27; see also 12:13]. Here in 12:1, Paul urges his readers to be what he has already told them they are: set apart and consecrated for the Lord (i.e., "holy").

Paul also describes his readers' [self-]sacrifice as "pleasing to God." He describes the Philippians' gift(s) to him, delivered by Epaphroditus, in similarly cultic terms: "a fragrant offering, an acceptable sacrifice, pleasing to God" (Phil 4:18). In six of the eight uses of *euarestos* in the Pauline corpus, the person being pleased is explicitly "God" or

---

6. BDAG (s.v.).

"the Lord."[7] Both instances of *euarestos* in the LXX (Wis 4:10; 9:10) also have God as the person being pleased. This word, then, is especially appropriate for describing an offering that is given with the hope of being acceptable and pleasing *to God*.

Third, as far as I can see, a "sacrifice" [*thysia*] is never described as "living" [*zōsan*], neither anywhere in the LXX nor elsewhere in the NT. This certainly makes sense; the verb *thyō* ("sacrifice, slaughter") necessarily involved the death of the sacrificial victim. "Because sacrificial animals or portions of animals—and human beings also—were burnt, *thyō* also assumed the meaning to slaughter for cultic ends."[8] In the LXX, *thysia* could refer to a cereal offering rather than an animal offering, but Paul's emphatic language—"present *your bodies* [*ta sōmata hymōn*] as a sacrifice"—clearly understands *thysia* in terms of animal rather than plant sacrifice. "Living sacrifice," then, ought to strike our ears as oddly as "meatless bacon," "deafening silence," or "freezer burn." Furnish describes this language as a "remarkable image" and rightly connects this with other moments in Romans in which life follows death: "the selves to be put at God's disposal in the world are precisely those which, having 'been brought from death to life' (6:13), are indwelt by the life-giving Spirit (8:1–13) and are 'alive to God in Christ Jesus' (6:11)."[9] This unique collocation—*living sacrifice*—evokes the similar idea from the Gospels, in which Jesus instructs anyone who would be his disciples, "let them deny themselves and take up their cross and follow me" (Mark 8:34).[10]

Fourth, the language of "sacrifice" [*thysia*] obviously belongs within a cultic context (i.e., within the sphere of the sacrificial system, with its various prescriptions and proscriptions relating to personnel, offerings, dates and festivals, etc.). *Latreian* ("act of worship") is also a cultic term. In the LXX, *latreia* refers to the Passover service (Exod 12:25–26; 13:5), to the temple service in general (1 Chr 28:13), to sacrificial systems more generally (Josh 22:27), or even to the entire system of Jewish religious

---

7. Rom 12:1; 14:18; 2 Cor 5:9 [*autō*]; Eph 5:10; Phil 4:18; Col 3:20. Of the remaining two uses of *euarestos* in the Pauline corpus, Rom 12:2 certainly has "pleasing to God" in view, but the object is not quite explicit; Titus 2:9 refers to slaves being pleasing "to their own masters" [*idiois despotais*].

8. Thiele, "θύω" (part), 3:417.

9. Furnish, "Living to God," 194.

10. These two passages, Rom 12:1 and Mark 8:34, do not share any of the same vocabulary. The connection between them is only thematic; they both use a *mortal* metaphor to describe the commitment involved in *living* as a follower of Jesus.

practice (1 Macc 2:19, 22).[11] Jews were famously protective of the sanctity and purity of the temple and the cultic system centered in Jerusalem. According to Acts, Paul runs into trouble when some Jews accuse him of defiling the temple by bringing gentiles beyond the Court of the Gentiles (Acts 22:28). Josephus describes the layout of the temple and mentions a balustrade separating the first court from the inner courts. This balustrade had inscriptions in both Greek and Latin warning that any non-Jew who proceeded into the inner courts would have only himself to blame for his death (see *Ant.* 15:417; *J.W.* 5:193–94). How fascinating, then, that Paul, a religiously observant Jew from the late Second Temple era, writing to gentiles in Rome, would use this cultic language in his exhortations to them. Despite the fact that gentiles could not travel to Jerusalem to offer sacrifices within the temple (they would have to find a Jewish male to offer the sacrifice to the priest on their behalf), Paul instructs his audience not just to *make* an offering to Israel's God but to *be* an offering! Paul tells them to do *spiritually* precisely what they could not do *literally*.

Paul builds on his original exhortation—to present your bodies as a sacrifice: living, holy, acceptable to God, a reasonable act of worship—by contrasting the shape of this sacrificial way of life with lifestyles characteristic of the current sociopolitical order. Furnish draws a helpful contrast between Paul's exhortation for his gentile readers in Rome, whose minds are (or ought to be) renewed, and the "worthless mind" that Paul describes in Romans 1.[12] Similarly, Linebaugh speculates that the author of the Epistle of Enoch (*1 En.* 92:1–5; 93:11—105:2) would object to Paul's view of justification: "From this perspective, the Pauline announcement of a divine righteousness that justifies the sinner is a theological oxymoron. In a shocking display of forensic schizophrenia, the judge identifies sinners as sinners (3:23) and then immediately overturns his accurate verdict with the seemingly unjust word of justification (3:24)."[13] Linebaugh later describes this divine legal drama in terms of God's act of creation:

> "But now the righteousness of God has been revealed apart from law." This is a new righteousness, a different righteousness, as peculiar as is it [sic] paradoxical. This righteousness is *descriptive* insofar as it identities [sic] the object of its saving action as a sinner (3:23), but it is *declarative* in that it renames

---

11. We get our English word "liturgy" from the related Greek word *leitourgia* ("service").

12. Furnish, "Living to God," 195.

13. Linebaugh, "Debating," 125.

> that object. It is the one identified as a sinner who is called righteous. The divine righteousness that Paul proclaims locates and labels unrighteousness only in order to create its opposite. . . . Justification, therefore, can be said to be an act of creation, or at least creation-like act. God does not call the sinner righteous even though he or she is not; God calls the sinner righteous and thereby constitutes him or her as such. God's forensic word is right, not because it describes the empirical, but because, as God's word, it establishes reality.[14]

Paul can countenance this "forensic schizophrenia" because his readers have experienced the "renewal of their mind" (12:2), they have received the "Spirit of adoption" (8:15), and they have been "set free from sin and are now serving God" (6:22). What follows in the remainder of Romans 12–15 (and especially in Romans 12–13) provides some specific and concrete explanation of "the will of God" and what that will looks like as it is lived out in communities of gentile followers of Christ.

The Exercise of God's Gifts (Rom 12:3–8)

> **3** For I am speaking to everyone among you by the gift that was given to me: do not think more highly of yourself than is necessary to think; instead, think so that you might be well-reasoned, [giving consideration] to each person as God apportioned a measure of faith. **4** For just as we have many members in one body, and these members do not all have the same function **5** —in the same way we, who are many, are one body in Christ, and we, individually, are members of one another— **6** let us exhibit our various gifts in accordance with the grace that was given to us, whether prophecy ([let us exhibit it] according to the proportion of [our] faith) **7** or service ([let us exhibit it] in service). If someone teaches, [let that person exhibit their gift] in teaching; **8** if someone encourages, [let that person exhibit their gift] in encouragement. Let the one who shares do so sincerely; the one who leads, diligently; the one who shows mercy, cheerfully.

Having just referred to "the renewal of the mind" [*hē anakainōsis tou noos*], Paul proceeds to describe what that renewal looks like. The first step, which will also lay the groundwork for the ethical admonitions throughout the next four chapters, is to avoid thinking too highly of oneself. The syntax of v. 3 is somewhat confusing, but the general thrust is clear enough. The

---

14. Ibid., 126; original italics.

imperatival infinitive, "do not think more highly of yourself" [*mē hyperphronein*; lit. "not to think too highly of yourself"], clearly refers to having too high a view of oneself while keeping too low an opinion of others. What, specifically, Paul means by "more than is necessary to think" [*par' ho dei phronein*] is unclear, but at the very least we can say that Paul does not have a completely self-effacing view of self. Rather than having *too high* a view of oneself [*hyperphronein*], Paul tells his readers to think with the purpose of being a reasonable or sensible person.[15]

The adjective *hekastō* ("to each person") presents a problem. Either it is the indirect object of the verb "he apportioned" (see the NET, NIV[?], NASB, etc.), or it is the indirect object of an implied verb that has to be supplied from the immediate context. The ESV and NRSV imply that the verb "to think" should be understood at the end of 12:3: "think with sober judgment, each [person thinking] according to the measure of faith that God has assigned."[16] Both readings are right about one thing but wrong about another. The adverb *hōs* ("like, as") that follows *hekastō* makes it highly doubtful that this adjective functions in relation to "he apportioned" (*pace* the NET, *et al.*). However, the ESV and NRSV wrongly treat *hekastō* as the subject rather than the object of the verb. If we supply the implied verb "think, give consideration to" and render *hekastō* as the object rather than the subject of that verb, the phrase becomes, "giving consideration to each person as God apportioned a measure of faith." Paul urges his readers in v. 3 to evaluate people as though each of them were the recipient of God's gift of faith (since they are!). The danger posed by "thinking too highly of oneself," then, is precisely that we fail to treat those around us as the objects of God's blessing.

In Rom 12:4–8, Paul turns to one of his favorite metaphors for the community of faith: a singular and unitary body made up of multiple and diverse members. He uses a similar image in 1 Corinthians 12: "For just as the body is one even as it has many parts, all the parts of the body, despite being many, are one body. So also is Christ. For also by the one Spirit we all were baptized into the one body, both Jews and Greeks, both slaves and free people. All of us were made to drink of the one Spirit" (1 Cor 12:12–13). This metaphor—one body with many parts—is immediately relevant for Paul's argument in Corinthians, namely that the division and disunity fracturing the community of believers in Corinth ran contrary to

---

15. See BDF §402(2).

16. I have added the words in brackets to make clear the assumption of the verb that both the ESV and the NRSV leave implied.

Living Sacrifices

the unified essence of that community. The metaphor is less appropriate for Romans, though Paul will shortly turn to the relation between different factions among the Romans (see Rom 14:1—15:13). Why, then, introduce this metaphor here, at the beginning of Romans 12? In light of our reading of Rom 12:1-2, in which Paul's ethical vision surveys the entire landscape of Christian living and attempts to describe that landscape in its entirety, we should note that Paul's first *specific* moral instruction concerns the essential unity of the community of believers in Rome. When Jesus' followers present themselves as living sacrifices pleasing to God and allow themselves to be transformed by the renewal of their minds, one of the first effects will be a unified community comprised of diverse members with various gifts, passions, and ministries, all working for a common cause. This is what it means, after all, to be "one body in Christ" and "members of one another" (Rom 12:5).

Paul closely links the metaphor "one body, many parts" with the issue of a plurality of gifts [*charismata . . . diaphora*; Rom 12:6], just as he had done in 1 Corinthians. Paul's gift, of course, is the apostolic vocation, by which he procures the obedience of faith among all the gentiles (see Rom 1:5). He has explicitly mentioned his gift just at the point when he began giving concrete moral instruction to his readers: "For I am speaking to everyone among you by the gift [*charitos*] that was given to me" (12:3). Just a few verses later he likewise urges his readers to join him in "exhibit[ing] our various gifts in accordance with the grace that was given to us" (12:6). Their responsibility, then, is to discharge their gifts "according to the proportion of [their] faith" (v. 6) and also in conjunction with the very nature of those gifts.

The Expression of God's Love (Rom 12:9-21)

> **9** Love must be sincere. Abhor what is evil; cling to what is good. **10** Be devoted to one another in brotherly love, and hold each other in greater honor. **11** Do not shrink from showing diligence. Be enthusiastic in spirit. Give service to the Lord. **12** Rejoice in hope, endure affliction, and persevere in prayer. **13** Shoulder the needs of the saints, and pursue hospitality. **14** Bless those who persecute you; bless, and do not curse them. **15** Rejoice with those who rejoice; weep with those who weep. **16** Be in harmony with one another. Do not set your minds on being proud; instead, associate with the lowly. Do not consider yourselves especially wise. **17** Repay no one evil for evil. Have regard for what is good in the sight of all the people. **18** If

it is possible on your own account, make peace with everyone. **19** And do not seek revenge, beloved, but rather leave space for God's wrath. For it is written, "'Judgment is mine; I myself will repay,' says the Lord" (see Deut 32:35). **20** Rather,

> "If your enemy is hungry, give him something to eat;
> if he is thirsty, give him a drink,
> for in doing so you will heap burning coals upon his head"
> (Prov 25:21–22).

21 Do not be overcome by evil; rather, overcome evil by means of the good.

Another similarity between Paul's moral instructions in Romans 12 and in 1 Corinthians is the close link between the exercise of spiritual gifts (see 1 Corinthians 12, 14), on the one hand, and the expression of love between members of community of believers (see 1 Corinthians 13). The link between gifts and love in Romans 12 results in the probably imperatival clause, *hē agapē anypokritos* ("Love must be sincere"; lit. "the love without hypocrisy"), which immediately follows Paul's brief instructions on the discharge of spiritual gifts. A series of participles, again probably with imperatival force, unpacks for Paul's Roman readers what "sincere love" looks like.

Paul uses actual imperative verbs for the first time since v. 2 in Rom 12:14: "Bless those who persecute you; bless, and do not curse them" [*eulogeite kai mē katarasthe*]. Paul's imperatives clearly echo ethical instructions in the Jesus tradition, particularly the Sermon on the Plain (Luke 6:20–49): "But to you who are listening, I say: Love your enemies; those who hate you, treat them well. Bless those who curse you [*eulogeite tous katarōmenous*], and pray for those who mistreat you" (Luke 6:27–28; cp. Matt 5:43–48). The double-imperative of Rom 12:14 serves nicely not only as an example of sincere love (see 12:9) but also as a heading for the moral instructions in the remainder of the chapter.

The exhortations in Rom 12:15–19 exhibit numerous links with other passages in Romans, some nearer and some further removed. Here we simply note two of them. First, "do not consider yourselves especially wise" (v. 16) reproduces exactly Paul's motivation for disclosing "this mystery" in the previous chapter, namely "so that you might not consider yourselves especially wise" [*hina mē ēte* [*par'*] *heautois phronimoi*; 11:25]. Second, Paul's exhortation for his readers to "leave space for God's wrath" [*tē orgē*] (v. 19) echoes the beginning of the letter: "For the wrath of God [*orgē theou*] is being revealed from heaven against all human ungodliness and injustice" (1:18). Such links provide occasion for us to appreciate that the hortatory instructions in this section provide the ethical embodiment of the rhetorical argument earlier in the letter.

The end of Romans 12 wraps up this section's discussion of the response of faith to opposition (Rom 12:14–21) by citing Prov 25:21–22. The seemingly sinister motives for doing good to one's enemy seem to contradict the imperatives of v. 14 ("bless those who persecute you . . ."). After all, what kind of blessing seeks to heap burning coals [*anthrakas pyros*] on someone's head?! More significantly, given how Paul opened this paragraph ("let love be sincere"), Paul seems to open himself to the charge of being *in*sincere in his motives for nourishing one's enemy.

The dissonance between the larger context of Romans 12 and the reference from Proverbs, however, is more apparent than real. With the exception of the word *psōmizō* ("feed") in place of the original *trephō* ("feed, nourish"), Paul cites Prov 25:21–22 LXX verbatim. However, the very next line of Prov 25:22, which Paul did not quote but which he surely must have known, reads, ". . . and the Lord will repay you with good things" [*ho de kyrios antapodōsei soi agatha*]. This promise—that the Lord will repay [*antapodidōmi*] those who show love for their enemies—balances nicely with the similar promise in Rom 12:19 that the Lord will repay [*antapodidōmi*] those who oppose his people. In other words, providing food and water for one's enemy corresponds to leaving space for God's wrath. The promise that God will repay one's adversaries *and* that he will also repay one's good deeds make it possible for love to be sincere, since the person showing love can act without giving thought to whether or not the recipient of one's love will reciprocate.

We should notice, however, that Paul does not address this promise to "some *one*." Rather, he picks up the second-person singular ("you") from Proverbs 25 and continues it through the final verse of Romans 12: "Do not be overcome by evil; rather, overcome evil by means of the good" (v. 21). Paul still imagines himself addressing his interlocutor. In contrast to the interlocutor's dilemma in 7:14–25, Paul admonishes him to master evil, and to do so not by strength of will [*enkrateia*; "self-control, self-mastery"] but "by means of the good" [*en tō agathō*].

The Submission of God's People (Rom 13:1–7)

> **1** Let everyone be submissive to the authorities in positions of power, for there is no authority except by God, and those that do exist have been arranged by God. **2** So then, the one who opposes the authority has opposed the ordinance of God; such people will receive judgment for themselves. **3** For rulers are not a source of fear for the good deed but for the evil. So, do you want not to fear the authority? Then practice the good, and you will have its praise, **4** for it is a servant of God for you, for your good. But if you do practice the evil, be afraid! For it does not bear the sword in vain. For it is an avenging servant of God, bringing wrath against the one who practices the evil. **5** Therefore, it is necessary for you to submit yourselves, not only because of [God's] wrath but also because of [your] conscience. **6** For this reason, then, you ought also pay taxes, for they are administrators who are devoted to this very thing. **7** Give to everyone their due. To the one due tax, give tax. To the one due tribute, give tribute. To the one due respect, give respect. And the one due honor, give honor.

Paul's treatment of the Roman believers' relation to the state (or to "civil authorities") is often taken out of context and offered in support of the idea that Christians should exhibit good citizenship toward governing authorities.[17] I have no desire to contradict that general thesis. However, when we appreciate the location of Paul's comments in the larger context of the letter as a whole, we will see that Paul in no way encourages abject submission to Rome (in the first century CE) or to the government (in contemporary political contexts).[18] John Marshall, drawing on the concept of "hybridity" from post-colonial hermeneutics, rightly insists, "The man thrice 'beaten with rods' (a punishment meted out by Roman municipal

---

17. For example, Stein notes some thematic and lexical links between Romans 12 and 13:1–7, but then, as if it were self-evident to everyone, claims, "Even if there are ties with the immediately surrounding materials, it must nevertheless be admitted that the ties are at best loose" (Stein, "Argument," 326). Not only am I not willing to admit this looseness, I think Stein is exactly wrong, as I hope to demonstrate in what follows. Other interpreters have not felt compelled, apparently, to concede this looseness, including Bailey ("Political Paraenesis"), Dunn ("Quietism"), Engberg-Pedersen ("Stoicizing Politics"), Horrell ("Peaceable"), Olree ("Government"), Marshall ("Hybridity"), and Yoder (*Politics*, 197–200).

18. Draper ("Humble Submission") offers a reading of Rom 13:1–7 explicitly in order to critique the political context of late-1980s South Africa. Despite very real differences between Draper's reading and mine, I applaud him for explicitly and intentionally keeping this one pericope within its larger literary (as well as sociological) context (see pp. 33–35).

Living Sacrifices

lictors) and bearing the 'marks of Christ on his body' (scars, punitive tattoos? 2 Cor 11:25, Gal 6:17) is not simply a partisan of empire."[19] Paul's stance *vis-à-vis* Roman imperial authority was much more complicated than either acquiescing to their power outright or resisting it wholesale.

William Herzog has warned against assuming, as do surface-level readings of Rom 13:1–7, that Paul wrote "in an open environment that valued reflection on good citizenship and encouraged free and unhindered inquiry into such matters. . . . The fact of the matter is that neither Tiberius nor Nero was interested in free inquiry or ethical treatises on good citizenship. They were interested in obedient and servile subjects."[20] Herzog will go on to stretch too far the point that Paul, who was not a member of either Judea's or Rome's social or political elite classes, dissembled, that is, he "feign[ed] obedience and loyalty to the colonial overlords while pursuing [his] own hidden agenda."[21] Instead, Paul often enough writes boldly enough, even in situations where we might have expected him to dissemble.[22] Therefore, we can read Rom 13:1–7 straightforwardly. What is more, when we attend more closely to this passage *within its literary context*, rather than reading it as an independent unit, we will find Paul's political rhetoric surprisingly strong.[23]

Paul begins, "Let everyone [*pasa psychē*; lit. "every soul"] be submissive to the authorities in positions of power" (Rom 13:1). As a general principle of civil conduct, this seems a stark admonition. However, we should not let the chapter division obscure the fact that Paul has just

19. Marshall, "Hybridity," 170.

20. Herzog, "Dissembling," 340.

21. Ibid., 341. Similarly, Elliott ("Political Christology," 41) describes Paul's "positive" comments on "the existing political authorities" as "anomalous." Such a perspective, however, cannot answer the question why Paul should raise the issue of the believer's stance *vis-à-vis* governing authorities.

22. For example, in Phil 2:6–11, in which Paul writes from a Roman (?) prison and sings of God's exaltation of Jesus, bestowing on Jesus "the name higher than every other name" (2:9) and requiring that every knee bow and every tongue confess that Jesus—*and not Caesar!*—is Lord. Luke similarly portrays Paul as a frank and bold speaker who does not dissemble before Roman governors or native kings (see Acts 25–26).

23. Herzog ("Dissembling," 351) apparently agrees that Rom 13:1–7 is not an independent block of material; (*pace* Käsemann, *Romans*, 352; Stein, "Argument," 326), though his own analysis emphasizes his reconstructed political context and neglects completely the place of this pericope within the broader scope of Romans 12–15. Draper provides a better perspective: "Firstly, Romans 13:1–7 fits under the general heading of 12:1–2. . . . Secondly, Romans 13:1–7 is located within Paul's teaching on love as the mark of the Christian life and the fulfillment of the law (12:3–21; 13:8–14)" (Draper, "Humble Submission," 35).

been expanding the instruction to bless those who persecute, to leave space for God to take vengeance, and, more implicitly, to trust that God will repay those who persist in faithful obedience with good things.[24] Immediately on the heels of admonishing his readers to provide for their enemies' needs, to resist evil and not be overcome by it, and in fact to overcome what is evil by means of what is good, Paul urges the Romans to subject themselves to the governing authorities, "for there is no authority except by God [*hypo theou*], and those that do exist have been arranged by God" [*hypo theou tetagmenai*]. Ekkehard Stegemann makes an interesting distinction here. When Paul enjoins a particular relation to governing authorities for his readers, he uses *hypotassō* ("be subject"; Rom 13:1, 5), but when he urges a particular relation to God and/or Jesus, as Lord, he uses words like *pistis* ("faith, trust, reliability"), *pistos* ("faithful, trustworthy, reliable"), and so on:

> [I]t is revealing that Paul applies the word-stem *pist-* only to relationships between humans and the God of Israel or Christ, and probably also between Jesus (Christ) and God.... A (Roman) ruler, however, is not characterized as *pistos* ["faithful"] and he does not deserve *fides* ["faithfulness"] either. According to Romans 13, he only deserves obedience, fear and honour.[25]

Paul's admonition is more subversive than it first appears.[26] Rulers frequently claimed divine legitimation for their political power. But Paul does not quite say that Caesar—in 57 CE, that would be Nero—exercises divinely legitimate political power over the Empire. Instead, Paul is saying (rather plainly, we might add) that the Roman emperor reigns at the good pleasure of Israel's God. Paul "repeatedly identifies civic officials

---

24. Similarly, see Engberg-Pedersen, "Stoicizing Politics," 168, cited as the epigram to the present chapter.

25. Stegemann, "Coexistence and Transformation," 20, 21.

26. *Pace* Stein ("Argument," 329), who takes at face value Paul's basis of the rulers' authority in "a general truth of creation rather than upon Christological or eschatological grounds.... It is because of the fact that all authority comes from God that every person should be subject to these authorities." The basic point is right, but since Stein overlooks our pericope's literary context he fails to link this passage with other things Paul has said about God's wrath and his relation, as Creator, *vis-à-vis* creation (e.g., at Rom 1:18-32). More significantly, Stein does not acknowledge that the (human) rulers are themselves subject to the source of their authority, Israel's Creator God. Carter reads 13:1-7 as politically subversive, but he does so primarily by rejecting the "face value" of Paul's rhetoric ("Irony"). My own reading affirms both the authenticity of our pericope's surface level and recognizes the political subversion resting immediately below (rather than running contrary to) that surface level.

as God's 'servants' (*diakonos* in vv. 4a and 4b; *leitourgoi* in v. 6), thereby implying that they are *accountable* to God."[27] By way of contrast, the Stoic philosopher Seneca wrote a letter to the young Emperor, Nero, just one or two years before Paul wrote Romans. Seneca describes the Emperor's position in terms of him having been "chosen to serve on earth as *vicar of the gods*."[28] "Vicar of [Rome's] gods" might very well be a position of honor. Paul, however, relegates the civil authorities to the position "vicar of [Israel's] God." Given Israel's subjection to Rome's power, Paul's affirmation of the emperor's ruling privileges seems, at the very least, back-handed. Ekkehard Stegemann has noted this dynamic: "If we take Rom 13:1 . . . seriously, then Paul does not deny the present Roman rulers' appointment or ordinance by God. But, at the same time, it is apparent that his gospel declares only Jesus Christ as the Son of God in power and as 'our Lord.'"[29]

More significantly, we can say with some confidence that Paul does not imagine the Roman civil authorities as uniquely or solely instilled with divine authority to rule, to reward the good, or to punish the evil. We might recall at least two moments from earlier in Romans.

- First, in the letter's address, Paul identifies himself as a "slave of Christ Jesus" (Rom 1:1), and he immediately proceeded to identify Jesus as "the descendant of David according to the flesh" who was "declared son of God [*huiou theou*] with power according to the Spirit of holiness by the resurrection from the dead" (1:3–4). As we have already seen,[30] these terms ("son of David"; "son of God") functioned as royal epithets, much like the English word "majesty" can function as a designation of royalty (as in the formal address, "Your Majesty"). This is no throw-away idea, perfunctorily referred to in the letter's opening but without any lasting effect on Paul's thinking or rhetoric. At the climax of Paul's exposition of the adoption of the gentiles into the family of Israel's God, he wrote, "For as many as are led by the Spirit of God, these also are children of God" [*huioi theou*; 8:14], which attributes the same title—"son(s) of God"—to believers in Jesus as to Jesus himself. And Paul makes this coincidence of titles explicit just a few verses later, referring to his readers as those whom God "chose beforehand[31]

27. Furnish, "Living to God," 198; original emphasis.

28. *Clem.* 1.1.2 (LCL; my emphasis), cited in Engberg-Pedersen, "Stoicizing Politics," 167.

29. Stegemann, "Coexistence and Transformation," 6.

30. See my discussion of Rom 1:3–4 in chap. 2, above.

31. Paul uses *proorizō*, a compound form of the same verb he used of Jesus in Rom 1:4 [*orizō*].

to be conformed to the image of his son, so that he would be the firstborn among many brethren" (8:29). In other words, Paul uses the same words to describe Jesus as God's viceroy—one who rules on God's behalf—as well as to attribute that same status to Jesus' followers.

- Second, at the beginning of his exposition of the sovereignty of God's election of and love for Jacob, Paul emphasized that God's choice of Jacob rather than Esau preceded even their birth, "so that the plan of God [*prothesis tou theou*], according to his choice, might remain" (Rom 9:11). As part of his demonstration of how God's plan works itself out in history, he appeals to a ruler, Pharaoh, who resisted God's purpose for Israel. God hardened Pharaoh's heart as a result of Pharaoh's opposition to God, which we explained in reference to God's promise to Abraham in Gen 12:1–3. That is, God promised to bless those who bless Abraham (and his descendants) and to curse those who curse him. Pharaoh, choosing to oppress rather than release the Hebrew slaves, became the epitome of God's curse on those who mistreat Israel. But more to the present point, Pharaoh provides an excellent example of how God (and God's people) relate to an oppressive ruler who fails to recognize the truth that Paul asserts in Rom 13:1, that "there is no authority except by God, and those that do exist have been arranged by God."

These two moments from Romans—(i) Jesus' place as God's viceroy, the firstborn among many brethren, and (ii) the warning of Pharaoh, who resisted God's plan—cast the present pericope in a new light. Rather than elevating the ruling authorities and encouraging his readers to submit themselves to them, Paul *demotes* them by placing them under YHWH's authority and, by implication, under the authority of Christ and those who follow him (*viz.* Christ's *adelphoi* ["brethren"; 8:29]).[32] Paul admonishes these people—those who reign as children of God—to subject themselves to the ruling authorities immediately after having instructed them on how

32. Horrell ("Peaceable," 88) makes this point admirably: "[H]erein lies one of the enduring and intrinsic ambiguities of this text, enduring despite the efforts of exegetes to resolve its meaning one way or the other: the (Jewish) strategy Paul adopts *both* legitimates *and* limits the state's authority at one and the same time. Insofar as Paul—along with many other Jewish writers—regards rulers as there because God has given them their position, he does add a certain divine legitimation to Roman imperial rule. But equally, by insisting that it is God who has granted the rulers their role, Paul, again along with the same Jewish writers, relativizes their position: it is theirs not on the grounds of their own might or (pseudo-divine) status, but only because God has chosen to allow it to be so; and what God has granted God can equally take away—and may well do so soon (cf. Rom 13:11–14; 1 Cor 2:6; 15:24; 1 Thess 5:2–3)."

to appropriately respond to their persecutors and enemies (12:14-21). The result is a subtle—but not *too* subtle—encouragement to trust that God sees their plight and will respond appropriately, whether at the *eschaton* or, as with Pharaoh, in the midst of history.[33]

Given this view of the ruling authorities, and especially in light of the exhortations in Rom 12:14-21 that God will exact vengeance on the enemies of his people and, by implication, repay good things to those who provide for their enemies, we might not be surprised to find that Paul casts disobedience to the ruling authorities as disobedience to God himself (13:2). Clearly Paul has in view the Roman believers and their response to Roman civil authorities. Paul's readers, as they live out the obedience of faith that Paul works to procure from among all the gentiles (see Rom 1:5), should exhibit a positive mode of citizenship that is not defiant to civil order. But, given the larger literary context of 13:1-7, Paul *also* has in mind the Roman civil authorities—including the emperor—and their response to the gospel of Israel's Messiah (= king), Jesus. Paul's readers, as they live out the obedience of faith under the civil authority of the Roman Empire (and especially the emperor), should live in the confidence that God will hold the ruling authorities to account, whether at the *eschaton* or, as with Pharaoh, in the midst of history.[34]

Paul goes on to explain in vv. 3-4 the proper function of civil authority (perhaps to the interlocutor).[35] These verses support my thesis,

---

33. Again, *pace* Stein ("Argument," 331; see also p. 336), who forces a choice between "logical" and "eschatological" judgment. Stein never explains why Paul must have *specifically* and *only* one of these senses of *krima* ("judgment") in view rather than a less precisely defined conception. I read Paul more openly, not claiming that he has *both* senses of *krima* in view, but also not forcing him to mean one and not the other. Rather, his use of *krima* is simply more open-ended than Stein's comments allow. Interestingly, one of the early concerns in Seneca's *De Clementia* (1.1.3-4) is that Nero should be able to give an account to the gods for how he has exercised his authority on their behalf, that "he has positively let clemency (*clementia*) as opposed to (in itself justified) sternness (*severitas*) have the upper hand" (Engberg-Pedersen, "Stoicizing Politics," 167).

34. I want to emphasize: I do not think Paul delays all satisfaction for injustice, whether perpetrated by the state or otherwise, to the *eschaton* (including the final resurrection and Jesus' *parousia*). After all, despite his clear expectation that the restoration of creation was yet to come (see Rom 8:18-30), Paul also clearly thinks God is currently revealing his wrath against human ungodliness and injustice (1:18-32). I see no reason to suppose that Paul thinks immoral gentiles can experience God's vengeance (see 12:19) in the present age, but immoral civil authorities cannot. Despite the clear call for Paul's readers to subject themselves to the governing authorities, Paul nevertheless leaves room for the exercise of God's judgment against those authorities when they exhibit the ungodliness and injustice against which God is currently revealing his wrath.

35. Winter ("Christian Benefactors," 94) reads the second-person singular address

stated in my discussion of v. 1, that this pericope is surprisingly subversive because it subjects the Emperor to the rule of Israel's God. (Of course, Israel [= Judea] is currently under *Rome's* authority, so the idea that Caesar might be *YHWH*'s servant [*diakonos*] would certainly strike Paul's readers [*in Rome!*] as remarkable.) Jonathan Draper, appealing to the idea of a "social contract" in which two socially unequal parties agree to relate to each other in mutually beneficial ways, rightly recognizes the provisional quality of Paul's comments about the power of civil authorities. "If the concept of 'social contract' is what really underlies Paul's legitimation of the state in Romans 13, then a state which ceases to reward virtue and punish vice, which ceases to protect its citizens but preys upon them, would also cease to receive legitimation."[36] We might go even further: such a state would become the *object* of God's wrath rather than the *servant* (= *instrument*) of that wrath.

Given the confidence Paul has just exhibited that God would exact his vengeance [*ekdikēsis*] upon evil (Rom 12:19), Paul performs a surprising rhetorical maneuver and identifies Caesar—Rome's emperor!—as God's instrument for exacting his vengeance [*diakonos . . . ekdikos* ("avenging servant"; 12:4)]. In fact, these verses help explain why Paul finds it so important that his readers submit themselves to Rome's authority: it would be an odd situation if the pagan emperor in Rome had to bring God's wrath to bear upon the community of Jesus' followers![37] Paul's exhortations are meant to avoid this situation. After all, God's wrath is being revealed against all human ungodliness and injustice (1:18); God's wrath [*orgē*] should not also apply to Jesus' followers. The expression of the civil authorities' wrath against injustice is, Paul says, God's wrath; "[s]ince the state is a servant of God (13:1b and 13:4a), there is indeed a sense in which its judgment is God's judgment."[38]

---

in Rom 13:1–7 as a tacit acknowledgement that "[t]he cost of a benefaction was very considerable and would be beyond the ability of some, if not most, members of the church." In other words, Paul addresses a particular (but still rhetorical) person, "you," who has above-average access to resources (esp. material resources). Perhaps. But given the regular and consistent appearance of Paul's interlocutor since Rom 2:1, I find it more likely that the second-person singular language in 13:1–7 provides a continuity across the entire letter (rather than that Paul introduces a second, and different, dialogue partner in [and for] this pericope).

36. Draper, "Humble Submission," 37.

37. This is precisely the problem with Israel. Her subjection to foreign (= pagan) nations as a punishment for her covenantal unfaithfulness is exactly backwards; God's covenant people, and *not* foreign nations, ought to be God's servant.

38. Stein, "Argument," 331. I do not share Stein's ambivalence ("there is a sense . . .").

But we might say something about Paul's reference to "the good deed" [*to agathon ergon*]. Draper rightly points out that Paul's language throughout this pericope has secular (= human) power structures rather than spiritual or angelic powers in view. Included in this secular political language, "'good works' are the mark of good citizenship."[39] As "the mark of good citizenship," we might already recognize that Paul is not actually saying that civil authorities reward those citizens who live morally upright lives—who love their families well, who work faithfully and diligently at their occupations, etc.[40] Rather, Paul acknowledges that political power structures reward people not for being morally upright but for exhibiting the marks of good citizenship.

Bruce Winter goes even further. Winter argues that "good works" refers to acts of public benefaction and that civil authorities were expected to reward public benefactors. "[N]ot only did rulers praise and honour those who undertook good works which benefited the city, but at the same time they promised likewise to publicly honour others who would undertake similar benefactions in the future."[41] The provision of some act of kindness to a municipality, always at considerable personal expense, put local authorities in their benefactor's debt, a debt that the authorities paid by publicly honoring their benefactors.[42] This is a key point: *civil authorities experienced social and cultural pressure under the expectation that they would repay benefactions (= good works) with public displays of honor.* Inscriptions that celebrated some act of public beneficence also made sure to state explicitly that "the city had met its *obligation of gratitude*

Rather, as I already explained, the state's wrath against injustice is God's wrath against injustice; the state is, after all, the avenging servant of God. However, when the civil authorities become the *perpetrators* of injustice rather than its *avengers*, the response of the people of God to the governing authorities necessarily changes.

39. Draper, "Humble Submission," 35.

40. It would be absurd to suggest that governments monitored and rewarded moral behavior among their citizenry. Cranfield appears to recognize the absurdity as he tries to walk away from exactly this reading of Rom 13:1-7: "Paul means that consciously or unconsciously, willingly or unwillingly, in one way or another, the power will praise the good work and punish the evil" (Cranfield, "Observations," 245; cited in Winter, "Christian Benefactors," 93). Olree ("Government," 95) makes a similar point vis-à-vis the punishment of "the evil deed": "whatever Paul meant when he said governments (including the Roman government) are established by God to 'bring punishment to the wrongdoer,' he could not have meant that governments are established by God for the purpose of outlawing all sin, or even most sin."

41. Winter, "Christian Benefactors," 87; see also my comments on Rom 5:7; 8:28, above.

42. See ibid., 91-92, for a discussion of "The Praising of Benefactors."

for the present public work bestowed on it."[43] Similarly, Philo, writing about Moses, but in the context of Roman-era Alexandria, may suggest that the reward [*epainoi kai timai*; "praises and honors"] due to benefactors is a legal obligation [*syn nomō*; "in accordance with law"].[44] Therefore, I read Paul as enjoining positive civic engagement among his readers rather than individual, private morality *vis-à-vis* the governing authorities. Believers in Rome ought to be more than morally upright individuals; they ought to be positive social and cultural influences more broadly.

"Therefore," Paul says, "it is necessary for you to submit yourselves, not only because of [God's] wrath but also because of [your] conscience. For this reason, then, you ought also pay taxes, for they are administrators[45] who are devoted to this very thing. Give to everyone their due. To the one due tax, give tax. To the one due tribute, give tribute. To the one due respect, give respect. And to the one due honor, give honor" (Rom 13:5–7). The end of the pericope draws the appropriate behavioral consequences from the preceding discussion. The submission to civil authorities ought not solely serve the negative function of avoiding wrath; rather, it serves the positive function of conforming to conscience. The contrast with Paul's speech-in-character in Rom 7:14–25 seems deliberate: Paul, speaking *as* (rather than *to*) his interlocutor, found himself unable to achieve the dictates of his conscience:

> 21 Therefore, here's what I discover about Torah,[46] which I discovered because I wanted to do good: evil dwells in me.

---

43. Ibid., 90; my emphasis. A little further on, Winter continues, "Literary sources strongly support the epigraphic evidence. They show that great importance was attached to meeting the obligation with gratitude. This obligation was not seen simply as a cultural convention, but *some saw it as 'a law'. Benefactions could be called 'loans' which were repaid with gratitude, and they should be reclaimed with monetary compensation if not properly acknowledged*. Such was the expectation of the benefactor that due recognition would be given in the appropriate way. Others saw failure to acknowledge public works adequately as a sin" (ibid., 90–91; my emphasis).

44. Philo, *Mos.* 1:154, cited by Coleman, "Binding," 308. If, on the other hand, the phrase "in accordance with law" [*syn nomō*] modifies *katorthountōn* ("those who act rightly" in accordance with law) rather than *epainoi kai timai* ("praises and honors" in accordance with law), then Philo's relevance for the current discussion disappears.

45. "'[M]inister' (*leitourgos*) refers to junior authorised officials in the state service" (Draper, "Humble Submission," 35). Paul continues to demote the elite Roman imperial authorities, calling them *leitourgoi* (= bureaucrats?) who, as he has said, exercise not their own authority but the authority of the Creator God of Israel. More importantly, Paul uses the same word to describe Roman imperial authority, on the one hand, and his own position *vis-à-vis* Israel's God (see Rom 15:16), on the other.

46. Romans 7:21 opens: *heuriskō ara ton nomon* (lit. "I find, therefore, the law"). But

> **22** For I delight in the Torah of God in my innermost being, **23** but I see a different Torah at work in my members, which wages war against my mind's Torah and takes me captive by means of Torah's judgment in my members against sin. (Rom 7:21–23)

In contrast to the hopeless situation of the gentile who sets out to submit to the full yoke of Torah-observance, which Paul chronicled in Romans 2–7, here in 13:1–7 Paul fully expects his interlocutor to be able to submit to God's authority, not only to avoid the experience of [God's] wrath, but also to act in full accordance with his conscience.

Of course, the difference between Romans 7 and Romans 13 is precisely the presence and function of the Spirit, which Paul discussed at length in Romans 8. That Spirit, here in 13:1–7, results in the full submission of Jesus' followers to civil authorities, authorities that "have been arranged by God" (13:1), which are "God's avenging servant [to bring] wrath against the one who practices the evil" (13:4), but which are themselves subject to God's authority and, if they do not fulfill their civil responsibilities appropriately, will experience God's vengeance (see 12:19).

One last point on this pericope: Thomas Coleman focuses his attention narrowly on the language of obligation in v. 7, and he divides the fourfold list of obligations (tribute, tax, respect, honor) into two kinds. The first two encompass physical or material obligations to the civil authorities, while the latter two entail relational or social responsibilities.[47] Here, however, I am only interested in Paul's reference to "tribute" [*phoros*].[48] Coleman stresses—rightly, in light of the lexicographical evidence[49]—that the payment of *phoros* carried "overtones of subjugation. . . . [T]ime and again in both Jewish and non-Jewish authors, we read of nations and cities that were conquered and forced to pay, quite begrudgingly, *phoros*."[50] This

---

Paul's (or, more accurately, Paul's *persona's*) point is not that he has found "the law" (= Torah) but rather that he has found something *about* "the law." Hence my translation, "Therefore, here's what I discover about Torah"; similarly, see Wright, "Romans," 569.

47. Coleman, "Binding," 309, passim.

48. "[T]hat which is brought in as payment to a state, with implication of dependant status" (BDAG, s.v.). Similarly, LSJ (s.v.) defines *phoros*: "*that which is brought in, tribute*, such as is paid *by subjects to a ruling state*, as by the Asiatic Greeks to Athens." They go on to translate *phorou hypoteleis* as "subject to pay *tribute*." LN (s.v.) agree: "a payment made by the people of one nation to another, *with the implication that this is a symbol of submission and dependence*" (my emphasis).

49. See the previous footnote.

50. Coleman, "Binding," 310, 311. Coleman (ibid., 312–13) goes on to read Paul's

concluding reference to *phoros* in v. 7 reintroduces the issue of submission, with which our pericope began in v. 1.[51] By submitting to the payment of *phoros* to the governing authorities, Paul's readers provided a concrete and verifiable demonstration of their loyalty to the state. However, Paul's exhortation for his readers to provide this demonstration comes in precisely that place where he explains to his readers that the civil authorities are under God's authority and that, if they are not faithful as servants [*diakonos*] or ministers [*leitourgoi*] to a higher authority, they will experience the very wrath which Paul has already said is now being revealed from heaven (see 1:18).

The Full Measure of Torah (Rom 13:8–14)

> **8** Owe no one anything, other than the debt to love one another, for the one who loves his neighbor has fulfilled Torah. **9** For the [requirement], "You shall not commit adultery" (Deut 5:17 LXX), "you shall not murder" (Deut 5:18 LXX), "you shall not steal" (Deut 5:19), "you shall not covet" (Deut 5:21), even if there is any other commandment, it is summed up in this saying: "You shall love your neighbor as yourself" (Lev 19:18). **10** Love for a neighbor does not produce [any] evil. Therefore, love is the full measure of Torah.
>
> **11** So then, since we know the time—that the hour has already arrived for you to arise from slumber, for now our salvation is nearer than when we [first] believed; **12** the night is far gone, and the day has drawn near—therefore, let us lay aside the practices of the darkness, and let us arm ourselves with the weapons of the light. **13** Let us walk decently, as befits the day, sated with neither food nor drink, neither sexually immoral nor licentious, neither contentious nor envious. **14** Instead, arm yourselves with the Lord Jesus Christ, and do not make any provision for the flesh, which leads to lust.

Hot on the heels of urging his Roman readers to fulfill their "obligations" [*opheilas*]—whether of tribute and tax [*phoros* and *telos*, respectively] or

---

reference to *phoros* in Rom 13:7 in terms of the Jewish component of Paul's audience. However, given the lack of any evidence *internal to Paul's letter itself* that Paul imagined himself writing to an audience that included Jewish believers, I am not well-disposed to the conclusions Coleman offers to his otherwise very helpful discussion.

51. Dunn ("Quietism," 60, 66) highlights the turbulence regarding taxes (esp. indirect taxes [i.e. *telē*]) in the years leading up to 58 CE and notes the timely relevance of Paul's exhortation regarding payment of taxes in Rom 13:6–7.

Living Sacrifices

respect and honor [*phobos* and *timē*, respectively]—Paul summarizes the principle underlying Rom 13:7: "Owe no one anything, other than the debt to love one another" (13:8a). Easy enough (in principle, if not in practice), though we should recognize that Paul, having elevated believers' civic responsibilities to a theological principle (disobedience to governing authorities = disobedience to God), now elevates the debt to love to an even higher position. One's debts [*opheilai*] to the state can (and should) be paid; one's debt [*opheilō*] to love remains perpetually outstanding and is always due.[52]

Paul takes a surprising turn in v. 8b: "for the one who loves his neighbor [*ton heteron*; lit. "the other, someone else"] has fulfilled Torah." Paul refers to Torah [(*ho*) *nomos*] often enough.[53] His references to Torah, however, diminished abruptly after Rom 7:7-25, and he has not mentioned Torah since 10:4-5.[54] In fact, the disappearance of the *nomos* from Romans corresponds closely with the appearance of the *pneuma* ("Spirit, spirit").[55] In other words, precisely at the moment when Paul's rhetoric begins to focus on the presence and function of the Spirit in God's economy, he stops concentrating on the presence and function of Torah. Hence my description of v. 8b as "a surprising turn." As Paul describes the community of those who walk according to the Spirit (see Rom 8:4), he brings the community's ethic back to Torah. This seems contradictory. On the one hand, Paul rejects outright that his gentile interlocutor should pursue righteousness by keeping Torah. Instead, the righteousness of God is being revealed "apart from Torah . . . through the faithfulness of Jesus" (3:21–22). On the other hand, Paul says plainly that love of neighbor, broadly referred to as *ton heteron* (lit. "the other"), "fulfills Torah" [*nomon peplērōken*].

On closer inspection the apparent contradiction comes to naught, and in actual fact Paul has been making precisely this point all along. Despite the marginalization of Torah implicit in some of Paul's affirmations (especially that the revelation of God's righteousness now takes place "apart from Torah"), we have also noted that Paul reserves an honored and

---

52. See Engberg-Pedersen, "Stoicizing Politics," 169–71.

53. Paul uses *nomos* seventy-four times in fifty verses across the whole of Romans.

54. "For Christ is the *telos* of Torah unto righteousness for everyone who believes. For Moses writes concerning the righteousness that is [revealed] by Torah, that 'The person who does them shall live by them'" (Rom 10:4–5, citing Lev 18:5).

55. Paul uses *pneuma* thirty-four times in twenty-seven verses across the whole of Romans. Whereas 92 percent of Paul's references to Torah (sixty-eight of seventy-four) occur in or prior to Rom 8:1–11, 85 percent of Paul's references to Spirit (or spirit; twenty-nine of thirty-four references) occur in or after 8:1–11.

privileged place for Torah in the fulfillment of God's promise to Abraham. Torah, in conjunction with the Prophets, offers testimony on behalf of God's righteousness (Rom 3:22), makes sin known for what it is (3:20; 7:13), and is established by means of the faith [*pistis*] that is both the basis of and the response to the gospel Paul preaches (3:31). We may perceive contradiction in Paul's treatment of Torah across the whole of his letter to the Romans precisely because Paul makes two overlapping arguments simultaneously:

- On the one hand, the fulfillment of God's promises to Abraham (esp. Gen 12:1–3) fulfills Torah's purpose, which was to reveal God's righteousness by means of Israel's faithfulness and obedience to YHWH, the Creator God.

- On the other hand, Israel's faith-less-ness to Torah obscured rather than revealed God's righteousness, and so the efforts of Paul's gentile interlocutor to keep Torah's terms and conform to the righteousness of God by means of "works of Torah" could never have succeeded.

Given these two arguments, we could rightly say that Paul describes gentile believers in Jesus as "those who keep Torah" [*hoi poiētai nomou*; lit. "the doers of Torah" (see Rom 2:13)] even as he insists without equivocation that God accomplished the very thing Torah was unable to accomplish, and he did so "by sending his own son in the likeness of sinful flesh" (8:3). We saw earlier that Paul reduces Torah to worshipping the Creator God rather than the created gods of the gentiles.[56] In Rom 13:8 Paul reduces Torah to love of neighbor: the person who loves another person, by means of that act of love, accomplishes Torah's purpose. How, then, might we understand both phenomena—(i) worshipping the Creator God rather than the created gods of the gentiles, and (ii) love of neighbor—both as the fulfillment Torah?

Recall Paul's description, in Romans 1, of the consequences of gentile idolatry and their worship of created images in place of the Creator God. Those who refuse to worship YHWH "are filled with all unrighteousness, wickedness, greediness, and malice; they are full of envy, murder, strife, treachery, malevolence. They are gossipers, slanderers, haters of God, insolent, arrogant, boasters, contrivers of evil deeds, disobedient to their parents, senseless, faithless, heartless, merciless" (Rom 1:29–31). If failure to worship Israel's Creator God leads to such antisocial behavior, then the proper recognition of the relationship between God, as Creator, and the

---

56. See our discussion of Rom 2:13–15 in chap. 3.

Living Sacrifices

works of his hands must lead to pro-social behavior. Paul assumes a rather close link between worshipping the Creator God, on the one hand, and loving others, on the other. Throughout the course of his letter, Paul likens the fulfillment of Torah in terms of both: right worship of God in Romans 2; right relationship with others in Romans 13.[57]

Paul then encapsulates the Decalogue (see Exod 20:1-17; Deut 5:6-21)[58] as Torah's epitome. More than this, he goes on to epitomize even the Decalogue by citing the love commandment from Leviticus: "Even if there is any other commandment, it is summed up in this saying [*en tō logō*]: 'You shall love your neighbor [*ton plēsion sou*] as yourself'" (Rom 13:9, citing Lev 19:18). The emphasis on love of neighbor helps explain Paul's references to only the second half of the Decalogue ("you shall not commit adultery; you shall not murder; you shall not steal, you shall not covet"; Rom 13:9, all of which pertain to horizontal (person-to-person) relationships more directly than to the vertical (person-to-God) relationship. However, in light of the connections we noted in the previous paragraph between proper worship of the Creator God and appropriate interpersonal

---

57. Without suggesting any kind of formal or literary link between Paul and the Synoptic Gospel tradition, I simply note the similarity with Jesus' response to the question of the greatest commandment (see Mark 12:28-34; Matt 22:34-40; cf. Luke 10:25-28).

58. The following table lays out the basic contents and order of the Ten Commandments in Exodus and Deuteronomy. According to this data, Paul apparently reproduces the Deuteronomic form of the Decalogue, though I think it likely that Paul cites the Decalogue from memory rather than from a written text.

The Decalogue in Romans 13

	Exodus 20:1-17	Deuteronomy 5:6-21	Romans 13:9
1.	No other gods before me (v. 3)	No other gods before me (v. 7)	
2.	No graven images (vv. 4-6)	No graven images (vv. 8-10)	
3.	Do not take the Lord's name in vain (v. 7)	Do not take the Lord's name in vain (v. 11)	
4.	Remember the Sabbath (vv. 8-11)	Keep the Sabbath (vv. 12-15)	
5.	Honor your father and mother (v. 12)	Honor your father and mother (v. 16)	
6.	Do not commit adultery (v. 13)	Do not commit adultery (v. 17)	Do not commit adultery
7.	Do not steal (v. 14)		
8.	Do not commit murder (v. 15)	Do not commit murder (v. 18)	Do not commit murder
[7.]		Do not steal (v. 19)	Do not steal
9.	Do not bear false witness (v. 16)	Do not bear false witness (v. 20)	
10.	Do not covet your neighbor's wife or other possessions (v. 17)	Do not covet your neighbor's wife or other possessions (v. 21)	Do not covet

relationships, I would not make very much at all of his focus on love of neighbor and, in contrast to Mark 12:28–34 parr., Paul's elision of love of God. In contrast to the disastrous consequences of suppressing the truth of God (see 1:18–32), "Love for a neighbor does not produce [any] evil" (13:10). Paul then goes on to draw an important conclusion, which conclusion strongly echoes his argument back in 2:6-11: "Therefore, love is the full measure [*plērōma*] of Torah" (13:10).[59]

The conclusion of Romans 13 resumes the high-level, abstract ethical admonitions like those we saw in Rom 12:1–2 (in contrast to the comparatively detailed, concrete exhortations of 12:3—13:10). The language of v. 13—"sated with neither food nor drink, neither sexually immoral nor licentious, neither contentious nor envious"—befits the rhetoric of self-mastery. Recall that Paul, speaking as his proselyte interlocutor, found Torah utterly useless for equipping him to resist the onslaught of his fleshly passions (see 7:15, 18–19). How do we explain the change in Paul's expectations? Something "apart from (= other than) Torah" has now equipped his gentile readers to overcome the lusts of their flesh and to master their passions. The militaristic connotations of the rhetoric of self-mastery fit our current context, since Paul urges his readers to join him in "arm[ing] ourselves with the weapons [*ta hopla*][60] of light." Rather than engaging the lusts of the flesh armed with Torah and its practices, Paul exhorts his readers, "arm yourselves with the Lord Jesus Christ." Paul enjoins his readers (gentile believers in Rome) to engage this particular battle (against the lusts of the flesh), and to do so equipped with this particular armament (the weapons of light and the Lord Jesus Christ).

---

59. Romans 13:10, comprised of just twelve Greek words, shares two key terms with Rom 2:6-11. Both passages mention *kakon* ("evil [thing]"; 2:9) and *ergazomai* ("do, accomplish"; 2:10). Paul also uses the compound verb *katergazomai* ("do, accomplish") in 2:9, for all intents and purposes a synonym with *ergazomai*.

60. The related word *hoplitēs* refers to "*a heavy-armed foot-soldier, man-at-arms, who carried a large shield (hoplon), whence the name*" (LSJ, s.v.).

14

The Offering of the Weak

Paul and the Particular Assemblies in Rome

> There is almost universal agreement (it appears to be an almost unquestioned fact) that the "weak" were Christian Jews *who still practiced the Law and Jewish customs (with most maintaining that this group would have included "God-fearing" gentiles as well)*, and that the "strong" were Christian gentiles *(as well as Christian Jews like Paul who have supposedly abandoned Jewish practices)*.[1]

We find ourselves once again at the beginning of a section that has often been removed from its literary context and read as an independent pericope. Paul's exhortations regarding welcoming the weak [*ton asthenounta*; Rom 14:1] and the preservation of fellowship between the weak and the strong [*hoi dynatoi*; 15:1] are usually read in terms of identifying the former as "Jewish-Christians," or "Judaizing Christians," while the latter are often equated with "gentile Christians." For example, Richard Longenecker refers to Paul's "ethical appeals in 14:1—15:13 to 'the strong,' who seem to be Gentile Christians, asking them to express Christian love and tolerance toward 'the weak,' who seem to be Jewish Christians."[2] I have some reservations about this reading of Romans 14–15. In particular, this

---

1. Nanos, *Mystery*, 87.
2. Longenecker, *Introducing*, 77.

interpretation relies on the ambiguity of the word "seem" without any discussion about *why* we should think Paul means "gentile Christians" when he says "the strong" and "Jewish Christians" when he says "the weak."[3] Paul would certainly have agreed that Jewish and gentile followers of Jesus should value their fellowship together more highly than they value any of their distinctive practices. However, nothing in the letter so far—and we have come quite a long way indeed—has required or even suggested that Paul has in mind an audience with a Jewish component. It would be strange if, at this late moment, Paul set his focus on the relation between two groups who have not figured in the letter up to this point. In this section, then, we will have to face anew the question: what is Paul on about?

Romans 14–15 and Paul's Encoded Audience

Let us first observe an inherent circularity regarding Paul's intended audience, on the one hand, and the function of this section of the letter (*viz.* Rom 14:1—15:13), which has undergirded the popular reading of this text.[4] Richard Longenecker, for example, explicitly begins his discussion of Paul's intended audience by turning to data *outside* the text itself in order to develop a hypothesis about "Rome in Paul's day," "Jews and Judaism at Rome," and "Christianity at Rome."[5] Not surprisingly, then, Longenecker gives priority to material *other than* Romans to develop an idea of Paul's intended audience *for* Romans itself.[6] The evidence leads us to conclude that, by the time Paul wrote Romans in 57 CE, the Jewish population of

---

3. Similarly, see Watson, "Law in Romans," 106.

4. See Longenecker's reference to "mirror reading" (*Introducing*, 55). Thorsteinsson notes rightly, "There is not much in the text itself that suggests that Paul is here dealing with groups of 'Jewish Christians' and 'gentile Christians.' He certainly does not identify them as such" (*Interlocutor*, 97).

5. Longenecker, *Introducing*, 56–75.

6. Thorsteinsson acknowledges that "[A]rguments for Jews being among Paul's intended audience have both been based on Romans itself as well as external sources for the historical circumstances behind the letter. The arguments are basically centered on the following 1) the identity of the 'weak' and the 'strong' in Romans 14–15; 2) Paul's greetings at the end of the letter; and 3) various aspects of chapters 1–11 which, together with certain implicit addresses, allegedly indicate a Jewish readership. The first two focus mainly on external factors, *viz.* the potential composition of 'Roman Christianity' at the time when Paul wrote his letter, whereas the last claims to be mostly concerned with internal elements" (*Interlocutor*, 89). Even so, advocates for a Jewish component of Paul's implied readers usually emphasize external factors in their reconstructions of Paul's audience.

Rome had begun to recover from the Edict of Claudius (49 CE), so that there were both Jewish and gentile Christians in the city. For this reason, Longenecker infers that Paul must have intended to address the whole Roman church, with its mix of Jewish and gentile constituents. But Longenecker does not answer this question: even if there were Jews in Rome in 57 CE, does Paul necessarily have them in mind as recipients of this letter? The argument, in effect, is that since both Jewish and gentile believers in Jesus must have lived in Rome in 57 CE, Paul must have been writing to both Jews and gentiles.

We can contrast Longenecker with Andrew Das's approach to the question of Paul's audience. Das takes seriously the fact that, "[A]t several key points in the letter, Paul identifies or describes the members of his audience as gentiles," and so he *begins* with the evidence internal to the letter itself.[7] Only after he has taken account of the data from Romans itself does he turn to consider the external evidence with which Longenecker began.[8] Within the text of Romans itself, Das concedes that 14:1—15:6 offers "some of the strongest evidence for a Jewish constituency in the Roman congregations."[9] He notes that the language of 14:1—15:6 clearly reflects Jewish practices, including the distinction between "unclean" [*koinos*] and "clean" foods [*kathara*] and abstinence from meat and wine "in hostile circumstances where [Jews] had no control over their diet."[10] However, if Paul's references to and descriptions of his audience in Romans explicitly identify them as gentiles, then Romans 14–15 does not address the problem of Jewish practices *per se* but rather the observance of Jewish practices *by gentiles*.[11] Kathy Ehrensperger rightly admonishes us to appreciate that

7. Das, *Solving*, 53–114 (p. 54 quoted).

8. See ibid., 149–202; Das, "Gentile-Encoded Audience," 40–44.

9. Das, *Solving*, 106.

10. Ibid., 106–7. For a careful discussion of the meaning and translation of *koinos* ("impure, unclean, defiled, polluted"), see Thiessen, *Contesting Conversion*, 126–31. Gentiles also distinguished animals that were acceptable for food or days that were special or holy. For example, Plutarch discusses the (apparently peculiar) Roman practice of abstaining from eating woodpeckers (*Quaest. rom.* 21). However, the vocabulary Paul uses to talk about the distinctions between "clean" [*kathara*] and "unclean" [*koinos*] are distinctive to marking and describing specifically Jewish practices (Das, *Solving*, 107–8; *pace* Klein, "Paul's Purpose," 36). See also Dunn, *Romans*, 2:800; Jewett, *Romans*, 859–60.

11. Das, *Solving*, 109; see also Das, *Paul*, 67–69. *Pace* Witherington, who moves too quickly from Jewish dietary regulations to Jewish Christians: "Even more to the point, the term *koinon* in Rom 14:14 is used in contexts where Jewish dietary rules involving clean and unclean food are in view. This means that Paul is indeed dealing

"[r]itual and cult"—including purity rules and dietary taboos—"are not only significant aspects of a Jewish way of life; they are key aspects of life for all Mediterranean and Near Eastern cultures in antiquity."[12] Paul may use terminology distinctively appropriate to *Jewish* discourse and praxis, but that does not mean that *only* Jews observed such distinctions.[13]

Reading Romans 14–15 in terms of Paul's encoded gentile audience avoids portraying Paul as coy and indirect, referring to "the strong" and "the weak" rather than explicitly and plainly naming his audience. These labels—"the strong" and "the weak"—are not code for "gentile Christians" and "Jewish Christians."[14] As Das explains:

> Because the weak are gentiles observing certain Jewish ritual observances, *of course Paul does not identify the strong as gentiles and the weak as Jews,* and of course, in view of his more than adequate description, Paul assumes the addressees will recognize who the weak and strong are.[15]

---

with a situation in Rome that involves the *kashrut* laws. In short, Paul is dealing with a Jewish Christian versus Gentile Christian issue here" (Witherington and Hyatt, *Romans*, 333–34).

12. Ehrensperger, "Called to Be Saints," 94.

13. "Requirements of purification, or adhering to either rituals to restore, or maintain, certain patterns of behavior to preserve a state of purity, is [sic] thus obviously not a specific concern of Jews but of all peoples around the Mediterranean in the ancient world. Thus purity regulations as such are not exceptional and would not have distinguished the Jews from any other group or people" (ibid., 95). That is, Jews were not unique in the Roman Mediterranean for differentiating the holy from the profane (or clean from unclean) but rather only for the distinctive ways they marked that differentiation. Our reading of Romans 14–15 suggests some of the gentiles to whom Paul is writing—who were already accustomed to distinguishing pure from impure—were positively disposed toward Jewish patterns of differentiation.

14. Wright provides a helpful nuance, even amidst a reading that accepts both Jewish and gentile elements among Paul's audience: "The best reading of this problem, I think, is that the divisions Paul knows to exist within the Roman church have at least a strong element about them of the Jew/Gentile tension that has been underneath so much of the letter. This is by no means to say that 'the weak' are Jewish Christians and 'the strong' are Gentile Christians. Paul is himself a Jewish Christian who sees himself as one of the 'strong'; and, if Galatians is anything to go by, there might well be Gentile Christians whom he would categorize as 'weak.' Rather, the matters about which disagreement has arisen, threatening to thwart united worship of the one God from people of all sorts, stem not principally from other types of cultural pressures, but from the continuing varied influence of the Jewish law within parts of the Christian community" (Wright, "Romans," 731).

15. Das, *Solving*, 109; emphasis in the original.

The Offering of the Weak

This reading also avoids the inherent circularity of the more traditional reading of Romans 14-15 in terms of a mixed Jewish/gentile audience. According to the traditional reading:

- Paul addresses a mixed audience of Jews and gentiles because the letter addresses Jewish concerns.
- Therefore,
  Paul uses "the strong" to refer to gentile Christians, whose faith is unhindered by scruples about things like Jewish dietary practices and Sabbath observance, and "the weak" to refer to Jewish Christians, who care about such things.
  Therefore,
- Paul addresses a mixed audience of Jews and gentiles . . .

Against this circularity, Das takes seriously Paul's encoded audience of gentile Christians, and when he comes to Rom 14:1—15:13, he reads the division between "the strong" and "the weak" in terms of the audience Paul has already explicitly addressed.[16] In other words, Rom 14:1—15:13 does not provide evidence against our thesis that Paul writes Romans for a gentile audience. Instead, the data that led us to conclude that Paul wrote for a gentile audience, including Rom 1:5-7, 13-15; and 11:13, now lead us to read 14:1—15:13 as a part of Paul's admonition for gentile Christians in Rome. Moreover, this section of Romans actually preserves evidence that, *even here*, Paul imagines himself writing for a gentile audience.[17] All of this confusion about Paul's audience arises in the tension between two relatively uncontroversial observations. First, Paul only ever explicitly re-

---

16. Klein also rejects reading Rom 14:1—15:13 as a division between "strong" gentile Christians and "weak" Jewish Christians ("Paul's Purpose," 36) for multiple reasons, including: "according to 14:1-14ff., not the 'weak' but the 'strong' seem to be on the offensive." See also Karris in the same volume ("Occasion," 65-84).

17. "[I]n Rom 15:14-18, when Paul apologizes to the narrative 'you' for the intermittent harshness of the epistle, he links his manner of writing to 'you' with his ministry 'to the Gentiles.' This correlation suggests at the least that the intended audience in 15:14-18 is Gentiles, which makes it reasonable to conclude that *the intended audience is the same in the immediately preceding 15:7-13*. . . . Paul's exhortation in Rom 14-15 culminates in a call for the 'weak' and 'strong' parties to 'welcome one another, just as Christ welcomed *you*' (15:7), a second person plural which no doubt corresponds to the Gentiles indicated by the repeated second person plural pronouns in 15:14-18 (Garroway, "Circumcision," 307, 311; my emphasis). Garroway goes on to immediately draw the relevant (and significant!) conclusion: "In that case, Paul's message about reconciliation in 15:7-13 *is directed at Gentiles*. He bids Gentile believers in Rome to put aside their differences and to welcome one another" (ibid., 307; my emphasis).

fers to his audience in Romans as gentiles; commentators and historians who posit a Jewish component among Romans' implied readers infer that component from aspects of the letter other than Paul's own statements identifying his audience. Second, Paul clearly discusses issues and quotes from/alludes to the Hebrew Bible in ways that are appropriate to a letter for Jews (or an audience that includes a Jewish component), regardless whom Paul identifies as his audience. Caroline Johnson Hodge provides a helpful synthesis of these two observations, which synthesis accounts for all of the data of our letter:

> I think it is possible for Jews to have been in the historical audience, and for Paul to have used references to Scripture, and still to understand Paul's arguments aimed solely at Gentiles. Indeed there are Jews among the believers in Rome, as is clear from Rom 16 where Paul greets some of them, but this does not mean he is necessarily addressing them. And he often uses Scripture and discusses the law, but this makes perfect sense in a missive to people who have pledged loyalty to the God of Israel. Paul even talks *about* Jews, especially in Rom 9–11, but not *to* Jews.[18]

Conflicting Expressions of Faith (Rom 14:1–12)

1 Welcome the one who is weak in faith, but not for disputes over opinions. **2** On the one hand, one person has faith and so eats anything, but the one who is weak [only] eats vegetables. **3** The one who eats ought not despise the one who does not eat, even as one who does not eat ought not condemn the one who eats, for God has welcomed him. **4** But who are you to condemn someone else's domestic slave? He stands or falls before his own master. Moreover, he will be made to stand, for his master is able to make him stand. **5** On the one hand, one person distinguishes one day from another, while someone else judges every day. Let each person be fully persuaded in their own mind. **6** The one who observes the day observes it for the Lord. Similarly, the one who eats eats for the Lord, for he gives thanks to God. Also, the one who avoids eating avoids it for the Lord, since he also gives thanks to God. **7** For none of us lives for himself and no one dies for himself. **8** If we live, we live for the Lord. If we die, we die for the Lord. Whether we live or die, then, we belong to the Lord. **9** For Christ died and lived for this very reason: so that he might reign over the dead and the living. **10** So why do you condemn your sibling? Or you, why do

---

18. Johnson Hodge, "Light to the Nations," 171; emphases in the original.

you despise your sibling? For we will all stand before the judgment seat of God, **11** for it is written,

> "'I myself live,' says the Lord, 'that every knee shall bow before me, and every tongue shall give praise to God'" (Isa 45:23).

12 So then, each one of us will give an account of himself [to God].

Against the backdrop of Paul's exclusively gentile audience, let us turn to the text. First, we observe that Paul takes a remarkably conciliatory tack. By way of contrast, compare Paul's aggressive tone in Galatians 5, where Paul is clearly addressing a gentile Christian audience under pressure from Jewish forces (whether Christian or not) to submit to Torah's yoke:

> **10** I have confidence in you, by the Lord, that you will come to no other conclusion. Instead, the one who is stirring you up will bear judgment, whoever he may be. **11** But if I, brethren, am still proclaiming circumcision, why am I still being persecuted? If so, then the scandal of the cross is removed. **12** *If only those who are troubling you would go ahead and emasculate themselves!* (Gal 5:10–12; my emphasis)

Galatians 5:12 contains some of the most biting and sarcastic rhetoric anywhere in the NT. In Genesis 17 YHWH gives circumcision as the sign of his covenant with Abraham and his family, and that sign is taken up in the Mosaic covenant (Lev 12:3; see also Deut 10:16; 30:6 MT). At the same time, anyone with mangled or mutilated genitalia is prevented from serving in the temple cultic service (Deut 23:2 LXX||MT; English translations = 23:1). Their condition rendered them unfit to enter the presence of the Lord. Notice, then, the irony: Paul confronts those who tell gentiles they have to be circumcised to be acceptable to God, and he wishes these people would render themselves unacceptable to God. (Paul likely thought them already unacceptable to God!)

This assertive, even aggressive, tenor seems more characteristic of Paul's personality, as I understand him. In Romans 14–15, however, Paul takes a strikingly conciliatory tone, urging his readers (i) to follow the dictates of their conscience and (ii) to accept others whose consciences lead them to observe a different practice. This conciliatory tone reminds us of Romans 2, in which Paul distilled the essence of Torah as separating the Creator God from his creation and honoring him as Creator.[19] If we

---

19. See my comments on Rom 2:14–15, above. According to Dunn, "[t]he parallel

should attribute any "assertive aggression" to Paul's tone here, it would certainly be in the imperative, "*Welcome* [*proslambanesthe*] the one who is weak in faith" (14:1).

Despite the "somewhat pejorative description"[20] of a person as "weak in faith," Paul does not offer any criticism or complaint against their weakness. Instead, the onus of Paul's exhortation falls on those who, presumably, are *not* weak in faith, whom Paul will soon refer to as "the strong" [*hoi dynatoi*; Rom 15:1]. Rather than confront their weakness and challenge them for being weak, Paul urges a largesse of spirit that not only accepts "those who are weak in faith," even in their weakness, but also that makes concessions for them, avoiding practices that in themselves do not rupture one's relationship with God. Hence the end of v. 1: "but not for disputes over opinions."[21] When "the strong" welcome "the weak," they should do so genuinely, without the ulterior motive of persuading them of their weakness. Jewett rightly notes: "[I]t must have been apparent to Paul's audience that he intended to reverse the shameful status of the 'weak.' Such a reversal required Paul to employ the discriminatory epithet evidently created and employed by groups opposing the 'weak in faith.'"[22]

Paul does not offer any explanation why he perceives a certain group of people or a certain kind of person as "weak" in Rom 14:1, but he does offer a hint in v. 2 by drawing a contrast between "the weak" and "one who has faith": "On the one hand, one person has faith [*pisteuei*] and so eats anything, but the one who is weak [only] eats herbs." Dunn interprets their weakness in terms of their reliance on something other than God. "In this case the weakness is trust in God *plus* dietary and festival laws, trust in God *dependent* on observance of such practices, a trust in God which leans on the crutches of particular customs and not on God alone, as though they were an integral part of that trust."[23] But this is almost certainly wrong, if only because everywhere else Paul vehemently opposes any implication that trust in God is insufficient.[24] A more charitable reading of "the weak

---

[in Rom 14:1–12] with the sequence of thought in chap. 2 is striking and probably deliberate" (*Romans*, 2:797), though he has in mind specifically the "rebuke against judging others" at the beginning of Romans 2.

20. Ibid.

21. Jewett, *Romans*, 836. Dunn (*Romans*, 2:798) offers the translation, "though not with a view to settling disputes."

22. Jewett, *Romans*, 836.

23. Dunn, *Romans*, 2:798; emphases in the original.

24. For a better assessment, see Jewett, *Romans*, 835. Ehrensperger ("Called to Be

in faith," and one that better accounts for Paul's amicable tone in this section, understands their faith as expressed *through* (rather than dependent *on*) dietary or calendrical observances (see also v. 6, below).

Paul's rhetoric, which exaggerates the positions of both parties as eating, on the one hand, "everything" [*panta*], or, on the other, only "herbs" [*lachana*], "enable[s] each group to smile and feel included in the subsequent argument."[25] In other words, Paul does not differentiate two groups and identify with one over the other;[26] he exaggerates both groups and so unites them in the space between the exaggerations. Moreover, Paul unites both groups as part of his discussion of the communal (sacramental?) meal in which Christians eat together and therefore have to take some consideration of how other members of the community will perceive their dietary practices. Jewett explains Paul's comments about "food" [*brōma*] in terms of their communal meal:

> The word *brōma* ("food"), used twice in this verse, refers to whatever a person or group chooses to eat in the context of the "full love-feast." Although this context is overlooked by recent commentators, it is clear that what a Roman Christian consumed in his or her private lodging would not be expected to give offense to a "brother."[27]

Paul does not offer generalized instructions for one's personal ethic in Romans 14–15. Paul is addressing the communal meal in which Jesus' followers gather together and fellowship together. In *this* context, what one chooses to eat (and how one reacts to others' choices) becomes especially significant.

Saints") provides a very helpful discussion of the problematic presuppositions underlying traditional interpretations of Rom 14:1—15:13 (esp. 14:14, 20).

25. Jewett, *Romans*, 838.

26. *Pace* Dunn, *Romans*, 2:797–98. Witherington also struggles with this point: "As in 1 Corinthians, Paul identifies with the strong *to a certain degree* in terms of the freedom issue, but he also wishes to defend the weak" (Witherington and Hyatt, *Romans*, 327; my emphasis). The problem with this traditional reading is two-fold: First, it fails to notice Paul's exaggeration of both parties' stances, which Jewett helpfully describes (Jewett, *Romans*, 837–38). Second, it assumes that Paul characterizes Jewish forms of religious expression and piety as "weak," though we have no reason for attributing this perspective to Paul. In fact, the one time Paul explicitly mentions both "the weak" and "the Jews," these are clearly two different groups (see 1 Cor 9:20, 22; see Thiselton, *Corinthians*, 705–6).

27. Jewett, *Romans*, 860, citing Godet, *Romans*, 461.

Both parties—"the one who has faith" and "the weak"—place their trust in God, which explains why Paul exhibits no need to rebuke or correct either party. Instead, he offers a balanced set of imperatives directed toward both: "The one who eats ought not despise [*mē exoutheneitō*] the one who does not eat, even as the one who does not eat ought not condemn [*mē krinetō*] the one who eats" (v. 3). The verbs are appropriate for the ones to whom Paul directs them; *exoutheneō* fits a situation in which a more cosmopolitan, worldly-wise constituency within the Roman church(es) feels no compunction regarding diet and who mock and/or dismiss those who express their faith by avoiding certain foods. The animosity, however, runs both ways, and Paul turns simultaneously to instruct more scrupulous Christians not to condemn [*krinō*] those who feel no need to avoid certain foods. Paul's exhortation for "the weak" to refrain from judging the one who eats parallels a similar injunction in the Jesus tradition: "Do not judge [*mē krinete*], so that you may not be judged" (Matt 7:1||Luke 6:37).[28] Both parties "think more highly of themselves than is necessary"; neither party considers the other "as one to whom God has apportioned a measure of faith" (see Rom 12:3).[29] As a result, the means by which both parties express their faith in God—whether eating all things or eating only herbs—becomes an obstacle to the unity of the body of Christ in Rome (see Rom 12:3–8).

In response to both parties, Paul says, "God has welcomed him [i.e., the other]" (Rom 14:3c). He then goes on to use the example of a domestic slave [*oiketēs*] who has been welcomed by his master but condemned by someone other than his master (see 14:4). Paul does not suggest a scenario where one person passes judgment on the house-slave of another person of comparable social status. Rather, Paul portrays an even less justifiable situation: one domestic slave is passing judgment on another slave![30] Thus Witherington rightly notes,

---

28. Jewett, *Romans*, 840.

29. *Pace* Dunn, who argues that "Paul's exhortation here (v 3c) is a rebuke particularly to the condemnatory attitude of the weak (vv 3b, 4): the one with the much tighter understanding of what is acceptable conduct for God's people would think that God has *not* accepted the other" (*Romans*, 2:803). Paul appeals to the example of God, who "has welcomed him" [*auton proselabeto*], in order to draw on God's universal welcome of both "the strong" and "the weak." Dunn himself will recognize that Paul addresses both groups mutually in Rom 14:13 (see ibid., 2:817), but he does not apparently notice that v. 13 continues the mutual address from earlier in the chapter. The mutual address begins no later than v. 3.

30. The judgmental slave's audacity is exacerbated by Paul's use of *oiketēs* ("house-slave, domestic slave") instead of *doulos* ("slave, servant"). "The former denotes a

[Verse] 4 thus suggests that one's fellow Christian has one hierarchical relationship to be concerned about, and that is with his or her master—Christ. Now, if Christ is the only person in the socially superior position, then all Christians are at the same social level—they are all simply slaves or servants. The weak have no business judging someone else's household slave, nor do the strong. Neither has a superior position over another in Christ; they are in the very same position with regard to the Master.[31]

This will become clearer in just a few verses (see v. 7). But we should also remember Paul's point back in Romans 6, where he reminded his interlocutor that the gentiles had once been "slaves to sin" (6:17). Gentiles have now been freed from their slavery to sin, but they are not free. Instead, "Now that you are freed from sin, you are enslaved to righteousness" (6:18). In Romans 14 we have one slave to righteousness passing judgment on another slave to righteousness. In contrast to this mutual judgment, Paul expresses confidence that either slave will "stand or fall before his own master" and that the master (= the Lord) is able to make both stand.

Paul provides a second example of different expressions of faith (see 14:5). This second example continues the key word *krinō* ("judge, condemn, distinguish") from the first example in vv. 2–4. We can assume, therefore, that Paul has not left one subject (dietary scruples) and moved on to another (observing certain days). Instead, he provides a second example to make the same point. Paul confirms the continuity of his discussion in vv. 6–12, where he leaves behind the two examples to draw his conclusion. We can make a couple observations here. First, despite the "somewhat pejorative" language of "the strong" and "the weak" (and the fact that Paul clearly identifies with "the strong"; see Rom 15:1), Paul clearly portrays both groups of believers as actively engaged in expressing their faithfulness to God in concrete and specific ways.[32] In fact, one is hard-pressed to explain at all why Paul calls them "weak," since they, like the "strong," "live for God." If Paul is picking up the word "weak" from Roman cultural prejudices against foreign religious scruples, then he does so ironically, mocking the wider cultural judgment of them as "weak." Earlier in the letter, when we found occasion to explore the theme

---

normally inalienable member of the household, including slaves who function almost as family members, whereas the latter is ordinarily limited to slaves and hired servants, whether in the household or in other service" (Jewett, *Romans*, 841–42). In other words, Paul portrays a situation that involves intra-familial condemnation.

31. Witherington and Hyatt, *Romans*, 335.

32. See Moo, *Romans*, 843.

of self-mastery,[33] to be weak—that is, to lack self-control or to succumb to one's passions—was part of the problem that Torah condemned and for which the gospel provided the solution. In Romans 14–15, however, Paul attaches no negative connotation to the word "weak." Both "strong" and "weak" alike live and die "for the Lord" [tō kyriō].

Second, despite his magnanimity toward both "the strong" and "the weak," we should not miss that Paul does not accept *everything* about these two groups. He is remarkably willing to accept those gentiles who avoid meat and keep Sabbath as expressions of their faithfulness in (or to) God, and he is just as remarkably willing to accept those gentiles who eat meat and neglect Sabbath-observance as expressions of their faithfulness in (or to) God. But he reinforces the imperatives of Rom 14:3—"The one who eats *ought not despise* the one who does not eat, even as the one who does not eat *ought not condemn* the one who eats" (emphases added)—with implied rebukes in v. 10. In other words, Paul is willing to accept eating or not eating meat, or keeping or not keeping Sabbath, as part of one's expressions of piety. But he is *not* willing to accept division within the one body of Christ. Anyone, whether "strong" or "weak," receives Paul's chastisement for despising and/or judging another believer with a different practice of piety. Whereas we would expect Paul to praise "the strong" and critique (or at least instruct) "the weak," he accepts both even as he offers correction to both.

Third, Paul subsumes everything—even life and death—to the sovereignty of Jesus [ho kyrios], so that both living and dying are done "for the Lord" (v. 8). We have already identified how Paul picks up the theme of the gentiles' freedom from slavery to sin and weakness and enslavement to righteousness from Romans 6. We saw Paul's exuberant confidence in Romans 8 with respect to the gentiles' adoption into the family of God. We saw that same confidence in Rom 11:28–32 (esp. v. 29) with respect to the surety of the Jews' relation to God. In Rom 14:8, Paul gives that confidence its ultimate expression: "Whether we live or die, then, *we belong to the Lord* [tou kyriou esmen; my emphasis]." This confidence is, ultimately, faith in the sovereignty of God and of the Lord Jesus. Paul assures both "the strong" and "the weak" among his readers, as those under the reign of Jesus, that their expressions of faith please God, whether they eat all things or only herbs, or whether or not they differentiate one day from another.

Fourth, once again Paul's moral exhortations are rooted in a particular reading of Israel's sacred written tradition. "A particular reading" is

---

33. See especially our discussion of Romans 6–7, as well as Stowers, *Rereading*.

key here. Paul could have turned to a number of texts to make a different point. For example, Isaiah writes,

> "And to those foreigners [*allogenesi*] who attach themselves to the Lord,
> to serve him and to love his name
> in order to be with him as male and female slaves,
> And all those who keep my Sabbaths so as not to defile them,
> and those who hold to my covenant,
> I will lead them onto my holy mountain,
> and I will delight them in my house of prayer.
> Their whole burnt offerings and their sacrifices will be acceptable on my altar,
> for my house shall be called a house of prayer for all the nations,"
> Said the Lord, who gathers the dispersed of Israel,
> for I will gather for him a gathering. (Isa 56:6–8 LXX)

It would not be difficult to conclude from Isaiah 56 that both Jews and gentiles ought to observe the Sabbath as part of their participation in the covenant. But Paul does not. Instead, he pulls from another part of Isaiah (see Isa 45:23) and focuses on God's sovereign status over all people ("every knee" [*pan gony*] and "every tongue" [*pasa glōssa*]). Since everyone—surely we can add "first the Jew then the Greek"—will give an account to God, Paul allows both "the strong" and "the weak" to honor God how they see fit.

This laissez-faire attitude is at least a bit surprising, especially given the social and symbolic value of dietary regulations and Sabbath observance in Second-Temple Judaism. Since at least the time of the Maccabean revolt (167–160 BCE), in which the Jews (= Judeans) sloughed off Greek (= Seleucid) rule, the most conspicuous markers of a person's fidelity to the ancestral covenant were *kashrut*, resting on the Sabbath, and circumcision, and in popular memory these markers of fidelity were often quite costly.[34] Paul has already identified "gentiles who do not have Torah" and attributed to them the virtue of "doing the things of Torah" (see Rom 2:14–

---

34. As perhaps the most famous example, see the story of the martyrdom of the mother and her seven sons in 2 Maccabees 7. Dunn (*Romans*, 2:800–801) has a helpful discussion of "the considerable importance of dietary laws for Jews of this period." However, Dunn does not explain why (or how) this "considerable importance" relates to Paul's point in Romans 14–15. In our reading, it relates to Paul's discussion inasmuch as gentiles interested in Jewish *theologoumena* (Israel's Messiah, Torah, *kashrut*, Sabbath observance, etc.) would have picked up on this importance for the Jews and accepted it for themselves.

16). Presumably Paul is not seriously suggesting that Torah-less gentiles observe Torah's distinctive regulations regarding *kashrut*, Sabbath observance, and circumcision. For Torah-less gentiles, fidelity to Torah must be measured according to a different standard. We have already discussed how Paul reduced fidelity to Torah on the part of the gentiles down to one thing: distinguishing the Creator God from his creation and worshiping only the former. In light of this essential reduction of Torah—that is, this reduction of the essence of Torah—Paul's live-and-let-live attitude toward the expression of faith among "the strong" and "the weak" fits perfectly well.

Celebrating the Faith of All the Gentiles (Rom 14:13–23)

> **13** Therefore, let us no longer condemn one another. Instead, you should make this determination: to not place a stumbling stone or a cause for offense before your brethren. **14** I know and am convinced by the Lord Jesus that nothing is unclean on its own, except for the person who considers a thing unclean. For that person, it is unclean. **15** If your brethren suffer because of food, you are no longer walking in love. You ought not destroy those for whom Christ died just for the sake of food! **16** Moreover, do not let your good thing be reviled. **17** For the kingdom of God is not food and drink but rather righteousness and peace and joy in the Holy Spirit. **18** For in this way the one who is subject to Christ is pleasing to God and approved by people.
>
> **19** So then, we pursue the things of peace as well as the things of one another's edification. **20** Do not destroy the work of God just on account of food. Everything, then, is clean, but it becomes evil to the one who stumbles and eats. **21** It is good to avoid eating meat, drinking wine, and any other thing by which your brethren stumble. **22** But you, the faith that you have on your own, have it before God. Blessed are those who do not condemn themselves by what they approve. **23** But anyone who wavers is condemned if they eat, since their eating is not by faith. Everything that is not by faith is sin.

Paul has used the verb *krinō* ("judge, condemn, differentiate") in his exhortation to "the weak" (see v. 3); for his exhortation to "the strong" he used the verb *exoutheneō* ("despise, disdain"). He now uses *krinō* again to enjoin two negative actions: (i) do not condemn one another, and (ii) do not cause others to stumble. "Therefore, let us no longer condemn [*mēketi ... krinōmen*] one another" (Rom 14:13a). We could understand v. 13a as an injunction primarily for "the weak," to whom Paul has already given instruction not to condemn [*krinō*] those who eat (v. 3). Two factors, however, push me to read Rom 14:13 as Paul's exhortation for both "the strong" and "the weak." First, Paul uses the first-person plural in the first part of the verse: "Let *us* no longer condemn one another." Second, the imperative in v. 13b, which we will discuss presently, is clearly directed at least toward "the strong," whose less restricted practices threaten to undermine the faith of those for whom eating meat is not an act of faith (see 14:20-23). So when Paul urges, "Let us no longer condemn one another," he is addressing his entire gentile audience, both "the strong" and "the weak."[35]

Still in Rom 14:13, Paul adds a second negative imperative onto the injunction not to despise and/or condemn one another (vv. 3, 10, 13a): "you should make this determination [*krinate*]: to not place a stumbling stone or a cause for offense before your brethren" (v. 13b). The remainder of the paragraph unpacks this exhortation. On the basis of the word play on *krinō* in Rom 14:13—"condemn" in v. 13a, but "make this determination" in v. 13b—and the shift from the first-person plural to the second-person plural, Dunn argues that Paul "signals a narrowing of the focus of address to 'the strong.'"[36] This suggestion makes little sense, however, since Paul included himself among "the strong" rather than "the weak" (see 15:1). Why, then, would "we" include both "the weak" and "the strong," but "you" (plural) include only "the strong"? Jewett provides a better comment: "The argumentative function of v. 13 is to provide a thematic admonition to both the weak and the strong, which is elaborated and explained through the rest of the pericope."[37]

Paul expresses a striking conviction in the truth of v. 14, and he underscores that conviction with the two verbs, "I know and am convinced" [*oida kai pepeismai*]. Paul identifies the source of his confident conviction as "the Lord Jesus." The content of Paul's conviction ("... that nothing is unclean in itself") appears to come from the tradition of Jesus' teaching.

---

35. Dunn presents his comments on Rom 14:13-23 under the heading, "The Responsibility of 'the Strong'" (ibid., 2:815-35). Some verses do indeed address "the strong" specifically (e.g., vv. 15-16), though many of Paul's instructions are equally appropriate for "the weak" as well (e.g., vv. 13-14, 23). However, Dunn does acknowledge, "[t]he exhortation [in v. 13] is probably to both groups" (ibid., 2:817).

36. Dunn, *Romans*, 2:817.

37. Jewett, *Romans*, 856-57 (p. 56 quoted).

If You Call Yourself a Jew

We have to be careful here because, according to an impressive scholarly consensus, all four canonical Gospels were written after Paul's letter to the Romans.[38] So we cannot say that Paul alludes to or quotes from any of our written Gospels. However, he does appear to reproduce the same tradition that we find in Mark 7:

Mark 7:18–19:	Rom 14:14:
[18] And he said to them, "In this way do you still not understand? Do you not know that everything from outside that enters into the person is not able to defile [*koinōsai*] them, [19] because it does not enter their heart but into the belly, and it exits out into the toilet?" (As a result, he cleansed all foods.)	I know and am convinced by the Lord Jesus that nothing is unclean [*koinon*] on its own, except for the person who considers a thing unclean [*koinon*]: for that person it is unclean [*koinon*].

These passages differ sufficiently so that we can be confident that Paul is not depending on one of Mark's written sources. Nevertheless, the most distinctive feature of Mark 7:19 is Mark's interpretive comment inserted into the middle of Jesus' teaching: "As a result, he cleansed all foods." The parallel account in Matthew does not include this interpretive comment. In Luke's loose parallel to Mark 7:19, Jesus tells his Pharisaic host, "Instead, give the inward things as acts of charity, and behold! All things are clean [*kathara*] for you" (Luke 11:41).

If we step back for a moment, we can appreciate what we have here. Mark inserts an interpretive comment into Jesus' teaching that impurity proceeds from within: according to Mark, Jesus rendered all foods acceptable.[39] Some time later, Luke goes even further and claims that Jesus

---

38. A very small minority of scholars dates one or two Gospels earlier than Romans. For example, James Crossley argues that Mark was written in the early 40s CE; see Crossley, *Date*. However, this is a very minority view.

39. Crossley (ibid., 183–205) argues that the authorial aside in Mark 7:19 does not nullify Torah's proscriptions against eating certain foods; instead, the phrase "he cleansed all foods" [*katharizōn panta ta brōmata*] declares "all foods *that are permitted to eat in the Torah* to be clean thereby denying the role of *handwashing*" (ibid., 192; emphases in the original). Crossley provides a complex discussion that depends on a careful and nuanced reconstruction of theories of impurity transmission in rabbinic literature. However, at the end of the day Mark did not limit the scope of Jesus' catharsis to "all foods that are permitted to eat in the Torah." Crossley's argument depends too much on his general impression that, "[i]f Mark wanted to reject the biblical food laws, as is generally assumed, he would have to be a lot more explicit than the editorial comment in 7:19" (ibid., 191; Crossley often plays the he-would-have-to-be-a-lot-more-explicit card; see pp. 84, 88, 91 n. 28, 93, 94, 103, 107, 108, 113, 167 n. 25).

himself declared (or rendered) all things clean. For Luke, this is not an interpretive conclusion drawn from Jesus' teaching but rather a clear declaration straight from Jesus' lips. Paul, writing about a decade before our earliest written gospel, says that he is persuaded *by the Lord Jesus* [*en kyriō Iēsou*] that nothing is unclean in itself. What renders something unclean is the act of considering it unclean. We can now draw two conclusions:

- First, Paul provides independent and antecedent corroboration for Mark's claim that Jesus himself taught that the source of impurity lies within a person rather than outside them. Jesus' followers could apply this teaching in various ways depending on the circumstances in which they found themselves. In Luke (and, to a lesser extent, in Mark), this meant that the conditions of one's cutlery and flatware—washed vs. unwashed—had no bearing on one's standing before God. Moreover, Mark gives the implication that Jesus' teaching effectively abrogated the entire system of Mosaic food legislation.[40] However, we should note the possibility that Mark's audience might not have necessarily interpreted v. 19b as a flat declaration that the distinctions maintained by *kashrut* no longer applied. For those whose hearts convicted them that eating pork (for example) contradicted God's commandment, eating pork would defile them because what was "coming out of them" (*viz.* willful disregard for a commandment of God) was defiling. "These distinctions are relevant for those who deem them relevant because they are aspects of their identity-shaping relationship with the one God."[41] On the other hand, those who felt no compunction eating pork have nothing defiling "coming out of them," and so they are not defiled.

- Second, Paul makes largely the same point as Mark, though he attributes this point more directly to the Lord Jesus himself (v. 14a). Mark, writing for a mixed audience of Jews as well as gentiles, gives the implication that the dietary regulations that applied to the former were not necessarily binding on the latter. Mark releases any gentiles among his audience who may have balked at the idea of having to take on distinctively Jewish eating habits from having to. And any Jews who still felt obligated to observe *kashrut* could engage them in fellowship because these gentiles were not defiled by what they consumed (and

40. But see the previous footnote.

41. Ehrensperger, "Called to Be Saints," 99. She continues: "Such a restricted perspective on the relevance of these distinctions has nothing to do with obliterating or undermining their significance for those for whom they are and remain significant."

so were not a source of defilement to any Jews at the table). Paul, writing for a thoroughly gentile audience, some of whom were particularly attracted to a Mosaic ethic and who considered submitting to Torah's yoke, informs his philo-Semitic gentile readers that gentiles who did not take on Mosaic practices were not any less acceptable before God.

Interestingly, there is no hint in Romans 14 that Paul condemns or chastises some of his gentile readers for eating "only herbs" or for distinguishing some days (= Sabbaths) from others. Instead, his concern is that their decision will result in suspicion or condescension toward gentiles who do not make the same or similar decisions.

Paul turns quickly on his heels from primarily addressing "the weak" in Rom 14:14 to focusing on "the strong" in v. 15. If "the weak" need to accept that, despite their conscientious objections, nothing is unclean on its own, "the strong" need to be aware of the impact of their decisions on those around them. Paul identifies two potential consequences: (i) that what "the strong" eat will cause other members of the community to suffer [*lypeomai*; lit. "be grieved"] or even result in their destruction [*apollymi*],[42] and (ii) that whatever "the strong" identify as good and for which they give thanks to God (recall v. 6) will be reviled or spoken of evilly [*blasphēmeō*].

Paul shifts the focus of the ethical discussion among Roman gentile Christians away from issues of what they are eating (and/or drinking) to issues of righteousness, peace, and joy (Rom 14:17). He has already used these first two nouns—"righteousness" and "peace"—at key moments in the letter.[43] Though this is the first time he has used the noun *joy* [*chara*] in Romans, Paul has urged his readers twice to "rejoice" [*chairō*; 12:12, 15]. In other words, here in v. 17 Paul diverts his readers' attention away from potential conflicts over the specific vehicles by which they express their faith and back toward themes on which he has been focusing throughout the entire letter: righteousness, peace, joy. "For in this way the one who is subject to Christ is pleasing to God and approved by humanity" (14:18).

The language of being "subject to Christ" [*douleuōn tō Christō*] in Rom 14:18 picks up Paul's earlier language that we are no longer slaves to sin (6:6), that we serve in newness of spirit (7:6), and that his readers ought to give service to the Lord (12:11). We find another, more salient link between 14:18 and Romans 12: being subject to Christ results in being "pleasing to God" [*euarestos tō theō*] and gains the approval of

42. Jewett rightly describes *apollymi* ("destroy") as a "powerful verb" (*Romans*, 861).

43. For righteousness, see 1:17; 3:21–27 (4x); and 6:12–23 (5x), among others; for peace, see 5:1 and 8:6, among others.

The Offering of the Weak

other people. Paul opened the exhortational section of Romans with one of his most well-known passages, which includes the only other two uses of *euarestos* in the letter:

> ¹ Therefore, I urge you, brethren, through the mercies of God, to present your bodies as a sacrifice—living, holy, and pleasing to God [*euareston tō theō*]; this is your reasonable act of worship. ² And do not be conformed to this age; rather, be transformed by the renewal of your mind, so that you might approve what is the will of God, which is good and pleasing [*euareston*] and perfect. (Rom 12:1-2)

The current section draws a number of themes together and offers the ethical capstone of the whole letter, as we can tell because of the multiple links with other parts of the letter (especially Romans 12). That is, what it means to "present your bodies as a sacrifice—living, holy, and pleasing to God," to let love be sincere, to be appropriately subject to governing authorities as well as to God, is most clearly seen in the community that subsumes its ethical decisions to the principle of "walking in love" (Rom 14:15) and subsuming personal freedoms to the needs and scruples of others.

Paul continues to unpack the exhortation of v. 13 through the end of the chapter. He offers more than simply the *negative* imperatives of keeping from condemning one another and causing others to sin (see Rom 14:13). Paul proceeds to offer a *positive* ethical vision for his readers to pursue in vv. 19-23. The obverse of "no longer condemning one another" (Rom 14:13) is "pursuing the things of peace" (v. 19). Paul has already argued that his readers, who have been justified by faith, have peace with God (5:1). Now, he affirms that his readers also pursue peace with one another and build one another up, though I suspect this affirmation bears imperatival connotations.[44] If a "weak" person—someone with dietary or calendrical scruples—has peace with God and is justified by a faith that expresses itself in the acts of avoiding certain foods or observing certain days, then for someone who is "strong"—someone without those scruples—to destroy that person amounts to "destroying the work of God" [*katalye ton ergon tou theou*; 14:20]. As Jewett explains: "The building metaphor in [v. 19] is carried over in the reference to the congregations of Rome as *to ergon tou theou* ("the work of God"). . . . [I]t is the divine

---

44. Jewett (*Romans*, 853-54, 865) argues that the indicative *diōkomen* ("we are pursuing"), which enjoys strong attestation, including ℵ and B, is more likely the original reading, instead of the subjunctive *diōkōmen* ("let us pursue"), which may make better sense contextually.

275

edifice of apostolic work through the gospel, as 1 Cor 3:10–15 indicates."[45] Paul enjoins his readers to build up rather than tear down the "divine edifice" of the community of Jesus' followers.

Paul makes a significant transition in Rom 14:21. Earlier Paul referred to the meat that "the strong" eat as "your good thing" [*hymōn to agathon*; v. 16], and he urges "the strong" not to let their good thing be spoken against. Now, five verses later and still talking to "the strong," he uses a similar word to identify another thing as "good" or "beautiful": "It is good [*kalon*] to avoid eating meat, drinking wine, and any other thing by which your brethren stumble" (14:21). Without negating the goodness [*agathon*] of that for which "the strong" give thanks to God, Paul attributes goodness [*kalon*] to unity among his audience and deference for the consciences of others in the community. He goes even further in 14:22. The imperative, "have [or 'keep'] your faith before God" certainly does not mean that the truest or most authentic expressions of faith are private, internal, or in any way disconnected from the larger community of faith.[46] Paul never exhibits this individualized, privatized conception of faith. In this context he is thoroughly focused on the social and communal aspects of faith, and especially the consequences when "the strong" show insufficient regard for "the weak" and "the weak" condemn "the strong" for not observing their expressions of piety.[47] As a result, I interpret "have [or 'keep'] your faith before God" as Paul's injunction to express one's faith in ways that edify, rather than destroy, other members of the community.[48] Kathy Ehrensperger provides an exemplary expression of Paul's point here:

> Paul does not in principle "undermine the law," or even declare part of the law, as related to food, to be irrelevant in Christ. Paul rather argues within the parameters of Jewish reasoning. He is talking about the realm in which those who are in Christ now

---

45. Ibid., 866.

46. Similarly, see ibid., 870.

47. Recall also that Paul is addressing the context of the early Christians' communal meal (see ibid., 860, cited above).

48. *Pace* Dunn (*Romans*, 2:827): "The 'stronger' the faith (that is, the more unconditional the trust), the less dependent is it on observance of particular traditions; the 'weaker' the faith, the more dependent on such customs. . . . Because faith has the character of immediate reliance on God *it need not be displayed in public*: the relationship of the 'strong' can still be without dependence on these traditional rulings even when observing them for the sake of the 'weak'" (my emphasis). Paul, however, can scarcely be imagined as suggesting that faith works apart from specific and concrete acts, or even that "it need not be displayed in public"! Moo (*Romans*, 861–62) provides a better analysis.

live, that is, the realm of a holy community. The food laws, and purity laws more generally, have something to do with this realm, but in different ways for Jews and Gentiles. It certainly does not imply that Paul denies the validity of food laws in Christ. The issue is something else. That which actually threatens the realm of holiness in Christ is neither adherence nor non-adherence to the law, neither eating nor not-eating, but "injuring the brother and sister."[49]

If this is the right reading, then we can interpret Rom 14:22b in a way that fits entirely within the larger context of Romans 14–15: "Blessed are those who do not condemn themselves by what they approve." Paul has just flatly declared, "All things are clean" [*panta men kathara*; 14:20]. His reference to people "condemning themselves [*krinōn heauton*] by what they approve" puts a question mark against the earlier declaration that all things are clean. That is, if all things are clean, how could eating meat or not observing Sabbath result in condemnation? On one's own, the answer must be: they cannot. But in community, where someone else's faith may be put in jeopardy by such things, the result is condemnation both for the one who eats apart from faith (v. 23) and for the one whose faith caused someone else to stumble (v. 22). A person is condemned by what they approve when their approval results in the destruction of another person's faith. In light of Paul's exuberant exclamation, "there is now no condemnation [*katakrima*] for those who are in Christ Jesus" (8:1), the warning of 14:23 becomes particularly striking. "Anyone who wavers is condemned [*katakekritai*] if they eat, since their eating is not by faith" (14:23). In the very same letter where Paul dismisses all condemnation for anyone in Christ Jesus, he warns of potential condemnation for anyone who violates a conscience informed by faith. Paul places a premium on communal faith and mutual deference for one another.

A Mutually Deferential Faith (Rom 15:1–13)

> **1** We who are strong ought to bear the weaknesses of the powerless and not please ourselves. **2** Let each of us please our neighbor, for good and for edification. **3** For Christ also did not please himself, but just as it is written, "The insults of those who insult you fell upon me" (Ps 68:10 LXX). **4** For whatever was written beforehand was written for our instruction, so that, through the perseverance and the encouragement of the Scriptures, we

---

49. Ehrensperger, "Called to Be Saints," 104.

> might have hope. **5** But may the God of perseverance and encouragement grant you all to agree with one another according to Christ Jesus, **6** so that all together with one mouth you might glorify the God and Father of our Lord Jesus Christ.
> **7** Therefore, welcome one another, just as Christ also welcomed you into the glory of God. **8** For I say, Christ has become an agent of circumcision for the truth of God, in order to confirm [his] promises to the patriarchs **9** so that the gentiles glorify God for [his] mercy, just as it is written,
>
> "Therefore, I will acknowledge you among the gentiles,
>   and I will sing praises to your name" (Ps 17:50 LXX).
> **10** And again he says,
> "Rejoice, you gentiles, along with his people" (Deut 32:43).
> **11** And again,
> "Praise the Lord, all you gentiles,
>   and let all the peoples give him praise" (Ps 116:1 LXX).
> **12** And again Isaiah says,
> "There will be a shoot of Jesse,
>   and one who rises up to rule over the gentiles.
> The nations will place their hope upon him" (Isa 11:10).
> **13** Now, may the God of hope fill you with all joy and peace as you believe, so that you would abound in hope by the power of the Holy Spirit.

Despite the new chapter, Romans 15 continues the exhortational section that began in Romans 14. In fact, Romans 15 *expands* the exhortations from the previous chapter by generalizing from the interaction between "strong" and "weak" Christians in Rome to the international scope of God's people, consisting of both Jews and gentiles. Since Rom 14:7 Paul has been writing in the first-person plural ("we"), though not consistently so.[50] Here in 15:1, Paul explicitly identifies himself with "the strong" [*hēmeis hoi dynatoi*; lit. "we who are able," or "we who are powerful"].

Typically, in light of Romans 14, commentators have read 15:1 as Paul identifying with those who eat meat and/or do not observe the Sabbath.[51] However, earlier in Romans Paul has emphatically affirmed his Jewish identity (9:1–5; 11:1, 14). It would be strange indeed if Paul

---

50. For example, Paul shifts from a first-person plural hortative subjunction ("Let *us* no longer condemn . . .") to a second-person plural imperative ("*you* should make this determination . . .") in the span of a single verse (14:13).

51. Jewett, for example, says, "The subject of this obligation explicitly includes Paul *along with the Gentile Christian majority* of the Roman churches" (*Romans*, 876; my emphasis).

identified himself with "the strong" (= those who are free of distinctively Jewish dietary and/or calendrical scruples) and separated himself from "the weak" (= those who observe Jewish norms of piety).[52] In light of the mutual obligations of both "the strong" and "the weak" toward each other in Romans 14, I would cautiously suggest that Paul shifts the referent of "the strong" here in Romans 15:1. Now, "the strong" refers to those who are able "to bear the weaknesses of the powerless" (15:1).[53] Wright comes close to this same proposal when he rightly critiques the translation of both the NRSV and the NIV at 15:1:

> Paul has not suggested that "weakness" is a "failing"; to pull the text that way is to slant his argument. Better to see, now, *a subtly new point*: "these 'weaknesses' I have been speaking of—the people who possess them are 'powerless.' They are who they are, and at the moment they can't help it. Thus we who are 'strong' have an obligation to support and help them." . . . The meaning then is that the strong must help those who, through their own current powerlessless [sic], have these "weaknesses." They must support and encourage them, not browbeat them with demands for more "strength" than they can presently muster.[54]

Under the shadow of Romans 14, where Paul has enjoined both "the strong" and "the weak" not to judge one another nor to place obstacles before the others' faith, "the weak" in Romans 15 become those whose weaknesses must be borne by others.[55] Jewett offers a helpful comment

---

52. According to Nanos, "the strong" = Christians, and "the weak" = non-Christian Jews (*Mystery*, 85–165). I disagree with Nanos's reading for the same reasons that I disagree with the traditional reading: Paul has affirmed his Jewish identity earlier in Romans, so here it would be strange if he distinguished himself now from the Jews, Christian or otherwise.

53. Thus we avoid the problem of restricting Paul's general exhortation ("Let each of us please our neighbor, for good and for edification"; Rom 15:2) to only one faction, as if only "the strong" were supposed to "please their neighbor" while "the weak" continued to inflict the dictates of their consciences on others. Since Paul clearly expects both "the weak" (= one who only "eats herbs"; 14:2) and "the strong" (= one who "believes to eat all things"; 14:2) to "please our neighbor" (*pace* Moo, *Romans*, 866–67), the meaning of "the strong" [*hoi dynatoi*] in 15:1 clearly cannot be identical with "the one who eats" in Romans 14.

54. Wright, "Romans," 745; my emphasis.

55. Paul's rhetoric already pointed in this direction, even in Romans 14, where "it must have been apparent to Paul's audience that he intended to reverse the shameful status of the 'weak'" (Jewett, *Romans*, 836, cited above). Moreover, despite the pejorative label "the weak," Paul implicitly sides with "the weak" in 14:1 when he forestalls "the strong" welcoming "the weak" in order to convince them of their weakness. "In these

here, despite very real differences between our readings of Romans 15: "Paul reverses the ordinary structure of obligation. Rather than the weak being forced to submit to the strong as was typical in Greco-Roman culture, the powerful are here under obligation to 'bear/carry' (*bastazein*) the weaknesses of the powerless."[56]

Paul makes this shift clearer in the end of Rom 15:1 and in v. 2. He identifies "we who are strong" with "we who do not please ourselves" and instead "please our neighbor" [*tō plēsion aresketō*]. His instruction here echoes Jesus' use of Lev 19:18: "And the second is this: You shall love your neighbor [*ton plēsion sou*] as yourself" (Mark 12:31). More importantly, it echoes Paul's own summation of Torah in Rom 13:8: "Owe no one anything, other than the debt to love one another, for the one who loves his neighbor [*ton heteron*; lit. "the other, someone else"] has fulfilled Torah." "The strong" in faith are no longer those who do or do not do any particular thing. "The strong" are those who submit themselves to the needs of others within the community.

Paul turns to the example of Jesus in Rom 15:3-4, and he applies the language of Ps 69:9 to explain Jesus' attitude of self-sacrifice (Rom 15:3). The psalmist bemoans opposition from "those who hate me without cause" [*hoi misountes me dōrean* (68:5 LXX; = 69:4 MT)]. He expresses his solidarity with, and commitment to, YHWH by accepting onto his own shoulders "the insults of those who insult you." Paul, however, transforms the psalmist's commitment to God into a prediction of Christ's service of others. That is, Paul recontextualizes the quote from the psalm so that now, rather than accepting contempt intended for God, the psalm now portrays Christ accepting contempt intended for "the weak." Although a number of commentators argue that Paul applies Ps 69:9 to Jesus' relationship to God,[57] the context of Paul's argument in Rom 14:1—15:13 makes this exceedingly unlikely. Rather, "[i]n the context of Rom 15, the selection of this quotation serves perfectly to sustain a mutually accepting attitude between the 'weak' and the 'strong.'"[58] Christ therefore becomes the paradigmatic instance of "the strong," which further confirms our

---

verses it is the opinions/reasoning (*dialogismoi*) of the 'weak' that are under scrutiny by the dominant group.... In the context of welcoming fellow believers to love feasts, he flatly repudiates the ulterior motive of doing so in order to induce the weak to adopt the opinions of the strong" (ibid.).

56. Jewett, *Romans*, 877.

57. For example, Dunn, *Romans*, 2:839; Moo, *Romans*, 868; Schreiner, *Romans*, 747; *inter alios*. For a helpful discussion, see Jewett, *Romans*, 880 n. 56.

58. See Jewett, *Romans*, 879–80; p. 880 quoted.

interpretation of 15:1, that "the strong" now refers to those who bear the weaknesses of "the weak" (= "the powerless") rather than those who feel no dietary or calendrical scruples. In light of this shift, the highest Christian ethical value becomes unity [*to auto phronein en allēlois*; 15:5; lit. "to think the same thing among one another"], and Paul offers a prayer in vv. 5-6 that "the God of perseverance and encouragement" would bestow this value among the Roman Christians.

Paul now moves to conclude this lengthy ethical exhortation, which spans the entire length of Rom 14:1—15:13. Paul opened the section with the exhortation, "Welcome [*proslambanesthe*] the one who is weak in faith" (14:1), and he drew upon the example of God himself, who also welcomed [*proselabeto*] both "the weak" and "the strong" (14:3). He now picks up the same word in the closing paragraph, and again he sets an imperative before his readers and appeals to the example of Christ: "Therefore, welcome one another [*proslambanesthe allēlous*], just as Christ also welcomed you [*proselabeto hymas*] into the glory of God" (15:7). As we have seen in earlier sections of Romans, Paul focuses narrowly and consistently on the full inclusion of gentiles among those who worship God (see 15:8-12).[59]

Again, we see a catena of references to Hebrew biblical traditions, in which Paul cites four texts in four verses.[60] Richard Hays argues (rightly, I think) that, in light of the appeal to the example of Christ in this pericope, Christ is the "I" who is speaking in the psalm citations in Rom 15:3 and 9.[61] "In Paul's reading of Ps 69:9, it is the Christ, speaking in the first person, who addresses God through the words of the biblical text."[62] In Rom 15:9, Paul portrays Christ as quoting the words of Ps 18:49 (LXX = 18:50) to announce, "Therefore, I will acknowledge you among the gentiles, and I will sing praises to your name." Christ then turns to Paul's gentile audience and exhorts them, in the words of Deut 32:43, "Rejoice, you gentiles, along with his people,"[63] and again, in the words of Ps 117:1 (LXX = 116:1),

---

59. See Garroway, "Circumcision," 309-10.

60. Ps 17:50 LXX; Deut 32:43; Ps 116:1 LXX; and Isa 11:10 in Rom 15:9-12, respectively.

61. Similarly, see Matera, *Romans*, 321, 324.

62. Hays, *Conversion*, 101-18, p. 102 quoted.

63. Both here and in v. 11, "his people" or "the people" [*ho laos (autou)*] refers to Israel, God's chosen people, rather than to people in general. "To the translators of the LXX the term *laos*, derived from the language of high style and ceremony, and infrequently used in the [Greek] of their time, seemed ideally suited for expressing the relationship of Israel to Yahweh. *Laos* serves in the overwhelming majority of cases as a translation of the [Hebrew] '*am* and means Israel as the chosen people of God, just

"Praise the Lord, all you gentiles, and let all the peoples give him praise." In agreement with the Christ, Isaiah prophesies, "There will be a shoot of Jesse, and one who rises up to rule over the gentiles. The nations will place their hope upon him" (Rom 15:12, citing Isa 11:10). Wright also follows Hays here: the citation of Psalm 18 in Rom 15:9 "mak[es] the central point that the Messiah himself, understood as the one praying in this psalm, is standing there, surrounded by Gentiles, singing God's praises."[64]

The thread running throughout Rom 15:8–12 is the coming together of both Jew and gentile to praise the God of Israel, which is the chief consequence of the gospel. We should notice the development across the whole of Romans. At the beginning of the letter Paul quoted Isa 52:5 as part of his complaint that the gentile proselyte's circumcision actually transgresses Torah, and that his transgression resulted in the name of God being reviled among the gentiles (Rom 2:24). Here toward the end of the letter, Paul quotes the exclamation of praise from Ps 17:50 LXX: "I will praise you among the gentiles, Lord, and I will sing of your name." The unity that flows, first, from God's welcome of both Jews and gentiles and, second, from the mutual welcome and acceptance of God's people toward each other results in the worldwide praise of God. Paul closes with a prayer that "the God of hope" would fill his people—Jews and gentiles—with joy and peace, in order to increase their experience of hope.

---

as, on the other hand, the [Hebrew] *gôy* is used particularly for the Gentiles (*ethnē*)" (Bietenhard, "λαός," 2:796; see also pp. 2:799–800).

64. Wright, "Romans," 748.

15

In Sum...

The End of Paul's Rhetoric and of His Letter

> *There can be no question ... that Paul here described his ministry in priestly terms. That however should not be taken to indicate that he thought of himself as a priest in a special way distinct from the ministries of other believers. There is no suggestion of that anywhere else in Paul. The whole imagery of priesthood has clearly been transposed entirely out of the cult and applied in its transformed sense to Paul's ministry of preaching the gospel to Gentiles.*[1]

With the rhetorical argument of the letter now complete, Paul begins to bring his letter to the Romans to a close. As Paul sets aside his rhetorical persona (either as a Jew in dialogue with a gentile proselyte to Judaism, or as the gentile proselyte himself) and resumes his authorial role, we encounter a flurry of cultic terms taken from Judaism's sacrificial systems and applied directly onto Paul's kerygmatic program among the gentiles. As we will see presently, Paul casts himself in the role of a priest officiating over the sacrifice of the gentiles, which sacrifice has been rendered pleasing and holy by the same Spirit that effected their adoption into the family of God, their grafting into the Israel-tree. Moreover, despite Dunn's concerns to the contrary (cited in the epigram, above), Paul puts

---

1. Dunn, *Partings*, 107.

himself forward as *the* priest who presents the offering of the gentiles, "the apostle to the gentiles" (Rom 11:13), who now writes to gentile believers in Rome in order to bring them under the authority of his commission to the nations.[2]

"In Sum..." (Rom 15:14–33)

14 I myself am convinced about you, my brethren, that you yourselves are full of goodness, filled with all knowledge, even able to admonish one another. **15** But I wrote to you even more boldly, in part as one who reminds you because of the grace that was given to me by God, **16** so that I would be a priestly servant of Christ Jesus for the gentiles, offering priestly service on behalf of the gospel of God, so that the offering of the gentiles might be acceptable, sanctified by the Holy Spirit. **17** Therefore, I have [this] boast in Christ Jesus: namely, my service for God. **18** For I will not dare to speak of anything except what Christ accomplished through me for the obedience of the gentiles, in word and in deed, **19** with the power of signs and wonders, with the power of the Spirit [of God], so that I have fulfilled the gospel of Christ from Jerusalem and circling around as far as Illyricum. **20** In this way I aspire to proclaim the gospel where Christ is not [already] called upon, so that I would not build upon another person's foundation. **21** But just as it is written,

> "To those whom it was not announced about him, they shall see,
>   and those who have not heard, they shall understand" (Isa 52:15).

22 Therefore, I have often been hindered from coming to you. **23** But now, since I no longer have any place among these regions and since I have had the desire to come to you for many years, **24** I may go to Spain. For I hope to see you as I pass through and to be assisted by you, after I have enjoyed your company for a while. **25** But now I am going to Jerusalem in order to serve the saints. **26** For Macedonia and Achaia were pleased to have some fellowship with the poor among the saints in Jerusalem, **27** for they were pleased, and they are also in their debt. For if the gentiles fellowship in their spiritual matters, they ought to serve them also in their fleshly matters. **28** Therefore, when I have completed this task and have certified this fruit for them, I will depart through you on my way to Spain. **29** But I know that, since I am coming to you with the fullness of the blessing of Christ, I will come [to you].

30 So I urge you[, brethren,] through our Lord Jesus Christ and through the love of the Spirit, to contend together with me in your prayers

---

2. See Das, *Solving*, 55.

> to God on my behalf, **31** so that I would be delivered from those who are disobedient in Judea and my service for Jerusalem would be acceptable to the saints, **32** so that, as I come to you with joy through the will of God, I might find some rest with you. **33** So may the God of peace be with you all. Amen.

Robert Jewett refers to this section of Romans as the *peroratio*, or the summation, in which Paul recaps some of the key themes of the letter and begins to draw it to a close. As the letter winds down, Paul leaves behind his rhetorical stance as a dialogue partner and resumes his authorial stance as a letter-writer. His letter "reminds" his readers [*epanamimnēskōn hymas*] of what they already know; after all, his audience is "full of goodness" and "filled with all knowledge" (Rom 15:14). He bears the responsibility to remind them of what they know "because of the grace that was given to me by God" (15:15). Paul's reference to "the grace" [*tēn charin*] he received from God picks up his earlier references to his apostolic vocation as "grace." Romans 12 began with Paul appealing to "the grace that was given to me" (Rom 12:3) as the basis of his moral authority and as the basis on which each person exercises whatever spiritual gift God has given them (see Rom 12:6). More importantly, Paul began his letter to the Romans with reference to the "grace and apostleship" he received from Jesus (see 1:5), and he identifies the purpose (or goal) of his grace and apostleship as "the obedience of faith among all the gentiles." As we noted in chapter 2, Paul portrays himself as an ambassador dispatched on behalf of Jesus, Israel's king, to procure allegiance ("the obedience of faith") from all the nations of the earth. At the end of Romans, Paul once again describes the purpose of the grace he was given:

> ... so that I would be a *priestly servant* [*leitourgon*] of Christ Jesus for the gentiles, *offering priestly service* [*hierourgounta*] on behalf of the gospel of God, so that *the offering* [*hē prosphora*] of the gentiles might be *acceptable* [*euprosdektos*], *sanctified* [*hēgiasmenē*] by the Holy Spirit. (Rom 15:16)

Paul piles up cultic language (i.e., language related to the temple cult) to describe himself. I identify five cultic terms, all of which apply to priestly service in the temple of God.

- "priestly servant" [*leitourgon*], which refers to "one engaged in administrative or cultic service."³ In the LXX, *leitourgos* may refer to an attendant to the king (e.g., 3 Kgdms 10:5) or a prophet's attendant (e.g., 4 Kgdms 4:43; 6:15), but it often refers to temple personnel (see 2 Esd 7:24; 20:39; Sir 7:30; Isa 61:6).⁴ Inexplicably, Jewett argues that Paul's self-presentation as a *leitourgos* "points more clearly to the role of a 'public functionary' of a city, regent, or God, an agent who provides benefaction without remuneration in a particular role," and he casts Paul in an ambassadorial rather than priestly role.⁵ However, in the very next paragraph Jewett will have to walk this argument back and concede that the participle, "offering priestly service" (see the next bullet point) "modifies the preceding clause and characterizes Paul's ambassadorship as a 'verbalized' form of priesthood."⁶

- "offering priestly service" [*hierourgounta*], or "to act in some cultic or sacred capacity."⁷ This NT *hapax legomenon* does not occur in the LXX,⁸ but it occurs frequently in Philo and Josephus (thirty-two and eleven occurrences, respectively). "[I]n Philo and Josephus it consistently denotes the priestly offering of sacrifice . . . though it should be noted that for both Philo and Josephus *hierourgein* is something the whole people can do."⁹

- "the offering" [*hē prosphora*], which refers either to "the act of bringing as a voluntary expression," or "that which is brought as a voluntary expression."¹⁰ Both definitions can be rendered "sacrifice" or "offering." Commentators generally agree that Paul is using *prosphora* in the latter sense.¹¹ It is less clear whether Paul envisages the gentiles *bringing*

---

3. BDAG s.v.

4. I would also include LXX Pss 102:21 ("Bless the Lord, all his hosts, his ministers [*leitourgoi*] doing his will") and 103:4 ("He who makes spirits his messengers, and flaming fire his ministers [*leitourgous*]"; both translations taken from the NETS) as cultic uses of *leitourgos*.

5. Jewett, *Romans*, 906–7 (p. 906 quoted); see also p. 915.

6. Ibid., 907.

7. BDAG s.v.

8. Though see the variant reading at 4 Macc. 7:8: "those who serve Torah as priests" [*tous hierourgountas ton nomon*; discussed in Dunn, *Romans*, 2:860].

9. Ibid.

10. BDAG s.v.

11. See, e.g., Dunn, *Romans*, 2:860; Matera, *Romans*, 332.

the offering or *being* the offering.¹² Either way, Paul casts himself in the role of a priest who officiates over "the offering of the gentiles."

- "acceptable" [*euprosdektos*], which "pert[ains] to being capable of eliciting favorable acceptance."¹³ This adjective often describes an offering or sacrifice, as it does here (see also 1 Pet 2:5). Paul has also used the near-synonym *euarestos* ("pleasing") twice in Rom 12:1–2 to describe the Romans' self-offering as living sacrifices.¹⁴

- "sanctified" [*hēgiasmenē*], for which BDAG (*s.v.*) offers four definitions, the first two of which are explicitly cultic: "set aside someth[ing] or make it suitable for ritual purposes," and "include a pers[on] in the inner circle of what is holy, in both cultic and moral associations of the word."¹⁵ This word "is almost exclusively a biblical word. It denotes the act of setting apart, dedicating to God, so as to be his alone, or used solely for his purposes."¹⁶ In Romans, Paul uses *hagiazō* only here, and I find it striking that Paul explicitly uses this "exclusively biblical word" to describe gentiles. But then again, the means by which God has sanctified the gentiles and rendered them "acceptable" to himself is the primary theme of Romans.

~

How does Paul, a Benjamite Jew (see Rom 11:1; Phil 3:5), cast himself in the role of an officiating priest of Israel's Creator God, given that priests come exclusively from the tribe of Levi? Dunn attributes this perhaps shocking development to an eschatological transformation:

> [T]he cultic language is transformed (not merely spiritualized) by an eschatological fulfillment; that is to say, the division between cultic and secular (together with that between sacred and

12. See ftn 15, below, for a suggestion that Paul envisages both meanings.

13. BDAG s.v.

14. Incidentally, we could construe Rom 15:16 as confirmation that Paul has been addressing a purely gentile audience in Rom 12:1–2 and, by extension, throughout the entire letter. In Romans 12 Paul urges his readers to offer themselves as living sacrifices to God. Then, in 15:16, Paul casts himself in the role of the officiating priest who presents "the offering of the gentiles," which clearly implies that *both* those who bring the offering *and* those who are the offering in 12:1–2 are gentiles.

15. I would not press the distinction between the "cultic and moral associations" of *hagiazō*; the figurative (= moral) use of the word draws upon the literal (= cultic) use. BDAG's third and fourth definitions are "to treat as holy," and "to eliminate that which is incompatible with holiness," both of which also have clear cultic connotations.

16. Dunn, *Romans*, 2:861.

profane, clean and unclean—14:14, 20) has been broken down and abolished as part of the breaking down of the (in large part cultically determined) distinction between Jew and Gentile.[17]

Perhaps, but Dunn has missed the larger point of Paul's appropriation of Israel's story and "the establishment" [*histanomen*; see Rom 3:31] of Torah in Paul's proclamation of the gospel. We have already had numerous occasions to mention YHWH's promise to Abraham in Gen 12:3: "I will bless those who bless you, and those who curse you I will curse. And in you all the tribes of the earth will be blessed." We have also referred to all or part of the Ten Commandments (Exodus 20) on multiple occasions, though we have not yet mentioned their narrative introduction in Exodus 19. As the people of Israel encamp at the base of Mt. Sinai and YHWH prepares to establish his covenant with them, God instructs Moses to tell the people, "you shall be to me a royal priesthood [*basileion hierateuma*] and a holy nation" (Exod 19:6 LXX). Levites functioned as priests mediating between YHWH and Israel, but Israel *as a whole* functioned (or was intended to function) as priests mediating between YHWH and all the nations.[18] Paul casts himself in the role of a priest officiating over "the offering of the gentiles" just as Israel was always supposed to do.[19] The cultic language of Rom 15:16 has not been "transformed" so much as it has been fulfilled![20] Paul reflects the view, already evident in Leviticus, that "'holiness' is not confined to the boundaries of the sanctuary and that of the cult but ex-

17. Ibid., 2:859–60.

18. Himmelfarb rightly identifies "a certain tension" at work in Exod 19:6 "between the idea of the entire people of Israel as priests and the actuality of what the Torah dictates, a system in which the priesthood is the possession of a limited group of Israelites" ("Kingdom of Priests," 90–91). Jews could manage or resolve this tension in any number of ways. Paul appears to have applied the relationship between Levi and the people of Israel to his own relation to the people of the nations/gentiles. Similarly, [Trito-]Isaiah casts Israel in this same role *vis-à-vis* the gentiles (ibid., 100).

19. Bird attributes a similar view to Philo of Alexandria: "The vocation of Israel is to be a prophet and priest for the salvation of the whole world" (see Bird, *Crossing*, 103–9; p. 108 quoted).

20. Frank Matera makes a similar argument, though without reference to Exodus 19: "Although Paul was not a priest, and could not be a priest since he belonged to the tribe of Benjamin rather than to the tribe of Levi, he employs cultic language here and elsewhere to highlight the new creation that God has brought about through the death and resurrection of Christ. In this new age, the eschatological people of God, believers drawn from Gentiles as well as Jews, is the temple of God and the dwelling place of God's Spirit (1 Cor 3:16). In this temple, believers offer themselves to God as a living sacrifice, and by proclaiming the gospel, Paul acts in a priestly capacity" (Matera, *Romans*, 333).

pands into 'the everyday life of common people.'"²¹ The innovative aspect of Paul's gospel focuses on the dynamics by which people—first the Jew and also the Greek—find themselves included in and circumscribed by "holiness."

This cultic metaphor is hardly one aspect of Paul's self-conception among many other aspects.²² Paul presents himself fundamentally as a priest of Israel's God who procures the offering of the gentiles and instructs them how to go about being and/or bringing that offering. The entire letter to the Romans has been focused on the basis of the gentiles' acceptability to God, and specifically whether or not Torah mediated that acceptability. Moreover, Paul began the exhortational section of the letter in cultic terms, and he returns to that language as he draws the letter to a close. Paul describes the scope of "the gift given to him by God"—that is, his apostolic vocation—as extending "outward from Jerusalem and circling around as far as Illyricum" (Rom 15:19). When he describes his ambition in terms of "proclaiming the gospel where Christ is not [already] called upon" (15:20), he is making an ethnic point as well as a geographical point. That is, he takes the gospel even to gentiles who have no affinity for Moses or Torah. When he says he does not want to "build upon another person's foundation" [*allotrion themelion*; 15:20], his point is not that he wants to avoid spreading the gospel in places where there are already followers of Jesus. After all, he is planning to visit Rome, a city with churches that he did not plant, endeavoring to "impart some spiritual gift" among them and to reap some fruit from among them (see 1:11, 13). Instead, the "other man's foundation" refers to Moses: Paul's apostolic vocation is a priestly endeavor that procures "the offering of the gentiles" and so extends well beyond the Mosaic foundation of the people of God. Paul's quotation from Isa 52:15 (see Rom 15:21) makes this point exactly.

But I would not push the distinction between the ethnic and the geographic understanding of Rom 15:20 too far. Paul pushes the geographic point to an extreme in order to push the ethnic point: He is going to Spain, the western frontier of the then-known world, because the gospel appeals

21. Ehrensperger, "Called to Be Saints," 102; citing Willis, *Leviticus*, 171.

22. So similarly Wright: "This sudden rush of sacrificial and cultic imagery can hardly be accidental; it is not, it seems, one metaphor taken at random. Paul is after all on his way to Jerusalem to bring a highly significant, and hence contentious, gift of money; the thought of going up to the temple, like a Diaspora Jew going on pilgrimage, is clearly in his mind. But he is talking about more than a single trip or a single gift. *He is talking about his entire vocation*, to gather up the Gentile world and present it as a surprising but appropriate offering before the world's creator and its rightful Lord" ("Romans," 754; my emphasis).

to all gentiles, even those most distant. Paul's ministry evokes, perhaps only negatively, the story of that other "apostle to the gentiles," Jonah, who fled to Spain (= Tarshish) to avoid God's call to Nineveh. Jonah fled because he anticipated God would show compassion to the Ninevites if they repented (see Jonah 4:2). Now Paul plans to go to Spain to take this very message to them, that Israel's Creator God extends his mercy even to them. The result is a spiritual bond that unites Jew and gentile into one people, and Paul reflects this unity both in his ministry to the gentiles (taking the gospel to them) as well as in his service to the Jews (gathering an offering from gentile believers in Asia and Europe to take to Jerusalem; see Rom 15:25–29).

Romans 15 closes with a final admonition that follows naturally from the mutual fellowship of vv. 23–29: Just as the gentile believers in Macedonia and Achaia benefitted from and were indebted to the saints in Jerusalem, so also Paul urges his gentile readers in Rome to "contend together with me [*synagōnisasthai moi*] in your prayers to God on my behalf" (15:30). We began the previous chapter noting that commentators often read Rom 14:1—15:13 in terms of divisions and conflict between Jewish and gentile Christians, and we noted that this reading is based on a circular argument rather than any real data. In Rom 15:30–33 we have a genuine appeal for inter-ethnic unity, as Paul (a Jew) appeals to his readers (gentiles) for their prayers as he takes an offering from Macedonia and Achaia (more gentiles) to the believers in Judea and Jerusalem (more Jews). When Paul asks for prayers that God deliver him "from those who are disobedient [*apo tōn apeithountōn*] in Judea" (15:31), Christian readers need to be careful to appreciate that Paul is *not* asking for safety from "the Jews." After all, he is engaged in ministry "to the saints" who are "in Jerusalem," the vast of majority of whom were Jews. As students of Romans (and of the NT more generally), we have to *un*learn reading value-laden terminology (such as "the disobedient") in ethnic terms.

Sincerely Yours, Paul (Rom 16:1–27)

1 Now, I present to you Phoebe, our sister, who is also a minister of the church that is in Cenchrea, **2** so that you would welcome her in the Lord, worthily of the saints, and help her in whatever way she might have need from you, for she also has become a patroness of many, even including me.

3 Greet Prisca and Aquila, my coworkers in Christ Jesus, **4** who stretched out their own neck for my life's sake, for whom I do not give thanks alone, but so do all the churches of the gentiles. **5** Also, greet the church that meets in their house. Greet Epaenetus, my beloved, who is the firstfruit for Christ in Asia. **6** Greet Mary, who labored profusely on your behalf. **7** Greet Andronicus and Junia, my fellow countrymen as well as my prisonmates, who are prominent among the apostles, who also were before me in Christ. **8** Greet Ampliatus, my beloved in the Lord. **9** Greet Urbanus, our coworker in Christ, and Stachys, my beloved. **10** Greet Apelles, who is approved in Christ. Greet the members of Aristobulus's household. **11** Greet Herodion, my fellow countryman. Greet the members of Narcissus's household who are in the Lord. **12** Greet Tryphena and Tryphosa, who are laborers in the Lord. Greet Persis, the beloved, who labored profusely in the Lord. **13** Greet Rufus, who is chosen in the Lord, as well as his mother (who was also a mother to me). **14** Greet Asyncritus, Plegon, Hermes, Patrobas, Hermas, and the brethren who are with them. **15** Greet Philologus and Julia, Nereus and his sister, and Olympas and all the saints who are with them. **16** Greet one another with a holy kiss. All the churches of Christ greet you.

17 Now I urge you, brethren, to look out for those who stir up dissensions and enticements contrary to the teaching that you learned. Stay away from them. **18** For people such us this do not serve our Lord Christ but rather their own belly, and through their smooth talk and flattery they deceive the hearts of the naïve. **19** For your obedience has reached everyone. Therefore, I rejoice over you. I want you to be wise with regard to what is good but innocent with regard to what is evil. **20** And the God of peace will crush Satan under your feet, and soon! May the grace of our Lord Jesus be with you.

21 Timothy, my coworker, greets you, as do also Lucius and Jason and Sosipater, my fellow countrymen. **22** (I, Tertius, the one who wrote this letter, greet you in the Lord.) **23** Gaius, my host, along with the whole church greets you. Erastus, the city treasurer, greets you, as well as Quartus [our] brother.

25 Now to the one who is able to strengthen you according to my gospel and to the proclamation of Jesus Christ, according to the revelation of the mystery which has been kept silent in times eternal, **26** but which is now revealed through the prophetic Scriptures according to the command of the eternal God for the obedience of faith and which is made known to all the nations, **27** to the only wise God, through Jesus Christ, to whom be glory forever. Amen.

The textual history of Romans 16 is complex and convoluted.[23] Problems include (i) whether or not the grace-formula of 16:20b is original, (ii) whether or not the grace-formula of 16:24 is original, (iii) whether or not the doxology of 16:25–27 is original, (iv) whether or not 16:27 ends with a grace-formula, or even (v) whether or not Romans 16 was originally part of Paul's letter to the Romans. We cannot solve any of these problems here. Instead, we will comment on the form of the text printed in NA[28], which (i) prints the grace-formula in 16:20b, (ii) omits the grace-formula in 16:24, (iii) prints the doxology in 16:25–27 in square brackets, (iv) omits the grace-formula at the end of 16:27, and of course (iv) includes Romans 16 as part of the letter.[24]

Romans 16 begins with a letter of reference, of sorts, for Phoebe, "our sister" [*tēn adelphēn hēmōn*], a deacon[ess] of the church in Cenchrea, "most probably to be identified as the eastern port of Corinth."[25] Jewett rightly describes Phoebe as the "congregational leader" of the Cenchrean church; the title "deacon[ess]" should not lead us to imagine her occupying a secondary or subservient role within the church.[26] He writes on her behalf, almost certainly, because she carried the letter from Paul, in Corinth, to the gentile Christians in Rome. "Ancient epistolary practice would therefore assume that the recommendation of Phoebe was related to her task of conveying and interpreting the letter in Rome as well as in carrying out the business entailed in the letter."[27] Witherington offers an interesting reading of Paul's acknowledgement of Phoebe's patronage in light of Paul's on-going practice of tentmaking:

> Paul has rejected patronage in Corinth from the church itself, choosing rather to continue his tentmaking trade. But he accepts it from Phoebe. This suggests that Paul has very great

---

23. See Longenecker, *Introducing*, 15–42. There are real problems (even errors) with Longenecker's discussion; see Foster, "Major," 97.

24. These text-critical decisions reflect, for example, the original reading of Codex Sinaiticus.

25. Jewett, *Romans*, 943.

26. See ibid., 944–48. In light of the greetings from Corinth/Cenchrea that Paul conveys in Rom 16:21–23, in which he names Timothy, Lucius, Jason, Sosipater, Gaius, Erastus, and Quartus, Paul apparently had access to some important, high-status believers in Corinth. The fact that Paul mentions her first among all those he identifies by name in Romans 16—and the likelihood that he entrusted her with the task of delivering (and reading?) his letter to the Romans—supports the argument that her position as *diakonos* ("deacon[ess]") was a high-status position, her gender notwithstanding.

27. Ibid., 943; see also Grieb, *Story*, xii, 144.

respect for and trust in Phoebe and does not fear that she will treat him merely as a client who has obligations to her and who must keep the reciprocity cycle going.[28]

Elizabeth Johnson goes further than both Jewett and Witherington; she describes Phoebe as "the minister of the church at Cenchreae" and Paul's "emissary, commissioned to set up a base of operations for him as he plans to travel to Spain."[29] In other words, Phoebe goes not just to convey Paul's letter to the Roman churches but also to prepare them for his arrival and recruit them for his mission. Paul urges the Roman Christians to welcome Phoebe, to receive her and the letter she bears from him, and to provide her the hospitality Paul anticipates they will show him when he arrives in Rome.

Paul extends greetings to a number of individuals in Rom 16:3-16, or more accurately, he asks his readers to extend his greetings to a number of individuals. If we interpret the phrases "the brethren who are with them" [*tous syn autois adelphois*; v. 14] and "all the saints who are with them" [*tous syn autois pantas hagious*; v. 15] as references to assemblies of Christians (= churches), Paul offers greetings to twenty-eight individuals, three churches, and two households in the span of fourteen verses.[30] We can make a number of observations about the names in 16:3-16. Paul mentions nineteen men and seven women by name, with two other women mentioned but not named: Rufus's mother (v. 13) and Nereus's sister (v. 15). Paul explicitly identifies three people as Jews (Andronicus and Junia [v. 7] and Herodion [v. 11]), in addition to others whom we can confidently describe as Jews (e.g., Prisca and Aquila). Despite arguments to the contrary, Paul's greetings to Jews in Rome do not provide an obstacle to our reconstruction of Paul's audience as thoroughly gentile. Thorsteinsson notes the second-person plural form of Paul's epistolary greeting and argues,

> This is the form of an indirect salutation in which the sender of a letter bids the reader(s) to greet certain people on his or her behalf. What is to be noted here is that this type was used when the sender wanted greetings to be delivered to someone who

---

28. Witherington and Hyatt, *Romans*, 384.

29. Johnson, "Covenant Faithfulness," 158.

30. The difference between churches and households in Paul's list of greetings should not be pressed. Robert Jewett rightly refers to "five house or tenement churches," and he lists the three churches and two households mentioned in vv. 5, 10, 11, 14, and 15 (Jewett, *Romans*, 953).

was not among the immediate audience. This aspect of Paul's greetings in Romans 16:3–15 has been entirely overlooked by interpreters of the letter. If Paul's choice of salutatory form is to be taken seriously it must be concluded that, instead of being descriptive of the letter's audience, these greetings suggest that the persons meant to be greeted should *not* be counted among those to whom Paul wrote the letter.[31]

The most famous issue arising from Paul's greetings in Rom 16:3–16 occurs in v. 7. Editors have famously read Rom 16:7 as offering greetings to "Andronicus and Junias." The latter name would then be an abbreviated form of the common masculine name, Junianus, though as Jewett notes there is no evidence "that the name Junianus was ever contracted."[32] Since at least the late 1990s, however, the editors of both the Nestle-Aland and the United Bible Societies Greek New Testaments have read v. 7 as offering greetings to "Andronicus and Junia," with the latter clearly describing a woman as "prominent among the apostles." Whatever our theology of men, women, and their respective roles in the church, Rom 16:7 clearly names a woman and likely identifies her "among the apostles." Moreover, she is not the only woman active in ministry in Romans 16 and not even the only high-status woman.

After this lengthy list of greetings, Paul offers (another) concluding exhortational section, which ends with the grace-formula of v. 20. Paul spent a chapter and a half urging his readers not to judge one another (14:13) and to "welcome one another" (15:7), and here at the close of the letter he cautions them to avoid those who create division. When he describes such people as "serving their own bellies" [*douleuousin . . . tē heautōn koilia*], we should not try to figure out if these are licentious Christians who indulge in every worldly pleasure or ascetic Christians who shun every trace of luxury. Instead, as in Rom 14:1—15:13, Paul's problem with these people is that they elevate food or drink above the unity and well-being of the community. Unlike "the naïve" who are influenced by people who engage in "smooth talk and flattery" [*dia tēs chrēstologias kai eulogias*; v. 18], Paul's Roman readers have exhibited noteworthy obedience, and the report of their obedience has spread "to everyone" (v. 19). Twice Paul has defined his apostolic vocation in terms of procuring the obedience of the gentiles (see Rom 1:5; 15:18). Even though Paul has never visited the Roman churches, his commendation in 16:19 suggests

---

31. Thorsteinsson, *Interlocutor*, 98–99; *pace* Watson, "Law in Romans," 105.

32. See Jewett, *Romans*, 950, and the literature cited there.

In Sum . . .

he includes them within the ambit of his apostolic authority and approves of their performance.

Paul then relates greetings from people with him in Corinth, including Timothy "my coworker" [*ho synergos mou*], Lucius, Jason, and Sosipater. Paul identifies all four of these individuals as Jews [*hoi syngeneis mou*; lit. "my fellow countrymen"], and we should appreciate that Paul—another Jew—relays their greetings to his gentile readers. In other words, the entire communicative moment represented by the letter to the Romans is an example or an instance of the mutual, inter-ethnic acceptance that Paul prayed for in Rom 15:30–33 and the more general acceptance for which he has argued throughout the entire letter, not just in 14:1—15:13.

Paul's amanuensis, Tertius, "the one who wrote this letter" [*Tertios ho grapsas tēn epistolēn*], also sends along his greetings to the gentile readers of Romans.

Last of all, Paul conveys the greetings of Gaius (his host in Corinth), the whole Corinthian church, Erastus (the Corinthian city treasurer), and Quartus, all three of whom are likely (i) gentile Christians and (ii) of significant social and/or political status.

Romans concludes with a doxological statement that wraps up a number of themes that ran the length of Paul's letter.[33] First, in his opening Paul described the gospel of God as "promised beforehand through his prophets in the Holy Scriptures" (Rom 1:2), and here in the closing he identifies the vehicle of divine revelation as "the prophetic Scriptures" [*graphōn prophētikōn*; 16:26]. Second, later in the letter's opening, Paul reveals his desire to visit the Roman Christians in order to impart some spiritual gift to them, "in order to strengthen" them [*eis to stērichthēnai*; 1:11]. He then uses the same word again in the letter's closing as he describes Israel's God as "the one who is able to strengthen [*stērixai*] you according to my gospel and to the proclamation of Jesus Christ" (16:25). Third, earlier Paul employed a disclosure formula to identify and draw his readers' attention to "this mystery" [*to mystērion touto*], which he identified as Israel's partial hardening in order to create space for "the fullness of the gentiles" (11:25). The partial hardening of Israel and the fullness of the gentiles works to achieve God's ultimate purpose for Israel: "And in this way all Israel will be saved" (11:26). Here in the closing doxology he once again mentions the "mystery" that has been kept silent but that is now made known. These and other links between the doxology in vv. 25–27

---

33. Moo (*Romans*, 936–38) provides a helpful chart that illustrates the thematic links between the doxology in Rom 16:25–27 and the rest of the letter.

and the rest of the letter make this an appropriate ending to this, Paul's lengthiest and, arguably, most important letter:

> **25** Now to the one who is able to strengthen you according to my gospel and to the proclamation of Jesus Christ, according to the revelation of the mystery which has been kept silent in times eternal, **26** but which is now revealed through the prophetic Scriptures according to the command of the eternal God for the obedience of faith and which is made known to all the nations, **27** to the only wise God, through Jesus Christ, to whom be glory forever. Amen. (Rom 16:25–27)

Bibliography

Adeyẹmi, Fẹmi. "Paul's 'Positive' Statements about the Mosaic Law." *BSac* 164.653 (2007) 49–58.
Adkins, A. W. H. *Moral Values and Political Behaviour in Ancient Greece: From Homer to the End of the Fifth Century.* London: Chatto and Windus, 1972.
Bailey, Daniel P. "Jesus as the Mercy Seat: The Semantics and Theology of Paul's Use of Hilasterion in Romans 3:25." *TynBul* 51.1 (2000) 155–58.
Bailey, Jon Nelson. "Paul's Political Paraenesis in Romans 13:1–7." *ResQ* 46.1 (2004) 11–28.
Barclay, John M. G. "'I Will Have Mercy on Whom I Have Mercy': The Golden Calf and Divine Mercy in Romans 9–11 and Second Temple Judaism." *EC* 1 (2010) 82–106.
Barrett, C. K. *A Commentary on the Epistle to the Romans.* 2nd ed. BNTC. London: Black, 1991.
Barth, Karl. *The Epistle to the Romans.* Translated by E. C. Hoskyns. London: Oxford University Press, 1933.
Bauer, Walter, Frederick W. Danker, William F. Arndt, and F. W. Gingrich, eds. *A Greek-English Lexicon of the New Testament and Other Early Christian Literature.* 3rd ed. Chicago: University of Chicago Press, 2000.
Beasley-Murray, George R. "Baptism." In *DPL* 60–66.
Betz, Hans Dieter. "Transferring a Ritual: Paul's Interpretation of Baptism in Romans 6." In *Paul in His Hellenistic Context,* edited by Troels Engberg-Pedersen, 84–118. Minneapolis: Fortress, 1995.
Bietenhard, Hans. "λαός." In *NIDNTT* 2:795–800.
———. "ὄνομα (part)." In *NIDNTT* 2:648–55.
Bird, Michael F. *Crossing over Sea and Land: Jewish Missionary Activity in the Second Temple Period.* Peabody, MA: Hendrickson, 2010.
Bird, Michael F., and Preston M. Sprinkle, eds. *The Faith of Jesus Christ: Exegetical, Biblical, and Theological Studies.* Milton Keynes, UK: Paternoster, 2009.
Blass, Friedrich, Albert Debrunner, and Robert Walter Funk, eds. *A Greek Grammar of the New Testament and Other Early Christian Literature.* Chicago: University of Chicago Press, 1961.
Borgen, Peder, Kåre Fuglseth, and Roald Skarsten. *The Philo Index: A Complete Greek Word Index to the Writings of Philo of Alexandria.* Grand Rapids: Eerdmans, 2000.
Braaten, Laurie J. "The Groaning Creation: The Biblical Background for Romans 8:22." *BR* 50 (2005) 19–39.
Brown, Colin, ed. *The New International Dictionary of New Testament Theology.* Grand Rapids: Zondervan, 1975–85.
———. "ἱλάσκομαι (part)." In *NIDNTT* 3:151–60.

Bibliography

Bultmann, Rudolf. *Der Stil der Paulinischen Predigt und die kynisch-stoische Diatribe.* FRLANT. Göttingen: Vandenhoeck & Ruprecht, 1910.

Burk, Denny. "Is Paul's Gospel Counterimperial? Evaluating the Prospects of the 'Fresh Perspective' for Evangelical Theology." *JETS* 51.2 (2008) 309–37.

Campbell, Douglas A. "The Faithfulness of Jesus Christ in Romans 3:22." In *The Faith of Jesus Christ: Exegetical, Biblical, and Theological Studies*, edited by Michael F. Bird and Preston M. Sprinkle, 57–71. Milton Keynes, UK: Paternoster, 2009.

Campbell, William S. "Did Paul Advocate Separation from the Synagogue? A Reaction to Francis Watson: *Paul, Judaism, and the Gentiles: A Sociological Approach*." *SJT* 42.4 (1989) 457–67.

———. "The Rationale for Gentile Inclusion and Identity in Paul." *CTR* 9.2 (2012) 23–38.

Caragounis, Chrys C. "Romans 5:15–16 in the Context of 5:12–21: Contrast or Comparison?" *NTS* 31.1 (1985) 142–48.

Carter, Timothy L. "The Irony of Romans 13." *NovT* 46.3 (2004) 209–28.

Carter, Warren. *John and Empire: Initial Explorations.* London: T & T Clark, 2008.

———. *The Roman Empire and the New Testament: An Essential Guide.* Nashville: Abingdon, 2006.

Charlesworth, James H, ed. *The Old Testament Pseudepigrapha.* 2 vols. ABRL. New York: Doubleday, 1985.

Clarke, Andrew D. "The Good and the Just in Romans 5:7." *TynBul* 41.1 (1990) 128–42.

Coleman, Thomas M. "Binding Obligations in Romans 13:7: A Semantic Field and Social Context." *TynBul* 48.2 (1997) 307–27.

Collins, John J. "Eschatologies of Late Antiquity." In *DNTB* 330–37.

Cottrell, Jack. *Romans.* 2 vols. College Press NIV Commentary. Joplin, MO: College Press, 1996.

Cranfield, Charles E. B. *A Critical and Exegetical Commentary on the Epistle to the Romans.* 2 vols. ICC. Edinburgh: T & T Clark, 1975.

———. "Some Observations on Romans 13:1–7." *NTS* 6.3 (1960) 241–49.

Crossley, James G. *The Date of Mark's Gospel: Insight from the Law in Earliest Christianity.* JSNTSup 266. London: T & T Clark, 2004.

Das, A. Andrew. "The Gentile-Encoded Audience of Romans: The Church Outside the Synagogue." In *Reading Paul's Letter to the Romans*, edited by Jerry L. Sumney, 29–46. RBS 73. Atlanta: Society of Biblical Literature, 2012.

———. *Paul and the Jews.* LPS. Peabody, MA: Hendrickson, 2003.

———. *Solving the Romans Debate.* Minneapolis: Fortress, 2007.

de Lacey, Douglas R. "Circumcision." In *DLNTD* 226–30.

Deffinbaugh, Robert L. "The Coming Wrath of God: Self-Righteousness Is Unrighteousness (Romans 2:1–29)." No pages. Online: https://bible.org/seriespage/3-coming-wrath-god-self-righteousness-unrighteousness-romans-21–29.

deSilva, David A. "Patronage." In *DNTB* 766–71.

Dillon, Richard J. "The Spirit as Taskmaster and Troublemaker in Romans 8." *CBQ* 60.4 (1998) 682–702.

Doering, Lutz. *Ancient Jewish Letters and the Beginnings of Christian Epistolography.* WUNT 1.298. Tübingen: Mohr Siebeck, 2012.

Donaldson, Terence L. "The 'Curse of the Law' and the Inclusion of the Gentiles: Galatians 3:13–14." *NTS* 32.1 (1986) 94–112.

———. *Judaism and the Gentiles: Jewish Patterns of Universalism (to 135 CE)*. Waco, TX: Baylor University Press, 2007.
Donfried, Karl P. *The Romans Debate*. Revised and expanded ed. Grand Rapids: Baker Academic, 2002.
Draper, Jonathan A. "'Humble Submission to Almighty God' and Its Biblical Foundation: Contextual Exegesis of Romans 13:1–7." *JTSA* 63 (1988) 30–38.
Dunn, James D. G. "Adam and Christ." In *Reading Paul's Letter to the Romans*, edited by Jerry L. Sumney, 125–38. RBS 73. Atlanta: Society of Biblical Literature, 2012.
———. *Jesus and the Spirit: A Study of the Religious and Charismatic Experience of Jesus and the First Christians as Reflected in the New Testament*. Philadelphia: Westminster, 1975.
———. *Romans*. WBC. 2 vols. Nashville: Thomas Nelson, 1988.
———. "Romans 13:1–7: A Charter for Political Quietism?" *ExAud* 2 (1986) 55–68.
———. *The Partings of the Ways: Between Christianity and Judaism and Their Significance for the Character of Christianity*. 2nd ed. London: SCM, 2006.
Eastman, Susan G. "Whose Apocalypse? The Identity of the Sons of God in Romans 8:19." *JBL* 121.2 (2002) 263–77.
Ehrensperger, Kathy. "'Called to Be Saints': The Identity-Shaping Dimensions of Paul's Priestly Discourse in Romans." In *Reading Paul in Context: Explorations in Identity Formation. Essays in Honour of William S. Campbell*, edited by Kathy Ehrensperger and J. Brian Tucker, 90–109. LNTS 428. London: T & T Clark, 2010.
———. "Scriptural Reasoning: The Dynamic That Informed Paul's Theologizing." *Journal of Scriptural Reasoning* 5.3 (2005). No pages. Online: http://jsr.lib.virginia.edu/?s=ehrensperger.
Eisenbaum, Pamela M. *Paul Was Not a Christian: The Real Message of a Misunderstood Apostle*. New York: HarperOne, 2009.
Elliott, Neil. "Paul's Political Christology: Samples from Romans." In *Reading Paul in Context: Explorations in Identity Formation. Essays in Honour of William S. Campbell*, edited by Kathy Ehrensperger and J. Brian Tucker, 39–51. LNTS 428. London: T & T Clark, 2010.
———. *The Rhetoric of Romans: Argumentative Constraint and Strategy and Paul's Dialogue with Judaism*. Minneapolis: Fortress, 2007.
Engberg-Pedersen, Troels. *Paul and the Stoics*. Louisville: Westminster John Knox, 2000.
———. "Paul's Stoicizing Politics in Romans 12–13: The Role of 13.1–10 in the Argument." *JSNT* 29.2 (2006) 163–72.
———. "The Reception of Graeco-Roman Culture in the New Testament: The Case of Romans 7.7–25." In *The New Testament as Reception*, edited by Mogens Müller and Henrik Tronier, 32–57. Sheffield, UK: Sheffield Academic, 2002.
Evans, Craig A., and Stanley E. Porter, eds. *Dictionary of New Testament Backgrounds*. Downers Grove, IL: InterVarsity, 2000.
Feldman, Louis H. *Judean Antiquities 1–4*. Flavius Josephus: Translation and Commentary 3. Boston: Brill Academic, 2000.
Finamore, Steve. "The Gospel and the Wrath of God in Romans 1." In *Understanding, Studying and Reading: New Testament Essays in Honour of John Ashton*, edited by Christopher Rowland and Crispin H. T. Fletcher-Louis, 140–45. JSNTSup 153. Sheffield, UK: Sheffield Academic, 1998.
Fitzmyer, Joseph A. *Romans*. AB. New York: Doubleday, 1993.

Bibliography

Foster, Paul. "Major Critical Issues in the Study of Romans (review of Richard N. Longenecker, *Introducing Romans*)." *ExpTim* 123.2 (2011) 96–97.

Frankfurter, David. "Jews or Not? Reconstructing the 'Other' in Rev 2:9 and 3:9." *HTR* 94.4 (2001) 403–25.

Frey, Jean-Baptiste. "Inscriptions Inédites Des Catacombs Juives de Rome." *Rivista Archaeologia Cristiana* 7 (1930) 235–60.

Furnish, Victor Paul. "Living to God, Walking in Love: Theology and Ethics in Romans." In *Reading Paul's Letter to the Romans*, edited by Jerry L. Sumney, 187–202. RBS 73. Atlanta: Society of Biblical Literature, 2012.

Garroway, Joshua. "The Circumcision of Christ: Romans 15.7–13." *JSNT* 34.4 (2012) 303–22.

———. *Paul's Gentile-Jews: Neither Jew nor Gentile, but Both*. New York: Palgrave, 2012.

Gathercole, Simon J. "A Law unto Themselves: The Gentiles in Romans 2.14–15 Revisited." *JSNT*.85 (2002) 27–49.

———. "After the New Perspective: Works, Justification and Boasting in Early Judaism and Romans 1–5." *TynBul* 52.2 (2001) 303–6.

Godet, Fréderic Louis, and Talbot W. Chambers. *Commentary on St. Paul's Epistle to the Romans*. Grand Rapids: Kregel, 1977.

Gombis, Timothy G. *Paul: A Guide for the Perplexed*. London: T & T Clark, 2010.

Goodwin, Mark. *Paul, Apostle of the Living God: Kerygma and Conversion in 2 Corinthians*. Harrisburg, PA: Trinity, 2001.

Green, Joel B., Scot McKnight, and I. Howard Marshall, eds. *Dictionary of Jesus and the Gospels*. 1st ed. Downers Grove, IL: InterVarsity, 1997.

Grenz, Stanley J. *Theology for the Community of God*. Grand Rapids: Eerdmans, 1994.

Grieb, A. Katherine. "The Righteousness of God in Romans." In *Reading Paul's Letter to the Romans*, edited by Jerry L. Sumney, 65–78. RBS 73. Atlanta: Society of Biblical Literature, 2012.

———. *The Story of Romans: A Narrative Defense of God's Righteousness*. Louisville, KY: Westminster John Knox Press, 2002.

Günther, Walther. "ἁμαρτία." In *NIDNTT* 3:577–83.

Hagedorn, Anselm C., and Jerome H. Neyrey. "'It Was Out of Envy That They Handed Jesus Over' (Mark 15:10): The Anatomy of Envy and the Gospel of Mark." *JSNT* 69 (1998) 15–56.

Hahn, Hans-Christoph. "καύχημα." In *NIDNTT* 1:227–29.

Harris, Murray J. "Appendix: Prepositions and Theology in the Greek New Testament." In *NIDNTT* 3:1171–1215.

Harrison, J. R. "Paul and the Imperial Gospel at Thessaloniki." *JSNT* 25.1 (2002) 71–96.

Harrison, Roland K. "ὠδίνω." In *NIDNTT* 3:857–58.

Hawthorne, Gerald F., Ralph P. Martin, and Daniel G. Reid, eds. *Dictionary of Paul and His Letters*. Downers Grove, IL: InterVarsity, 1993.

Hays, Richard B. *The Conversion of the Imagination: Paul as Interpreter of Israel's Scripture*. Grand Rapids: Eerdmans, 2005.

Hellholm, David. "Enthymemic Argumentation in Paul: The Case of Romans 6." In *Paul in His Hellenistic Context*, edited by Troels Engberg-Pedersen, 119–79. Minneapolis: Fortress, 1995.

Herzog, William R, II. "Dissembling, a Weapon of the Weak: The Case of Christ and Caesar in Mark 12:13–17 and Romans 13:1–7." *PRSt* 21.4 (1994) 339–60.

Bibliography

Himmelfarb, Martha. "'A Kingdom of Priests': The Democratization of the Priesthood in the Literature of Second Temple Judaism." *Journal of Jewish Thought and Philosophy* 6 (1997) 89–104.

Horrell, David G. *An Introduction to the Study of Paul*. 2nd ed. London: T & T Clark, 2006.

———. "The Peaceable, Tolerant Community and the Legitimate Role of the State: Ethics and Ethical Dilemmas in Romans 12:1–15:13." *RevExp* 100.1 (2003) 81–99.

Hurtado, Larry W. "God." In *DJG* 270–76.

Ito, Akio. "Romans 2: A Deuteronomistic Reading." *JSNT* 59 (1995) 21–37.

Jervis, L. Ann. "The Spirit Brings Christ's Life to Life." In *Reading Paul's Letter to the Romans*, edited by Jerry L. Sumney, 139–56. RBS 73. Atlanta: Society of Biblical Literature, 2012.

Jewett, Robert. *Romans*. Hermeneia. Minneapolis: Fortress, 2007.

———. "The Anthropological Implications of the Revelation of Wrath in Romans." In *Reading Paul in Context: Explorations in Identity Formation. Essays in Honour of William S. Campbell*, edited by Kathy Ehrensperger and J. Brian Tucker, 24–38. LNTS 428. London: T & T Clark, 2010.

Johnson, E. Elizabeth. *The Function of Apocalyptic and Wisdom Traditions in Romans 9–11*. SBLDS 109. Atlanta: Scholars, 1989.

———. "God's Covenant Faithfulness to Israel." In *Reading Paul's Letter to the Romans*, edited by Jerry L. Sumney, 157–67. RBS 73. Atlanta: Society of Biblical Literature, 2012.

Johnson Hodge, Caroline. "'A Light to the Nations': The Role of Israel in Romans 9–11." In *Reading Paul's Letter to the Romans*, edited by Jerry L. Sumney, 169–86. RBS 73. Atlanta: Society of Biblical Literature, 2012.

Karris, Robert J. "Romans 14:1—15:13 and the Occasion of Romans." In *The Romans Debate*, edited by Karl P. Donfried, 65–84. Revised and expanded ed. Peabody, MA: Hendrickson, 1991.

Käsemann, Ernst. *Commentary on Romans*. Translated by G. W. Bromiley. Grand Rapids: Eerdmans, 1980.

Keesmaat, Sylvia C. "Exodus and the Intertextual Transformation of Tradition in Romans 8.14–30." *JSNT* 54 (1994) 29–56.

———. "Reading Romans in the Capital of the Empire." In *Reading Paul's Letter to the Romans*, edited by Jerry L. Sumney, 47–64. RBS 73. Atlanta: Society of Biblical Literature, 2012.

Kim, Tae Hun. "The Anarthrous Υἱὸς Θεοῦ in Mark 15,39 and the Roman Imperial Cult." *Bib* 79.2 (1998) 221–41.

Kirk, J. R. Daniel. "Reconsidering *Dikaiōma* in Romans 5:16." *JBL* 126.4 (2007) 787–92.

Kittel, Gerhard, and Gerhard Friedrich, eds. *Theological Dictionary of the New Testament*. Translated by Geoffrey W. Bromiley. Grand Rapids: Eerdmans, 1964–76.

Klein, Günter. "Paul's Purpose in Writing the Epistle to the Romans." In *The Romans Debate*, 29–43. Revised and expanded ed. Peabody, MA: Hendrickson, 1991.

Kraemer, Ross S. "On the Meaning of the Term 'Jew' in Greco-Roman Inscriptions." *HTR* 82.1 (1989) 35–53.

Krentz, Edgar. "The Name of God in Disrepute: Romans 2:17–29." *CurTM* 17.6 (1990) 429–39.

Kruse, Colin G. "Persecution." In *DNTB* 775–78.

Bibliography

Liddell, H. G., R. Scott, and Henry Stuart Jones, eds. *A Greek-English Lexicon*. Oxford: Clarendon, 1996.
Linebaugh, Jonathan A. "Debating Diagonal Δικαιοσύνη: The Epistle of Enoch and Paul in Theological Conversation." *EC* 1 (2010) 107–28.
Longenecker, Richard N. *Introducing Romans: Critical Issues in Paul's Most Famous Letter*. Grand Rapids: Eerdmans, 2011.
Louw, J. P., and E. A. Nida, eds. *Greek-English Lexicon of the New Testament: Based on Semantic Domains*. 2 vols. 2nd ed. New York: United Bible Societies, 1989.
Marshall, John W. "Hybridity and Reading Romans 13." *JSNT* 31.2 (2008) 157–78.
Martin, Ralph P., and Peter H. Davids, eds. *Dictionary of the Later New Testament and Its Developments*. Downers Grove, IL: InterVarsity, 1997.
Martin, Troy W. "*The Good* as God (Romans 5.7)." *JSNT* 25.1 (2002) 55–70.
Matera, Frank J. *Romans*. PCNT. Grand Rapids: Baker Academic, 2010.
Mayer, Reinhold. "Ἰσραήλ." In *NIDNTT* 2:304–16.
McFadden, Kevin W. "The Fulfillment of the Law's *Dikaiōma*: Another Look at Romans 8:1–4." *JETS* 52.3 (2009) 483–97.
McGrath, Alister E. *Christian Theology: An Introduction*. 4th ed. Malden, MA: Blackwell, 1993.
Metzger, Bruce M. *A Textual Commentary on the Greek New Testament*. 2nd ed. Stuttgart: German Bible Society, 1994.
Meyer, Ben F. "The Pre-Pauline Formula in Rom. 3:25–26a." *NTS* 29.2 (1983) 198–208.
Moo, Douglas J. *The Epistle to the Romans*. NICNT. Grand Rapids: Eerdmans, 1996.
Morales, Rodrigo J. "'Promised through His Prophets in the Holy Scriptures': The Role of Scripture in the Letter to the Romans." In *Reading Paul's Letter to the Romans*, edited by Jerry L. Sumney, 109–24. RBS 73. Atlanta: Society of Biblical Literature, 2012.
———. *The Spirit and the Restoration of Israel: New Exodus and New Creation Motifs in Galatians*. WUNT 2.282. Tübingen: Mohr Siebeck, 2010.
Morris, Leon. *The Epistle to the Romans*. PNTC. Grand Rapids: Eerdmans, 1988.
Nanos, Mark D. "'Callused,' Not 'Hardened': Paul's Revelation of Temporary Protection until All Israel Can Be Healed." In *Reading Paul in Context: Explorations in Identity Formation. Essays in Honour of William S. Campbell*, edited by Kathy Ehrensperger and J. Brian Tucker, 52–73. LNTS 428. London: T & T Clark, 2010.
———. "Grafting the Olive Brance (11:17–24)." *The Jewish Annotated New Testament*. Edited by Amy-Jill Levine and Marc Zvi Brettler. Oxford: Oxford University Press, 2011.
———. *The Mystery of Romans: The Jewish Context of Paul's Letter*. Minneapolis: Fortress, 1996.
———. "To the Churches within the Synagogues of Rome." In *Reading Paul's Letter to the Romans*, edited by Jerry L. Sumney, 11–28. RBS 73. Atlanta: Society of Biblical Literature, 2012.
Novenson, Matthew V. "Did Paul Believe in Judaism". Paper presented to Paul Seminar of the British New Testament Society. London, 2012.
Olree, Andy G. "Government as God's Agent: A Reconsideration of Romans 12 and 13." *SCJ* 8.2 (2005) 181–97.
Park, Eung Chun. *Either Jew or Gentile: Paul's Unfolding Theology of Inclusivity*. Louisville, KY: Westminster John Knox, 2003.

Bibliography

Porter, Stanley E. "The Argument of Romans 5: Can a Rhetorical Question Make a Difference?" *JBL* 110.4 (1991) 655–77.

———. *Idioms of the Greek New Testament*. 2nd ed. Sheffield, UK: Sheffield Academic, 1994.

Rodríguez, Rafael. *Oral Tradition and the New Testament: A Guide for the Perplexed*. London: Bloomsbury Academic, 2014.

———. *Structuring Early Christian Memory: Jesus in Tradition, Performance, and Text*. ESCO. LNTS 407. London: T & T Clark, 2010.

Roetzel, Calvin J. "Paul and *Nomos* in the Messianic Age." in *Reading Paul in Context: Explorations in Identity Formation. Essays in Honour of William S. Campbell*, edited by Kathy Ehrensperger and J. Brian Tucker, 113–27. LNTS 428. London: T & T Clark, 2010.

Schneider, Johannes. "στενάζω, στεναγμός, συστενάζω." In *TDNT* 7:600–603.

Schoedel, William R. *Ignatius of Antioch: A Commentary on the Letters of Ignatius of Antioch*. Hermeneia. Philadelphia: Fortress, 1985.

Schreiner, Thomas R. "Did Paul Believe in Justification by Works? Another Look at Romans 2." *BBR* 3 (1993) 131–58.

———. *Romans*. BECNT. Grand Rapids: Baker Academic, 1998.

Silva, Moisés. "Old Testament in Paul." In *DPL* 630–42.

Song, Changwon. *Reading Romans as a Diatribe*. StBL 59. New York: Lang, 2004.

Stegemann, Ekkehard W. "Coexistence and Transformation: Reading the Politics of Identity in Romans in an Imperial Context." In *Reading Paul in Context: Explorations in Identity Formation: Essays in Honour of William S. Campbell*, edited by Kathy Ehrensperger and J. Brian Tucker, 3–23. LNTS 428. London: T & T Clark, 2010.

Stein, Robert H. "The Argument of Romans 13:1–7." *NovT* 31.4 (1989) 325–43.

Stendahl, Krister. "The Apostle Paul and the Introspective Conscience of the West." *HTR* 56.3 (1963) 199–215.

Stowers, Stanley K. *The Diatribe and Paul's Letter to the Romans*. SBLDS 57. Chico, CA: Scholars, 1981.

———. *A Rereading of Romans: Justice, Jews, and Gentiles*. New Haven: Yale University Press, 1994.

———. "Romans 7:7–25 as a Speech-in-Character (προσωποποιία)." In *Paul in His Hellenistic Context*, edited by Troels Engberg-Pedersen, 180–202. Minneapolis: Fortress, 1995.

Sumney, Jerry L. "'Christ Died for Us': Interpretation of Jesus' Death as a Central Element of the Identity of the Earliest Church." In *Reading Paul in Context: Explorations in Identity Formation. Essays in Honour of William S. Campbell*, edited by Kathy Ehrensperger and J. Brian Tucker, 147–72. LNTS 428. London: T & T Clark, 2010.

Thiele, Friedrich. "θύω (part)." In *NIDNTT* 3:417.

Thiessen, Matthew. *Contesting Conversion: Genealogy, Circumcision, and Identity in Ancient Judaism and Christianity*. Oxford: Oxford University Press, 2011.

———. "Romans 2:17 and the Identity of the So-Called *Ioudaios*." Paper presented to the Pauline Epistles section of the Society of Biblical Literature Annual Meeting. San Francisco, 2011.

Thiselton, Anthony C. *The First Epistle to the Corinthians*. NIGTC. Grand Rapids: Eerdmans, 2000.

Bibliography

Thorsteinsson, Runar M. *Paul's Interlocutor in Romans 2: Function and Identity in the Context of Ancient Epistolography.* ConBNT 40. Stockholm: Almqvist & Wiksell, 2003.

Trebilco, Paul R. "Diaspora Judaism." In *DLNTD* 287–300.

Wallace, Daniel B. *Greek Grammar beyond the Basics: An Exegetical Syntax of the New Testament.* Grand Rapids: Zondervan, 1996.

Wasserman, Emma. "Paul among the Philosophers: The Case of Sin in Romans 6–8." *JSNT* 30.4 (2008) 387–415.

Watson, David F. *Honor among Christians: The Cultural Key to the Messianic Secret.* Minneapolis: Fortress, 2010.

Watson, Francis. "The Law in Romans." In *Reading Paul's Letter to the Romans*, edited by Jerry L. Sumney, 93–107. RBS 73. Atlanta: Society of Biblical Literature, 2012.

Williams, Sam K. "The 'Righteousness of God' in Romans." *JBL* 99.2 (1980) 241–90.

Willis, Timothy M. *Leviticus.* AOTC. Nashville: Abingdon, 2009.

Winkler, John J. *The Constraints of Desire: The Anthropology of Sex and Gender in Ancient Greece.* New York: Routledge, 1989.

Winter, Bruce W. "The Public Honouring of Christian Benefactors: Romans 13:3–4 and 1 Peter 2:14–15." *JSNT*.34 (1988) 87–103.

———. *Seek the Welfare of the City: Christians as Benefactors and Citizens.* Grand Rapids: Eerdmans, 1994.

Witherington, Ben, III, and Darlene Hyatt. *Paul's Letter to the Romans: A Socio-Rhetorical Commentary.* Grand Rapids: Eerdmans, 2004.

Wright, N. T. "The Letter to the Romans: Introduction, Commentary, and Reflections." In *The New Interpreter's Bible: A Commentary in Twelve Volumes*, edited by Leander E. Keck, 10:393–770. 12 vols. Nashville: Abingdon, 2002.

———. *The New Testament and the People of God.* COQG 1. Minneapolis: Fortress, 1992.

———. "Paul's Gospel and Caesar's Empire." In *Paul and Politics: Ekklesia, Israel, Imperium, Interpretation*, edited by Richard A. Horsley, 160–83. Harrisburg, PA: Trinity, 2000.

Yoder, John Howard. *The Politics of Jesus.* Grand Rapids: Eerdmans, 1972.

Index of Authors

Adeyẹmi, 200
Adkins, 102

Bailey, 82, 83, 242
Barclay, 70, 180, 181
Barrett, 40
Barth, 22, 25-26
Beasley-Murray, 109, 110
Betz, 109, 110
Bietenhard, 48
Bird, 38, 51, 79, 288
Borgen, 120
Braaten, 162
Brown, 82
Bultmann, 36
Burk, 98

Campbell, D., 78
Campbell W. S., 36, 53, 144, 221-22, 223
Caragounis, 106
Carter, 44, 244
Clarke, 102-3
Coleman, 250, 251-52
Collins, 43
Cottrell, 96, 139
Cranfield, 33, 34, 220, 249
Crossley, 272

Das, ix, 5, 6, 8-9, 10-11, 20, 45, 52, 56, 59, 75, 123, 147-48, 159, 172, 173, 185, 187, 190-91, 222, 225, 226, 229, 259-61, 284
Deffinbaugh, 39
deSilva, 165
Dillon, 151, 162
Doering, 18

Donaldson, 5, 52-53
Draper, 242, 243, 248, 249, 250
Dunn, 28, 29, 33-34, 41, 43, 49, 55, 67, 69, 71, 87, 97, 100, 101, 102, 106, 107, 110, 111-12, 114, 116, 117, 132, 135, 137, 138, 156, 164, 171, 173, 176, 183, 186, 192, 194, 198, 201-2, 203, 207, 208, 220, 242, 252, 259, 263, 264, 265, 266, 269, 271, 276, 280, 283, 286, 287-88

Eastman, 161
Ehrensperger, 2, 56, 75, 90, 188, 259-60, 264, 273, 277, 289
Eisenbaum, 5, 200, 222
Elliott, 49, 51, 54, 60, 81, 94, 243
Engberg-Pedersen, 135, 143, 232, 242, 244, 245, 247, 253

Feldman, 175
Fitzmyer, 113, 150
Frankfurter, 49
Furnish, 28, 54, 78, 232, 235, 236, 245

Garroway, 10, 26, 36, 39, 45, 49, 50, 59, 61, 72, 75, 77, 88, 91, 176, 180, 194-95, 226, 229, 261, 281
Gathercole, 45-46, 54, 86
Goodwin, 29
Grenz, 209
Grieb, 2, 7, 10, 22-23, 29, 70, 76, 84, 91, 96, 133, 140, 141, 233, 292
Günther, 192

Hagedorn, 220
Hahn, 86
Harrington, 175

Index of Authors

Harris, 162
Harrison, J. R., 98
Harrison, R. K., 162
Hays, 90, 281
Hellholm, 110
Herzog, 243
Himmelfarb, 20, 288
Horrell, 1, 2, 242, 246
Hurtado, 156

Ito, 92

Jervis, 148, 150, 158
Jewett, 13, 22, 23, 27, 28, 29, 40, 42, 49, 55, 63, 78–79, 82, 85, 86, 87, 98, 99, 103, 105, 106, 110, 111, 113, 114, 115, 117, 119, 123, 124, 128, 129, 132, 135, 136, 139, 151–52, 154, 155, 163, 164, 172, 173, 174, 175–76, 177, 178, 179, 181, 183, 184–85, 186, 187, 188, 189, 194, 195, 198, 200, 201, 203, 205, 209, 210, 213, 220, 259, 264, 265, 266, 271, 274, 275–76, 278, 279–80, 285, 286, 292, 293, 294
Johnson, E., 173, 183, 187, 191, 201, 208, 216, 293
Johnson Hodge, C., 169, 262

Karris, 261
Käsemann, 133, 243
Keesmaat, 36, 158
Kim, 98
Kirk, 153
Klein, 259, 261
Kraemer, 53
Krentz, 55
Kruse, 198

Linebaugh, 75, 186, 236
Longenecker, 6, 7, 11, 123, 257, 258–59, 292
Marshall, 242–43
Martin, 103
Matera, 16, 38, 49, 55, 62, 64–65, 82, 84, 85, 86, 87, 102, 106, 107, 149, 150, 151, 152, 157, 167, 281, 286, 288

Mayer, 187
McFadden, 153
McGrath, 209
Metzger, 97, 157, 188
Meyer, 82
Moo, 41, 47, 49, 86, 87, 106, 132, 135, 136, 151, 173, 176, 178, 181–82, 185, 187, 189, 267, 276, 279, 280, 295
Morales, 69, 70, 173, 180, 186, 188, 200
Morris, 179

Nanos, 52, 184, 213, 221, 223, 226, 229, 257, 279
Neyrey, 220
Novenson, 49, 193

Olree, 242, 249

Park, 75
Porter, 106

Rodríguez, 202, 216
Roetzel, 144

Schneider, 162, 163
Schoedel, 53
Schreiner, 29, 33, 34, 41, 47, 49, 55, 79, 106, 132, 135, 136, 194, 200, 203, 280
Song, 37, 64, 65
Sprinkle, 79
Stegemann, 20, 27, 98, 244, 245
Stein, 242, 243, 244, 247, 248
Stendahl, 86, 136, 139
Stowers, 8
Stowers, ix, 36–37, 39, 44, 47, 49, 62, 63, 64–65, 68, 70, 71, 73, 74, 78, 97, 101, 119–20, 121–22, 125, 134, 135, 136, 137, 139, 141, 144, 268
Sumney, 82

Thiele, 235
Thiessen, 49, 50, 55, 56–59, 61, 72, 259
Thiselton, 145–46, 265

Index of Authors

Thorsteinsson, ix, 8, 9, 33, 34-36, 38, 41, 49-50, 126, 134, 161, 179, 219, 258, 294
Trebilco, 117

Wallace, 80, 143, 193
Wasserman, 108
Watson, D., 220
Watson, F., 8, 77, 78, 258, 294
Williams, 76
Willis, 289
Winkler, 141

Winter, 164-65, 247, 249-50
Witherington, 38, 39, 49, 78, 106, 195, 198, 203, 206, 211, 259-60, 265, 266-67, 292-93
Wright, 23, 78, 95, 96, 98, 128, 129, 136, 137, 138, 139, 140, 141, 143, 145, 146, 150-51, 152-53, 160, 162, 164, 167, 172, 174, 179, 183, 188, 190, 194, 199, 201, 202, 206, 251, 260, 279, 282, 289

Yoder, 242

Index of of Ancient Documents

HEBREW BIBLE/OLD TESTAMENT

Gen

1–3	105
1:26–27	160, 166
1:28	155
2:7–8	184
2:16–27	144
3	133
12	91, 155
12:1–3	23, 24, 107, 182, 201, 246, 254
12:2–3	2
12:3	x, 90, 150, 212
15	74
15:4–5	174
15:5	89
15:6	2, 89
16:2	175
17	91, 263
17:5	89
17:12	58
18:14	170
21:12	170, 175
25:23	170
50:24	90

Exod

4:21	182
4:22	3, 18
6:3	203
7:3	182
7:22	182
8:15	182
9:12	182
9:16	177, 183
9:35	182
10:1	182
10:20	182
10:27	182
11:10	182
12:25–26	235
13:5	235
14:4	182
14:8	182
14:17	182
19	204, 288
20	288
20:1–3	216
20:1–17	255
20:2–3	55
20:2–6	132
20:13	56
20:15	56
20:17	132
22:1	57
25:22	83
32–34	181
32:13	90
33:1	90
33:13	180
33:18	182
33:19	180–81
40:34–38	100

Index of of Ancient Documents

Lev

12:3	58, 263
16:2	83
18	202
18:4–5	202
18:5	253
19:18	252, 280
20:26	15

Num

7:89	83

Deut

1:8	90
5:6–21	255
5:17	252
5:18	252
5:19	252
6:4–9	88
6:10	90
7:8	177
7:25	55
9:5	90
9:27	90
10:16	263
21:15	177
21:16	177
23:2	263
28–32	74, 92, 107, 114, 150, 201
29:3	214, 217
29:12	90
30	205, 230
30:6	263
30:14	204–5
30:19	68
30:20	90
32	77
32:21	207, 209, 210–11
32:35	240
32:43	278, 281
34:4	90
30:11–14	203–4
30:17–18	107
30:19–20	24, 115, 142
31:24–30	107

Josh

22:27	235

1 Kgdms

2:2	68
12:22	215

2 Kgdms

7:12–16	3, 17
7:14–15	77

3 Kgdms

8:10–11	100
10:5	286
19:10	214
19:18	214

4 Kgdms

4:43	286
6:15	286

1 Chr

28:13	235
29:13	86

2 Chr

5:13–14	100

Job

9:12	177

Ps

2:2	17
2:7	3
5:10	67, 69
9:28	67, 69
13	68
13:1–3	67, 68
13:4	69
14:1	28
14:7	69

Index of of Ancient Documents

17:50	278, 281, 282	29	184
18	209, 282	29:10	214, 217
18:2	210	29:16	177
18:5	207, 209	29:22	15
18:49	281	45:9	177
31:1–2	89	45:23	269
35:2	67, 70	49:5–6	5
43:23	167	52:5	3, 60, 282
50:6	64, 65	52:7	207, 208
51	77	52:15	284
52:2–4	67, 68	53:1	16, 207, 208–9
61	41	54	128
61:12	40	56:6–8	269
68:5	280	59:7–8	67, 69
68:10	277	59:13	69
68:22	218	59:20–21	225, 227
68:23–24	214, 217	61:6	286
68:28	218	65:1	207, 209, 211
69:9	280, 281	65:2	207, 209, 211
93:14–15	215		
102:21	286	## Jer	
103:4	286		
116:1	278, 281	3:1–13	128
139:4	67, 69	4:31	162
		7:29	215
## Prov		9:5	57
		9:6	57
1:16	68	12:13	86
16:31	86	18:1–11	184
24	41	31	77
24:12	40	31:3	177
25:21–22	240, 241	38:31–33	4

Eccl

Lam

7:20	68–69	3:31	215

Isa

Ezek

1:9	178, 201	5:8–11	215
8:14	191, 195–96	16	128
10	193	16:1–63	76
10:22–23	178, 201	16:12	86
10:22b–23	188, 196	16:17	86
10:22b	205	16:39	86
11:10	278, 281, 282	23:26	86
19:1	30	23:42	86
27:9	225, 227, 228	24:25	86
28:16	191, 195–96, 206	36:22–23	3

Index of of Ancient Documents

Ezek (continued)

45	16
48	16

Hos

1–2	193
1:2—3:5	76
2:1	178, 188
2:23	177
3:1	177
9:15	177
11:1	18, 177

Joel

2:26–29	101
3:1	101
3:5	197, 206–7

Jonah

4:2	290

Hab

2:4	22–23, 27

Mal

1:3	177

Mal

1:2–3	170, 176–77, 179

APOCRYPHA

Bel

1:5	31

2 Esd

7:24	286
20:39	286

1 Macc

2:19	236
2:22	236

2 Macc

7	269
7:20–21	141

Sir

7:30	286
31:10–11	86

Wis

4:10	235
9:10	235
12:12	177
14:8	30

NEW TESTAMENT

Matt

2:15	18
5:17	88, 201
5:43–48	240
7:1	266
22:34–40	255

Mark

3:5	226
7	272
8:34	235
12:28–34	255, 256
12:31	280
14:26	156

Luke

6:20–49	240
6:27–28	240
6:37	266
10:25–28	255
11:41	272

Index of of Ancient Documents

Acts

2	206
10	206
15:23	18
22:3	135
22:28	236
23:6	135
23:26	18
25–26	243

Rom

1	224
1–4	206, 216
1–8	206
1:1	5, 245
1:2	295
1:3–4	150
1:4	245
1:5–7	261
1:13	197, 233
1:13–15	261
1:16	209
1:18	179, 248, 252
1:18–32	47, 55, 60, 67, 209, 219, 244, 247, 256
1:18—2:16	47, 92
1:18—2:29	146
1:19	133
1:19–20	209
1:23	166, 193
1:24	128, 182, 184, 217
1:26	128, 182, 184, 217
1:28	128, 155, 182, 184, 217
1:29–31	254
1:32	133
2–7	251
2:1–5	47
2:1–16	60, 219
2:4	219
2:6–11	256
2:13–15	254
2:17	ix
2:17—4:21	47
2:24	60, 282
2:25–29	91
3:1–8	190
3:2	204
3:3–4	217
3:4	65, 187, 229
3:8	189
3:9	228
3:9–20	67
3:10	28
3:10–18	209
3:20	131, 146, 254
3:21	131, 170
3:21–22	202, 253
3:21–24	186
3:22	79, 131, 218, 254
3:22–23	192, 228
3:23	236
3:24	236
3:25	219
3:26	161
3:29–30	206
3:31	130, 170, 254, 288
4:1	195
5	228
5:6–11	101
5:7	249
5:10	228
5:12–21	146
5:13–14	133
6	40
6–7	30
6:1	205
6:4	108
6:11	235
6:13	235
6:17	267
6:18	267
6:20	146
6:22	237
6:23	144
7	206
7:1	233
7:4	233
7:5	144
7:7–25	157, 178, 253
7:10	144
7:12	170
7:13	144, 254
7:14	170
7:14–25	241, 250
7:15	256

313

Index of of Ancient Documents

Rom (continued)

7:18–19	256
7:21	157
7:21–23	251
7:24	157, 228
8	40, 210
8:1–11	253
8:1–13	235
8:3	254
8:4	233, 253
8:12	197, 233
8:12–17	190
8:14	228
8:15	158, 237
8:15–17	211, 220
8:18–30	247
8:28	249
8:29	166, 197, 246
8:29–30	215
9–11	206, 213, 225, 262
9:1–5	135, 220
9:3	171
9:6	190, 201, 205, 211
9:7–8	182
9:11	176, 246
9:13	177
9:14–16	181
9:15	180
9:25–26	193
9:27	205
9:27–28	193
10:1	233
10:4	199–201
10:4–5	253
10:5–13	202
10:12	206, 218
10:15	208
10:16	208
10:18–21	214
11:1	287
11:17–24	221
11:25	233, 240
11:28–36	190
12–15	40
12:1–2	205, 275, 287
12:3	285
12:19	248
13:8	280
14:1—15:13	239
14:11	5
15:30–32	191
15:30–33	295

1 Cor

1:22–24	119
3:10–15	276
3:16	288
10:32	119
11:7	166
12	238, 240
13	240
14	240
15	112
15:49	166
15:56	145

2 Cor

2:9	100
3:6	4
3:18	166
4:4	166
5:9	235
6:2	5
11:25	243
13:3	100

Gal

1:1	11, 14
1:6	123
1:10	15
1:13–14	136
1:15	15
2:1–10	11
2:7	75
2:12	15
2:15	119, 135
2:16	79
3:1–5	56
3:10–14	200, 201
3:13	128, 171
3:15	123
3:16	174
3:27	108
3:29	174

4:4–5	128
4:6	156
5:12	123, 263
6:17	243

Eph

2:18	97
3:12	79, 97
4:5	108
4:18	226
5:10	235

Phil

1:1	15
2:6–11	243
2:8	112
2:22	100
3:5	287
3:5–6	135
3:6	80
3:9	79
4:18	235

Col

2:12	108
3:20	235

1 Thess

2:14	119

Titus

1:1	15

Heb

9:4	82
9:5	82

Jas

1:15	132
2:10–11	56

1 Pet

1:2	19
2:5	287

2 Pet

1:2	19

2 John

3	19

Rev

1:4	19

PSEUDEPIGRAPHA

Apoc. Abr.

24:9	132
24:10	132

Apoc. Mos.

19:3	132

1 En.

92:1–5	236
93:11—105:2	236

Jub.

14:21–24	174
15:15–16	174
15:19	174
15:21	174

L.A.B.

8:1	175
8:3	175

L.A.E.

19	132

4 Macc.

2:6	132
7:8	286

JOSEPHUS

Ag. Ap.

1:168–71	58

Ant.

1:188	175
1:191	175
1:222	174
8:260–63	58
15:417	236
20:38–39	50

J.W.

2:409–10	21
2:463	193
5:193–94	236

PHILO

Creation

152	132

Decalogue

142–43	132

Mos.

1:154	250
2:18–20	121

Sacr. Abel

15	121

Spec. Laws

1:2	58
1:172–76	120
1:190–93	120
2:195	121
4:84–94	132

APOSTOLIC FATHERS

Barn.

9	58

Ign. *Phld.*

6:1	53

Mart. Pol.

3:2	198

GRECO-ROMAN AUTHORS

Aristotle, *Eth. nic.*

7.1150b 20	144

Epictetus, *Discourses*

3.15.10	52

Herodotus, *Hist.*

2.104	58

Plutarch, *Quaest. rom.*

21	259

Seneca, *Clem.*

1.1.2	245
1.1.3–4	247

Seneca, *Lucil.*

20:2	38–39
31:5	40

Strabo, *Geog.*

17.2.5 — 58

Virgil, *Aen.*

1:278–79 — 43

Xenophon, *Cyr.*

7.5.45 — 97

www.ingramcontent.com/pod-product-compliance
Lightning Source LLC
Chambersburg PA
CBHW030433300426
44112CB00009B/981